WHAT IT LOOKS LIKE

A Memoir

An awakening through
love and trauma
war and music
sports and history
politics and spirituality

MARTA MARANDA

Alchemadhi
Publishing

The publisher is not responsible for websites or their contents that are not owned by the publisher. Internet sources are frequently archived or deleted and some may not be available at the time of publication.

Grateful acknowledgment for permission to reprint previously published material is made to the following:

EVERYONE WILL CRAWL: Words and Music by Charlie Sexton and Tonio K. Copyright © 1995 Sony/ATV Music Publishing LLC, Sextunes Music, WB Music Corp. All rights on behalf of Sony/ATV Music Publishing LLC and Sextunes Music administered by Sony/ATV Music Publishing LLC, 8 Music Square West, Nashville, TN 37203. All rights reserved. Used by permission.

GOOD SOULS: Words and Music by James Walsh, James Stelfox, Barry Westhead, and Benjamin Byrne. Copyright © 2002 EMI Music Publishing Ltd. All rights for the U.S. and Canada controlled and administered by EMI April Music, Inc. All rights reserved. International copyright secured. Used by permission. Reprinted by permission of Hal Leonard Corporation

I WILL SURVIVE: Words and Music by Dino Fekaris and Frederick J. Perren. Copyright © 1978 Universal–Polygram International Publishing, Inc. and Perren–Vibes Music, Inc. All rights controlled and administered by Universal–Polygram International Publishing, Inc. All rights reserved. Used by permission. Reprinted by permission of Hal Leonard Corporation.

OVERVIEW OF DEVELOPMENTAL IMMATURITY ISSUES: Copyright © Pia Mellody. Used by permission.

PAIN CYCLE: Adapted by Clint Withrow from *I'll Quit Tomorrow: A Practical Guide to Alcoholism Treatment* by Vernon E. Johnson. Used by permission.

THE SIX PILLARS OF SELF-ESTEEM by Nathaniel Branden. Copyright © 1994 by Nathaniel Branden. Used by permission of Bantam Books, a division of Random House, Inc.

Library of Congress Control Number: 2015903378

ISBN: 978-0-9857814-2-2
Also available as an e-book.

Cover design by Greenleaf Book Group and Debbie Berne
Typesetting by Fiona Raven, www.fionaraven.com

Printed in the United States of America
Second Edition

To my mother and father,
who gave me the courage and passion
to say, this stops here.

That intellect which knows when to act and when not to act, what is to be done and what is not to be done, what is to be feared and what is not to be feared, along with the knowledge of bondage and liberation, is wisdom.

—*Bhagavad Gita 18:30*

"Who are you?" he was asked.
His reply was simple.
"I am awake."

—*Buddha Shakyamuni*

It's not true that life is one damn thing after another; it's one damn thing over and over.

—*Edna St. Vincent Millay*

If nothing has changed, then nothing has changed.

—*James Hollis, PhD*

Never think you've got it all figured out.

—*Phil Simms*

Outside noisy, inside empty.

—*Chinese proverb*

As I turn to you and I say,
Thank goodness for the good souls,
That make life better.
As I turn to you and I say,
If it wasn't for the good souls,
Life would not matter.

—*"Good Souls," Starsailor*

The moment you see how important it is to love yourself, you will stop making others suffer.

—*Mallika Sutta*

It's a long, hard road
From creation to the grave
Too many lost souls down here
Too few of them are saved
It's a real big picture
Starring one and all
Everyone here will play the fool
Everyone will crawl
Everyone will crawl

It's a mass production
It's everywhere you are
From the slaughter of the innocent
To the burning of the farm
Nothing is for certain here
And everybody's armed
The only thing that's guaranteed
Is everyone will crawl
Everyone will crawl

Yes we crawl through the heartbreak
We're crawling through the weeds
We crawl towards the love
Through the prejudice and greed
From queens and kings and presidents
The greatest to the small
Everybody, everyone
Everybody, everyone
Everyone will crawl

I dreamed I was flying
I dreamed I was found
Beyond the barbed wire
High above the underground
I dreamed I was flying
I dreamed I was free
Flying higher and higher
As the world fell below me

I climbed up on the mountain
And I snuck up on the Man
With my notebook of stone wide open
And my chisel in my hand
I said how come things are so tough down here
How come we all must fall
He said how you gonna learn to walk
How you gonna learn to run
How you gonna learn to fly
Until you learn to crawl

— *"Everyone Will Crawl," Charlie Sexton*

Contents

Note from the Author

This book is an unconventional memoir. It was my intention to not only tell my story, but to become a facilitator of the stories of others who have touched my life—including those from a distant time and place—with the hope of finding different ways to present the book's two main themes: connections and consequences. Parts I and II focus primarily on my individual healing, and the tools, lessons, people, and places that changed my life along the way. However, the book takes a detour early in Part III and delves into global connections and consequences from a historical perspective before continuing on to the conclusion of my personal story.

The year I left the clinic, our country was in the midst of a presidential election and two wars, and there was no escaping any of it. Between the vitriolic presidential campaigns and debates, and the global violence, the upheaval that surrounded me felt very similar to the internal unrest I felt while in the clinic. Because of this similarity, I decided to apply the same tools I used to resolve my personal confusion to help me better understand my country, government, and the political choices facing me at the time. Just as I had to go back to my childhood to understand myself as an adult, I relied on history to explain in part how my country, my children, and my future grandchildren ended up with the world we have today.

The historical section was the topic of many discussions throughout all phases of writing and publishing this book. Some believed it was important to include the examples of how every connection and consequence of both healthy and dysfunctional choices that apply to an individual work exactly the same way in every family, community, and nation, and how they affect the entire world. Others felt the historical section detracted from, rather than enhanced, my story.

To me, not including this section would have resulted in half a story, because while my healing may have begun with me, it didn't end there. The more I read about and researched our current events, the farther back the connections and consequences took me. Whether from George W. Bush's time as governor of Texas to his choices as president, or from historical Africa and Afghanistan to current-day Pakistan and Iraq, the journey I made from past to present was an essential contribution to my politics, my spirituality, and my personal and professional relationships. I felt it might be beneficial to others as well. But the historical section and departure from my story might not resonate with all readers. If this is true for you, feel free to skip from the break at page 232 to the break at page 307 (though I hope you will consider revisiting these pages at a later time). The remaining pages will take you through the changes in my personal politics, spirituality, and relationships, and to the conclusion of my story.

One of the most difficult parts of writing this book was determining how much to include on George W. Bush, who was running for re-election during my stay in the clinic in 2003. Too little would mean glossing over the significant events and realizations that occurred during the years immediately following my leaving the clinic. Too much could be construed as political bias or personal attacks. The truth is, I am apolitical. I do not belong to or endorse a particular political party, and I have yet to find a candidate from any party whom I feel is worthy or capable of properly leading and representing this country. George W. Bush was president during the time that my life, and especially my political awareness, were going through great change. My questions and my exploration would have been the same whether our president had been Barack Obama, Bill Clinton, or Ronald Reagan. And with each passing election, it's hard not to believe that the lack of truth, openness, and accountability would have been the same as well.

While this book contains both fact and opinion, it is not my intention to change your thinking. Only to ask you that when forming your own opinions about political candidates, our country's involvement in past and current events, and other countries whose races, religions, or political beliefs differ from yours, please include the information I offer here. It is not all-inclusive and it may not be perfect, but I do feel it is worth consideration. Also, as you read, if you feel further clarification, details, or examples would be helpful, please refer to "Notes" in the back of the book.

All of the stories from or about the addicts, both in and outside the clinic, are composites, and some details have been changed to protect identities. Two stories about addicts in the clinic were relayed to me after I had left. The exact words spoken by me, my family, friends, peers, and counselors have been lost to time, and I've written the quotes more from intuition than memory. Unless specifically expressed, the uses of masculine pronouns are gender neutral.

Since an accurate and adequate way of referring to God has yet to be found, I sometimes rely on the convenient language of our times, which assigns God both form and gender (Him). I use an uppercase "G" when referring to a spiritual God or a God of consciousness, and a lowercase "g" when referring to a material god or a god of unconsciousness.

A special note to sexual abuse survivors: The willingness of many of you, as well as the media, to no longer enable sex offenders to hide behind secrecy and silence has contributed greatly to both individual and world healing. However, with the public attention comes the very real potential for the resurrection of painful memories and the reopening of old wounds. During times of high media exposure of sexual abuse cases, be mindful of what and how much you open yourself up to, and stay connected to your support system, whether it be your family, friends, or therapeutic or spiritual communities. And to sex offenders: Please get help now. Not only do the rest of us deserve it, so do you.

Introduction

It's called the Holy Hammer. The Hammer part I got right away because it smashed into my life with such force there was barely the thinnest shred left to hold onto and say, "I can rebuild the life I had with this," which I'd soon learn was the point all along. Holy I wouldn't understand until much later. There were no glory-filled visions, no sounds of grace, no sweetness on my tongue, no smell of hope, and nothing sacred I could feel before me as I reached out my hands to keep from falling. It was hell. And hell looks, and sounds, and tastes, and smells, and feels like fear.

The Holy Hammer comes as a catastrophic event to remind us to live our lives in truth, and uses accountability to do it. You can block your ears, jam your eyes shut, or cover yourself in denial hoping not to be seen. But you'll have only so much time to accept what is being asked of you before It breaks everything open, exposing all things ghastly and glorious over and over and over, until you do.

I wrote those words several months after leaving the one place I never thought I'd find myself. I don't drink, smoke, use drugs, or have destructive sexual patterns. I am committed to exercise, eat healthfully, and have never had a cup of coffee in my life. But in November 2003,

I checked into a five-week inpatient addiction treatment center one week after my former husband, in for substance abuse, checked out. What began with me attending his Family Week to vent my pain and frustration and to get answers to my questions ended with only more questions. Realizing I couldn't answer them on my own, the clinic seemed the best place to begin looking for help. So I admitted myself into the full program without force or intervention, and I was sober. Because of these two occurrences, my observations and interpretations of the recovery process and my ability to grasp and absorb the clinic's teachings may be very different from those who arrived under other circumstances. What I learned was that the tools and teachings of recovery are universal, not just for addicts. They are for those who want to understand why we do what we do and think what we think, why what we say looks vastly different from our behavior, and why we continue to live lives we don't want to live. And for those who want to know what self-esteem and a healthy childhood really look like, who understand the necessity of telling one's story, and who believe in the relentless and unconditional need for authentic truth from a healthy mind if we are to live our best lives.

Rebuilding and refining a life is as much a cycle as a process. We first heal our individual dysfunction, use our new inner health to view and act in the world differently, then bring what we have learned in the world back into our lives to support and continue individual healing. And after the clinic, I brought the changes within me into everything around me. Politically I went through elections, war, Iraq, Afghanistan, Pakistan, and the Congo; spiritually through Christianity, Buddhism, and Hinduism; and personally into relationships I didn't think possible even a few years before. But whether politically, spiritually, or personally, I could always unravel the consequences of the present by looking at the foundations we—as individuals, families, communities, and nations—had laid in the past, and through the eyes of truth, accountability, authenticity, and openness.

However, my journey since leaving the clinic has often been messy, unattractive, and difficult to understand. I was many times lonely and scared, and there were long stretches where it seemed I made nothing but mistakes. But this is what breaking dysfunctional patterns and healing a life look like.

Still, there is incredible beauty in this alchemical process where one moment, one choice, one life, then relationships, entire families, communities, and nations are honed ever closer to a harmonious brilliance. It is in this never-ending process where you keep yourself honest. Where you are reminded that love and fear cannot breathe the same air, so you choose love. Where a painful word or act from another will not leave you writhing for years, because you know who you are. And where your power, your joy, and your sense of self come from that highest place inside of you, rather than the low place others fall to after you've kicked them down.

I welcome you into my process of questions and confusion; the falling, climbing out, and falling back again; and the unmatchable joy of every clear step forward. Each of us is responsible for revealing our own secrets, mistakes, and triumphs. Some will do this timely and honestly. Some may never do it. But the Holy Hammer came into my life and left me no choice. And this is what it looks like.

Part I

The End

I spent my childhood being cut down to fit a space where I never belonged in the first place. I spent the rest of my life searching for someone to tell me what to do with the scars. Eventually my need to know why I so often tried to heal my wounds with things that should have only enhanced my life, not defined it, would become as much of a calling as my need to write about it. And I would learn that, for me, creating authentic and lasting change meant I first had to make peace with the memories.

I am Italian and German, which seemed like genius on God's part. I got the full range of human possibility, from passion and emotion to pragmatism and logic, and I looked to my parents to help me figure out when to use which to create balance. The problem was they were busy with problems of their own.

My father, the Italian, was the youngest of eleven children. If he were alive today, he'd be diagnosed an addict with multiple addictions. My mother is one of the strongest people I have ever known, and coping with an illness, a husband swinging from gloom to fury, and five children caught in the middle convinced her she could only hold us together with an iron will void of all attention and affection.

The result was I learned how to keep secrets, would do anything to protect those I love, could fix any situation through sheer control, and could make myself believe something that wasn't true; and so began the patterns for the next forty years of my life. Over and over, they controlled everything from my relationships and professional life to my political and spiritual beliefs, until the time came when I was asked to create a new life with unbroken pieces.

My journey of rebuilding and refining has been a maze of many possibilities. Some filled with new people and words that would at times confuse me and at others set me on a path so straight I could sense the light and clarity even when I couldn't yet see it. And some filled with the same old patterns that plunged me into a darkness so blinding I stumbled back again and again to a place I thought I'd left long ago.

Along the way, many told me that much of what I thought was real and true about myself and my life wasn't. As I waded through the depth and density of consciousness and unconsciousness; awareness and ego; self and Self; impermanence and nonexistence; form and emptiness; wisdom and ignorance; freedom and boundaries; abundance and balance; commitment and surrender; God and Universe; living in the moment; the inner child and wounded child; core issues and trauma; and the redefining of everything from love and home to confidence and power, I would have to decide which I'd have to adapt to—either now or later when I was more open to accepting them—and which would have to adapt to me.

In the beginning, all I knew of the rebuilding and refining processes I had learned through something that may seem an unlikely teacher for someone like me, but it was, and continues to be, the one place I feel most at home. There is a common adage, "Life is like . . ." where you complete the sentence with whatever most inspires you. To a musician, writer, or painter, life is like art. To a scientist, life is like an observable experiment. To me, life is always like sports.

My father wanted sons. That I was his third child, and his third girl, was not the way he'd hoped his life would unfold. And while two boys would eventually follow, my father would pass on to me his love of sports through a connection that would never break, despite our willingness to either destroy or abandon nearly everything else between us.

However, I have never played organized sports, not even in school. It was less about our education system's struggle to accept the newly adopted Title IX than the struggle in my own head over what I was capable of, what I was allowed to do, what I was supposed to do, and who or what had the final say about it all. In my life, there has been no larger presence than my father, and as far back as I can remember, he simply didn't believe I could do much of anything. So I became an observer. While others watched manufactured life through episodic television and so-called reality shows, I watched real life through professional sports. It was my comedy and drama; my family, friend, and mentor; the source of all lessons and answers.

My first glimpse of what the refinement process looked like was at the beginning of the third quarter in professional football games. Here I saw the results of halftime discussions about where to make offensive and defensive adjustments, and when to stick with the original game plan. When I realized the problems in my life were not because of the faults or failings of others but because of my own, I also knew I had to learn what to change because it wasn't true or wasn't working, and what I could never change because it was part of the Original Plan and would always be true, would always work, if I got out of the way and allowed it to.

But I could only stand back and watch the refinement processes of others outside my childhood home, because inside there was no such thing. And by not participating in healthy change as a child, I never understood how to put it into practice as an adult. I was not shown what to do by loving example and then set free to do it—only what not to do through their opposites: pain and fear.

It was through rebuilding a house that I began to understand the process of rebuilding myself. We had been married five of our ten years when we broke ground on the home I created as a gift to my husband. Men with sweaty faces and thick-skinned hands dug and filled with concrete the foundation trenches, reminding me that nothing valuable or lasting can happen without the commitment to solid ground or the willingness to work through the inevitable pain.

Many people were part of the rebuilding. Some came for just a short time. Some stayed from beginning to end. Of those who were with me day in and out, three transformed my thoughts and feelings into concrete and paint. I would bring a page, a photograph, a piece of cloth, or simply describe what I saw in my head. One would create the proper boundaries needed for all of it to work. One would draw inside those boundaries the patterns and flow that turned empty walls, ceilings, and floors into art. One would build it.

And into the refinement process I stepped, though I wouldn't fully see or understand its brilliance then. The four of us—the contractor, architect, assistant, and I—met nearly every day in a tiny singlewide trailer set up on the property. We'd unroll plans and drawings and look at them through the eyes of each new day. A big change here, a few small ones there, and the sense to know what to leave alone. Over and over, day after day. The hope, of course, was to catch the problems before they became concrete. That didn't always happen. And it was trust, acceptance, and forgiveness that allowed us to break apart something that wasn't working and turn it into something that would.

I was able to picture much of the house in my mind from the start. I took my thoughts and feelings about the good things in life and used everything that touched my senses to translate it all. The color of sand at sunset on the walls; the taste of cinnamon and apples in the kitchen; the touch of my beloved Bonnie Blue's face in the fabric. When you walked into any room, you could feel what was in my heart through your eyes.

The union of talent, trust, respect, and commitment that I forged with those rebuilding my home was new to me. Never before had I been in a relationship like this, nor understood the fundamental need for such an environment to bring anything to its highest potential. Though it would be a very long time before I would know this again, at that moment, I not only knew what it looked like, but that I could be a part of it.

The level of detail I asked for was extraordinary. So much of what I do is big. I create big. I love big. I fail big. I hurt big. Sometimes this bigness worked on paper but not on walls. And sometimes there wasn't enough paper to hold all I wanted to say, and I had to go to the walls themselves and add until it felt right. I remember being alone in the house the day after it was finished, looking around and realizing there wasn't a blank space anywhere from top to bottom. I had filled it to its rim with the overflow of what I carried inside me.

While the four of us worked much of this process together, ultimately I was responsible for the changes that would create a healthy and happy home. Alone I searched through countless lumber and marble yards, fabric houses, furniture stores, art galleries, and antique shops. There were times I'd bring a sample or photograph, or move or add or take away, and look up to see raised brows and doubting eyes. But always at the core was the belief that we would never let each other be a part of something that didn't reach its highest potential.

During the years it took to rebuild our home, my husband, our two Abyssinians, Punkin and Bonnie Blue, and I lived on the construction site on the top floor of a neighboring house measuring not much beyond 1,000 square feet. What I wouldn't know until later was that I was in the midst of living two very separate lives—one being built through trust, the other shattering through addiction. It was a violent pulling apart and smashing together, a bloody emotional battle that wouldn't leave anyone feeling victorious. By the time it was over, I couldn't begin to know the total dismantling my life would require. I thought I knew what truth was. I thought I knew what love was. I thought I knew who *I* was—my place, my purpose. It was only when I admitted myself into the same clinic my husband had entered for substance abuse that I found I had lived my entire life through wishful thinking. And that everything about to confront me on the surface was necessary to get me to face the truths that lay far below.

What I knew of addiction I'd learned from my father, but the word "addict" was never a thought and "alcoholic" never spoken. My father simply drank. And all the buried secrets and lies of being a dysfunctional, non-relational family floated around us, unable to be grasped or surrendered.

Because of the depth of denial, and an even deeper layer of secrets, there is a vague knowing of something being wrong, or of not being right; a knowing that often leads to a constant and conscious willingness to turn away. But every step away in denial or fear only brings us two steps closer to everything we are trying our hardest to escape.

It would take me a while to realize that my thoughts of repairing and rebuilding were about houses and other people, not myself. For most of my life I believed if I could just fix someone else, I would fix everything else, but most of all my relationships.

Being a part of the professional relationships founded on trust and commitment while rebuilding our home encouraged me to look more closely at all of my relationships, hoping to bring what had worked professionally into the rest of my life. Slowly, and not always successfully, I worked to take my time when deciding to accept or discount another's idea or opinion or suggestion, to give my instincts much more respect and attention, and most importantly, to ask hard questions and listen more closely to the answers. And my first conscious attempt at trying to do any of this, even if I was not entirely sure of how to do it, was through sports.

Every NFL season, it becomes a sport unto itself for media opinionists to question whether an athlete has earned his high draft pick or multimillions or on-field praise. Maybe he's living off a college reputation that hasn't yet translated to the pros. Maybe he's getting credit that should really be going to a strong offense or defense. Maybe it's the color of his skin. But to me the question is much broader: Why do we—as individuals, couples, families, organizations, or nations—give someone a pass, accept the unacceptable, or assign credit where it isn't earned or deserved?

Because he is family?
Because he is a friend?
Because he has the same skin color?
Because he is the same nationality?
Because he or she is the same gender?
Because he belongs to the same political party?
Because he has the same religious or spiritual beliefs?
Because he went to the same schools?
Because he is professionally powerful?
Because he is athletically gifted?
Because he is rich?
Because he is famous?
Because he is the enemy of our enemy?

Sports have provided, if not clear answers, at least situations that have helped me ask better questions.

Steve Howe was a hard-throwing left-handed pitcher, two-time All–Big Ten selection at the University of Michigan, 1980 National League Rookie of the Year, rookie record holder, World Series Champion, alcoholic, and drug addict. He was suspended seven times for drug and alcohol abuse during his seventeen-year career. After his seventh suspension in 1992, he became the first player banned from baseball for life for drug abuse. An arbitrator reinstated him about five months later. In April 2006, Steve Howe died when his pickup truck rolled over in a one-vehicle accident. The toxicology results found methamphetamine in his blood.

Can we change someone by believing in him more than he believes in himself?

Fifty-seven minutes into the sixteenth and final game of the 2001 regular season, New York Giants defensive lineman Michael Strahan needed only one more sack to pass Mark Gastineau's single-season record of twenty-two. He got it. But it was said that, while Strahan may have deserved it, he didn't earn it; that Green Bay quarterback, Brett Favre, constructed a play that allowed Strahan a clear path to him, which resulted in an easy tackle. Some said the sack was orchestrated and believed it cheapened the seventeen-year-old record and the integrity of the game. Others said it was a gesture of goodwill that shouldn't be a cause for concern. Favre claimed the sack that forever erased Mark Gastineau's name from the record books was legitimate.

Can giving a pass to favorably change the destiny of one person negatively alter the destiny of another person, family, community, or nation?

Just shy of four weeks after the Mitchell Report investigating steroid use in Major League Baseball was released naming Roger Clemens eighty-two times, he went on *60 Minutes* to declare his innocence and decry what he thought was the public's presumption of his guilt. "I'm angry that what I've done for the game of baseball . . . that I don't get the benefit of the doubt. . . . You'd think I'd get an inch of respect." Clemens, whose twenty-four-year pitching career brought him seven Cy Young awards and two World Series Championships, had been a certainty for the Baseball Hall of Fame before the report was released.

Should the appearance of what someone is in public be more important than the truth of what he is in private?

This was my introduction to two valuable lessons I would have to remain aware of for the rest of my life: Every hard question I ask someone else, I must also ask myself; and every time I look outside for the answer, the truth and the change must always come from within me.

Within the world of addiction, giving a pass to others is the full-time occupation of an enabler. Enablers accept behaviors a healthy person would find unacceptable in order to get something else, such as security, love, companionship, self-esteem, or at least the appearance of these things. I am an enabler. For most of my life, I have accepted almost any unacceptable behavior in exchange for "something else." While I didn't yet know that missing piece, I was only moments away from beginning my journey toward awareness—and years away from understanding.

After its completion, our new home was an accomplishment—this I knew. It was big. It was beautiful. But I wasn't sure what it meant. Was it an ending, or a part of still more to come? When the last of the crew and equipment had gone, I tried to understand my thoughts and feelings. And though there were a few times when I stood in the moment and connected to this place of hope, of beauty, of trust, of commitment and fulfillment, mostly its completion simply felt like I had changed it all into more of the same; a feeling I could neither appreciate nor make sense of at the time. But what do you think when faced with something you can't understand? Sometimes nothing. Sometimes, you just stop thinking.

We had been in our new home for two years when my life ended and began in the same moment. The first few days after my husband entered the clinic, I buried myself in all the things I normally did with my life. I would later be told that constant busyness is a form of denial. But to deny something requires a thought process, and I had no thoughts. I simply floated. My hands opened mail, typed letters, wrote checks. My feet took me from this room to that. And I have no idea who told them to.

Loss and change in private are vastly different from loss and change in public. Private loss and change are shared with close family and friends who are part of your history. Their physical, emotional, and spiritual threads are densely woven with yours, creating a reciprocal relationship of strengths and weaknesses, questions and answers, choices and consequences. Love lives here.

Public loss and change can make people whom you don't know and who don't know you turn truth into assumption, fact into opinion, compassion into mercilessness. But it can also create connections and inviolable bonds with those you would never have known otherwise. And the connection that had to happen before any true understanding or healing in my life could begin was between the rehab clinic now treating my husband and me.

A counselor called within days after my husband had entered the clinic. The call seemed long, though I'm not certain it was. But it was awkward. And strange. I didn't understand why he spoke so little of my husband, whom I thought all of this was about, and so much about me. He asked how I was doing. I said I was fine. He asked it in a different way. I answered in a different way, but I was still fine. He said he knew how hard all this was and that he was there for me, anything I needed, anytime.

Anything I needed. Anytime.

I needed my own words and my own voice and someone else's open heart. And apparently, I needed them now. Suddenly every buried word, thought, and emotion came smashing through a surface thickened by years of self-neglect and denial. Things I'd held inside for weeks, years, and all of my life; things I didn't even realize I remembered; things that had never made sense. And the questions. Always the questions. But mostly one question.

Why?

By the end I was exhausted, and any movement from any part of me seemed impossible. But my body, heart, and mind kept repeating the only truth I knew at that moment: I can't stay and I can't go.

The counselor called me often during the next few weeks. I don't remember when I realized the reason why. There was no blast of clarity or even a gradual dawning as each piece slowly pulled together. It was just something I came to know. I was in therapy. I didn't understand it. And I didn't like it. After all, I was not the one with the problem.

I never mentioned my discovery to the counselor. He continued to call and ask questions about me, and I continued to let him, thinking that for every question he asked about me, I would ask one about my husband. But it never seemed to work that way. He'd ask a question about me, my marriage, my parents, or my childhood, and I'd answer; every word like pebbles tumbling off a mountainside, bringing me just the slightest bit of relief.

Within each conversation, the counselor mentioned something called Family Week. The fourth week of the clinic's five-week rehabilitation program is for the addict and his or her family to come together in a safe environment to air their problems and, hopefully, learn to resolve them in a healthy way. My husband's Family Week was approaching and the counselor wanted me to attend, believing this was the most important, in fact the only, next step for us.

I had not been in contact with my husband since he'd left for the clinic nearly four weeks earlier, so somehow I had to make the decision whether to attend his Family Week based on what I wanted, when what I wanted seemed impossible to know. I couldn't figure out how to sort through all the thoughts, emotions, and memories that only seemed to multiply each day.

Of my family and friends, I knew of none who had faced a similar situation and to whom I could turn for guidance. But even if I had,

I wonder whether I would have sought them out. I was very young when I was taught to keep secrets, my family's and mine. And being forced to keep secrets also forces you to find survival tools and defense mechanisms to deal with confusing, frightening, and damaging situations on your own when you are often too young and inexperienced to do so. But I did find one place for my voice; one place where anything I wanted to say, in any way I wanted to say it, would be heard. With a pen and blank piece of paper I was free. I was safe. I was home.

I hadn't written anything either personally or professionally in the nearly ten years I'd been married. As I sat down at my computer one night after another conversation with the counselor, I didn't turn to writing even then. But it found me, gripping my heart and my hands so powerfully there was nowhere else to go. Soon I became consciously unaware. Conscious of writing, but unaware of the time or space I was writing in. There was no room, no chair, no desk or computer. Just the words, whose moment and reason to be had come.

Four pages later, I stopped and looked at what I had done. Behaviors and betrayals were lashed to the pages with so much pain it didn't feel at all freeing. It only felt like I had known this person before and understood why she wrote this way. She was much younger then, but just as broken and with no way to make sense of the pieces. She tried to resolve her frustration, confusion, and pain born of betrayed trust and stolen innocence in the only way she had ever known, had ever been shown—with anger.

At that time, I did not see this anger as misplaced, and I did not see as extraordinary that every word was about what had been done to me, and none about what I had done to myself. And it never occurred to me that anyone would see it any other way. But any thought I'd had of finding answers simply by writing showed itself for the illusion it was, because I still had only questions. I lifted my head and looked around, coming back into space and time, and I wondered where all the beauty and joy had gone, replaced by everything ugly and hopeless. How did a love so big I'd had to build a house to hold it all come to this? I knew that the answer to this question, more than any other, was the one I wanted to find. I also knew I wouldn't be able to find it alone.

I don't remember much about the five-hour flight or the hour drive from the airport to the clinic that Monday morning. But I remember clearly what happened when two staff members walked me toward the door of the room where my husband and two counselors sat waiting for me. I couldn't walk through it—and not because I was giving myself a choice. My body simply would not move through that door. I got close and a magnetic bolt shot from the top of my head to the soles of my feet and froze me to the floor. I could step back, but not forward. I tried again to walk through the door with the same result. My knees would not bend and my feet remained riveted to the floorboards. Over and over, I walked up and backed down until I became aware of a wailing sound that could only come from the deepest, blackest place where pain and heartache are buried under more pain and heartache. And could only have come from me.

With a person on each side of me, I walked to the doorway once more but put my hands on the sides of the doorframe to keep from going any further. My head was lowered. I could not look up. I was asking so much of my mind and body at that moment the command to lift my head was one too many. Standing at the doorway, hands clutching the frame, head bowed, breath choked and wet, I tried to understand what I was feeling. I was overwhelmed. I was hurting. And I was scared. But what was I scared of? Of my husband? Of the room? Of these people I didn't know? Of this place I had never been? Of this moment I could never have imagined myself in if I had lived a thousand lifetimes?

Slowly, step by tiny step, I walked into the room and sat down in a chair across from my husband. I still hadn't raised my head, and I was still choking on tears. I was later told I'd said out loud, "I am stronger than this." I don't remember saying it, but I do remember feeling that this was as broken as I could possibly get. I was wrong.

In fact, this was just the beginning of my being wrong about so many things, not because of intentional choices, but in my assumptions, expectations, and judgments, which were the only ones I could have had given my history, experience, and knowledge. And before now, I'd had absolutely no experience with or knowledge of rehab.

So I assumed. To the point that I fully believed I was simply coming to a week of therapy, which meant I talked about my problems with my husband and our marriage, and the counselors fixed them. But while talking about one's problems is part of the rehab process, it wasn't much of one at that moment. And if I were to come away from the clinic understanding just two things, the counselors would have considered my stay there a success. They wasted no time introducing me to the first one.

Sitting there, I tried to make my mind adjust to this new environment so I could think and act more clearly. The four of us further shrunk an already tiny room filled with too many chairs and too many pictures that were meant to be comforting, though not succeeding. And I had a fleeting sense of being underground, confined to a space where no one who truly knew what it meant to be alive would ever end up.

Everything unfamiliar found itself battling the memories that flooded my mind every time I looked at my husband, and I found I still only wanted to speak one word: Why? When no one answered, I asked again, and kept on asking until the counselors pointed to something they thought would help me understand.

On the floor, propped up in front of a chair between the counselors, was a large poster board chart with four vertical sections. The first section was titled Nature of the Child, and below it was a list of five characteristics: valuable, vulnerable, imperfect, dependent, and spontaneous.

One counselor turned to me and said that all children are born precious. To be precious is to be valuable. Yet children are also vulnerable, imperfect, dependent, and spontaneous. Their vulnerability requires another's protection to feel safe until they learn how to protect themselves and others. Their imperfection needs compassionate guidance so they learn to correct what they can and let go of whatever is beyond their control. Their dependency changes with each step toward independence until they find the balance between what they can do on their own and when they need to ask for help. Their spontaneity should never be lost, only refined to avoid a life of chaos.

Pointing to the second section labeled Core Issues, he further explained that each of the natural characteristics from the first section directly corresponds to a foundational trait each of us should have in our lives to be considered healthy. When a child is properly nurtured, guided, and lives a life free of growth-stunting trauma, his being valued leads to high self-esteem; his feeling vulnerable yet protected leads to understanding boundaries; his being accepted as imperfect leads to developing realistic perceptions; his healthy dependency leads to knowing when to be self-reliant and when to rely on others; and his spontaneity leads to also seeing the value in moderation and self-control.

What I saw in the connection between a child's properly nurtured natural characteristics and his corresponding core issues was what a healthy life looked like. What I saw next was how a sane life goes insane.

The counselor said childhood trauma, or anything "less than nurturing," arrests the development of the core issues. And it makes no difference if it is one large catastrophic event or many small ones that build up over time—the result is the same. The child grows, but the core issues become stunted and remain undeveloped, unable to function in any balanced way, seeking only extremes. Because when a child is consistently exposed to an environment of extreme and out-of-control behavior, his survival tools and defense mechanisms will inevitably be the same. And it is more certain than not that he will carry his immature core issues and corrupted survival tools with him into adulthood, and that they will look like this:

Less Than/Better Than
When caregivers create a dysfunctional sense of value, a child will respond by believing himself to be either less than or better than others. "Less thans" and "better thans" constantly compare themselves to others. While one determines he will always fail or never measure up, the other believes he is better, smarter, and more deserving than everyone else. Neither sees his worth as equal to another's, nor accepts that everyone has strengths and weaknesses, superior and inferior talents.

Too Vulnerable/Invulnerable

With proper nurturing and without trauma, a vulnerable child learns to develop boundaries—those healthy barriers we establish to keep people from abusing us, and us from abusing others. Trauma distorts boundary development, causing a child to become either too vulnerable or invulnerable. When too vulnerable, he makes himself a victim, blaming everyone and everything else for his pain, problems, and circumstances; when invulnerable, he puts up a false front of arrogance. One refuses to be held responsible or accountable. The other presents himself as confident through belligerence, which is actually an indication of weakness, not strength.

Rebellious/Perfectionistic

Imperfection is part of the human experience, but even more so for a child as he tests limits to discover what he is able and unable to do at any given moment. But if a caregiver's expectations exceed a child's ability or experience level, his sense of reality suffers. When a child's mistakes are repeatedly pointed out, when he hears he can't do anything right enough times that he believes it is true, he will live out the script his caregivers have written for him and either become rebellious and create a life of chaos and defiance, or constantly strive for perfection, which is unattainable even by those who require it of the child. Perfectionists look at mistakes not as essential for information gathering, learning, and growth, but as failures. And they repeat the responses shown them by their caregivers by being critical and demanding, setting up themselves and everyone around them for the very failure they wanted to avoid.

Too Dependent/Anti-Dependent

All children must depend on adults for survival until they have acquired what is necessary to survive on their own. But when a child is traumatized or raised by caregivers who pass on to him their own trauma, his development of appropriate dependency is damaged. If caregivers cling too tightly, enmeshing their child's life with their own, he doesn't learn independence. If they provide no support or always expect their

Overview of Developmental Immaturity Issues

NATURE OF THE CHILD	CORE ISSUES	SECONDARY SYMPTOMS	RELATIONAL PROBLEMS
Childhood trauma causes →	Immaturity both drive →	Unmanageability all three create →	Problems with being intimate
1. Valuable	1. Self-Esteem Issues (Less than vs. Better than)	1. Negative Control Issues	1. Relational Esteem Issues
2. Vulnerable (Protection)	2. Boundary Issues (Too vulnerable vs. Invulnerable)	2. Resentment Issues	2. Enmeshment & Avoidance Issues
3. Imperfect (Reality)	3. Reality Issues (Rebellious vs. Perfectionistic)	3. Spirituality Issues	3. Dishonesty
4. Dependent (Needs/Wants)	4. Dependency Issues (Too dependent vs. Anti-dependent or Needless/Wantless)	4. Addiction Issues/ Depression/ Physical Illness	4. Problems with Inter-dependence
5. Spontaneous and Open	5. Moderation/ Containment Issues (Out of control vs. Controlling others)	5. Intimacy Issues	5. Intensity Issues

child to learn "the hard way," he learns that his wants and needs will be ignored. One expects others to always take care of him, make his decisions, solve his problems. The other becomes anti-dependent, needing no one, wanting nothing, never asking for help no matter what.

Out Of Control/Controlling Others
One of the greatest gifts given to children is spontaneity, the sense of freedom that comes with not having much responsibility other than to absorb and rejoice in the world and all its wonder. But trauma causes a child to lose his ability to develop moderation and containment, and understand what is and is not within his power to control. With no containment, spontaneity becomes unmanageable impulsiveness. With too much, he goes beyond what he can control in his own life to trying to control everyone and everything around him.

Indicating the third section of the chart, the counselor said that the traumatized nature of a child and the damaged core issues together create secondary symptoms, which result in a life of unmanageability with control problems, resentment, spiritual confusion, addiction, depression, physical illness, and relational issues.

The fourth section showed how all three—a child's traumatized true nature, his damaged core issues, and secondary symptoms—come together to almost guarantee problems in all of his relationships. And how it all comes down to one word: intimacy.

I heard this word often while at the clinic. And what is necessary to be intimate in any relationship looks a lot like the true nature of a child and healthy core issues, such as valuing oneself and others, being able to be vulnerable, being compassionate with imperfection, finding the proper balance between dependence and independence, embracing spontaneity, and respecting boundaries. But when two broken adults come together, they bring their childhood trauma, damaged core issues, dysfunctional survival tools, and inappropriate defense mechanisms into their relationships and then wonder why they can't love each other, work together, communicate, resolve conflicts, raise healthy children, or stay married. And therein lies the first of the two things the clinic counselors wanted me to understand.

Those childhood survival tools resulting from trauma and damaged core issues work for a child for one reason: He cannot leave. When a child must stay in a hostile or traumatizing environment, he will develop tools and mechanisms to help him cope with and compensate for feeling worthless, repressed, unsupported, and unprotected.

As an adult he can leave. He can change his environment, his behavior, his thoughts, his choices, and the people he allows into his life and heart. But he will often hold onto his dysfunctional childhood survival tools—now directed toward abusing substances or behaviors such as alcohol, drugs, sex, food, tobacco, work, arrogance, or timidity—because they are the only anxiety management behaviors he knows. So in order to use his dysfunctional survival tools, which have become his only source of comfort and self-soothing, he must continually create or place himself in hostile environments that cause anxiety. Whether at work or home, with his spouse, children, friends, or co-workers, his mind will constantly see threats even where none exist.

It was clear what the counselors were trying to say: *We must replace our defective childhood survival tools with healthy ones if we are to become functional, relational adults.* It just wasn't clear to me then. Fortunately, enough curiosity about the effect of trauma on development would stay with me until I was ready to discover how it all applied to me. But at that moment, I was still waiting for the talking therapy to start.

This first meeting lasted about four hours, dominated by the discussion of core issues. When we all stood to leave, a counselor explained that, at the clinic, boundaries included asking another's permission to touch him or her, for instance, when wanting to give someone a hug. At first I didn't understand what he was saying. Did he mean this to apply only to strangers and unmarried couples, or to everyone, even a couple married nearly ten years? I learned the answer to my questions was yes when, one by one, they each asked me, "Can I give you a hug?" Apparently, to these counselors, replacing inappropriate childhood survival tools meant we started right now.

Like most outpatients, I stayed at a nearby hotel and was shuttled by clinic transportation. Before walking to the van, the counselors gave me a book on codependency. Unfamiliar with the word, I asked what it meant, then nodded as if I understood their explanation.

I must have checked in and found my room easily enough because the next thing I remember I was sitting on the bed, still holding the book the counselors had given me, fully understanding what the word "weary" meant. My body floated down, my head dropped to the pillow, and the weight of the day closed my eyes.

When I woke, it was nearing sunset. I was somewhat disoriented because my body clock said it should be much later with an already darkened sky, and I was hungry. Still wearing the clothes I'd arrived in, I went down to the hotel dining room for a quick dinner. Afterwards, I got into bed with the book on codependency thinking I'd read a page or two because I had said I would. By the time I'd gotten to page 135, I had dog-eared about thirty pages and filled the blank inside covers with notes and questions.

I struggled with the definition of codependency because it seemed to be so many things and could literally apply to everyone. But what I gathered was that codependency is the result of continuing to use the defective survival tools developed as a child to manage family dysfunction in our adult relationships with others who are doing the same. I learned how traumas and dysfunctional behaviors are passed on from generation to generation; why traumatic situations cause low self-esteem in some and arrogance and grandiosity in others; and that the most common type of esteem codependents have is called "other-esteem," meaning their sense of self comes from something external, such as their looks, their career, how much money they have, the kind of car they drive, who they know, or how attractive or powerful their spouse is. I read that it was fine to get enjoyment from these things, but not an identity. Though it seemed to me it would be easier to find the stars in sunlight than someone who didn't have other-esteem.

What fascinated me were the case histories in the book. Real people with real stories that connected their past childhood traumas to their present adult dysfunctional behaviors. I was continually amazed at how an adult would put himself in the same painful environment he experienced as a child in order to use the adaptive skills he had developed. Then I realized it had to be this way. He had no other skills to use. And he would be lost in any other environment, especially a healthy one, which would not only be uncomfortable but most likely unrecognizable.

I closed the book and closed my eyes. I was feeling a mix of apprehension and curiosity about my upcoming first full day at the clinic, though I was confident that it would be more about what I wanted to know and say rather than what the counselors wanted me to hear.

We started at 9:00 a.m. Tuesday with what was called a Feelings Check. Tacked to one wall was a list of eight feelings: anger, fear, pain, joy, passion, love, shame, and guilt. Several times a day counselors asked us what we were feeling, and we were to choose the appropriate one from the list. I usually felt more than one and they often conflicted. Though there are many more feelings than just these eight, I learned that all could be represented by one on the list. Feeling sad or lonely was really feeling pain. Feeling happy and hopeful was joy; threatened and overwhelmed was fear; compassion and tenderness, love.

It became very clear, very fast that feelings were the objective. Throughout the week, counselors often tried to pull us out of our heads and into our hearts with, "You've told me what you think, now tell me what you feel." They weren't very impressed with our logic or problem-solving abilities, or how we used our minds to get out of trouble, believing too much thinking was what got us into trouble in the first place. We constantly maneuver, manipulate, and control situations that we want to get into or out of, rather than choose to be honest about and unafraid of what we feel.

But many are afraid, even ashamed, of feelings. So much so that they will smash them down to pieces so small they become invisible to everyone on the outside. Thinking holds a high place, and there doesn't seem to be much room up there for feelings. But I would eventually learn that a life without heart isn't a life at all.

That morning I was feeling fear, pain, and the smallest bit of joy. The reasons for the first two were obvious. The last was because of what I had read in the book on codependency the night before. I knew I was far from getting answers, and even farther from understanding them, but for the first time I had the feeling they were out there. That was enough for me to make a hallowed vow, one that I must reaffirm every day of my life. I promised myself that, no matter what, I would continue this search for answers until I ran out of questions.

After the Feelings Check, one of the counselors said he wanted to tell us more about himself, and for over an hour I was absorbed in his story. Never before had I heard someone speak so openly, and in such detail, about his life. In my world, these were secrets, vulnerabilities, and weaknesses. But in his, this openness and truth looked like strength, confidence, and peace.

He spoke of how his parents used what they had learned from their parents to raise him: mixed messages about love and pain, abandonment from one and smothering from the other, addictions on both sides, and many other destructive behaviors no child should have as a foundation. There was also sexual abuse from a trusted family friend. These were his guides when forming relationships with his parents and siblings; choosing his career, friends, and lovers; and understanding what is acceptable and unacceptable behavior, which eventually became as mixed as his parents' messages. He described the behaviors he engaged in as an adult, which were so unimaginable to me I wasn't sure I should know this much about any person. But then he began making connections. As the case studies did in the book on codependency, he pulled a thread from every dysfunctional thought, behavior, or incident as an adult and tied it to a damaging thought, behavior, or incident from earlier in his life. And with each connection I heard the answer: This is why.

However, he was emphatic that we understand this wasn't the whole story, that there were good parts and happy times, and that his parents did exactly what could be expected of them given their own experiences and what they believed to be true at the time they were raising him. And this unearthing of things rotten and decayed was not to find excuses or someone to blame or reasons to become a victim. It was to bring everything destructive to the surface to let the open air transform it all into the beginnings of a new life.

When he finished, I had a speechless moment where I knew that anything I said would be miles from what I meant. I realized later it was because I wasn't thinking, I was feeling. And I was feeling honored. This man gave me something of great value that morning. He willingly and unselfishly showed me the worst parts of himself so I might one day live my best life.

The rest of the morning was spent on the Dance, which is how the counselors described the mechanics of an unhealthy relationship. In a dance to music, one leads and one follows. In an unhealthy love relationship, one withdraws and one pursues. The pursuer is called a Love Addict. The one who retreats is an Avoidance Addict. And their cycles are so diametrically opposed there isn't a teardrop's chance in hell they will ever connect in any healthy way.

The Avoidance Addict has an intense fear of intimacy with an underlying fear of being abandoned—the result of past trauma stunting emotional growth. The Avoidance Addict carries this emotional immaturity into adulthood, making it impossible for him to develop or function in a healthy relationship. He gets his value in relationships through taking care of needy people, though suffers a fierce conflict in the process. He feels guilty if he doesn't rescue or provide for others, but suffocated when he does because it brings them too close.

The Avoidance Addict gets into a relationship out of obligation, not love, and uses various means of external seduction, such as money, power, gifts, sex, or shallow attention. The Love Addict, not happy for long with these superficial pleasantries, moves closer, wanting something deeper and more substantive. The Avoidance Addict feels smothered and resists with anger or resentment. As the instability caused by these negative responses keeps his Love Addict partner at a distance, the Avoidance Addict looks outside the relationship for the excitement he craves in things like drugs, alcohol, sex, gambling, or work. If there is an event that disrupts his pattern, such as his partner threatening to leave if things don't change, he may return to the relationship out of guilt or fear of being abandoned, or move on to a new relationship altogether, where he begins the pattern again with someone else.

The Love Addict's anxieties are the reverse of the Avoidance Addict's. Her greatest fear is of being abandoned, with an additional fear of intimacy. Again because of dysfunctional emotional growth, she comes to the relationship feeling inferior to her partner, with an unquenchable desire to get closer to him and a need to be taken care of—and her cycle begins.

She is first taken in by the Avoidance Addict's superficial seduction, and surrounds the relationship in fantasy or fairy tale: "He's wonderful. He's perfect. He's The One."

She moves toward him and asks for more. The Avoidance Addict backs up, puts up walls, and diverts his attention to other interests. The Love Addict denies his behavior and continues to push forward, and may even use substances such as alcohol or drugs, or develop spending or eating disorders to ease the pain of the Avoidance Addict's unresponsiveness. Then something happens to shatter that denial into an imponderable number of pieces. When the denial is broken, the Love Addict goes through an emotional withdrawal from the fantasy much like the physical withdrawal of a substance abuser, and is overwhelmed with pain, anger, fear, and shame. The problem with love addiction is not that she loves, but who and how. She asks for intimacy and vulnerability, honesty and commitment from someone who cannot give them because of his lack of emotional and moral maturity, and which she can't authentically give or even accept herself because of her own trauma.

At this point, as with the Avoidance Addict, only two options are open to the Love Addict, and both keep her in the Dance. She either stays in the current relationship by mentally rebuilding the fantasy or gets into a new relationship and starts the cycle over again with someone else.

But there is a third way for both. They can stop dancing.

I thought of my vow to search for answers until I ran out of questions, but at this time I could only think of one. Why were they telling me this? First, I didn't fully fit into either the Love Addict or Avoidance

Addict cycles. Second, I'm not an addict at all, and I was starting to
believe the counselors had an addiction for everything and everyone.
I had made mistakes in my life, but there was one thing I knew. I grew
up with addiction. I know what it looks like, and it doesn't look like me.
I have spent my entire life making sure it didn't. I don't drink, smoke,
use drugs, drink caffeine, or overspend. I can walk away from any
craps table in any casino regardless of whether I'm winning or losing.
I eat well, exercise, vote, and love my kids, my country, and my cats.
I am the anti-addict. Though I was beginning to wonder if I was the
only one who realized this.

Days at the clinic were tightly structured and scheduled to the minute.
After spending significant time on the Dance, we stopped for lunch. My
husband walked me to the cafeteria, introducing me to a few people
along the way. This was the first time I had been beyond the room
where we held our sessions and in the main part of the clinic with the
rest of the patients. But I didn't see patients. I saw addicts, which was
exactly what I had spent every day of my life trying to avoid since
I last saw my father.

The cafeteria was typical: Formica tables, small chairs, and plastic
trays you slid down metal rails in front of glass-shielded food. The
food was low fat, high carbohydrate, and sugar-free. No caffeine was
allowed on the premises, which left water, juice, and decaffeinated tea
as the drink choices. I heard a few complaints about the food, but it
wasn't so bad.

Since I wasn't a patient some of the clinic was off limits to me,
including the bedrooms. We walked past the bookstore and the nursing station and into the TV room, where I learned the television was
only on during specific hours and that some programs and channels
were blocked because of the sex addicts.

I wish I could say how it happened that I had never heard of sex
addiction until that moment. How my life, my education, my experiences, my exposure to countless books and people had not even once

brought those two words into my consciousness. I remember looking at my husband and saying the words as if they didn't belong together, or at least didn't belong in my mouth: "Sex addiction? What is that?"

The simple explanation is that it is just like anything else you can't stop thinking about or doing to excess despite destructive consequences. Some sex addicts at the clinic were "non-offenders," meaning they had affairs or a pornography obsession. Others were there because of a court order. Sex addicts were the reason cigars weren't allowed, as some considered them a sex tool. Public displays of affection were also not permitted, even between patients and their spouses, because they could trigger a sex addict's fantasies.

With so much forbidden to protect the sex addicts from themselves, I couldn't help but wonder how they managed on their own once they left the clinic; what they did when they found themselves surrounded by Victoria's Secret commercials, adult video stores, cigar shops, and people kissing in public. What do you do with a life where coming in contact with anything that can be turned into a sexual trigger compels you to fantasize, masturbate, jump into bed with a person not your spouse, grab some porn, or worse?

So far I'd learned how childhood trauma affects our core issues, and how these stunted core issues turn our relationships into a heart-numbing, unfulfilling dance. But how do you recreate a childhood, rebuild a thought process, stop believing something you've believed all your life, change when you haven't the slightest idea what change looks like?

After the Dance lecture just a few minutes earlier I had defiantly thought, *I know what addiction looks like*. And at the time, it not only didn't look like me, it didn't look like any of this. In my world, it was alcoholism and drug addiction. But in here it was shopping, overeating, not eating, tobacco, work, love, relationships, sex, porn, gambling, gossip, the Internet, video games, and a never-ending list of everything else.

Who created this world? What created these people? And how had I never known it had come to this? This wasn't my father, the one alcoholic I'd known, nor the one drug addict I'd married. It was so many fathers, mothers, husbands, wives, daughters, and sons; countless neighbors, co-workers, and friends; the famous and the unknown; the wealthy, the middle-class, and the barely getting by. Suddenly, the secret I had helped my father and husband keep all these years was no longer rare, or even much of a secret.

We ended up sitting in a couple of chairs outside the cafeteria. It was a beautiful day. The air was dry and cool. The sky was without a cloud and made brilliantly clear by the sun. As I breathed in the mountain view, I learned more about the clinic—how every patient's luggage was searched for drugs, alcohol, and other contraband, and razors were confiscated and could only be checked out for forty-five minutes each morning. I thought it interesting that the clinic tried so hard to make sure patients didn't harm themselves or others by removing and monitoring the razors, but didn't mind the serrated butter knives in the cafeteria.

After lunch, the counselors opened the afternoon session with the Feedback Loop, which is the clinic's method for healthy communication during emotionally tense discussions. If the chart explaining the effect of trauma on our core issues told me how things went wrong, the Feedback Loop was the first step toward making them right again.

Anyone should be able to have an inoffensive conversation about something innocuous. But how do you keep from hurting someone, or getting hurt, during a discussion loaded with pain and anger? The counselors said the way is to express emotion or approach a sensitive subject without blaming or shaming the other, and the tool was the Feedback Loop.

There are three parts to the Feedback Loop:
1. Repeating what the person said or did that has caused pain.
2. Stating what you think about what was said or done.
3. Sharing what you feel about it.

And it sounds like:
1. What I saw (or heard) was . . .
2. What I thought about that was . . .
3. And I felt . . .

For example:

1. What I heard was that you gambled away the money meant to pay our house payment.
2. What I thought about that was that our marriage, our financial security, and your commitment to getting well are less important to you than your desire to gamble.
3. And I felt anger, pain, and fear.

It was most important to speak our thoughts and feelings from what they called the I Position, and to always keep the focus on the *situation* rather than the other person's personality or character traits, because the more your attention is on the person during an emotionally charged conversation, the greater the chance you'll blame, shame, or ridicule him or her. So saying "What I thought about that was that I was less important to you than your desire to gamble" is speaking from the I Position. "I think **you** are a jerk" is not. Once you follow "I" with "you" during a painful or tense discussion, it's almost certain something shaming is right behind it.

I quickly realized that hearing about this new way of communicating pain and anger non-confrontationally was much easier than actually doing it. So to help us get used to replacing our dysfunctional childhood communication tools with this new healthier technique, the counselors gave us homework. Using the Feedback Loop, we were to write down as many things that caused us pain and anger as we wanted, then choose the top three for the following day's discussion.

We spent the rest of the afternoon exploring the addict's mind and pain cycle. The cycle starts with a situation a person doesn't know how to resolve or can't confront. This causes pain. For a child, it can be anything from abuse to divorce to being unpopular at school. The child carries the trauma with him into adulthood, where it then serves as the foundation for a whole new set of problems. Trauma suffered in adulthood, such as war, illness, or an accident, can start the cycle later in life. Regardless of whether the pain comes from childhood or adult trauma, a person will try various things as a painkiller until he finds one or several that work, skyrocketing him into a state of euphoria—at least in the beginning. This is Phase I.

The brain has an innate problem-solving mechanism, part of our survival system, that is triggered by pain. When we feel either physical or emotional pain, it is a sign that something is wrong and needs to be remedied. When we tackle a problem with our natural abilities or ask for help from someone capable and trustworthy, our brains reward us with a genuine sense of accomplishment, well-being, and good feeling.

Addiction short-circuits the brain's natural problem-solving ability by using a substance or behavior to hide or suppress—rather than confront—the pain and the problem. The painkiller artificially activates the brain's reward system or pleasure centers. When a person takes the substance or engages in the behavior, he gets "rewarded" by feeling good, though without having earned it. The addict now has his confidence in the substance or behavior to bring him comfort and happiness, rather than his own problem-solving abilities.

Pain Cycle

Adapted by Clint Withrow from *I'll Quit Tomorrow* by Vernon Johnson

In Phase II, the painkiller is too valuable to stop because of the relief it provides, but it doesn't have the same effectiveness as the first dose. So the addict increases the substance or behavior attempting to reach that initial euphoria, which he never can again. Neither can he again return to his original "normal" baseline before he started using, but will drop below it after the effect of the substance or behavior wears off.

Over time, the addict builds up a tolerance to the substance or behavior and has to further increase the dose and frequency to break through the threshold to get his high. In Phase III, he barely gets beyond his original baseline when on the painkiller, and drops even further below it once the effects subside.

Eventually, substance abusers develop a physical addiction as well as the psychological addiction found in all addicts. In Phase IV, the addict no longer gets high at all but has to use the painkiller just to reach some level of normal functioning and to hold off withdrawal. At this point, getting and using the painkiller becomes a matter of survival, and nothing is off limits in the addict's pursuit of it. Morals and values don't matter. Character doesn't matter. Neither does spirituality. And the more he needs it, the more he's willing to risk until not even a marriage and family, a career, or jail make a difference. For many addicts, just as potent as the behavior or substance itself is the high they get from engaging in the risky or illegal situations that are a part of their addictions.

In addition to going to any lengths to acquire the painkiller, the addict must "protect his supply" from family and friends once he gets it, fearing they will take it away. If his supply is cut off, he will go through withdrawal and experience pain, which is what he began using the substance or behavior to avoid in the first place. He will lie, manipulate, and develop ways to put distance between him and anyone who might jeopardize his source of comfort—and the lying becomes habitual. He will lie when he doesn't need to. He will lie when the truth is easier. And the more the addict lies, the guiltier he feels. So he uses to keep from feeling guilty, lies to continue using, then feels guilty for using and lying, which causes him to use again. And on it goes.

A narcotic addict replaces what used to give him joy naturally with a drug because the reward, or high, he gets from real life is no longer enough. People, places, activities, intimacy, love, and sex pale in comparison to the pain-free euphoria of highly addictive narcotics like codeine, morphine, heroin, Vicodin, and oxycodone. Before long, the addict begins to resent anyone or anything that interferes with his drug acquisition and use, and develops a "drug personality." He harbors secret animosity, hatred, hostility, and paranoia. Events that are entirely benign to someone not on drugs may appear sinister or threatening to the addict. His moods swing. He isolates, constructing a life where he can be alone with the one thing he loves and the only thing that matters: his drug.

"But does all of this end when someone stops using the substance or behavior?" I asked.

I didn't get the emphatic "Yes!" I had wanted, though I got something even more valuable—a truth I would have to carry into all of my relationships for the rest of my life. A truth I knew, that we all know but still don't seem to think applies to us personally. Each person only has control over his or her own life and choices, and there will never be any way around that. I cannot and never will be able to force someone or love someone enough to get him or her to start or stop doing anything. One's choices are always one's own, even if I don't like them, even if I think there are better choices, even if they are deadly.

I thought of all the addicts in this place, of the addicts filling the thousands of clinics across the country, and tried to imagine their thought processes. How does someone make the kinds of choices that lead to heartache, broken homes, lost careers, legal trouble, even death? As we were leaving for the day, one of the counselors turned to me and said, "You know, the substance or behavior in this pain cycle can be a relationship, too. And it is a choice to have a healthy or a harmful one."

Back at the hotel, I sat on the bed, hardly believing I had been at the clinic only a day and a half. My body felt like it had always been there. It had absorbed the weight of the place, thick and oppressive from years of accumulating each patient's brokenness, sadness, pain, confusion, and wasted time.

I concentrated on trying to feel, not think, as I relived the day. I got to my feelings easily enough, but not the reasons for having them. Why did I feel like everyone was trying to say something without saying it? Why did I feel like I was the focus of all the lectures and discussions rather than my husband? Why did I feel even more off balance and confused in a place that was supposed to provide support and clarity? I didn't know what I should or shouldn't do, or even what I was allowed to do. What I thought I understood before I came to the clinic wasn't so clear anymore. Right and wrong, acceptable and unacceptable seemed to have switched places. What I had imagined Family Week would be like and what it actually was couldn't have been more different than if one were fiction and one fact. But if I'd learned only one thing from this day, the addict's pain cycle showed me that all these years I had been trying to fix something I didn't remotely understand.

We opened Wednesday morning with a Feelings Check, and I braced myself for another day of everything I didn't expect. We didn't start with our homework. Instead, we all spent the morning telling our stories just as the counselor had done the day before.

I didn't understand at the time how important stories—mine as well as everyone else's—would become to my life and healing. We learn about ourselves not just through self-examination, but also through the lives of others. In rehab or twelve-step meetings, you show where you are in your recovery, or whether you are in recovery at all, by your story. And you are not in recovery if the story you told on your last day at the clinic is the same story you told on your first.

In the beginning, denial, fear, justification, and anger keep a story focused on others: "I am an addict because he did this; because she said that; because of my parents, my spouse, my kids, my job, *you*." It is in this first step of revealing trauma and releasing pain where you find your voice, the ability to say the things, however clouded and corrupt, out loud and in your own words that you never could before. But no one can recover by staying here. Moving past the pain and trauma, the blaming and shaming, and all the false perceptions and distorted thinking that make you a victim gives you the power to heal yourself rather than others the power to keep you broken.

As painful as it is, telling others who *you* are—all the things you've thought, felt, said, and done that you've spent years hiding through lies, denial, isolation, and addiction—helps you get from finding your voice to using it for its highest and most healing purpose. It's where you begin to make the connections between what others did to you as a child and what you have done to yourself as an adult. And each time you tell one more secret, one more truth, you bring your story one step closer to authenticity, and your life one step higher toward your true purpose. This is where you'll begin to find resolutions. Where you'll first glimpse awareness. Where you'll know how you've been living, what you've done, and where you've been is no longer who, what, or where you want to be.

After many stories, I began to hear a difference between several of them and that first story I heard from the counselor during my husband's Family Week. His words seemed to free him, each one an open door rather than an obstacle. Each one used to heal himself rather than harm someone else. But far from freeing, some stories only seemed to add more weight to loved ones, as if the storytellers were just looking for a place to dump all the words, not use them toward a greater understanding. And in the end there was more pain, not less, leaving no room for connections, compassion, healing, or love.

By the time we finished our stories it was close to noon. As we walked to the cafeteria, I noticed something for the first time that seemed to contradict a rehabilitation clinic's very purpose: the smoke pits. Three small outside areas—one for men, one for women, and one co-ed—with wooden benches and folding chairs where the addicts went to smoke cigarettes. After lunch, I asked a counselor if this didn't work against their goal of transforming addiction and promote it instead. He said that, in the beginning, the clinic had either thought about or actually attempted to ban cigarettes from the premises. But because many addicts also have a nicotine addiction, administrators found most refused to check into rehab for their other problems if they couldn't smoke. So they chose to try to remove the substances and behaviors that put the addict in immediate danger first, and hoped the rest would eventually follow. But the paradox was startling: attempting to break addiction by allowing addiction.

Besides prison, rehab can be one of the most controlled and controlling environments imaginable. The administration takes away reading materials, television choices, music, phones, computers, and most free time. It controls what patients eat, see, and hear, and their access to the outside world. It makes choices for those who are not able to make healthy and balanced ones for themselves, while trying to teach them how. But in the beginning, the more I observed and heard about the smoke pits, the more I felt they actually encouraged bad choices for some addicts.

One thing known about addiction is that it's about substitution, not elimination. Substituting harmful environments, behaviors, feelings, thought processes, and patterns with healthy ones. And balance is the key to all of it. Even seemingly healthy substitutions, like exercise or religion, can quickly become unhealthy and off-balance with extreme perceptions, thoughts, and behaviors. But from what I had now learned about the effects of trauma on core issues, addicts don't know healthy and can only function in extremes. And when what an addict has turned to for years to act as a barrier between himself and his pain is taken away, he will only care about replacing it with whatever will rebuild that barrier the fastest.

And healthy is not fast.

The path to the highest purpose of every choice—finding the real truth rather than what we imagine it to be, and what is wanted from us rather than what we want for ourselves—is a very slow process of unraveling one misperception, one mistake, one untruth, and one twisted pattern, thought, behavior, and feeling at a time and replacing it with what is balanced and healing. It was interesting to see which substitutions some of the addicts preferred when nearly every quick fix was taken away from them, and when they were given the opportunity to choose for themselves from what was left. Some cigar smokers with a distaste for cigarettes and those who smoked them now spent their free time at the smoke pits, first bumming cigarettes from others, then eventually purchasing packs of their own. And some addicts who had checked into the clinic as non-smokers left with nearly a pack-a-day habit.

The smoke pits were also where many addicts used the lives of others to keep from looking at their own. Through gossip they could pass judgment on someone else's recovery or behavior, keep their focus on everything outside rather than inside their own hearts and minds, and use their words to shame others rather than heal themselves.

I would later see the value in giving addicts breathing room to make some of their own choices, then stepping back to watch as they made them. Much like being able to tell where an addict is in his recovery by his story, you can also tell how committed he is to getting well from where he chooses his substitutions: those that lead to sobriety or those that keep him addicted.

We were now well into the third day of my husband's Family Week. Every day I brought with me a manila envelope holding the four pages I had written before I left, and every day I asked the counselors for the chance to read them. They always said no. Sensing another opportunity after lunch, I asked again. Our Feedback Loop homework was to list all the things that had caused us pain. I had already done that in these pages. It may not have been in the form they wanted, but at that time I thought I deserved, had even earned the right to read it the way I felt it. Once again, they said no. Unlike the freestyle format we used to tell our stories, our Feedback Loop homework was to be discussed within a specific structure and for an intended purpose, and what I was asking to do didn't fit into any of it.

In a healthy discussion there are two roles: one who speaks and one who listens. These roles are to be carried out literally. If you are in the "speaking chair," you alone speak. If you are in the "listening chair," your only task is to listen. There is no interrupting, talking over each other to say the first reactive or defensive thing that comes to mind, or focusing your attention on your response rather than the speaker. Replacing our dysfunctional communication methods with productive ones allows the person listening to listen with honor and the person speaking to share with respect.

The speaker first communicates what has caused him pain using the Feedback Loop. Once the speaker has finished, the listener puts what he's heard through a mental filter. If the listener believes the statement is true, he opens his boundaries and responds by expressing his thoughts and feelings through the Feedback Loop. If he believes it is not true, he refuses to let the statement in by closing his boundaries, deflecting it back to the speaker. The listener can now see the statement as something the speaker is saying about himself rather than about the listener. For instance, if an addict accuses an honest person of stealing from him, the listener keeps his boundaries intact and reminds himself that the addict is actually revealing the truth of his own dishonesty. If the listener is unable to determine whether the statement is true or not, he asks for more information until he can.

For so many, the listening chair is one of the most difficult parts of the recovery process. Regardless of how well it is said, this is where you will hear how much you have hurt others when you, if the addict, may still not be willing to accept responsibility for your part, or you, if the enabler, are still feeling so much pain of your own. This is where the counselors hope for healthy and honest communication, which can be glorious to see. But sometimes there is a disconnect so great it's hard to know if it's because there is so much in between keeping everyone apart, or nothing there to begin with.

It was late afternoon when my time in the listening and speaking chairs ended, and I remember feeling so tired. I told the counselors I wanted to read what I had written before coming there and then go home. They said I could read it the following day, but they asked me not to leave. There was still so much good work ahead, so many positive and healing moments that could occur. Miracles happen every day.

On the drive back to the hotel that afternoon, I wondered why the counselors had spoken of miracles. Why they had just spent three days trying to rid me of my expectations, fantasies, and illusions only to add one more. But I could tell them about miracles—what it means to hope for one because you've got nothing left to hope for, and what it feels like when the miracle never comes.

It was hard to get out of bed the next morning, but I knew the sooner I did, the sooner I could say what I had come to say and go home. I missed my house. And my kids. And Punkin. But most of all, I was feeling the loss of my beloved Bonnie Blue, who had passed away just a few months earlier. I wanted just one thing in my life that made sense. Just one thing that felt and smelled and sounded familiar.

After the Feelings Check, I pulled out my pages and read. Today, what was written on those pages would be much different. But at that moment, I let out a lifetime of buried pain, broken trust, and a confusion so profound I believed I'd lost my mind and soul, and three hours of Feedback Loop instruction would never have been enough to hold it back.

In the span of a year, I would be asked three questions that would change my life. After I'd finished reading, and after a silence that was too long to be comfortable, a counselor asked the first one: "What about you?"

And there it was. In just three words he said what both counselors had been trying to say in a million different ways all week.

"What *about* me?" I asked, barely believing I had heard the question at all. "You have ripped open my life and told me everything I did out of love wasn't really love. What I thought was right was wrong. What I thought was helping only made things worse. I am truly trying my best to understand what is happening here, but I am not the drug addict. I have never betrayed my husband or broken our vows. All I've done these past ten years is try to do my part to make our marriage work and do it as honorably as I can. I don't understand why this is so bad."

I then heard the second question that changed my life: "Why did you stay?"

If I knew then what I know now, I would have been able to answer that question. I would have seen that blaming my husband, judging his life and his choices, was easy, and giving myself a pass, ignoring my own questionable choices and motivations, was even easier. I would have spoken of what I'd learned about truth and denial, wisdom and ignorance, the acceptable and unacceptable. And I would have realized the second thing the counselors wanted me to understand if I were to have a successful Family Week: It is about me.

By Family Week, the addict has already been a part of the program as an inpatient for three weeks. He's already heard the Dance and the Pain Cycle; already been using the Feedback Loop; already been to weeks of group therapy, psychiatry sessions, and daily twelve-step meetings; already told his story dozens of times. While the addict's program is still far from over, the clinic hopes Family Week is just the beginning for his family members. But just like banning cigarette smoking would keep most addicts from coming to rehab, telling family members that there is never just one sick person in a sick relationship or family, and that the week is about each of them discovering his or her own part in the dysfunctional system, would keep many of them from coming anywhere near Family Week.

But Family Week was about me in an even more important way. It was about my thoughts and behaviors, my words and feelings, my choices and patterns, my motivations and intentions, my mistakes and adjustments, my refinement, my journey, my redemption, my highest purpose, and the first step toward awakening to all of it. But all I said was, "Please. I just want to go home."

When I first got to the clinic, I was asked to fill out several pages of family history. The questions ranged from the number of siblings I had and their ages, my parents' names, their ages, and if they were still married and living, to asking for specific examples of abuse. Still not understanding why they wanted to know so much about me, I answered what I knew about my family and then simply wrote *yes* without much detail for the questions about abuse.

It was this history the counselors now used, hoping to convince me not only to stay, but stay for another week. They said I had too many unresolved things from my past, and working through them could heal my life as well as help my marriage. I asked how they could be unresolved if I had never denied or suppressed them, or used a substance or behavior to make believe they never happened.

"I know what is there," I assured them. "But it is done, and I can't change any of it. And I don't want to let what happened back then control my life now by reliving it."

They said there were things I knew and things I didn't, and what I didn't know was controlling my life now, whether I wanted it to or not. As long as I kept myself uninformed, my choices were not mine. They weren't even choices, but reactions to situations all those things I didn't know, or hadn't resolved, kept putting me in over and over. I was trying to stay one step ahead of something that was already beyond my reach, and would continue to escalate until the day I resolved not only to know, but know why, and how to change. I could say I had accepted my past, I could say I had moved on, but my behavior said something entirely different. To authentically accept my past as well as use it to my benefit, I had to reconcile what I know with what I do.

They believed the way for me to begin was through Survivors Week, which would delve into my childhood from birth to seventeen years old. They compared Family Week to surgery, where I was cut open and the dysfunction, like a disease, was exposed. Survivors Week would get to the source of the dysfunction, give me the tools to understand and repair it, and close me up again so the healing could begin.

But I could only be amazed that the counselors had found yet another way to ask the "What about you?" question. I wanted to say I thought they were crazy. I wanted to say I thought *they* were the ones who needed more rehab. What I said was no. But I found that "no" to a therapist means "please ask again." And they did. They said if I went home now, raw as I was, I would be walking into a place that would seem more a haunted house than a haven. I told them they couldn't possibly know what my home meant to me. It was my sanctuary, my refuge, the one place I felt protected. But they believed when I closed the door to that house, I wouldn't be keeping out everything that hurt me, but locking myself inside with every bit of it.

"It is everywhere," a counselor said. "In every color, piece of fabric, and painting. It is a monument to pain. It is what you wanted so badly as a child, a happy home, but couldn't create no matter how hard you tried, and still can't create in your marriage. But there is a way to understand it and Survivors Week will help you. You can change it. You can rebuild. But you have to start with yourself."

I still said no to Survivors Week, but the counselors did convince me to stay for the last day of Family Week, which was when we would discuss our negotiable and non-negotiable issues, express what we liked and loved about each other, and make amends for our transgressions.

Later that night, I found it much easier to write down what was negotiable than what wasn't. It was the finality of saying *this* is non-negotiable. No discussion. No compromise. Because this time, I knew it wouldn't be about my husband standing by his commitments to me, but me standing by my commitments to myself.

In time, I would learn how other addicts and their wives confronted a non-negotiable issue. Addicts who are still deep in their addictions see anyone wanting to discuss limits as controlling. It doesn't matter how reasonable the request is, how much sense it makes, or how intrinsic it is to a healthy relationship or life. There can be no lines in the sand, no ultimatums. Addicts "don't like surprises," meaning anything they can't control or that may interfere with their addiction. And they will not tolerate challenges to their belief systems and defense mechanisms. So they develop ways to shut down anything non-negotiable. Some will appear to abide by a non-negotiable by replacing one addiction with another. For instance, an addict may stop using drugs but escalate his sex addiction, which to that point had been masked by his drug use. Others will use a very potent manipulation tool to silence anyone requiring limits or restrictions: guilt. Sometimes the guilt is based on personal information or a sensitive issue that is particular to one person; sometimes it is based on a collective idea of what is socially desirable—and there are no accusations a man can use to more effectively suppress a woman's question, request, or requirement than those of emasculation and control.

Wives of addicts tell how they feel unable to move beyond the limbo their marriages were mired in, and unable to express what they would no longer accept in the relationship for fear of being branded something a woman often has no defense against: a domineering bitch. If she questions the addict's conflicting words and behaviors, he says she is questioning his manhood by treating him like a child. If she sets limits on what she will accept from her husband, he says she is trying to change him and control his life. To which I've heard more than one frustrated wife respond, "If I were controlling you, you wouldn't be an addict."

Relationships are made of a constant flow of interactions, and any interaction will be about either power or force. Power is movement and progress. Force creates stalemates and decay. One leads to growth, the other to inevitable demise.

But many confuse force with power. The difference is in your intention. Force only benefits you. It's about what you want, even when you try to make it look like what you're doing is meant to help someone else, and your motivation comes from fear. You are afraid of being abandoned, unloved, unwanted, unappreciated, of not belonging, of not having enough, of not getting your share, of the unknown. It's when you must have everything your way because controlling others is where you find your self-worth. Force is coercion and manipulation. Force is guilt and threats. Force is fear and control. Force is ridicule, shame, and blame. And when one person dominates another there is no power or balance, only weakness and instability. There is no love. And there is no relationship.

Power is where you want the decision, the discussion, the process to benefit everyone, not just you; where you want everyone strengthened, everyone to find balance, everyone to speak, act, and live from truth and clarity rather than fear; where cooperation is better than control; where sharing the relationship is better than owning it; where you don't need to manipulate or coerce or ridicule someone to provide your value because who you are comes from what you give yourself, not what you steal from someone else; where even if they don't want you, don't love you, want the exact opposite of what you want, you can let go—even walk away if you have to—without fear. Because power is knowing there is a place and enough for everyone, and knowing that everything good comes from relationships that are built on love, truth, trust, respect, humility, accountability, and openness.

I've heard it said that a compromise is where nobody wins. But this can only come from one whose self-worth is so low he has to force himself on others to become elevated in his own eyes. By making himself the only one with the right words and the right way, others are always wrong, their input always without value. So he ceases to accept new perspectives and ideas. Feeling discounted, others cease to provide them, and all growth stops.

A negotiable has both parties backing off and moving forward. It is within this flow where new ideas and information arise, where integration occurs, or where what has gone before is refined or discarded for something more appropriate. The joy comes from creating something powerful that takes a step toward benefiting everyone, not forcing something that provides a fraudulent sense of self-worth for just one.

Within a marriage, negotiables show whom and what your spouse values, what he or she hopes to strengthen, and where the focus lies: on the marriage, on you, on him- or herself, or on all of it. But non-negotiables are almost impossible to properly present or understand if they aren't spoken and heard through clear and healthy minds—and rehab is not a place for either clear or healthy minds.

We discussed our negotiable and non-negotiable lists the rest of the morning. After lunch came our likes, loves, and amends. My husband went first, and it went fast. I kept thinking there was more to come. Some grand gesture or big finish. So I sat and waited for that miracle the counselors had spoken of. There was none.

After I read my likes and loves and had made amends, there was nothing more to discuss or diagram; no more stories, lessons, or lectures. Family Week was over. But looking back, it seems the miracle may have come after all.

I had to leave soon if I was to be on time for my flight home. As I stood, both counselors spoke again about my staying for Survivors Week. I didn't hear much of what they said, only my own voice within asking, *Why does nothing feel resolved? What did I miss? And what do I do now?* I didn't know what I'd missed, what message I hadn't heard, but I did remember my vow to never stop until I ran out of questions. The problem was that the place I was being encouraged to look for answers was the clinic. I didn't want to return, but I didn't know of an alternative. I turned to the counselors and told them I would attend Survivors Week, but I had to go home for the weekend first. I had a house to take care of, bills to pay, and I needed to see my kids and Punkin. They weren't happy with the compromise, afraid that once I was home I wouldn't come back. But I knew I had to go, and that I would come back. Just as the counselors had taught me, this was what a negotiable looked like, and it would only succeed if we both kept our word.

It was late when I got home that Friday night. I walked in the door and called out for Punkin. She came running, as happy to see me as I was her. I picked her up and buried my face in her fur. I'd missed everything about her, and I wished so much that Bonnie were there. I carried Punkin upstairs to the bedroom and stood in the doorway. It was hard to step through it, and I remembered feeling the same way my first day of Family Week. I closed my eyes and said to myself, *I am home*. And with Punkin in my arms, walked into the room.

The weekend was barely there before it was over. I spent it unpacking and repacking and wondering why I had agreed to return to the clinic for another week. My children were as confused about it as I was. When they asked why I was going back, all I could say was that it had made sense at the time.

By Saturday night I had taken care of everything necessary. It was late and Punkin was already in our bed, curled up and fast asleep. I joined her but simply lay there. Knowing I had to leave the next day for the clinic did little to encourage sleep. I thought of the name, Survivors Week, and found nothing comforting or hopeful in those words.

By morning I was tired, I was anxious, but I was going. I grabbed my bag, kissed Punkin goodbye, and took my first step toward something that didn't look much like a miracle at the time. There was no epiphany, no rays of Jesus light streaming through the clouds, no angels, no choir. But this moment would transform me by inches, through stretches of pain and confusion, through flashes of peace and understanding, for the rest of my life.

On the first day of Survivors Week I was taken to the same building where I'd spent my husband's Family Week, but a different room. It was packed. I saw an empty seat and thanked God it was in the back. Seated at the front of the room, facing us, were several counselors. One by one, they introduced themselves and told their stories. They were big stories of multiple addictions over decades, broken marriages and broken laws, mental breakdowns and deteriorating bodies, relapse after recovery attempt after relapse. And I didn't belong here.

After the last story, one of the counselors said it was our turn to introduce ourselves and say why we were there. An animal both chained and caged could not have had any more fear than I at that moment. They started at the front row. Name. Alcohol and sex addiction. Name. Drug addiction and theft. Name. Gambling and debt. Name. Depression and suicide. Name. Eating disorder and overspending. Name. All of the above. When my turn came I wanted to shout, "NONE OF THE ABOVE!" Instead I said, "Marta. Codependent, maybe?"

The counselors then divided us into smaller groups, assigning each group a counselor and the room number where we were to meet after lunch. I got to the room at the designated time and found our counselor and a few patients already there talking lightheartedly, almost as if they knew each other. Some of them did. There were six in my Survivors group. Some were staying in hotels and attending the workshop as an outpatient as I was. Others were patients in the clinic and this was week two of their five-week program.

Our counselor introduced herself again but did not retell her story. I liked her right away, for no particular reason. She opened the afternoon by explaining what we could expect from the week. Survivors had three parts. The first was a deeper exploration of boundaries. What I'd learned in my husband's Family Week was how to use them to effectively communicate in the present. Survivors Week concentrated on the boundaries of my childhood and how their violation might have led to trauma and, eventually, to where I was today. But boundaries at any age and in any situation are about protection. We protect ourselves from having our boundaries breached by others, and we protect others by containing ourselves within proper boundaries. Our external boundaries shield us from the physical, verbal, and emotional violations of others, such as standing too close, improper touching, eavesdropping, offensive sexual comments, leering, and forced or abusive sexual activity. But we harm others when we violate our own internal boundaries through lying, sarcasm, ridicule, manipulating, interrupting, and breaking commitments.

However, children are not born with developed or functional boundaries and take their cues from their caregivers. And if the parents' boundaries are dysfunctional, chances are good the child's will be as well. When parents repeatedly breach a child's boundaries, he learns this is how he should be treated and how he should treat others.

The second part of Survivors, called Debriefing, began the following morning. For the next two days, we were to dig as far back as we could remember and pull up the boundary violations, those "less than nurturing" experiences from which we were not protected. I didn't have to look very far. I have always known what shouldn't have happened, but I didn't know how I was going to say the words loud enough for strangers to hear.

Rather than choose from among us, our counselor asked for a volunteer to go first. One woman, an outpatient in her early fifties, raised her hand. She told her story, and then two more went after her. They showed me how to tell a story one has never told before, how to say out loud the words that were never spoken even inside one's own heart and soul.

The remaining three of us told our stories the following day. However, each time the counselor asked for a volunteer, my hand never felt light enough to lift. I was the last to tell my story.

I was a cute little girl with long, ringed hair and big, soft, brown eyes. There was a clover field with a pond near where I lived. I used to sit alone in that field for hours and make clover chains. I'd bring mason jars to the pond to catch tadpoles, always letting them go after a day or two because I knew their families missed them. But my favorite time was the first snow. Looking out into the black night, watching the flakes fall, always felt like Christmas to me because I knew I would wake up the next morning and see that God had wrapped the world in white and laid it as a gift outside my front door.

In winter, I had to wear one of those pointy knit caps with a fringed ball on top and a big, puffy coat that always took too much time to climb into; my restless excitement to get outside before my older sisters made it take even longer. Being the first one out in fresh snow was the best thing I had ever known. Being the first one to make a snow angel was even better. Through my snow angel I saw my real angel, the one who watched over me night and day. The older kids said it was stupid. Real angels wouldn't lie down in snow when they have wings to fly. But I knew air made angels invisible. Snow made them real.

My earliest memory was when I was four years old, and it was the first snow. I wriggled into my coat and hat and blasted out the front door, slamming it behind me. My father was in the living room watching television. I knew better than to slam the front door. I had been told a hundred times. There were two steps from the front door to the front yard. My feet had barely touched the first one before my head was yanked back by my hair, lifting me off the ground. In the split second it took for my feet to touch ground again, my father had taken one side of my head in his hand and rammed the other into the front door. "I told you not to slam the door!" he said. I let out a scream that brought my mother running. She took me inside and looked for something to make an icepack. Then she put me in bed and sat beside me, holding the ice to my head until I stopped crying. I missed the first snow. And I didn't get to make a snow angel or see my real angel, the one who watched over me night and day.

Many years passed before I made the connection between my father's drinking and his anger and disappointment with his life. When you're a child of an alcoholic, you don't look for connections or explanations or reasons. You only look for two things: a way to make him happy and a way out if you can't. There are things I remember doing at a very young age, like waiting out of sight when my father drove up to see what kind of mood he was in. And things I remember feeling, like my chest pulled tight and my stomach aching. None of these are what a little girl who only wanted to make clover chains and snow angels should have known.

But I didn't understand that then. It was just the way things were. I was small and my father was big. He was right and I was always doing something wrong. Life was about his happiness and ability to do exactly what he wanted when he wanted. As long as I didn't interfere with that, he wouldn't hurt me with his hands or his belt.

I was eleven and just entering puberty the first time my father treated me like his wife instead of his daughter.

I had to stop and catch my breath. I looked at the counselor, hoping for a reprieve. I didn't want to go any further. She looked back full of compassion and unafraid for me; she believed I could do it. I wasn't sure. I took another breath and went on.

I was eleven. We were in the living room, which was used only for guests and special occasions. It was mid-evening and my father and I were playing gin. My family loved games of any kind and we were all very competitive. We always wanted to play against my father, especially cards, because he was so good—and if you could beat my father, so were you. I had never beaten him. I was sitting cross-legged on the floor. He was stretched out, his back against the front of an upholstered armchair. He kept moving his feet in such a way to try to open my legs. Eventually he did. Before, during, and after each hand I would close them again, but he would always get them uncrossed either by prying them open or, when I resisted, by telling me to. It went on like this for hours.

Why didn't I tell him I was uncomfortable? Why didn't I get up and leave? Because I didn't know I could. And because I was winning. So much that I had now won fourteen hands in a row. During number fifteen, my father looked at his cards and then looked again. He let out a laugh and called gin. He said he had to look at them twice because it had been so long since he'd won. By this time it was late and everyone had gone to bed, so I got up to leave. He pulled me down and on top of him in one movement.

My father was wearing thin gray slacks without a belt and a white, short-sleeved T-shirt. He was barefoot. His face was rough with stubble and his hair combed back and slick with tonic. He was wearing Old Spice aftershave. I can tell you where every blister, callous, and cut were on his hands and fingers. He touched me in places and with parts that should never have touched me, and I saw things I should never have seen. It happened twice more, in different rooms and under different circumstances. And each time, I burned every detail into my brain. I never wanted to forget because I never wanted him to say it didn't happen. I had learned one thing about my father. He lied. All the time. Even when he didn't need to. Even when the truth was easier.

I sat there for a while to see how I felt about what I had just done. I hadn't cried as I spoke, but each word was full of emotion. I looked around the room. I still had everyone's attention. The tears started to come when I admitted that I was ashamed I hadn't left, hadn't known I could, and that I should never have been wearing my favorite green shorts I am sure I'd outgrown the year before. It had taken me over thirty years to say what I had felt that night, and still felt on that day. It was my fault.

The counselor ended the day with a discussion on "carried shame." Because a child's boundaries—the very thing designed to protect him— are still undeveloped, he indiscriminately soaks up everything around him. So when coming in contact with trauma, he has no choice but to absorb his offender's behavior.

Panic-stricken, I quickly searched my mind for things I may have done to violate my children's boundaries and set them up for trauma. I was relieved when the counselor said all parents make mistakes. Obvious abusive, violent, or sexual trauma aside, it's impossible to always say and do the right things at the right time. But the difference between the mistakes of a functional parent and a dysfunctional one is what happens afterward. A functional parent will hold himself accountable for his behavior and explain that it wasn't the child's fault, thereby alleviating any guilt or shame the child may be feeling. A dysfunctional parent traumatizes the child and then walks away, leaving the child behind to wonder what he did to cause the abuse.

The counselor's point was that none of it was my fault. The adult me heard her clearly and knew what she said was true. But the eleven-year-old had lived with the guilt and shame for so long it was hard to believe anything else.

She went on to say that we were not here to blame our offenders or even determine whether the abuse was intentional. This week was about setting ourselves free from feelings that were never ours to begin with. And the Experientials, the final phase of Survivors Week, was where the liberation began.

The Experientials began on our fourth day and I watched as, one by one, three of my peers underwent the process. It was during these Experientials that I most understood the reason for not just visualizing boundaries, but making them as real, substantive, and purposeful as possible. I would later hear participants in other rooms describe their Experientials as uneventful, even a waste of time. Fortunately, this was not the case with my group. In the beginning, we were just as nervous and in the dark as everyone else about Experientials. But we were also committed to something larger than our fear: knowing and healing ourselves. This meant participating in every process to its fullest extent while trusting the counselors to keep us safe.

The counselor called my name on the final day. I went up to the front of the room and sat in the single chair. She pulled her chair next to mine, facing my side. Everyone else sat lined up against the left wall. The counselor began by asking us all to close our eyes and take a few deep breaths. She spent the next several minutes on relaxation, helping us work out the tension that saturates an emotional environment such as this. There were moments when I thought my nervousness would overwhelm me, but I kept my eyes closed and did the breathing as well as I could. Next came the boundary visualization, which was crucial for us all. Those along the wall knew my process was going to take me further into the abuse, and I knew I was going to come face to face with my abusers.

The counselor asked that we visualize an appropriate boundary for what we were about to experience. It could be anything, such as an unbreakable, impenetrable clear covering that kept out all painful emotion but still allowed one to see and be seen, or a diving suit that let an observer venture into the process with the participant but kept anything from soaking in. Some surrounded themselves in light, some in crystal, some in their God. When we had gone through the relaxation and boundary visualization, the counselor softly asked me what I had chosen as my boundary. It was armor.

My eyes still closed, she told me to go back to a childhood home and describe what I saw. It was a small, three-bedroom, red brick house. My parents slept in one room, my two younger brothers in another, my two older sisters and I in the last. Most of what I remembered centered on music, which is the first thing I was aware of that made me truly happy. It took over every one of my senses and I would be wherever the song said I was. Most of the time, it pushed all of my little girl energy out through my arms and legs and lungs, and I couldn't sit still or keep quiet no matter how many times my parents asked me to.

My sisters and I shared a small portable phonograph. My records of nursery rhymes and children's songs were fine, but I loved my oldest sister's records best and would play them whenever I thought I wouldn't get caught. Little Eva. The Four Tops. The Supremes. My favorite song was "Come See About Me," though I had no idea what Diana Ross was saying. It sounded like *bop beedle bop bee* to me, so that's what I danced to all around the house, singing as loudly as my little girl voice would allow.

The counselor then asked me to picture a place during this time where I felt safe and happy, such as a favorite room in the house, a dock by a lake, or a big tree in the back yard. I went back to the clover field. It was wildly in bloom, clover blossoms everywhere. I ran through them, brushed my hands over the tops of them, buried my face and body in them to get their smell on my skin. The counselor asked if I could see myself as a little girl in the field. I said yes. She wanted me to describe her. I was wearing one of my sister's old dresses that I loved because it had been worn so much that the fabric was thin and cloud soft. My brown hair was long, halfway down my back. It had been brushed and pinned up in the morning, but by then strands had pulled free and the soft curls were running wild. I was sitting in the middle of the field making a clover chain. It was almost the end of summer and the end of the day. Dusk had brought cooler air. The setting sun was ablaze in colors so close I could touch them. I lay on my back in the clover and lifted my arms high above me to grab the pink, orange, and yellow streaks that filled the sky.

She asked if I had a special name I wanted to call this little girl. I said Em, the phonetic spelling of my first initial. Em was the name I had used when I wrote stories as a child and, later, in my journal. She then asked if I would mind if Em sat in my lap. My reaction was immediate. I didn't want to hold her. I didn't want her close to me. But four others had gone before me—women who had suffered much worse abuse than I, grown men with childhood trauma of their own—and all had embraced a younger version of themselves. I swallowed hard a few times and had trouble staying still in my chair. Finally I said, "Yes, I will take her." With my eyes still closed, the counselor gently placed a pillow in my lap. It was soft and warm and weightless.

She asked if there was anything I wanted to say to Em. I said no, so we all sat in silence. After a while, she took the pillow from me. I was still back in my childhood, getting ready to leave the clover field and enter the small brick house. She had me visualize my boundaries to make sure they were up and intact. I took a mental look at myself.

I was covered head to toe in solid black metal inches thick, with only the smallest openings around my face so I could see, hear, speak, and breathe. The counselor then asked whom I wanted to speak to first. I said my parents. My eyes were still closed, but I heard the door open and shut. There were footsteps and the sound of two chairs being pulled across the floor and placed in front of me. She asked me to open my eyes to see if the chairs were a comfortable distance from me. They were too close, so I told her to move them back, and then back some more. I closed my eyes again and heard my parents sit down across from me.

They weren't really there, but they may as well have been. I could see them so clearly in my mind. I saw how they looked when I was four, so much bigger and smarter than I. I saw them at six when we moved to a new house. Then at seven when they put in a swimming pool and I loved them so much for that. And at eleven when the house became a sad and painful place.

I spoke to my mother first. We'd had many mother-daughter arguments. So many that she put the "mother's curse" on me during one of our fights, saying I would have a daughter just like me one day. As a teen, I was rebellious to my core. I didn't know why. But I did know very early that I was without protection. If I needed help, no one would come. And I knew that this was a world of scarcity, not abundance; that there was never going to be enough for me, and if I wanted anything I had to either get there first or fight for it.

I told all of this to my mother as she sat in that chair across from me. That more than anything, I needed her to stand in front of me when bad things happened to me, to be my armor. And that I should never have learned I had to fight for everything because it wasn't true, though during the times I had to, I wanted her to fight with me. But most of all, I should have learned that life never runs out of good things, that there is plenty for everyone, and it all should have been in that little red brick house: the hugs and kisses, the laughter and bedtime stories, my mother sharing my delight in tadpoles and the clover field, my excitement at the first snow, and my belief in my beautiful snow angel. Everything that would have looked like love to a little girl like me.

There wasn't much more I wanted to say, so I asked her to leave. I heard footsteps again and one chair scrape across the floor. The door opened and quickly closed. That left me alone with my father. My chest and stomach were hurting now, and at first I didn't know what to say. I hung my head down as far as I could and told him quietly, "You hurt me."

I heard the counselor whisper in my ear, "Tell him how he hurt you."

I started to cry in gasps and couldn't catch my breath.

She said again, "Tell him what happened and how you felt."

I snapped my head up and screamed out as loudly as I could, "YOU HURT ME. I WAS ELEVEN. I WAS ONLY ELEVEN. WHY? WHY DID YOU HURT ME? THEN HURT ME AGAIN? AND AGAIN? I WAS SO YOUNG. JUST A LITTLE GIRL. AND I WAS NOT YOUR WIFE. I WAS YOUR DAUGHTER. I TRUSTED YOU. I NEVER HURT YOU. NEVER."

At some point during this, I felt a bataka bat slip into my hands. I had seen the others before me use this foam-filled bat. I lifted it and hit the chair before me as hard as I could with each word. I kept hitting the chair even after the words stopped, leaving only tears and pain. I hit and hit until all the pain that had been in my chest and stomach moved to my arms. After a while, I felt no pain. The tears had stopped. Eventually, numbness and fatigue kept me from lifting the bat again.

I was breathing heavily. The counselor spoke, but I didn't hear what she said. I sat down, quieted my breathing, and slowly regained feeling and awareness. When I felt stronger I laid down the bat and asked my father to leave.

The counselor asked whom I wanted to speak to next and I said my husband. I heard him come in and close the door. As soon as the counselor told me he was in the room, my body clenched. It was too much for me to have my husband in the same room, sit in the same chair as my father, and in an instant they became the same person. With tight fists, I stood up and started to walk toward him. I heard the counselor call my name and tell me to stop. She brought me back to the present and back to my chair. She never explained why. But whatever the reason, everyone saw—except me.

After each Experiential, the rest of the group gave feedback using the Feedback Loop and offered unconditional support and acceptance. It was no different with me, except for one thing. They all said I needed to come back for the full five-week program. I felt myself collapse from a force both within and outside of me. I asked them why, what did they see? The word I heard most often was "deep." That the childhood wounds from both of my parents were so deep I couldn't get out, and as an adult I had surrounded myself with people who made sure I never would; and that the disconnect between the sad four-year-old, the damaged eleven-year-old, and the adult me was so immense that when the counselor put the pillow that represented my inner child in my arms, I held them out as far away from her as I could. I never hugged her. I didn't touch her. She just sat there in my lap—unprotected.

After the last Experiential, the counselor ended the day by giving us quarter-sized coins commemorating our work during Survivors Week. We all hugged and promised to stay in touch. I walked out of the room with mixed emotions. I understood more about the connection between my past and my present, and why I had to go back to my childhood to find the patterns in order to change them. But remembering bits and pieces of my life and dealing with singular memories as they arose was one thing. It was something else to have forty years dug up at once—all of it—from my father to my husband. And it was no life I, or anyone, should have had. This life was chosen for me when I was young, and when I got older and could have chosen any other life, I picked the same one for myself over and over.

I was sitting alone outside, waiting for a ride to take me to the airport, when someone from my group sat down beside me. We talked about the experience and how we felt about it. I said I still wanted to know why. What was the point of a life like that? What was a child supposed to do with experiences like those? The beautiful, innocent little girl that was supposed to be never had a chance. I could not change my childhood. I could not change my parents. I could not change one thing that happened. And I hated that part. Not only did I feel cheated, but I had cheated my children and my husband out of the chance to be with someone who was whole.

He listened quietly to it all, and afterwards said something like "everything happens for a reason," which I honestly didn't want to hear. But then he said this:

Let's assume the near-perfect family we all wanted even exists, and that's assuming a lot. Do you think all those with wonderful childhoods lead wonderful adult lives? They've got plenty of problems of their own, and some of these people are working them out in this clinic. They have a sense of entitlement to love since they only learned to take it, not give it. And they lack the strength and growth that only comes from adversity because their parents shielded them from as much pain as possible when they were children. This led them to shield themselves as adults with whatever made them feel good when the inevitable hard times came.

These people may be nice to be around for a while and seem normal enough in the beginning, but it isn't real. As long as they stay on the selfish bottom rung of life, they will be incapable of knowing how to be there for someone else, unless there is something in it for them. Your childhood adversity has made you loving, giving, and strong. If I had to choose someone to be in the trenches with, someone I trusted to be there in bad times as well as good, it would be you. Not someone who's only lived half a life and thinks the world owes him the other half. I would choose you precisely because you didn't just survive pain, but barreled through it on your own, and now have the courage to find the lessons in it all.

This was something I had never heard before, someone appreciating me *because* of my dysfunctional childhood. It was this very dysfunctional childhood that gave me the tools to survive it. And when all I had learned to survive in an unhealthy life no longer served me, it gave me the strength and courage to search for the new tools I needed to live a healthy one. So all that had happened to me as a child had to happen for me to understand that my entire life was going to be about making one choice: stay broken or heal. It showed me, through a constant flow of people and situations, how to change and make adjustments, and the consequences of not doing so when life demanded it. And it taught me that, if I were going to live my best life, I would never be done changing, learning, or growing, and that I could never do any of it alone.

Trying to create a life without pain is thinking with a child's mind, because there is no such thing. There was never supposed to be. We shouldn't seek out or wallow in it, but adversity is growth. Growth means greater strength and one step closer to a fulfilled life. And living our purpose gives us everything we need to face the next trial that comes along.

But there is a definite fork in the road with trauma. We can use it to make ourselves and others better by learning from it, or it can use us to make our lives and every life we touch worse by becoming a slave to it. My time had come to decide which way I was going to go.

Finally home later that Friday night, I was not as comfortable as I thought I would be. I kept hearing those in my Survivors group saying I should go back for the entire five-week program. It was unthinkable. I couldn't grasp how I had gone from my husband's Family Week to being told I needed to be in treatment myself. I could understand if I had told them I was drinking or drugging or sleeping around, but I wasn't doing any of that. I was just trying to be a good person and a good wife and, without question, I thought the two weeks I had already spent in the clinic were enough.

All day Saturday, I was back doing what I normally did to keep the house running. Late that night, I was alone in a big house and could only think about what lay ahead for me because I still didn't understand why. By morning, I realized that if I didn't go back, I might never know why. I called the clinic and they confirmed they had an available bed. Immediately the weight of the moment surrounded me. I knew that the very next words out of my mouth were going to affect me, one way or another, for the rest of my life. And that the choice—growth or brokenness, consciousness or ignorance, yes or no—was one only I could make. My silence grew, and I thought of how easy it would be to simply hang up. But instead, and with a heavy acceptance, I said I was on my way.

Part II

The Clinic

I thought it reasonable to assume that formally checking into the clinic wouldn't be too difficult since I'd already spent two weeks there, but it wasn't so. This would make sense to me later; spending time in rehab was not something I ever wanted to get used to. But I wasn't prepared for the total disorientation and lack of control. Going back to a hotel room every night during my husband's Family Week and my week in Survivors gave me the illusion I had some say in what was happening to me. There was no way to fool myself into believing that now.

I didn't walk in ranting, crying, giggling, puking, incoherent, or vacant like I would soon see others do. The clinic asked that substance abusers not quit cold before checking in to avoid body trauma. During my stay, I saw many addicts rebel against the clinic's authority, but this was one rule they enthusiastically embraced. Some got drunk on the flight over or at a bar in town. Others smoked or injected their drugs in the clinic parking lot. They checked in with the drink or drug between them and what was to come, and it stayed this way until the weaning off process was finished. I was told it was at least two weeks before drug addicts had their first drug-free day.

I wasn't sure how much some addicts remembered about their first day or even the first few weeks, other than where to pick up their medication and what time to be there. I remember much of it. I wasn't weaned off anything; didn't have a two-week, drug-induced stay in my comfort zone; nothing to numb the fear that the unknown brings.

I arrived on a Monday afternoon and was immediately separated from my luggage, which was taken to another room to be searched. They were looking not only for drugs and alcohol, but also for unauthorized books and magazines (which turned out to be anything not in the clinic's bookstore), music sources, prescribed medications, over-the-counter medicines, food (especially any with caffeine or sugar), mouthwash, aerosol cans, cell phones, cigars, and I wasn't sure what else.

I was escorted to the nursing station, which I quickly realized was the hub of the clinic. There was so much noise and so many people, and I wanted no part of it. I could easily have gone to my room and stayed there until my five weeks were up. One of the nurses asked me to sit in the chair in the corner. My eyes immediately looked to his for any sign that I was just one more crazy person he had to deal with that day, but there was none. He made small talk as he put the blood pressure cuff on my arm and took my temperature. I barely responded but concentrated on his voice to take my mind off the disquiet around me.

He then held up something I had grown very familiar with over the past two weeks and would now have to confront every morning: a list of the eight feelings in a Feelings Check. He asked me to look at the list and choose what I was feeling. I looked away instead. I said to myself, *Come on, Marta. This is the easy part.*

I said out loud, "I'm just really nervous."

"So, which on the list best describes that feeling?" the nurse asked again.

There was only one. What I'd been feeling for the past two weeks, and likely for most of my life but had never known it. I told him I felt fear.

He took me to a room off the main area containing only a small desk and two chairs and said someone would join me shortly. I felt like the biggest, most conspicuous thing in the room. I pulled my sweater tight around me and shrank down in my chair as far as I could. Just as I was wondering how I could get my luggage and myself out of there without anyone noticing, a different nurse with a perky smile and voice entered and asked how I was. I said I was fine, which we both knew was a lie. She was there to conduct my intake interview, basically a list of questions starting with, of course, a Feelings Check. But she also wanted to know what I was there for, what medications I was taking, and whether I had thoughts of harming myself or others. I must have answered everything correctly because they didn't tie me down or kick me out after we'd finished.

I was escorted back to the boomerang-shaped counter in the nursing station that separated them from the rest of us. The nurse who had taken my vitals walked up and talked me through how things worked there. He pointed to a small window in the wall to my right and said that was where I would pick up my meds. Whoa. This was not good.

"What meds?" I asked.

He told me I would be seeing a psychiatrist within the next couple of days, and that I would get any medications he prescribed for me at that window during the designated pick-up times. My back stiffened and I got that pressure in my chest whenever something I didn't like was happening. I wasn't interested in taking "meds," and I thought it bizarre that the clinic wanted to get the addicts off most drugs and put the one clean person in the place on them. But since I kept this to myself, we moved on.

The nurse said my psychiatrist's appointment would be written on the weekly schedule, which I'd find in my Group in-box on the wall across from the meds pick-up window. Each Group had a color designation. Mine was orange. Each Friday, my schedule would be in the orange-labeled in-box, which would tell me exactly where to be, when to go, and what I was doing every day from 6:50 a.m. to 9:00 p.m. for the following week. Administrative and counseling staff also used the in-box to relay messages.

He then said, "The other way we stay in touch with you is with this," and slid a small black pager across the counter. "You need to keep this on you at all times. We'll beep you with any special appointments or schedule changes. We'll also use it to let you know the time of your doctor's appointment for the blood work and physical exam, which will be sometime this week."

I took the beeper and held it in my hand, not wanting to attach it to any part of me yet. This little black box would give them access to me every moment, day or night. It seemed too much to give them so soon.

"There are three phones in the nursing station," he continued, pointing to one behind me. "The phones are turned on only during designated times, and it's first come, first served. If all the phones are in use, you need to put your name on the list and wait till one opens up. You can only make a call with a prepaid phone card, which we sell at the meds window. Each call is ten minutes, max."

To my left on the counter was a small basket that contained pink message slips folded in half and taped in the middle of the open end. The name of the person the message belonged to was written on the outside. He told me cell phones were not permitted, and anyone wanting to reach me had to call the nursing station and leave a message, which a nurse would take, but also inform the caller that, for confidentiality reasons, no one would confirm or deny I was a patient there.

He then said my luggage was being searched as we spoke and I would likely find some items missing. Finally, he handed me an ID badge that, like the pager, I was to wear at all times. I was now officially a patient in rehab.

After the nurse had finished, the only thing left was to show me to my room. We walked just a few steps to a doorway that led to a long hall with rooms on the right side, windows on the left. He opened the door to the first room, and I wondered what putting me right next to the nursing station meant. Did they want easy access to me, or want me to have easy access to them? I would never know.

I walked in, closed the door, and looked around, expecting the worst. The rooms and their contents had been described to me as being too small, too scratchy, too old, or too hard. But the room wasn't so small. It was big enough for two twin beds, two desks, a closet, and a bathroom with a window. There were fresh towels on each bed. They were white, smelled like bleach, and not so scratchy. I sat on the bed. I'd slept on worse mattresses for sure. This was home for the next month, and except for knowing I wouldn't be walking barefoot on the unnaturally gray carpet, it was better than I'd imagined.

I was happy to see my luggage just inside the door. I pulled it in front of the closet and opened it. By the looks of the contents, the staff had opened, felt, squirted, shaken, and smelled everything. My cell phone was indeed gone, as were my razor, birth control pills, caffeine-free aspirin, and all of my electric appliances. I got mixed explanations for the removal of my hair dryer and electric toothbrush. One was that the clinic checked them for faulty wiring that could cause a short. Another was that they dismantled them to search for contraband. Why didn't matter to me. But for some reason I became obsessed with getting my things back and neatly put away, and I didn't take my eyes off the nursing station until I had done so.

I took out my clothes, refolded some, and hung others. Stuck under a few shirts I found the one photo I had brought. I knew I would stay connected to my children through regular phone calls, which was better than a photo to me, and any others would have raised too many uncomfortable questions. I touched the glass in the frame, and for a moment, it felt like Bonnie Blue.

We had adopted Punkin first. She is a ruddy Abyssinian, so named because she's the color of freshly baked pumpkin pie and was considered the runt of the litter. Bonnie Blue arrived a year later, her name coming from her blue-gray color and one of my favorite movies. From the moment she arrived she was my girl, and we were inseparable. There was just something about her I understood.

While Punkin always seemed so proud of her sculpted muscles and glowing fur, Bonnie often looked not quite healthy. Her eyes were constantly wet, the result of being born without tear ducts I was told. There was always the danger that the damp around her eyes would breed bacteria and infection, so we'd wipe them clean all day, every day. Later we learned that Bonnie's knees were more on the sides of her legs than on the front, and one hip could pop out of its socket at any particular moment, for no apparent reason.

Whenever I was in the house, Bonnie was either by my side or where I could see her. One morning, when she was just five years old, I realized I hadn't seen her for quite a while. I called her name a few times, but she didn't come. I walked around the house calling to her. She still didn't come. I went down the stairway and found her on the landing, lying on her side in her own urine, paralyzed from the neck down. Bonnie had suffered a stroke.

The decision to let Bonnie go was one of the hardest I have ever made. Watching her ashes fall gently on the grass in our yard, I told her it was beyond measure how much I had loved her, how much happiness she had brought me, and how much she would be missed.

I had taken the photo I now held in my hands when she was ten months old. She had jumped up on a table to smell the fresh flower arrangement. The sun was streaming in through the glass doors and made everything about her shine. I grabbed my camera and called her name. She looked up and moved toward me. I snapped the picture and knew it was going to be a good one until I realized the flash hadn't gone off. By the time I was ready to take another, she had jumped off the table and the moment had passed. But after developing the film, I was thrilled the flash had chosen that time to fail. The sun had lit up Bonnie beautifully. The thought of her by my side like she used to be felt good, and I carefully placed the photo on the desk beside my bed.

The clock said it was almost time for dinner, which was from 5:00 p.m. to 6:00 p.m. I had only one decision to make at that moment—to go to dinner or not—and was having an impossibly hard time making it, being full of contradictions. I was hungry, but not really. I wanted to stay in the room, but sort of wanted to go out. I didn't want to be here at all, but coming had been my choice.

I felt my decision would have been much easier if there wasn't anyone else in the clinic, or at least in the cafeteria, during dinner. I didn't want to be around anyone tonight and was glad I didn't have a roommate. I couldn't have managed the cheery small talk I would have felt obligated to make.

I closed my eyes and wondered how someone who made hundreds, maybe thousands of decisions every day at home could have so much trouble with one decision about dinner. I then realized the dinner option was available to me for an entire hour, and it didn't take me an hour to eat. I would finish unpacking and get as settled as I could. If any time remained in the hour after that, I would go.

The fact that I'm intensely organized, and procrastination is as far from my nature as Antarctica blew any hope I had of buying myself time. The unpacking and settling in took a grand total of ten minutes. *Okay*, I thought, *I'll go to dinner. But I won't talk to anyone.* I hoped everyone else in the cafeteria felt the same.

I knew the way and the drill by heart. I walked in and walked up to the food line, grabbed a tray, some silverware, and told the servers what I wanted, which was most likely chicken. After filling a glass with water, I sat at an empty corner table in the back. I was alone for a full five minutes. Someone I knew from my week in Survivors sat down next to me and said hi and that it was good to see me. Three more people whom I didn't know but who knew her sat down shortly thereafter.

In rehab there is just one burning question: "What are you in for?" And it didn't take long for those at the table whom I didn't know to ask me. For me, there was just one answer; one that would let everyone know that, though we were in the same place, I was nothing like them. I rattled off my now memorized résumé.

"I don't drink, smoke, do drugs, excessively gamble, or overspend. I've never had a cup of coffee in my life, rarely eat sugar, and walk twenty miles a week."

Silence all around, then the inevitable, "Really. Then why are you here?"

A good question that deserved an honest answer. I said, "I guess I get into relationships with people like you."

Anywhere else, others might have been offended by my response, but in rehab they just nodded, understanding fully what I meant. They all had someone just like me at home.

The others talked while we all ate. They'd been here for several weeks already and had much more to say than I. There was someone's Family Week coming up, a good call and a bad call from home, and complaints about the food, the rules, the staff, and other patients. I listened to it all and wondered if this would be me in a few weeks, comfortably chatting about stuff that mattered and stuff that didn't with people I didn't know. But for now I just wanted to go back to my room. I finished my dinner then got up to leave, saying I'd see them all tomorrow.

Walking back to my room, I had the grounds nearly to myself. Most everyone else was either still in the cafeteria or at the smoke pits. I looked around and breathed in deeply. I didn't know what lay ahead for me, but I felt there weren't going to be many nights when I would be aware of anything but the pain this place uncovered. So I took this night, my first night, and made it a memory I could go back to when it got too difficult.

Fall air is truly miraculous no matter what part of the country you are in. On this night, I stood in front of a low wood-post fence, looking toward a skyline of clouds resting on half-mountains settled beside mountains so zealous they smashed through the windows of heaven. The dusky air was so welcoming, so giving, it made itself visible. Jack Kerouac called it blue air, and I knew just what he meant.

Whether I look forward to dawn or dusk is relative to my life at the moment. Dawn is anticipation and life unfolding. Dusk is the revealed and life at rest. Dawn was a force when I was building our home, a constant source of energy and motivation. I didn't have those feelings now. I was ready for the day to end.

Before going to my room, I checked my in-box and found my schedule already there. I glanced at it and saw it was full of the orange highlighting that indicated mandatory attendance. Back in my room, I took a longer look. Breakfast was from 6:50 a.m. to 7:30 a.m. and recommended but not required. The peer meeting began at 7:40 a.m. I had heard a few things about these meetings but not enough to make sense of them, and all I learned about them from the schedule was that they were mandatory and held every day but Sunday.

I found my alarm clock and set it to give me the minimum time to take a shower and eat breakfast in the morning, then got ready for bed. East Coast time said I should do this, but it was too early for that here. I had noticed a plastic bag on my bed when I first arrived. I opened it now and saw several books from the clinic's approved reading list. There was the same one on codependency given to me at my husband's Family Week that I had already read, another on healing, and two others on specific steps in the twelve-step program. The first was for Step One: "We admitted we were powerless over alcohol—that our lives had become unmanageable." I didn't need to read this. I wasn't an alcoholic. The other was for Step Four: "Made a searching and fearless moral inventory of ourselves." Great. Still another way to ask the "What about you?" question. I decided I'd rather admit I was an alcoholic.

I hadn't read very far before I remembered rattling off that list of everything I don't do earlier at dinner. I hoped it had sounded like I was self-disciplined, had mastered my behavior. Which is true I suppose, but only partly. Not drinking is mostly a result of my father's alcoholism. At some point during my life I had heard that addiction, especially alcoholism, is passed on from generation to generation and that the odds are not just good but great that children of alcoholics will become alcoholics themselves. All my life I had been told that I was just like my father, from looks to temperament. But from the moment I left the living room floor after fifteen hands of gin, I loathed my father. I didn't want to know his past or be part of his present, and I knew for certain we'd have no future since I'd planned to leave that house the day of my high school graduation. I made a conscious decision to never act like him, sound like him, be Italian like him. And there was no way I was ever going to be an alcoholic like him.

My father was a happy drunk for about four minutes. From the fifth minute on, he just found more and more to be angry about until he was raging. And it would never stop. He'd start to wind down, even turn around and walk away. But just as he got to the door he'd think of something else that made him angry, turn back, and start all over again. Sometimes with just words. Sometimes with his hand. Other times he'd unbuckle his belt and whip it through the belt loops so fast it caught fire and melted my skin into welts.

I didn't even think about drinking until high school, and even then, I only drank a couple of times. I remember both vividly. The first was sloe gin and 7UP. It tasted good. Not like liquor at all. I drank one sloe gin fizz out of my favorite tall A&W Root Beer mug, didn't feel anything, and drank two more. The second time I tried tequila shots, which tasted wretched, though I diligently worked past that until I'd had so many shots I couldn't taste anything. I remember these two binges well because, of course, I got violently sick.

I knew this was "typical" teenage excessive behavior. When I was in my twenties and still not drinking, people would say I'd certainly outgrown all of that; I was an adult now, with adult self-control, and I could enjoy drinking without getting drunk. The thing is, I didn't know whether I could have enjoyed drinking if I did it in moderation because, judging by my father, I wasn't sure I could actually drink in moderation. And drinking to find out just didn't seem worth it to me. So once again, I learned to skip over the middle ground and make a choice between extremes. I could either be a drunk like my father or not drink at all.

What was more interesting than my decision not to drink after high school was other people's reaction to it. It didn't matter where I was, whoever was drinking always wanted to know why I wasn't. Some were uncomfortably persistent in trying to get me to drink, saying I couldn't have any fun if I didn't. And I always thought, no *you* can't have fun unless you drink. I can.

However, I learned two things during my marriage. One is that I will be forever grateful to the Holy Roman Empire for carrying grapevines along with their weapons as they marched into France. There are French wines so extraordinary they deserve a moment of silence. You sense the very soil from which the vines grew, and become connected to the earth with every taste.

While still preferring not to drink at all, I also learned that I can drink in moderation, even and especially when it's a wine I love. I once heard a very wealthy man say that the worst thing about being rich is that you can have everything you want whenever you want it so nothing is special. But I never understood how money could make anyone take for granted those things that never cease to inspire or take one's breath away at the sight, sound, smell, touch, or taste of them; like fine wine and art, honesty and integrity, true friendship and love.

I was in high school in the 1970s, which should be enough for anyone to know what part drugs played in my life. We did drugs. Pot was common. Cocaine was getting that way. Acid was a must for any Pink Floyd or Led Zeppelin concert. The problem was I had problems when not on drugs. That didn't change when I was on them. I did my last chemical at age seventeen and never looked back.

I smoked cigarettes for twelve years, which I came to enjoy once I forced myself to. I quit when I was pregnant with each of my children and then started back up again after their births. I quit again cold and for good on my twenty-sixth birthday as a gift to my children and myself.

Craps came into my life late in my marriage. A sports broadcaster taught me to play during a Las Vegas charity event my husband and I were attending. Burning my money made more sense to me than playing slots, and blackjack and roulette didn't interest me for more than a few minutes. But craps grabbed my attention immediately; so much so that after my first try at the tables, I bought a book to research the game and developed my own playing style, though I kept my teacher's one uncompromising rule: Know when to walk away. You walk away when you've won enough and when you've lost enough. And if you say, "Just one more time," you should have walked away long ago. I like to play, but I like to win more, and the only way to win when you gamble at anything is to know when to walk away.

Not drinking coffee or soda was never a hardship. Their tastes didn't appeal to me. But there was a time I was more drawn to sugar than I am now. Before I came to know it did me more harm than good, I often wondered why I was attracted to something I didn't really want and that made me feel so bad. And I now remembered the counselors asking a similar question about my marriage during my husband's Family Week: If it didn't feel right, why did I stay?

I woke up starving. With my stomach making the first decision of the day for me, I got up and got ready for breakfast and my first day in rehab. The choices of scrambled eggs, Canadian bacon, and oatmeal were actually not bad, and breakfast would become my favorite meal of the day. Later in my stay, when some of my peers learned I didn't have a problem with the food, they suggested I get help for this by going to rehab.

The next stop after breakfast was the peer meeting, which turned out to be exactly what the name implied: a meeting for and conducted by the patients. No psychiatrists, counselors, nurses, or anyone else who hadn't paid the admission price. It was run by "the mayor," a patient selected by counselors and administrators who remained in place until his or her program was completed. No one knew the criteria for being chosen. There were three mayors during my stay, and I tried to find the similarities among them. They tended to be quiet, not speak unless spoken to, and isolate themselves from others. I assumed the staff used this position to get participation from those who wouldn't do so on their own, which I thought was a great idea. I went through nearly two weeks and two mayors before I realized I was still sitting in the back row, hadn't learned any of the songs, and didn't talk at all during the meetings, and that this was probably not a good idea for someone who absolutely did not want to be mayor.

That first peer meeting was baptism by earthquake and avalanche for me; seventy addicts in one room, all in different weeks in their programs and at different stages in their recoveries. I didn't know how I was going to fit in, or even if I wanted to. But I looked around the room and noticed a closeness among individuals, and the group as a whole, I hadn't expected.

In the coming weeks, I came to understand this bond and its power. It was from day after day of sitting in a room full of people we didn't know, slowly and painfully stripping away layer after layer until the worst we'd done and the worst done to us was exposed, leaving every inch raw and vulnerable. Then with humility and through tears, we asked, "Can you love me knowing this?" The bond developed because we all risked learning the answer. It was intimacy at its most frightening and most freeing. In time, I would be fortunate enough to become a part of it.

The meeting was structured but had a sense of ease about it. The jokes and one-liners started before the meeting and continued all the way through. But it was here I saw the first of many indications that the staff didn't trust us much—mostly for good reason, as I would later learn, but not always. We had to sign in upon arrival, but the mayor started every meeting by taking attendance to make sure those whose names were on the list were actually present instead of being signed in by someone else.

Someone read from a daily meditation book; new beginnings was a common topic, as were change, fear, and learning to surrender. Newcomers were then asked to stand, which was me and one other person on this day. The other person stood up reluctantly. I took the chance that no one actually knew this was my first day and didn't move. I was sitting so far in the back I didn't think anyone could find me even if they did know. I heard my name called by about seventy people and looked up to see that same number turned around, staring straight at me. I knew the sooner I stood up, the sooner I could sit back down. The group sang a song to welcome the other patient first, while I stood there feeling like an idiot. After he sat down, they sang it all over again to me.

Next, the peers who had completed the First Step in their twelve-step program stood and received a round of applause. I assumed this was for the alcoholics and was glad there was at least one thing I wouldn't be called out for. I still wasn't getting it.

The mayor then recognized those who had contracts. Contracts were directives from counselors to patients to help them start or stop a behavior. An alcoholic still in a depression because of a relationship that had ended two years earlier had a contract to smile non-stop for twenty-four hours. A drug and sex addict who used humor and sarcasm to keep from looking seriously at his problems couldn't use either for a week. Another addict who couldn't stop talking long enough to hear anyone or anything else wasn't allowed to speak for three days. And still another who couldn't find one kind thing to say about himself had to do so at every peer meeting. The purpose of going public with the contracts was so the rest of us could offer praise when patients were doing well and support when they weren't.

Just as I was beginning to wonder how, or even if, all of this benevolence could be sustained, the mayor asked for feedback. Those who had something positive to say about themselves or a peer or an experience went first, reading from narrow slips of paper pre-printed with the Feedback Loop format. Next came those who had a problem with something or someone, and the room went dead quiet. Hearing who was mad at whom and why seemed to be a high point of the meeting, as long as it was about someone else.

One morning, a peer spoke of how he felt betrayed by a fellow peer; someone he'd spent many long hours feeling compassion and empathy for, weeping and praying with, consoling and counseling as he listened to the peer's stories of abuse, of pain, even of his brother's near-fatal car accident, nearly all of which had turned out to be lies. He expressed his anger at this betrayal furiously and without mercy, and became the voice for many others in the room who felt the same way.

I wasn't sure which struck me more, the irony of the situation or the others' inability to see it. All of the addicts who felt so betrayed by this peer had spent much of their lives doing that very thing to their spouses, family, friends, and co-workers. Only now they knew what it felt like to be on the other side of betrayal, and none of them seemed to like it much.

In the clinic I had heard many addicts express anger at their family's reactions when they finally revealed their secrets. To them, forgiveness should have been instantaneous, love abundant, and all forgotten because of their newfound honesty. But they couldn't understand that by being untrustworthy, others no longer trusted or believed them; by breaking vows and promises, others viewed them as unfaithful; by trading their integrity for pills, alcohol, or sex, others saw them as without character or morals. Time after time, I watched addicts expect something for themselves they weren't willing to give to others.

The meeting ended with all of us dancing to Abba's "Dancing Queen." It was the strangest, most out-of-place thing I'd seen yet, and no one knew how it got started. But once the music began, we all found an open space and followed the step-by-step dance chart hanging in the front of the room or the two peers who had jumped on stage to act as guides.

It all seemed pretty ridiculous to me, though what was nonsensical at the beginning of my stay I saw as brilliant a few months after I'd left. Each part contained something we needed in our lives if we were going to get out of whatever problem we were in and stay out, and the meeting introduced them to us in slow, small, non-threatening ways.

Simply showing up for each meeting and signing in was a small thing with huge potential. Over and over, the counselors used words like truth, honesty, reality, and accountability, hoping to make it clear that these are the foundations for living a better life. But addicts must do the opposite in order to be addicts. They lie and break rules, vows, and even laws in order to get what they crave, because what they crave isn't socially or legally acceptable. Many have steeped in their lies for so long that lying becomes second nature, and they find a way to justify it all, believing they are simply different from everyone else. Special. Entitled. Above it all.

It took me a while after I had left the clinic to realize that telling myself and others the truth, accurately determining my motivation for each choice, word, act, or thought, is The Answer to every question. It is so crucial that it should have come to me, not just in initial caps, but accompanied by a blinding ray of light and epiphanic choir music. I was slow to understand because the whole idea seemed impossible to put into practice. I couldn't imagine checking my intentions for authenticity—consciously breaking through the denial and justification—every time I said, did, felt, or thought something. However, that's exactly what the counselors said I had to do, and that I was resisting, not because it couldn't be done, but because I didn't want to do it, didn't want to actually ask myself why I made the choices I did. And I definitely didn't want to hear the answers.

But how would I apply something like this? They said it could sometimes happen in an instant and other times take hours, days, or longer. But the more I authentically questioned the motivations for my words, thoughts, feelings, and behaviors, the better and faster I would get at making the right choices and correcting my mistakes.

We all have within us an internal alarm system that warns us in any number of ways when we are about to make a choice that escalates our dysfunction rather than supports our healing. But the signs are easy to ignore when they don't fit with what our dysfunction wants, and it wants nothing that won't bless our illusions, instantly intoxicate us, or allow us complete control. Even if complete control means we must keep breaking things—our relationships, our souls, ourselves—to have something to fix in order to feel powerful and in control again.

I knew I needed to better understand and have confidence in the ways of my own internal warning system, to see it as an ally in my healing so that I consistently and actively pursued and relied upon its guidance. And when I was unsure of the best choice, I needed to rely on another whom I trusted to make sense of what I couldn't at the time, and sometimes, rely on time itself. Waiting is a choice, too.

I slowly began to understand the clinic's teaching that only by speaking and acting honestly could we stop living two lives: the one we show others and the one we keep to ourselves. I knew a lot about living both a public and a private life, and my father was my first teacher. On the outside, we were a normal, middle-class, church-going family of seven. Inside, my father's addictions and rage made us anything but normal. Outside, my father never hurt me, hit me, touched me. Inside, it happened too often. His rule was that family business stayed in the family and questioning anything was forbidden. But I learned that if there is a difference between what someone says and what he does, always look to the behavior for the truth. Words can be manipulated, but eventually everyone will and must be who they really are.

The clinic hoped to teach us how to harmonize our two lives; make the private life match the public one, actually be the person we say we are. It's not that we aren't going to lie or manipulate or fall short of our morals and values. But we need to catch ourselves when it happens, correct it now rather than let it get to where the lying and manipulating become more of who we are than not.

Knowing that change is difficult for nearly everyone and big change can be overwhelming, the counselors started small: peer meeting attendance was required—we were to show up when we were supposed to, and be honest about when we didn't. But it wouldn't stay small. Eventually, every situation and interaction was aimed at getting us to tell the truth, and to rectify anything less as quickly as possible.

I can say with relative certainty that, before the clinic, none of us started our days with motivational readings and positive thoughts, or we wouldn't have been in there otherwise. You can't want to slowly kill yourself with drugs, drink, sex, work, tobacco, rage, ridicule, relationships, food, or a million other things if you feel good about who you are and your place in the world. And no amount of trying to make arrogance look like confidence will change that.

The source for this kind of thinking is still debatable. Is it genetic, environmental, or a combination of both? For some at the clinic, it was determined to be mostly biological, often coming in the form of depression, and eased with medication. But many of them, along with others without clinical depression, had lived in a negative environment from their earliest years.

I thought of those who'd had the most impact on my life. There is no question I was raised by people who weren't happy and who had made a living of covering me in their black cloud. When I had the chance to surround myself with those who were different, I didn't— though I now was able to apply something I'd learned in my husband's Family Week—I don't think I could have. I wasn't sure I knew what healthy people looked like, and if I had known, whether *they* would have seemed like the abnormal ones. In my world, what I'd felt was what I had always felt. Uneasiness was comfortable. Chaos was stability. Negativity was positive motivation for me to try harder, be better, make things right.

However, no one at the clinic said that motivational readings and repeating positive statements alone would change our lives; only that, when put together with all the other thought and behavior modification tools they would give us during our five-week stay, they would help.

The songs were not specifically designed to make us feel like idiots, but to point out that this was what we all felt when taking part in them. Most people are self-conscious, self-absorbed, consumed with negativity, and obsessed with projecting and controlling a particular image. That goes double for addicts. We were being shown that people don't want to mask who they are with a substance or behavior when they are at ease with themselves. And being at ease means you can be in silly situations not of your own making and not mentally break apart, laugh at yourself and your mistakes even if you aren't the one to point them out.

Developing true confidence and learning how to become less self-centered was going to take a lot more than a few songs and positive thoughts. The peer meeting also used the recognition of those who had completed the first of the twelve steps and the public airing of contracts to teach the benefits of supporting others—the most important of these being that if you are appreciative and focused on the value and accomplishments of others, you won't be as obsessed with your own. And the beauty of support is that it works both ways.

The gifts of completing the First Step only come from being as intellectually and emotionally honest as possible. It asks people who have spent much of their lives lying and denying to first tell the truth about who they are, and eventually tell all their secrets. For many in rehab, it is their first time admitting the things they've done to themselves and others through their addictions. For others, it is their first time actually admitting to being an addict.

The contracts took us one step beyond voicing the failures in our lives, to voicing our failures in the clinic. These said that even with all the individual and group therapies, affirmations, journaling, prayer groups, and twelve-step meetings, we still fell back into old habits and needed help. This was crucial. Many people in general, and addicts specifically, don't ask for help. For the addict, it goes back to living in extremes. Some are too arrogant to admit they need help. Others don't think they deserve it. So the person offering support learns how to give to others more often than take; sees that the world outside himself is much more wonderful than he believed; and realizes that it is not, and should not, always be about him. And the person needing support learns how to ask for and be honest about what he needs; trust himself and others enough to tell the truth; and know that authentically loving and living with others is better than living in isolation. This mutual support system rewards truth, humility, and camaraderie and is the beginning of knowing what intimacy is: honesty, vulnerability, and trust. There is no relationship, whether with oneself or others, without intimacy. And those who never know intimacy, never love.

One thing recovery doesn't do is eliminate problems. It only teaches you better ways to deal with them when they inevitably come along. If much of rehab is designed to get us to speak truthfully, and the Feedback Loop teaches us how, having the opportunity to do this every day in the peer meeting should reinforce both. It was easy when being complimentary, much harder when someone felt wronged. The two behaviors most people engage in when problems arise are to throw around a lot of words without thinking, or to say nothing at all. Ranting has never solved much, and saying nothing escalates anger and resentment until it eventually comes out and takes aim at something or someone it shouldn't.

The feedback part of the meeting provided many things: a safe place to express our feelings to keep them from building up, a clearly structured way to do it, and an opportunity to practice boundaries and surrender. Standing up for yourself does not mean you trample on someone else. But there is always the chance that even after properly saying what you must, the other person won't be empathetic. And it is here that you must decide whether it's something you can let go of, a time for compromise, or a deal breaker.

At first, I wanted nothing to do with "Dancing Queen." Music and dancing are a part of me at the deepest level, both coming from my parents. My mother's singing is so pure it should not be contained within anything human, and my parents so fully anticipated each other's moves and moods when they danced I never understood why it wasn't this way off the dance floor as well. Musical instruments were common in our house, each of us taking up one or another during our school years. And you could always tell who had gotten to the living room stereo first on any given day by what was on it: opera, polka, and Mantovani for my parents; rock, pop, country, Motown, and anything out of New York's Brill Building for the rest of us.

I did come to understand and accept the gifts of "Dancing Queen": those of giving a lot of adults who'd lost the ability to be childlike, spontaneous, in the moment, and unafraid of mistakes the freedom to be all of this—if only for a few minutes—and the rare experience of enjoying life without indulging in a harmful substance or behavior. But for some there was a sinister side to "Dancing Queen." One of the patients told clinic administrators that the song and the dancing triggered his sex addiction and he was uncomfortable attending the meetings. Without debate or discussion, the administrators decided the inability of one to overcome was more important than the success of the rest and put an end to "Dancing Queen."

I had some time between the peer meeting and my first lecture, so I sat in a chair facing the horse stable next to the clinic. This became the place I would go when I had no hope of understanding anything, and where the occasional glimmer would thankfully prove me wrong. I had a view of the mountains, the desert, the horses, and the aroma of it all. I was asked more than once how I could share my lunch with the smell of dung. I only knew that it was the first honest thing I'd had in my life in years.

All patients were required to attend the lectures held every weekday from 9:00 a.m. to 10:00 a.m. Sometimes a counselor or guest speaker gave them in person. Sometimes they were on videotape. Most often they were held in the same room as the peer meeting, which could be comfortable if it wasn't too cold and you got one of the padded chairs instead of a metal one. I remember four lectures—two well, one partly, and one only to the point where I walked out.

The lecture I enjoyed the most and draw upon to this day was on the love addiction/love avoidance cycles. Not because of the information, which was basically what I had heard in my husband's Family Week, but because of the fifty-something, laughter-filled warm blanket who gave it. This counselor had been married to an alcoholic for over thirty years and divorced from him for six. She was the codependent/love addict, he the addict/love avoidant. She wove together these cycles and their story, turning inanimate theories into real life, and she overflowed with laughter and humor—something missing in most of the clinic's counselors and everyone in high-level administration. We absorbed it all and overflowed with her. I laughed the entire hour, wondering how she could find her own betrayal and heartbreak so funny. How I could. But I guess that was how—it was her betrayal and heartbreak I found funny, not my own. I hoped I would be where she was one day. And I really hoped it wouldn't take six years to get there.

However, I realized something about the love addiction/love avoidance cycles I hadn't before. They described every relationship my family, friends, and I had ever had, and all those I'd seen on television and in movies, read of in books, and heard about in songs. All that filled the blank spaces in one's life would one day leave it empty again. Everything magnetic and vibrant that brought two people together would eventually tear them apart. When that time came, one would run away so fast that the other had no choice but to hold on as tightly as possible to keep from being thrown to the ground and trampled by everything that came after.

So, had all the writers, poets, artists, lyricists, and dramatists since the beginning of love gotten it wrong? If the divorce rate is any indication, at least half of us are getting it wrong now—and more than once. It's been said the promise broken most often is "I do."

One of the most disappointing things I've done with my life is to marry three times, and in a year, I will have been divorced three times. There is so much about this that is shocking to me even now, especially for someone who, until even a few years ago, felt born to be married only once to the love of her life, and destined to one day celebrate fifty years of a union that had grown even stronger with time, surrounded by our many children and grandchildren and great-grandchildren.

Even more important, it was never the example of love and marriage I had wanted to give my children; that commitment can be treated this recklessly, founded on the thoughtless, split-second connection of body parts rather than of hearts, minds, and souls, which joyfully takes a lifetime; that someone can fill and fulfill you, and when this stops, there is someone else. I'd heard it all often enough to know this isn't love, but somehow I didn't. It may be because we have so few examples of what love really is, or because what it is doesn't instantly feel as good as what it isn't.

What must I have thought of myself to have made these choices? To have only wondered, *Does he want me?* Never, *Do I want him?*

To not realize that while being the right one is a glorious thing, there is so much more. I deserved to wait for the right one too.

When asked, "Do you have any regrets about the choices you've made?" many people answer, "None at all," giving the reason that if they hadn't made those choices, they wouldn't be who they are today. I have regrets. I don't dwell on my bad choices, but I do regret them. And for me, these regrets were the first step toward trying to understand, correct, and eventually forgive myself for my mistakes. This process is long, and there are still times I am somewhere between understanding my relationship choices and correcting them.

Certain things from our childhoods make such a strong impression that they become embedded as truth, whether they are true or not, and what influences me in this way may not be the same for you. But between my parents' marriage, my sexual abuse, and whatever else felt hypocritical and wrong, I became convinced of the sacredness of sex and marriage. I rebelled against my father's message that sex and another's body mean nothing. To me they meant so much, enough to keep getting married until I got it right. But this wasn't the way to live what I believed.

My first two marriages, entered into without much thought, didn't end well. I married the first time at eighteen years old, had my first child at nineteen, my second at twenty-one, and divorced at twenty-two. It took my first husband and me over twenty years to make an attempt at coming to terms with this relationship and each other. I wanted to reconcile, not only to heal our children, but also myself. I needed to say out loud so I could hear that I had been wrong to be so careless with my life and the lives of others. I had to look at this man, the father of my children, and tell him I had never really known him. I was too young to even know myself, and the babies came so fast and we were so broke I was never able to find the time or place or desire to start. And when this marriage ended, I took the same lack of thought and knowledge about love and commitment into the next one.

I wouldn't know the outcome of my third marriage until my tenth wedding anniversary. And it was on this day, five months after leaving the clinic, that I had to decide whether everything I'd begun to learn about my relationships with men, women, family, friends, myself, and my God had failed me or would ultimately save me.

The clinic's director of sexual disorders gave the other lecture I most remember. He apparently had some national prominence in this field. He definitely had celebrity status among most of the patients, many of whom spoke of him with near reverence. I had never heard of him, and I got an uncomfortable feeling that I had checked in with more sex addicts than anything else. Eventually, I'd learn that all addicts are the same; only what they use to manage pain and trigger pleasure differs. But at this point I was still having trouble relating to some. Alcoholics I knew. Drug addicts, I was beginning to. Sex addicts, not a clue. And I felt very uneasy at the thought of having to sit through a lecture on sex addiction. I started squirming the minute he introduced himself and gave his credentials, among them being a recovering sex addict. But that was the last I heard of any reference to sex addiction or dysfunction. There were no stories about how his or anyone else's sex addiction manifested itself, no horrific examples of what we all knew no one should do, only an hour of some of the most thought-provoking guidance I would get during my stay at the clinic.

Aside from writing my thoughts and feelings before coming to my husband's Family Week, it had been nearly ten years since I'd written anything creatively or professionally. However, by this lecture I had been carrying a journal with me all the time. I wrote down anything that even remotely sounded like it could help me understand what had happened to my life. Much like Larry Darrell in *The Razor's Edge*, I better know the truth of things when I see them in print.

The focus of the lecture was change, and began with a discussion on blame. The value of removing blame from any situation cannot be overestimated. But it's human nature at this stage of our psychological evolution to find something or someone to fault, and it's rarely ourselves. We know we shouldn't do it. Blame only keeps us from learning the lessons we are meant to learn and puts others on the defensive, and a situation where someone is on the defensive can never end well. A defensive person feels threatened and will most likely have one reaction: dig in and fight, and someone who fights only wants to be heard, which means he isn't listening. So you have to dig in and fight to be heard, which means everyone is fighting, and no one is listening.

The Feedback Loop is supposed to defuse a highly charged situation by removing blame, but it's not foolproof. There are sure to be times when someone feels backed against the wall. But this counselor didn't want us to connect to blame in the first place. He said, "Don't ask whose fault it is. Ask how it happened."

I instantly saw a problem with this. The answer to, "How did it happen?" could be "Because he did this!" which is still blame, so it was clear that someone determined to point a finger could find a way. But this counselor hoped he wasn't talking to anyone like that today, that those present wanted something different from what they had now. Anyone serious about resolving conflict won't go the way of blame. Instead, they will look at the sequence of events for the miscommunication, the honest mistake, the unconscious choices, the difference in opinions, motivations, thoughts, and feelings. Looking honestly at these and asking how they came about is how we develop compassion and determine what is acceptable and unacceptable.

Although I didn't yet know how to properly and consistently resolve conflicts, I knew where to start. Every change I wanted to see in someone else had to start with me, and my first step would be to stand still. For much of my life, whenever I felt hurt or angry I either did what I saw my father do, which was overreact, or what I'd learned to do in response to him, which was either shut down or defend myself with a flood of words as if my life depended on finding the right combination. I needed patience. I needed to wait, to ask myself if what I felt or saw or heard was the truth. I needed to add thought to the emotion. But thinking did not mean playing and replaying a situation or comment in my head, building it up with layers of assumption and mind reading until I was agitated beyond anything manageable. It meant I needed to check myself again and again until I could trust myself to act, not react.

While I was contemplating all of this, I felt a shift in the lecture and realized the counselor and I had arrived at the same place at the same time. His focus was no longer on outside struggles, but on the one within each of us. There is unquestionably a need for honest evaluation and atonement for all we've done wrong. But today he wanted us to get past blaming and berating ourselves, which only causes us to stop moving, because if we can't move, we can't change. And we must change.

He was clear about why we don't change, why the same situations, same relationships, same problems keep happening to us again and again, and why some were in rehab for the second, third, or more times. *We can see there is a problem, we know what needs to be done, but we will not do it.*

I can assure you most everyone in that room knew they had to change, and wanted to desperately. Some had lost jobs, marriages, children, homes, or every cent they had. Others were close to losing them. Some had the government waiting for them on the outside, others the law. And all of us were dying physically, emotionally, and spiritually. But it was something else to know how to change. It is not enough to have the knowledge or desire, or even the willpower. What is the missing piece that turns knowing what to change into actual change?

This is where our minds, our fears, and our brokenness become our gods; where we allow all of these to create our excuses, denials, and justifications, and convince us there actually is a missing piece to stop us from doing what we know we *must* do if we are to live our lives within the goodness of our hearts rather than the destructive cravings of our minds. Because there is no missing piece, no empty space, no time lapse between knowing change and living it.

First you *make a decision* to change something, just one thing at first. The obvious change would be to eliminate the substance or behavior destroying your life. But again, the most important change is to start telling yourself and others the truth, the full truth, all the time. There are no small lies, white lies, or lies you tell to be kind. You have to realize to the depth of your soul that everything you are hiding will kill you one way or another. Be honest about the drugs, drink, sex, gambling, shopping, rage, and all the rest. But also be honest about all that is beneath them: the fear, the insecurity, the instability, the anxiety, the unknown.

Before deciding to check into the clinic, I had to sit in the raw, bloody, painful truth about my childhood, my marriage, and myself. I absorbed it all through skin to bone and knew I could be honest about at least one thing: My life of controlled chaos was now out of control, and I didn't know why. But I needed to tell someone, anyone, who could help me understand.

Since there is nothing between deciding to change and change itself, the next three parts of the process are directives to move. The first, and most controversial, is to *act as if*. The second is to *take action*. And if you didn't yet understand that you have to do more than just think about changing, the third is *it only works if you work it*.

There wasn't a person at the clinic who didn't have a problem with "acting as if." Every moment here was about telling and living the truth. Now we were being told to pretend to be something we didn't think we were. This wasn't the first time we had heard this or something like it, and we questioned it each and every time. But it wasn't like we didn't already know how to do this. I "acted as if" I was living a contented life for many years, and by this time, I'd heard many stories from my peers, all revealing they were equally skilled at pretense. But the counselors' answers were so vague and unsatisfactory that even after I had left the clinic, I still didn't understand what "acting as if" meant. That didn't mean it wasn't worth understanding. They said it so often I knew value lay in there somewhere. Though I am still unable to put together one clear sentence out of any of their explanations, I can give my interpretation—one that took me nearly a year to piece together.

If we didn't feel valuable or lovable or deserving of respect, the counselors wanted us to act as though we were. This was the chasm we didn't know how to bridge. It was only after I had gotten out of the clinic and become so conscious of telling the truth as often as I could catch myself that "acting as if" made any sense. My goal was to never again force others to provide my value or make me feel loved, and to live my life as honestly as possible, which meant everything from stopping myself before I told even the smallest lie to cutting the time between when I had, when I realized it, and when I corrected it. No longer could I be late for an appointment because I didn't leave in time, then blame it on traffic. No longer could I say something meant to hurt someone, then say I was only kidding. No longer could I tell myself I was neither able nor good enough to do whatever was before me. After time and failure, a little success then a little more, I became aware of a slow change. I began to trust myself with my thoughts, words, and actions. If I said no or yes to myself or to someone else, I could mean it, I could live with self-respect. Feeling valuable, confident, and worthy all came from this, and only from within myself.

Realizing this, I began to reconcile what the counselors had said and why I hadn't understood. They wanted us to act as though we had value while living honestly. We were trying to act valuable while still living lies, and that was why it rang false. You can't feel valuable when what you say and do is worthless. You can't act with self-respect when you don't trust yourself. And no affirmation to confirm your worth, wisdom, beauty, talent, love, and infinite potential will amount to anything when you know it's contaminated. So we had a choice. We could act to hide something or act to be something, but we could never be who we wanted without the truth.

"Take action" was easy enough to understand, but by the time I had heard "it only works if you work it," I'd almost had enough of pithy sayings. That's the downside of this kind of cleverness. Aphorisms so precisely sum up a meaning or solution that they sound trite, childish, and incredibly obvious, which makes them easy to disregard. But the undeniability of something coming together only if you work at it—actually put it into practice—would manage to stay with me and serve me well as I became more conscious of who was truthful, who I could trust for guidance, and who I would welcome into my life with emotional, spiritual, and physical intimacy. Because its purpose is to remind us that never again will simply saying something is so make it so. Every one of us has to back up our words with our actions. Saying one is a Christian, spiritual, honest, moral, ethical, compassionate, sorry, forgiving, loyal, loving, married, a parent, or in recovery isn't enough. We have to be these things. Failure to act on our beliefs doesn't mean our word must always be discounted or disregarded, but not consistently finding, understanding, and correcting the disconnect means it eventually will be.

But even working it wasn't enough for this counselor. He said if we really wanted to change we had to do whatever it took, go to any lengths to make it happen. We all had experience with this, too. I had done whatever was in, and sometimes beyond, my power to help those in my life—which I had learned was not help at all, but enabling—and all the addicts I had so far encountered had gone to the same extremes to get whatever they needed to destroy themselves. We were now being asked to use this same determination to heal.

He said to forget about half measures. There was no such thing as "I will try." *Should* had to become *must*. By the end of my time at the clinic, I realized just how daunting this task would be. Addicts have to change every thought. Every. Single. One. Because every thought they have is the opposite of what they should have. A drug addict trusts his supplier, not his loved ones; a sex addict sees a body as love, and a heart and soul as without value; an alcoholic believes the only God that exists is inside a bottle; and they all think it is the truth. The counselor was adamant that committing to change was the critical decision in our lives, and the result must be a total restructuring of our relationships with the truth and ourselves.

If everything I had heard for the past hour didn't seem difficult enough, what came next would be the hardest of all. He said the most important decisions are made without knowing what the outcome will be, and he used a quote from a popular movie at the time, *The Lord of the Rings*, to illustrate that we have never been alone in facing the unknown: "I will take the Ring, though I do not know the way."

We had to surrender, step into the mysterious and believe that something even more mysterious would help us take the next step. And know that when we intentionally or unintentionally wandered, we would be shown the way. Some would get a gentle nudge, others a life-changing jolt. But we would be shown the way.

He must have seen the doubt, the lack of confidence we had in our ability to do even one of these things with any success—or maybe it was because he had once felt the same way—because he reminded us of something that was too easily forgotten amid all the things we must do: We already had everything we needed to do them inside of us. Some heard or felt it as an inner voice, intuition, or divine guidance. Others called it Self, Atman, or Buddha Nature. But it is what we ignored time after time in our need to feed desire and ease pain. This time, he said, our highest nature, that inner voice, deserved respect. This time, we must listen.

He ended with words that still inspire me: "Be mindful of when you are at your best." He believed without a doubt that I would have a best day, at least one day when I made the right choices among all the others that made it look as if I hadn't learned a single thing. And if I had one day, I could have others. This is what change looks like.

As much detail as I remember from this lecture, there was another about which I remember almost nothing at all—not the topic, the purpose, or the point. I do remember the counselor. Everything about her said she had a story, that she'd been someplace dark, ignoble, and inhabitable only by those who could withstand the unimaginable.

I have an impression of what she was wearing. Black, no color. Pants, not a dress. Long sleeves, leather, or denim; no lace, ruffles, or bows. She had dark hair and dark-lined eyes and was younger than most of the other counselors. I didn't sense any vulnerability and not a lot of humility, only edges and angles and lines. A hard beauty inside and out.

She pulled up a chair to sit down, and I half expected her to turn it around and straddle it backside. But she sat in the forward-facing chair and, with elbows resting on thighs, leaned into us. She seemed unafraid of, even used to being physically close and open. I wondered how long it took her to become emotionally open as well. Her voice and words were honest and unflinching. Nothing added. Nothing withheld.

Her life had been an escalating fall from drugs to addiction, drinking to alcoholism, sex to sadism, masochism, and bondage. Pain to erase pain. I don't remember her details. It didn't seem important that I should, since the degrading parts of her life didn't move me as much as her redemption, which I felt she was fighting for even at that moment, a fight she'd have to continue tomorrow, and for many days thereafter.

If her details were unimportant, it seemed I was the only one who thought so. I looked around the room, especially at those I now knew to be sex addicts. If one was triggered merely by listening to "Dancing Queen," I could only imagine what listening to this could do. As she spoke all were quiet, never blinking, barely breathing.

Until then, I hadn't questioned any of the clinic's methods, especially not the value of telling our stories. But I left this lecture with an uncomfortable tug inside, though nothing I could yet put into words.

There was one other lecture that is memorable only because it was the only one I couldn't sit through. It was a video on sex addiction. We didn't know the topic or format of any lecture until we arrived. That day, the lights dimmed, someone pushed the play button, and the title and introduction left no doubt what the next hour would cover. By this time I had grown close to a few of my peers, one of whom was sitting next to me. We turned and looked at each other at the same instant, and I wondered if we were thinking the same thing. I knew we were when she said, "I don't have a good feeling about this."

The voice on the tape explained that this lecture would examine sex addiction on four levels: masturbation, pornography, prostitution, and predators. Everything inside of me tightened and began to vibrate. We turned and looked at each other again with much wider eyes.

"I don't want to stay. Do you think we can leave?" she asked.

I shook my head. "I don't know, do you think we can leave?"

"I don't know."

We continued like this for another thirty seconds until the introduction was over and the voice started discussing the first level. The thought of listening to a lecture on sexual dysfunction for an hour and to this extent made me more than uncomfortable. But what later surprised me was how we were unable to immediately follow the instructions of our minds, bodies, hearts, and inner voices all telling us to get out of there.

We both have a history of sexual abuse by someone we trusted, or should have been able to, and by someone in a position of authority. And because of this trust and authority we did what we were told to do. We didn't question, even when everything within us screamed for us to. We never ran or even walked away. We never said no. And we never told.

And here we were again. Not because of any abuse by the clinic, but because of our past abuse that had now become a second skin after weeks of connecting to it and pulling it piece by jagged piece to the surface, and because we saw the clinic as an authority. They were committed to their structure, the rules, an order to things. They had to be, or the chaos we all brought to the same place at the same time would take control and tear everything apart. They mapped out our days and nights, and when we strayed we heard about it in a note placed in our Group in-box, through the beeper, at our psychiatry sessions, or in a meeting with an administrative counselor if the insubordination was bad enough.

I was raised Catholic, and both of my parents were in the military. With just one of these there is a good chance of a strict upbringing. With both, it's a certainty. This can affect a child in one of two ways: He is comforted by the structure and welcomes it or is suffocated by it and rebels. Teenage years aside, I needed structure. I followed rules. I obeyed authority.

When the clinic said I had to work within their system, that was fine with me, but it was also now teaching me to trust myself. I could sit there frozen and afraid, or I could leave. When it began to hurt more to sit there than to break the rules, I said to my peer, "I have to get out of here." She stood with me, and we both walked out. We were the only ones.

Later that night at dinner, one of my peers in for sex addiction came up to me and asked, "Where did you go this morning?"

I said, "I just couldn't stay. Did you?"

"Oh yeah, till the end. It was actually very interesting." And the uncomfortable tug got a little stronger.

It wasn't until I had left the clinic that I learned of a potential downside to telling our stories. Euphoric recall is something that happens to those telling their stories who are still more in their addiction than in recovery. You hear it in their anxious voices and stream of tumbling words, see it in their wide, unfocused eyes as they get lost in remembering past addictive behavior. They still view the behavior as thrilling rather than dysfunctional, often glorify it, and don't acknowledge the enormous damage and negative consequences that resulted.

Euphoric recall is usually the first step toward losing sobriety and acting out the full-blown behavior, and sharing excessive detail about addictive behavior without professional supervision can affect more than the storyteller by spilling over onto listeners with similar behavior patterns, triggering their memories as well. There is no place for euphoric recall in healing or twelve-step meetings, which are for sharing only experiences of hope, courage, and optimism.

After every morning lecture we'd split up and walk to our designated meeting rooms, usually located in another building. Primary Group Therapy, which we shortened to either Primary or Group, was held twice a day at 10:00 a.m. and 2:00 p.m. and slotted to last an hour and a half, though my Group would often go two hours. Depending on the number of patients in the clinic at the time, a Group could consist of up to eight people.

One of the most potent gifts Group offered was the chance to see and hear in one place, through a small number of people and during a concentrated amount of time, the recovery process in all its different stages. The clinic itself was in constant movement with new patients checking in, graduating patients leaving, and everyone else moving one day closer to the end of their five-week program. It was the same in Group. Here, on any given day, you could see how far you'd come from watching and listening to those on their first day, how far you had to go from those on their last, as well as something from everyone at every level in between.

Just as interesting as what you could learn from each peer was watching how they chose to learn it, and there was one observation that never failed: Those whose decision to enter the clinic had been their own were much more open to the process and to receiving the full benefit of the program than those who were forced in or the focus of an intervention. By determining for themselves their time had come, they dropped their defenses sooner and were much more willing to listen to and incorporate into their lives what was being presented to them. Many who came here involuntarily kept most, if not all, of their resistance, arrogance, and defiance until their last day of the program, if they stayed that long.

My Group peers consisted of women only, most of whom had sexual abuse in their pasts. For both men and women, sexual abuse was a common thread in many of our stories. I remember being at a clinic Alcoholics Anonymous (AA) meeting one night when one of the patients scheduled to leave within a few days decided to share. He sat up straight, inched forward in his chair, opened his hands and his mouth, but nothing came out. He cleared his throat and tried again. He said today he had let go of his last secret, and it had taken nearly all of his five weeks in the clinic to be able to do so. He had been molested as a young boy, he didn't say by whom. But for almost thirty years he never told anyone, until that day. I knew the look on his face well, a mix of unimaginable liberation and immeasurable pain and every heartbreakingly joyful emotion in between. I thought about what lay ahead for him: grieving his lost childhood and innocence; revealing his thoughts of never feeling safe or loved; facing the abandonment, confusion, fear, and anger that he had carried with him everywhere and into every relationship, but also for the first time, the presence of a distant light showing him the way out of it all.

It was then I knew that many of our problems could be eliminated if grown men and women kept their minds and hands off little boys and girls. The amount of destruction and devastation to a child by this selfish and corrupt act is boundless. But that is the predator's goal. He doesn't have the courage or conviction to find a way to heal himself, and it isn't enough for him to destroy his own life. He has to take someone innocent, trusting, and vulnerable down with him.

We told our stories everywhere, but most often and in greatest detail in Group, and the telling and listening to stories was seismic. I saw huge shifts in understanding occur because of them. Whether someone told his story truthfully for the first time or heard someone else's, he could be thoroughly shaken out of his denial and detachment for at least that moment, and hopefully longer.

It wasn't a stretch to make a connection to our prehistoric ancestors with our storytelling. Cave dwellers squatting around campfires passed on stories of what they had seen and heard so that others might know what lay beyond and survive. And here we were, sitting in a circle under florescent lights, telling our stories so that others might know the truth about our lives, the danger of staying the same, and the chance of surviving through change.

Over time, the stories became precious inheritances that we assimilated into our lives. However, the value of stories is not in hoarding them but in telling them. You take what you need to learn, to grow, to heal, and then pass them on to others who also want to know themselves and the truth. Our stories make us all wealthy benefactors, enriching any who care to listen. There is no thinking one is too rich and famous, or average and mundane, or poor and inconsequential to tell his or her story, and I believe it is something we must all do. It can be to millions, a roomful, a handful, or just one, but there is someone who needs help somewhere, and you are the only one who can make the difference. Tell your story. Just take care that it is your story and not someone else's. Your story will go through all those who have touched your life for better or worse, but in every instance, it must all and always come back to you.

In the clinic, there were different parts to our stories. One was our history: our childhood, family background, and all the painful things we thought we had left behind with age, though found they not only had followed us into adulthood but had grown even stronger with time. These were the hardest for me to hear. I was still concerned about the damage I had unintentionally done to my own children.

Two stories were more common than I could have imagined. One was of parents abandoning their children, of one day walking away and never coming back, no reason, warning, or explanation; no phone calls to keep in touch; no birthday cards or letters; no showing up for little league, dance recitals, prom, or graduation, only a memory, now over twenty years old, of a father standing in a doorway as seen through the eyes of his nine-year-old son. Running down the driveway, the boy turns, waves, and shouts goodbye on his way to catch the school bus, never knowing this glimpse of his father will be his last. On this day, the father left a boy to do what he would not. And this boy would do a man's job, become protector and provider for his mother and two younger sisters, for the rest of his life. Every day he wondered why his father had left them, and what began as, "What was wrong with us?" soon became, "What was wrong with me?"

The boy thought if he did well in school and sports, did everything as perfectly as he could, his father would come back, would want to be a part of the family again. But his father never came back. Over the years, his mother dated and loved other men. One day when the boy came home after dark, he saw his mother through the big picture window lying on the sofa with another man, their clothes piled beside them on the floor, and he knew he had to try harder in every way so she wouldn't leave him for this guy or any other. So he became the best. He excelled in academics. He excelled in athletics. He excelled in alcoholism. Fortunately, he didn't succeed in his two suicide attempts.

The other story was a lie family members told a child that was guaranteed to shatter any sense of identity and ability to trust once he or she learned the truth. In one situation, and during a time when unwed motherhood was not as socially acceptable, some mothers and grandparents decided it was best if the child was told that mother was sister and grandmother was mother. The thinking was that this arrangement would protect the child, his mother, and the rest of the family from ridicule and shame. In another, a child's biological father was no longer a part of the family, and the mother filled the void by telling her child the father was someone else, usually the man in her life at the time. Eventually, the mother or other family members would tell the child the truth when they deemed him or her old enough to handle it.

But there would never be a right time to tell someone that her entire life has been a lie, and that the person she thought she was didn't exist. Stripped of her self-esteem and sense of self, one addict found an identity by taking on those of the men in her relationships and found her value in sex. She could be anything, would do anything anyone wanted, and when she lost interest in being someone she wasn't, or a man lost interest in her, she would find another. Eventually it wouldn't be just one other but many others—some lasting months, others weeks, most for just one night. She had spent her life trying to prove she was somebody, though on the inside she believed she was nobody. She needed constant attention, touching, verbal affirmation. She was obsessed with hearing positive answers to her non-stop questions, which provided a high much like a drink for an alcoholic or a pill for a drug addict. "Aren't I beautiful? Aren't I the best lover you've ever had? Aren't I somebody you'll remember for the rest of your life?"

Another with the same circumstance would have the opposite reaction. Even though he was married with children, being physically or emotionally close to anyone was unnatural to him, and what was uncomfortable in the beginning became painful, then impossible. Now in his fifties, he had no friends and had completely withdrawn from his family, choosing isolation over any chance of vulnerability. The stress of trying to maintain his distance while his wife and children demanded his attention, of separating himself not only from the life he'd created but from the one he refused to face and rebuild, plummeted him into alcoholism and depression. He wanted no one and didn't need anyone to want him, and everyone accommodated him by leaving. He was alone, but what at first had seemed like a good idea now scared him. The desire to be alone had escalated into the desire to be dead.

We were never supposed to compare our stories or trauma. Pain was pain no matter the source, and no one's pain was any more or less than anyone else's. But I couldn't help but be humbled by the abuse some of my peers had suffered, and their courage in trying to overcome it: the gang rape of one teenager rendered helpless by her heroin addiction in a dark room filled with dirty people; the abandonment of another by his parents when he told them he was gay; and story after story of incest and molestation by father, uncle, brother, stepparent, neighbor, teacher, minister, priest, principal, scout leader, coach.

Though we were often reminded that no one had the ultimate trauma, in the beginning I was less empathetic toward those whose stories seemed weak because there was no physical or sexual abuse. One drug and sex addict had a strict father and a loving mother. That was it—no molestation, no whipping, smacking, or punching, just a bellowing, critical father and an overbearing mother who always told him he was special. There were stories of mothers controlling or living vicariously through their children, and of confiding in and seeking comfort from their sons because their husbands weren't physically or emotionally available; of fathers who weren't there for soccer games, school plays, or teacher conferences because they were too busy with work or other interests, and who were mentally and emotionally elsewhere even when they were home. And what seemed to me as thoroughly surmountable circumstances had somehow plummeted others into life-threatening addiction.

However, one woman had the family many of us in the clinic had only dreamed of. Both parents were college-educated professionals, and between the two of them they had learned to balance their work and family lives. One parent or the other was home when their three children arrived home from school, available to help with homework, and present for extra-curricular activities. They lived an upper-class lifestyle with a large home, nice cars, and money to spare. But the parents believed that, though their children would take what was given to them, they would only appreciate what they earned. So to teach them independence and responsibility, the parents required each child to be employed during high school. And to teach them compassion and gratitude, the entire family took part in regular community service through their church. The parents said they were sympathetic through broken hearts and unfulfilled dreams, and firm with underage drug, sex, and alcohol experimentation.

In exchange for what they considered support, guidance, and

opportunity, which all of their children saw as a suffocating need for control and perfection, the parents expected them to be productive and find their purpose. They didn't care what it was as long as it included a college degree from a prestigious university, and a well-paying, high-end job. This meant good grades, better test scores, and a painstaking determination to make each step count toward the larger goal.

Two of their three children obliged, but they may as well have been asking their middle daughter to breathe under water. She didn't know who she was or what she wanted, but it wasn't even close to what her parents expected. She had hated school from her earliest memory of it. It was too restrictive, had too many rules, and she had no patience for the studying, homework, and test taking. And sitting in a business office, wearing a business suit, making business decisions wasn't even a remote possibility. Besides, she didn't have to prove anything to anyone. She loved her parents and siblings, and knew they wanted the best for her, but she wasn't one of them. They liked different things, different people, and had different priorities.

I don't know how her rebellion started, but I saw where it led. She was an intravenous crystal methamphetamine addict, and this was her third attempt at rehab. And I knew that everything she said was the rationale of an addict deep in her addiction; every skewed thought and word the result of years of drug-induced and drug-enhanced fear and paranoia. But no one starts out this way. It might have begun by trying to assuage feelings of awkwardness and alienation in small ways, and then escalated into the full-blown revolt it was today. But I would never know for certain, or ever learn the root of the problem—like whether she had a learning disability or something else that made her uncomfortable with any kind of structure, guidance, or authority—or what made her so unable to fit into her family in even the smallest way. I also tried to find the answer in either nature or nurture with no luck. I could argue that, while it appeared her parents had raised all of their children with the same good intentions and inevitable mistakes, maybe their style of parenting had done more harm than good to this child. She needed something different and it was up to the parents to adapt to the child, rather than the other way around. But then I looked at the other four members of this family, who seemed relatively healthy and well-balanced, and wondered if the problem wasn't some biological glitch.

For the most part and for the longest time, I didn't care. I understood her family's story much better than hers. They described how her addiction had ripped the family apart; how at first, everyone was on her side, wanting to do everything possible to help her get well. But each time she went back on her promise to stay sober, each time she lied to them, stole from them, manipulated them, pitted one family member against the other, she lost another ally until she'd made sure she had become the very outcast she'd always felt herself to be. The family now only felt anger and frustration and absolute bewilderment. No one knew what to do, how to do it, or even if they wanted to try anymore. Anything they did was never enough, never right, and never made one bit of difference. And what hurt worst of all was that she was rejecting them, accusing them, blaming them for all of her problems. I understood that her parents were asking her to be something she couldn't and still be true to herself, but I didn't understand a defiance so great that she would rather live in degradation as a crystal meth addict, be willing to die if it came to that, than come to some agreement with them.

I thought of the cosmic cruelty that had put me with my parents and her with hers. I was supposed to believe there was a good reason for this, but for the life of me I couldn't figure out what it was. I wanted to grab her shoulders and say, "Don't you see what you have? By luck you are where you are. By choice you have thrown it away. I would have given anything to be your parents' daughter. Anything." And I wanted to run to her parents, take their hands in my little-girl hands and beg, "Take me. Please. Take me."

It was the story of a peer whose parents had paid him no attention at all when he was a child that changed my thinking and my heart. There was no physical or sexual abuse, but the emotional and psychological abuse was just as damaging. He was so insignificant, so worthless, so nothing that he didn't rate being encouraged, hugged, told he was loved, or even looked in the eye during the few words he was granted.

He made his own bed, his own meals, and his own way in a world that was much too big and confusing for him to understand. There was no place in the home for the boy then and no place in the world for the man now. This I understood as well as any story of physical or sexual abuse.

I soon grasped why there was no value distinction in our stories and was able to empathize with all of my peers. What was common among us was more powerful than the details that differed. I always related to some part of someone's story. Even more compelling was that we were all in the same place, trying to do the same thing: heal our minds, bodies, hearts, and souls. We were bound by the courage it took to tell each other our stories at all, to be vulnerable and ask that, here, we not be abandoned or ridiculed or ignored like we had been by so many others before.

After hearing the stories, it was easy to see how our childhoods had directly impacted the adults we had become, but it was harder to separate our problems from someone else's, to fix what was ours and let go of the rest. And this had led to the patterns we kept repeating throughout our lives.

Initially, I blamed myself for my sexual abuse. As I grew older, I intellectually understood that it wasn't my fault, but by then I had already established the pattern. Whereas some people habitually blame others for their problems, I couldn't stop blaming myself. Whatever the situation it became painfully comfortable to tell myself that if I were smarter, prettier, better, less of what I was and more of what I should be, things would have been different.

However, seeing myself as the source of a problem actually made breaking my patterns much easier than if I'd been one who always blamed others. Eventually I realized that if I blamed others for the things I was unhappy with, I was also giving them the power to determine when, or even if, they would change. I was already able to consistently look within, and this courage would give me, and only me, the power to keep what worked and change what didn't. But I had to make one very important change. When I took inventory of my choices, behaviors, and patterns, I needed to do so as an objective observer rather than a merciless critic. I had already born the brunt of so much anger and violence from others and none of it had worked in my favor. I now had to give myself all the good things I deserved, especially when the patterns snuck back in after I thought I'd kicked them out for good. I had to gently take my own hand, wrap myself in my own arms, and not let go for as long as it took to get it right.

In addition to connecting our pasts to our patterns, our stories showed how both manifested in our adult lives through what we had done to ourselves and others. In the beginning it was hard for me to imagine anyone thinking up, let alone acting out, many of the behaviors others revealed. I would find the explanation in three accomplices: denial, justification, and arrogance.

I can't overestimate how big a part denial, or lying to oneself, plays in dysfunction and addiction: *Just once won't hurt. Just once more. I don't have a problem. I can stop any time. I am in control.*

When denial inevitably breaks, justification seeps through: *It's not my fault. Everybody drinks. All my friends smoke. Prescription drugs aren't illegal. Oral sex, online sex, phone sex isn't cheating. I never really loved her.*

And inverted thinking is rampant. An overweight person looks in the mirror and sees thin to justify more eating. An anorexic sees fat to justify starvation.

But it's arrogance that rears up whenever conscience stirs and allows addicts to go from betraying themselves to betraying everyone around them: *I can do what I want. I won't get caught. It won't matter if I do. I will get away with it—because I deserve to. I am different, special, gifted, better than all of you.*

And no matter what an addict has done, he will always point to someone he thinks has done something worse: *At least I have a job. At least I'm not paying for sex. At least I'm not selling drugs.*

The manipulation starts small and slowly as addicts see how much they can get away with. The more they get away with, the bolder they get, and they learn to deny, justify, and then become arrogantly unapologetic for each step. It's been said that an addict is like someone speeding recklessly down a highway, uncaring and unconcerned about the devastation and broken lives he leaves behind.

Some media have referred to the clinic where I stayed as "posh." That's not exactly the word I would use, but then again, I have nothing to compare it to. Those who have never actually stayed there might make that assumption because celebrities and professional athletes have been known to check in, and there were a few of those in at the same time I was. But the other nearly seventy patients were everything from miners and construction workers to lawyers and accountants to grandparents and housewives.

Some of the stories I heard were of lifestyles and behaviors stereotypically associated with hard-core drug addicts: no job, money, or home and willing to sell or do anything to get high. Although some of the heroin addicts also used prescription drugs, they were by far the respectable drugs of choice for the middle- and upper-class addicts, as well as an alarming number of young people. It may have been the type of person this clinic attracted, or an indication of society's changing and much bigger drug problem, but it seemed there were more prescription drug addicts there than those addicted to illegal drugs. They were able to go to work and be productive while using, at least in the beginning. And some attributed everything from their creativity to their athleticism to the drugs. Even better was that prescription drugs had legitimacy, which made them easy to justify. (*At least it's not crack.*)

Of all the stories, I became most curious about those from sex addicts. After listening to a lot of addicts, both in the clinic and out, I noticed the repetition of certain statements. Two not specific to any type of addict were "I am an observer of human behavior" and "I love to watch people." The addict says these statements as if they were positive attributes, and they would be, if he weren't an addict. But when said by a non-recovering addict they can be translated a few different ways: He observes people to determine the best way to manipulate them, to mimic them in an attempt to act normally, or to judge. An addict spends a lot of time looking at and judging others so he doesn't have to look at and judge himself.

There were some statements, however, that were particular to sex addicts. When heterosexual male sex addicts were asked whether their addiction indicated disrespect for both themselves and women, many responded, "But I love women," but then couldn't answer, "What do you love about them?" or explain how they connected to or were intimate with women out of bed. To them, women were simply objects or body parts, and an ass, leg, or breast man could reduce them to just one. What they loved was to use women to feed their addiction and ease their insecurities, pain, and fear because they were unable or unwilling to find out what needed to be changed about themselves and change it. So women became non-human, interchangeable with a pill or drink or slot machine.

And the sex addict has a lot of help. The compulsion among all media to attract that golden eighteen- to thirty-four-year-old male demographic has made sex the focus of commercials, magazines, movies, TV shows, even cable news. One sex addict and self-professed leg man said he watched cable news when at work, the airport, or any place he couldn't look at porn, and he was thrilled when the competition between the networks and willing women broadcasters resulted in even shorter skirts and more leg shots.

There was a time when, while no one could ultimately define pornography, most of us knew what it was; the distinction between what was publicly acceptable and what was covered in brown wrapper in the back of the newsstand was clear. But with commercials, catalogues, music videos, and cable TV blurring the lines, it's getting harder to differentiate between what is acceptable and what is porn. The good news is we haven't given up trying. The debate over what is acceptable was very much in evidence when a situation with a former president had us asking whether oral sex (or phone sex, computer sex, or a lap dance) is cheating, causing many to respond that if you don't want anyone to know you're looking at it, it's porn, and if you wouldn't do it in front of your spouse or mate, it's cheating.

The not-so-good news is that it's a tough climate in which to say sex is misrepresented and undervalued. We are overwhelmed with the most primitive uses of sex by those who are the most defined by or make the most money from it, and they will kick back hard and fast when offered a different perspective. First, the labels: prude, puritan, repressed, censorship. Then, the justification: I love my body and I'm not ashamed to show it; humans aren't meant to be monogamous; prostitution is a victimless crime; it's just sex; sex sells; it's normal. But just as the statements to justify sex without intimacy, meaningless nudity, adultery, prostitution, and the overall lowering of sexual standards seemed disingenuous to me, so did those portraying participating adults as victims.

When I lived in New York City, I one day crossed the street at the corner of Third Avenue and Lexington and found myself in the middle of a protest made up of about twenty women. There was a small table with pornographic photos and literature on women's rights. I kept walking until I saw an enlargement of *Hustler* magazine's infamous meat grinder photo, which was by then about twenty years old. The image was of a woman's body stuffed into a meat grinder, legs and hips sticking out of the top feed hole, the rest of her belching out of the front as raw bloody meat. I don't recall what the women were chanting, but the message was clear: Stop victimizing women.

It seemed the victimization manifested a few ways. One was that the images reduced women to less-than-human chunks of meat. Another was that when men viewed these images it led to an increase in rape and violence against women. So what I understood the protestors to be saying was that if there were an end to pornography, women would become more valued and violent crime against them would decline.

I felt conflicted over their message. It wasn't that I opposed their hoped-for outcomes of holding women in higher esteem and the lowering of violent crime against them, but rather how they wanted to solve the problem and whom they held solely responsible. And they blamed men for creating, selling, profiting from, and looking at pornography. There is no question that for many men, today's definition of being a man requires a disconnect between sex and love, thinking and feeling, and the treating of themselves and others as things rather than human beings. But the same can be said of just as many women. And my only thought after seeing the graphic photos and hearing the protestors' chants was that porn can't exist without those who make the choice to be photographed naked or having sex.

I've heard a justification for this from many women, many times, mostly from those who have just posed nude in a magazine or taken their clothes off in a movie. They love their bodies and aren't ashamed to show them. But I have never been able to connect the two. Why does not being ashamed of one's body have to mean scant clothing, nude photos, or filmed sex? How does taking your clothes off for the pathological pleasure of someone you don't know translate into love for yourself and your body or personal empowerment? Why are people considered uninhibited only if they can get physically naked in front of strangers or talk freely about sex and their bodies? And how and when did something as sacred and beautiful as our nakedness, our lovemaking, and our ability to love become so battered, broken, and backwards?

After every story we asked the question: Why do we do what we do? The answer was always the same: fear. And we fear nothing more than intimacy. We simply do not want to let others, or even ourselves, get close enough to see who we really are. Or at least, who we think we are.

Man or woman, when you are terrified to show anyone your heart, showing many your body is easy. There is nothing courageous or liberating about taking your clothes off or having sex with strangers or someone you don't love. It is facing and breaking through what scares you, all that paralyzes you, that will undoubtedly take every bit of strength and courage you have. If you want to be truly free, remove everything you have wrapped around your heart. Uncover your vulnerabilities and fears. Let them out so all that's left is honesty, understanding, forgiveness, and love. When you give these gifts of the heart first to yourself, and then to another, your body will follow.

But there is a catch to becoming emotionally naked. You must choose someone who is capable of receiving and reciprocating this gift—someone whose heart is as open and vulnerable as yours, and who understands the value and necessity of creating this circle of intimacy. While love is unconditional, intimacy is not. There is no such thing as a happy one-sided love affair.

I've heard many stories from those who felt unworthy of real love, from those damaged men and women who have hurt so much for so long it's the only thing they know. They are so convinced intimacy could never happen to them that they settle for sex and pretend it's love, only seeking or attracting the kind of person guaranteed to fulfill the prophecy. Someone who connects him- or herself to porn or strip clubs or places no value on sex cannot connect to a heart, and there is absolutely nothing anyone can do to make someone capable of intimacy. One either chooses to see intimacy as a gift rather than a threat, or doesn't. And we each make this choice alone.

Intimacy is knowing that, though opening your heart lets much flow out, much more floods back in. But for many it is easier not to take that chance. Or so one may think. Day after day for five weeks I saw the faces and heard the stories of those who found out there is no escape. All the running and hiding, and that constant, grinding fear of intimacy catches up with us all. No exceptions.

I believe the core of any group is ultimately responsible for identifying and correcting its own problems and offenses, which in turn benefits all those who are collaterally affected. Teachers will repair our education system, voters our political system, clean athletes and referees our professional sports. And pornography will stop when men redefine what it is to be a man. It will stop when women no longer believe this is all they are worthy or capable of. Strip clubs will shut down when women stop justifying working there by saying they can't make that kind of money anywhere else. And it will start when both truthfully answer the question: "Is *this* what I was put on this earth for?"

"But it's just sex." I've heard enough from those whose lives revolve around "just sex" to know there is nothing innocuous about it. They are controlled and ultimately destroyed by the minimization of something too profound to be minimized. There is no other act that so completely joins two bodies, one within another. The very essence of us, the substance of creation, flows toward our beloved then back again. Skin upon skin. Breath into breath. Binding beating hearts. For those to whom celibacy is not a way of life, this is how we let God know He wasn't wrong to entrust us with the gift of humanity, of self-respect,

respect for others, trust, integrity, commitment, appreciation, vulner-ability, joy, wonder, and love.

So, here lies the sex addict's dilemma: If sex and nudity are truly meaningless, why does he so desperately need them to fill a void? Why does he risk everything and give up so much more to feel completed by something that has no value?

It is not that sex has no meaning or value. It is that some must believe this is true to keep their distance from intimacy. They must disconnect sex from love, or else they would have to make the effort and commitment to be intimate and vulnerable and relational—experi-ence all the joy and pain that goes along with that—just like everyone else. They'd have to believe that "sex is not the search for something that's missing. It's the expression of something that's been found": a lifelong celebration of a living, breathing gift from God.

Sex is an expression of love, but sex is not love, and it seemed the sex addicts in the clinic were beginning to realize this. Without exception, every sex addict's story contained this one sentence: "I just want to be loved." The first few times I heard it, my heart broke. I too wanted them to be loved, to feel loved. With these words came their profound realization that even though love was missing from their lives, they now knew it was real and essential.

I then came to a realization of my own. Not one of them said, "I want to give love." So while each understood it was something they needed in their lives, none realized love is something you give; something you give first, give always, give without motive, and then you get. Because when you can't give love, you only get someone who thinks he or she is not worthy of receiving it, which means you only get someone who is as broken as you.

But you can only give something you own, something that lives in your heart and flows out of your hands in a loving caress, a nurturing hug; out of your mouth in words of praise and appreciation. It looks like a smile, open arms, tears of joy, acceptance, gratitude, listening, understanding, comfort, compassion. Love is not "out there" to be grasped. It is inside waiting to be released through your open heart.

It's never just sex. It's never "just" anything. There is a reason for every thought, word, feeling, and behavior, and trying to reduce any of it to zero to make our addictions, dysfunctions, and bad decisions acceptable doesn't change this. Our choices come from what we wish to embrace or avoid, and we get so much of it upside down. We are afraid of the good and nurturing things in life but jump soul-deep into everything destructive. Like accepting sex without intimacy, never caring that if sex means nothing to him or her, neither do you.

The key to intimacy is that you must first want to know who *you* are before you can be intimate with anyone else. This is the greatest self-imposed obstacle, not just for addicts, but for many others who don't consider themselves dysfunctional. They cannot be vulnerable, intimate, and unafraid of the unknown even with themselves, and they will do anything, put any substance or behavior or deliberate act of denial between themselves and an awareness of who they are to the point of emotional, spiritual, even physical death. Self-discovery is not a joy, but something to be avoided at all cost.

However, continual self-discovery is the greatest act of self-love, and the greatest gift you can give to others. Being unafraid to learn who you are, what to keep, what to change, and to forgive all of it is what nurturing looks like. You must know how to care for yourself before you can care for others. If you are afraid to learn who you are, all of the things you do for others—those thoughtful words and acts of kindness—will be filled with impure motive and intent. You do them not to give something to someone else, but to get something for yourself, like the feeling of being worthy or loved; like the power from controlling what others think of you; like circumventing the pain and hard work of change by manipulating others into believing you are something you haven't worked for, haven't earned, and really don't believe yourself. And whatever feelings of worth or love, whatever good opinions that may come from this betrayal of yourself and others, will not last.

Some sex addicts spoke of early childhood sexual humiliation or trauma, though most had difficulty determining the source of the addiction. But I had found that the memories of the first sex high from addicts both in and outside the clinic were often the same. They had discovered pornography or masturbation as a child, sometimes as young as five or six years old, and their lives were forever changed. But every time I heard this I had the same questions: What allows one person to successfully navigate the stages of emotional development and another to stay frozen with the sexual and relational skills of a child? And what allows one person to see sex as an enhancement to a relationship and another to see sex as the relationship itself?

While the consensus is that sex addiction is like any other addiction—one uses a substance or behavior, in this case sex, to self-medicate emotional pain, resulting in catastrophic consequences—the debate is still open as to its causes. Many have been raised in families with other addictions and dysfunctions, and often speak of either distant or uncaring parents or an overly strict household where sex was considered dirty or sinful. And more than eighty percent are sexual abuse survivors, so for most it starts with childhood trauma.

But it's not just those who were traumatized in childhood who are buying into the depreciation of sex. It sells just as easily to men and women of all ages who've had relatively normal, non-traumatic childhoods. There are far more people who accept that the body means little or nothing at all, that it doesn't need to be protected, respected, and held in high esteem than there are those who've been told it's dirty or sinful; and there are far more people comfortable with the ever-present messages of sex without love in magazines, movies, television, and advertising than there are sexual abuse victims. And they're not just buying. They're also selling it to the rest of us.

Sometime after I had left the clinic, I saw a commercial for a body spray targeting teenagers. A young man lavishly sprayed himself with the scent and then walked outside. Provocatively dressed women surrounded him in a frenzy as now easily recognizable porn music played in the background. It actually took me a while to figure out what they were trying to sell. Also in the room was a man in his thirties and his young daughter.

"It looks like porn is now mainstream and acceptable for kids," I said.

He replied, "What's wrong with porn?"

I stepped around the fact that his asking this question proved my point. "Would you want your daughter in it?"

"No," he said. "Of course not."

But he had no problem watching *your* daughter take her clothes off and have sex with someone she didn't know or love. This was acceptable to him, just as it was to his father, and his grandfather, and will most likely be to his children, and just as it is in advertising, music videos, movies, and television. Sex sells—because we allow it to.

In his book *Sex God*, Rob Bell explained that having sex with many women gives men "the feeling of being a man without actually having to be one." What separates adults from children in relationships is emotional maturity, the ability to be intimate. Children can have sex, but they don't have the emotional development to be part of a lasting and committed romantic relationship. But even that difference may no longer exist.

With every sex addict's story telling me he looked at love and sex exactly the same way he had the first time he'd masturbated as a child, I wondered: Is this really as far as we've gotten? That thirty-, forty-, fifty-, and sixty-year-olds can act the same way in a romantic relationship as they did when they were six or sixteen, with the same lack of self-control and self-esteem? The lust and excitement part of love we can do. So can any teenager. But is that all there is? Is there nothing more and does nothing change with time, age, and experience?

It doesn't take sitting in a rehab clinic with sex addicts to ask these questions. Somehow and at some point, we decided it was acceptable to bring those with arrested emotional and relational development—those who believe sex is better than love and better than a relationship, or that sex is love—into our homes and lives through advertising, television, movies, and other media.

But what's wrong with porn? Someone once asked a better question: What is normal in a dysfunctional society? And if pornography, from soft to hardcore, is now socially acceptable, can we consider ourselves healthy?

One night at an Al-Anon meeting I attended after leaving the clinic, I listened to a woman, clearly devastated, tell of dealing with her husband's alcoholism for over twenty years only to recently find out about his sex addiction. One of the first things I learned in the clinic was that many addicts have multiple addictions, and sex addiction and alcoholism are a frequent combination. The addict uses alcohol to lower inhibitions and reduce his fear of intimacy and rejection when seeking sex.

After the meeting, a few people stayed behind to talk with the woman and I heard her ask, "What would he do if there were no porn?" The question intrigued me and I asked it of a non-recovering sex addict, closely watching his reaction, knowing it would be more telling than the words that followed. For a split second I saw the wide, darting eyes of a mind in panic as he considered a life without not just flagrant porn, but everything he used to connect his mind to sex or nudity. Then came the inevitable justification: "As of now, porn and strip clubs are legal, and until that changes people have the right to have them in their lives."

While all of that sounded accurate, I couldn't help but think we were letting our lowest behavioral standards rather than our highest potential dictate what was acceptable, the results of which could have far-reaching consequences. I once read that if we don't model healthy choices in our behaviors and relationships for future generations to follow, they will not see making healthy choices as important or necessary. Children will recreate in their own lives the behavioral choices adults have shown them—even if those choices are dysfunctional.

National statistics indicate that sex offenses by juvenile offenders have risen forty percent over two decades, and that the offenders are younger and their crimes more violent. Offenses include sexual assault, attempted rape, statutory rape, fondling, and prostitution. And one school psychologist has asked the only question that matters: "How do these kids even know about this?" To which the only response is, "How could they *not* know about it?"

But disrespect for our bodies and sex and love is legal, and it was hard for me to think that changing this would make a difference. Eden's garden had been turned into a toxic waste dump, and there was no law powerful enough to change it back. But wouldn't keeping it legal and allowing people to turn away from the devaluation and misrepresentation of love and sex on their own be better indicators of our cultural health anyway?

If rehab was characteristic of the outside world, not many could turn away; not from magazines or movies or celebrity sex tapes or even from an attractive someone just walking by. An addict's mind is one of obsessive thought, and obsessive thought leads to destructive behavior. One of the clinic's goals was to teach an addict ways to arrest the obsessive thinking before it became destructive behavior. And for the sex addict, that meant the three-second rule. When sex addicts see an attractive person, they are to allow themselves no more than a three-second look before turning away, and that's the end of it. There is no second glance, no time for the image of stripping her naked or having sex with her to develop and take control of their minds, no chance to create one more fantasy. Just three seconds. Then the thought slips away or is replaced by one that is non-sexual.

The clinic kept finding small, simple ways to help us retrain our brains. Simple, but not easy. That look. The one from the beautiful someone we don't know and from whom not one word has been heard; the one movies show us we can build an entire relationship upon; the one our ego craves to feel valuable, appreciated, loved; the one that boosts our self-esteem, but only artificially, and only for that moment. And then we need another, and another . . .

I could never escape the belief that in a healthy relationship there is a difference between looking and "the look." The three-second rule was the first time I had heard that, far from benign, one of these could actually be damaging to people and their relationships. I eventually got the best explanation of how this works from a long-time recovering sex addict. In the meantime, my curiosity led me to gather the puzzle pieces on my own, and I wondered: How has it happened that we no longer fear death from starvation, wild animals, the elements, or many diseases, yet we stand by as our inability to be intimate and relational threatens our survival as couples, families, communities, and nations?

I once read a survey that asked people which person, living or dead, would they most want to spend time with. The overwhelming first choice was Jesus Christ, though he wasn't mine. I figured that since so many people would be talking to Jesus, I would eventually find out everything I wanted to know about him. It also meant the line to my first choice, Abraham Maslow, would be a short one. In fact, I doubted many, outside of those in the psychology and business communities, would even know who he was. But he was the closest thing to a mentor I've ever had. In my life, which was full of people who could only show me what not to do, he showed me what was possible.

I have turned to Abraham Maslow many times in my life to help explain what confused me, and at least twice while in the clinic. The first was to help me better understand this fear of intimacy, which by now seemed nearly epidemic.

I first heard about Maslow when I was an undergrad with a psychology minor. He didn't get as much lecture time as the behaviorists, cognitivists, and psychoanalysts, which, ironically, was why he had co-founded humanist psychology to begin with. He believed that psychology had become too focused on abnormality and pathology and had ignored those who were living healthy, fulfilled lives. Meaning, we had spent so much time looking at the worst in people that we knew what a sick life looked like, but not a healthy one.

There was much in Maslow's teachings that, for most of my life, I had no idea how to apply. I knew no one who was living a functional life through healthy thoughts and behaviors, no one living his highest potential—which has nothing to do with success, fame, money, or beauty—for me to follow.

But the thought of it. The thought that there was a more conscious me; that I could make my choices from this most high, balanced, and intuitive place, rather than let my lowest-level desires and knee-jerk reactions make them for me; that I could actually live the life, fulfill the purpose I was meant to. Maslow said I could do this. I hoped he was right.

He showed how it was possible through the Hierarchy of Needs, for which he is probably most well known. Maslow believed we move through a five-level process—from survival to fulfillment—to satisfy all that is necessary for a healthy life.

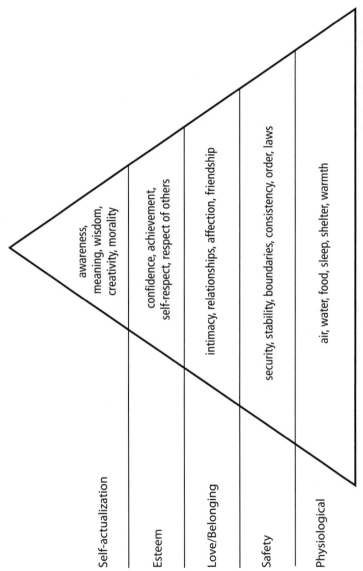

Hierarchy of Needs

Self-actualization — awareness, meaning, wisdom, creativity, morality

Esteem — confidence, achievement, self-respect, respect of others

Love/Belonging — intimacy, relationships, affection, friendship

Safety — security, stability, boundaries, consistency, order, laws

Physiological — air, water, food, sleep, shelter, warmth

Developed by Abraham H. Maslow

The first and most basic level consists of the physiological needs, such as air, food, and water. You will always seek to satisfy your survival needs first, meaning that if you are starving you will devote all of your time and energy to finding food, and have no interest in developing a relationship or your self-esteem.

Once your physiological needs are met, you move to the second level to satisfy your safety needs by establishing security, stability, and freedom from anxiety and chaos. You want to live in a home where you don't fear physical, emotional, verbal, or sexual abuse; in a neighborhood where you're not threatened with bodily harm or property damage from intruders; in a community that protects its residents; in a nation where all citizens are treated fairly and equally.

When you feel safe, the third level provides your love and belonging needs. Here your primary motivation is the desire to love and be loved, be a part of a family, get married, have children, bond with like-minded friends and co-workers, join an organization or group.

The fourth level contains the esteem needs. Once your survival needs are met and you feel safe and loved, you then desire a good and stable opinion of yourself and the respect of others. Feeling safe doesn't mean you never feel vulnerable. It means that you can be openly vulnerable and still feel protected by those who are closest to you. Once you feel safe enough to create intimacy with others through love and belonging, it's this mutual support system that allows you to take the next step toward building self-esteem. This is where you risk challenges, take chances, make choices, pursue dreams, fail a little, and succeed a little more; this is where healthy character is built, morals and values are tested.

Yet, even when these four levels are satisfied you may still feel a restlessness and discontentment—what Maslow calls the self-actualization need. It is here at the fifth level that you live life to its highest potential, where Maslow believes "what a man can be, he must be."

As I looked around I could say that all of us in the clinic, and many in this country, do not fear threats to our basic survival. We have supermarkets, soup kitchens, and restaurants; hospitals and law enforcement; homes with indoor plumbing, heat, and air conditioning.

We keep wild animals in cages and national parks, and have cars, televisions, radios, computers, and cell phones to keep us in contact with the rest of the world. We have done our part to satisfy Maslow's first level of the hierarchy and are now able to fulfill our safety needs.

But it is here, at our desire to feel safe, where we get stuck. If you don't feel safe—whether real or imagined, physically, mentally, or emotionally—you will not make the transition to authentically and intimately belong to another or a group of others. If you don't feel safe you will do whatever you need to do, develop whatever defense mechanisms necessary, put whatever you must between you and everything you're afraid of to protect yourself. And I wondered, if we have everything we need to ensure our survival, then why don't we feel safe?

Long before I knew why, I could see the effects of not feeling safe, which were evident through the Law of Escalation. This law is simple: Everything escalates. All thought, all speech, all behavior as individuals, families, communities, companies, organizations, and nations, whether good or bad. Literally everything. And everything continues to escalate without a conscious and constant effort to maintain balance, because balance is where healthy perception comes from, and healthy perception creates healthy thought, speech, and behavior.

I know the Law of Escalation is truth by a sentence I have heard often from people who want to justify unacceptable thoughts, words, or behaviors: Everybody does it. Everybody flirts, cheats on their spouses, cheats on their taxes, cheats at school. Everybody lies to friends, family, employers, on résumés. Everybody in professional sports is using performance-enhancing drugs, spying on their opponent, trying to get a just-beyond-the-rules edge. The Law of Escalation is what's behind the theory that obsessive thought leads to destructive behavior and the question, "What's wrong with porn?"

However, there was a time when everybody didn't do it or think it. Nothing begins at the extreme end of unacceptable or illegal. But because we as individuals, families, sports and business organizations, and nations don't maintain balance, we have to justify every lowest behavioral standard because now they've become commonplace. Because now—everybody does it.

So I applied the Law of Escalation to the fulfillment of our basic needs. The more prosperous and advanced we became, the more we redefined these fundamental needs. It was no longer just food for survival, but high-fat, chemically infused food; not just drink to quench thirst, but something to make us high or numb through sugar, caffeine, or alcohol; not just shelter, but two homes plus three cars, the latest technological devices, money, fame, and success.

All of these things, which should have freed us, enslaved us instead. And all of these things, which should have made us feel safe, left us too afraid to move, to breathe, to love. The escalation of possessions has created a barrier that alienates and disconnects us from ourselves and everyone else.

But possessions by themselves can't alienate us from anyone; we have willingly given them this power. It is easier to surround ourselves with material things that give us false security than look within to find out exactly what it is we are afraid of, which is the true path to safety. We will look for any way, acquire any thing, to keep from feeling afraid and powerless.

However, the answer isn't to stop progressing, producing, or acquiring, but to balance our material possessions with our emotional, intellectual, and spiritual growth. Acquisitiveness should be in harmony with altruism, a beautiful body with a beautiful mind, heart, and soul. But we've not learned to do this with any authenticity. By being intimate, we risk seeing in others the parts of ourselves we don't want to see and don't want to make the effort to change. So we have perfected pretending to be intimate, pretending to be part of a relationship or group, through our behavior. We know how to date, marry, have children, join churches and clubs. But it is not just the behavior that creates intimacy and fulfills the belonging need. It is also the mental and emotional connection. You can be married and not have the slightest ability to intimately relate to your spouse; have children but be more like a drill sergeant than a nurturing parent; be part of a club and still not belong; be in a room full of people and still feel alone.

So we are stuck between two levels of Maslow's hierarchy, between spending all of our time and energy on satisfying what we think are

our basic needs and trying to feel safe. And instead of building relationships through intimacy, we have added people to the list of possessions we think we must have to make our lives comfortable or secure
or "normal." Family, friends, and co-workers have become just one
more thing to own, rather than intimate connections to love, growth,
integrity, commitment, strength, and joy.

Sitting alone in my room one night after a long day exposed to
nothing but brokenness, I had an uncomfortable thought. Because of
the Law of Escalation, there are fewer healthy people every day—fewer
people to feel safe with, to build intimacy with, to create belonging-
ness. And every day, the number of sick people escalates. Sick people
are governing sick people. Sick people are teaching sick people. Sick
people are in relationships with sick people. Sick people are raising
sick children.

I began to understand why we don't feel safe. We aren't taught to.
We aren't shown what building our safety net through lifelong commitments to relationships and right choices looks like. Most everything
we come in contact with teaches us how to cover up what we're afraid
of rather than face it; how to disconnect from ourselves and others
rather than risk intimacy; that if we do the wrong thing, it's all right
because everyone else is doing it too. There is no safety at home. We
are raised by people who drink, drug, cheat, gamble, compulsively
shop, work too much, watch hours of TV and porn or vent their rage
through verbal, emotional, and physical violence. There is no safety
in our relationships; there is a fifty percent chance any marriage we
enter into will fail. Our culture constantly tells us this is the way it is
and the way it should be. Anything else is no fun, not cool, too religious, or boring. And anytime we get that feeling in our gut telling us
something different, we just take or do something to make it go away.

*We are lonely because we can't be intimate. We can't be intimate
because we don't feel safe. We don't feel safe because we haven't been
taught how.*

A few people in and outside the clinic helped me go even further into all of this—the lack of intimacy, the look, and the inability to feel safe. Some were addicts who had become counselors. Others were guest speakers at twelve-step meetings. A genuinely recovering addict is a profound source of honest information because breaking through the denial, defenses, excuses, and lies is the only real chance an addict has at getting healthy. Those who are serious about this will stand before you, tell it all, and tell it truthfully.

One guest speaker was an alcoholic and sex addict still sober after nine years. The alcohol was the easiest to let go of, but it took an immeasurable shift in his thinking to help him break his sex addiction. He said if we had come to this twelve-step meeting hoping to leave feeling better than when we came in, we had come to the wrong place. He was there to tell the truth. He said,

Whether you are an addict or enabler, the truth is you are where you are because you are lonely, you are scared, and you are angry. The truth is you will never get well if you don't admit this. I am getting well because I have.

I've been drinking since I was a teenager, and a sex addict since long before that. By the time I was barely an adult I could look at any woman who caught my attention anytime, anywhere, and picture her naked or having sex with me. I use the word "caught" intentionally. Once I made eye contact with a woman it was as if my brain snagged on a line that connected me to her, and through that line I felt a power and possibility I didn't feel anywhere else.

The power came with the first look. If she was real, rather than an image on a page or television or computer, and looked back, the power exhilarated me. The possibility came with the fantasy. She could be whoever and whatever I wanted. It took me years to figure out that the power and possibility I got from looking and fantasizing was a lie. It didn't make me, or anyone around me, better, stronger, or wiser. But through me and because of me, it diminished and could destroy us all.

So here's another truth. There is no such thing as "just looking." If you're looking, you're lonely. You're lonely because you're scared you aren't enough. And the fear that you aren't enough keeps you from doing all those things you want to do, like commit to an authentic personal and spiritual life, and excel professionally. So you hold back, which makes you feel even worse about yourself. Even if you are successful by today's flawed standard, if you got there through your dysfunction, you will try to stay there through your dysfunction. But it will always fall apart. So you live angry—and you are angry. If you weren't, you wouldn't be doing violence to yourself and others. And there is no doubt, all that stuff you're doing when you're alone in your room or in your head is violence as sure as if you were taking a knife to your own skin. That violence bleeds over onto others in your life, and those you demean by mentally stripping and violating because they never said you could. You can say you aren't lonely or scared or angry, but using someone or something to make yourself feel better says something different. You are all of these things, and it's up to you to find out why.

No one is saying you can't look. Appreciating beauty is a joy, and seeing beauty in all people and all things, not just the obvious, is a rare gift. But it's time to become conscious of *why* you look. Are you looking to appreciate, or to support your sickness, weakness, and low self-esteem? Are you looking to remind yourself to find beauty everywhere, or to use beauty for an ugly purpose? You have a choice. You've always had a choice.

I used to justify my choices, first by believing that what I did in my own mind was my business and I wasn't hurting anyone anyway; second by believing women wanted me to look, to use their bodies in my mind any way I wanted because of the way they dressed or walked or looked at me when I looked at them. Maybe some of them did. But the more I came to understand I was worth more than this destructive life, the more I realized they were too—even if they didn't know it. It may have been their choice to live their lives in a way that was less than they deserved, but I didn't have to help them do it. Doing the healthy thing for me meant I had to do the right thing by all women, which is putting my trust in truth, commitment, intimacy, and most of all boundaries. I learned there are places I can go and places I can't, both physically and mentally.

Eventually, the places I couldn't go became places I didn't want to go to after all. Even if everything a woman did was asking me to. I will support any woman who wants to be seen and valued as a whole person, but I will no longer support her need to be noticed just for her body, nor will I reduce a woman to this through my own thoughts and behavior. I may only be one person, but I am now a better one; and because of me, even though she'll never know it, so is she.

People always ask, "How did you change?" First, understand that I'm not done changing and never will be. I constantly have to work on taking my mind where I want it to go rather than where it wants to take me. The good news is, the greater your commitment to getting well, the easier it gets. But in the beginning, I was just like you. Not only did I not want to change, I didn't think I could.

Porn was hard to break, not because I didn't want to but because it seemed nearly impossible to get away from. Sexual images are an acceptable part of everyday life and invade nearly all we see, made possible by the many men and women eager to be seen as desirable and valuable because of the way they look naked, which has nothing to do with who they are.

Even more difficult was when I'd meet a woman through work or see one in a movie, TV show, interview, or even a commercial, who was not only beautiful but smart, well-spoken, funny, quirky, and doing something with her life and I'd think, *I should be with you*. As if, somehow, being with her would make everything in my life better, make me better. Then I'd carry her home with me in my mind and when we were alone, I would be better.

The thing is, I'm married. I felt confident I had given my wife a good life—kids, a nice house, a good income—and a pretty good husband once I stopped drinking. But there was one thing I never gave her: my presence. I may have been physically there, but not mentally and never emotionally. I never gave her one second more thought or attention than I had to, and even then it was only to keep her quiet and away from me. I saved my attention, charm, kindness, and enthusiasm for others.

But even with the others, this was as far as I'd go. Once they asked for something I didn't know how to fake, or asked anything from me at all, the whole thing lost its magic. I was never in this life for what I could give, only for what I could get. It was never about anyone else, but always and only about me.

That's why I loved my fantasies most of all. With fantasies, the possibilities were unlimited. I could get anything I wanted, and a woman could be anything I wanted, but mostly, she just wanted me, though I only wanted the *experience* of her. Not an investment of time or energy or emotion. While the thought of having that special relationship, of finding my soul mate, was intriguing, it always seemed like something I hadn't yet come across, rather than something I could have already had; like something I would get when I found the right one. It never occurred to me that I had to be the right one too.

There came a time when the answer to *I wonder what it would be like to have sex with her or see her naked* was *Just like every other woman I've had sex with or seen naked.* Because I could keep changing women, find new pictures, new celebrities, or someone new on the beach, but nothing would change until I changed.

I had to change what I thought and felt about women, about love and commitment, but most of all about myself. That's what this is really about. How you feel about yourself. With each new woman, new photo, new fantasy, you are saying, "I don't like who I am," over and over and over. Denying this doesn't make it any less true. There is not a woman alive, no matter how beautiful, smart, rich, or famous, who can make you love yourself. All they'll give you is a momentary high. If that's all you're looking for you're in luck, because there are plenty of women who think so little of themselves that they'll accommodate you.

I also had to stop thinking that what I did in my own mind wasn't hurting anyone. It was hurting everyone. There is nothing harmless about sexual fantasies, whether fueled by a picture or a real person. And they can escalate into having an affair or buying another human being when the fantasies stop being enough.

I had convinced myself that my fantasies were nothing more than my own personal entertainment, and that I had beaten my addictive and dysfunctional behaviors when I stopped drinking. Success in one part of your life can make you feel entitled to break the rules in another part. Even when my favorite mental pastime resulted in physical affairs, I could justify it. I had quit drinking, the bills were paid, and I always showed up where and when I was supposed to. I was giving all those in my life everything they wanted. This was for me.

Even if you're not acting on your fantasies they are just as dangerous and destructive, because you will always need more. They will become more intense and increase until they dominate you, your thoughts, and your behavior, and you'll cross boundaries no man should ever cross: your wife's sister, your best friend's wife, your daughter's best friend, your stepdaughter, your own daughter. You will cheat your boss out of time and money by looking at porn online when you should be working, and you will cheat your family out of any chance of being happy and healthy, let alone actually remaining a family.

And you *will* deny intimacy to your spouse or mate because all of your time and energy are spent nurturing your fantasy life rather than your real relationship. All of this erodes you, your wife, your marriage, the women you fantasize about, but most of all, your kids. Your behavior guarantees that your children will be future addicts or enablers.

Sexual fantasies are only harmless—have absolutely no control over you—when you aren't having them.

The power and possibility of fantasy is that not only don't

you have to get to know the other person, you don't have to have another person at all. You masturbate to a photo or fantasy often enough and you begin to believe having a relationship with a real person will only interfere with your life and diminish your sexual enjoyment. This is where the problem lies. Your ability to be intimate, to actually relate to another in an authentic and committed relationship, grows weaker with each fantasy until it becomes something you don't have the slightest idea how to do. And that constant empty feeling you have is there because you've invested nothing in this ability to have genuine and lasting relationships. You need true intimacy with a real person. It brings you right up against all the things you love and don't love about someone else. Those things are there for a reason—to teach you about what you love and don't love about yourself.

Fantasy is a conscious choice to deny reality, a deliberate intention to lie to yourself and insulate yourself from your own dysfunctions because you are too scared to face and fix them. Reality and intimacy will challenge you to grow, change, do what's right even when you don't want to, and learn something new about and see something beautiful in the person you've been waking up next to for years. When you have the real thing, you no longer need the fantasy.

That's how it worked for me. I took all the energy I put into my fantasies and relationships with other women and channeled it into my relationship with my wife, my family, my God, and myself. I can appreciate beauty in another, but that's all it is—an appreciation that someone was blessed with good genes or a sense of humor or the ability to make something of herself. I don't need her approval to boost my self-esteem. I don't need her to look at me, like me, or desire me sexually. Because I no longer need any of this, there's no reason to manipulate women to get it by flirting or lying or cheating. I really don't know this person, and she doesn't know me. That used to be a plus when I thought I couldn't get any worse and didn't want anyone to know me. But the healthier I get, the more I want everyone to genuinely *know* me; to know what I've been, what I am now, and what lies ahead; to know I'm worth loving and committing to because I can now do the same. Not through manipulation or some fantasy of what could be with a pretty someone who happened to be sitting next to me on an airplane, but with a real someone who wants to work as hard as I do at getting all of this right.

I know what has happened to me is rare. The odds of a recovering sex addict's relationship succeeding are low. They're zero for a non-recovering sex addict. Other than mine, I don't know of any other relationship that's survived. The reason I hear most often for this is that the addict didn't pick the right person, and for the longest time I believed the same thing. I thought I knew all there was to know about my wife and none of it interested me, and hadn't for a long time, if it ever did. What I did know I wasn't crazy about. Even worse, after a while I realized she had to be pretty sick herself to be with me. Any woman married to a man like I was shouldn't put up with it for even one day; not the looks, the jokes, the constant remarks about another woman's attractiveness or body; not the distance, the lack of love and respect, the lies and betrayal, or the manipulation forcing her to accept all of this as normal. If she does accept it, does see it as normal, her problem is as big as his.

Fortunately, my wife and I understood that we both played a role in our mess. I took responsibility for my part, and she took responsibility for hers. In the beginning, it was hard to admit we didn't know what we were doing. If we did we wouldn't have been in the situation we were in. We couldn't rely on what we believed was the right thing to do because everything we did or thought came from dysfunction. So recovery couldn't be what I wanted or what she wanted. We had to commit to turning over our lives to those who could genuinely help us. Since neither of us was totally convinced we'd be successful, we set a time limit. We'd give it our all and make a total commitment to recovery for one year, but if either one of us wanted out after that time, it was over. After nine years, we're both still here.

In addition to our individual counseling sessions, my wife and I met weekly with a therapist, but we could only discuss what we'd learned about the process and ourselves so far. These joint meetings were not a place to complain about, blame, or criticize each other. As a result, two valuable things happened. Since we were only allowed to talk about ourselves, we revealed things to each other we hadn't been able to before, slowly at first to test reactions, then a little more as our trust in each other grew. Trust, by far, was the hardest thing to build because we had never really trusted each other, anyone else, or even ourselves.

Keeping the focus on our process and ourselves also kept us from saying things about each other that we would have regretted later when we were deeper into our recoveries and thinking clearer. That didn't mean we didn't say them. There were no limitations in our individual therapy sessions. But it was in my own sessions where I learned that much of what I blamed my wife and others for was my problem after all, and that the power to change, to have a different and better life, was also mine.

In the beginning, you will fight hard to keep your old life. You need to take more than a second to think about what I just said. *You will fight to stay sick.* Very few sex addicts get well. Not because you can't, but because you won't. You will continue to manipulate others; continue to find ways to stay in your addiction by connecting your personal, professional, even spiritual life to sex while trying to convince yourself and others you are healing; and continue to spend every moment trying to get away with the unhealthy thoughts and behaviors that are destroying your life. If you have any hope of truly recovering, you will let go of all this. It is my goal every day to get away with absolutely nothing. That between me, my wife, and my support system, I stay on the right path. The only reason this would ever be a problem is if I wanted to live my old life, which I don't, and never will again. I make mistakes, but I own up to and learn from them. What's even better is I now make and own up to my right choices, and I make more and more of those every day.

Most people find the growth and recovery process excruciatingly slow and complain about the lack of quick or obvious change, but then, ironically, consciously choose to change through "baby steps" to slow it down even more. The process can be as fast or as slow as you want it to be. While you must commit to this process for a lifetime rather than days, weeks, or months, quick and obvious change is possible. The only one stopping it from happening is you and your need to hold on to some misguided idea of who you are and what you are capable of. As long as you are afraid of everything you are meant to be, you will never be free.

I hit the wall after all of my secrets were exposed, but my real recovery began with the answers to these two questions:

Do I want my son to be like me?

Do I want my daughter to marry someone like me?

If you're lucky enough to realize you've hit the wall, you can begin the long climb back to a place where neither you nor anyone else ever needs to be ashamed of who you are. But you really have to want it. I'm not telling you to be something you don't want to be. It's your life and they are your choices. I'm only asking you to look at whatever you choose honestly. If what you're doing is right, why aren't you telling everyone—your family, friends, and those you manipulate into having sex with you—what you do, what you think, what you are? A healthy life is nothing to be ashamed of or keep hidden. But you are as sick as your secrets.

There were other recovering addicts who wanted to tell the truth about their lives and behaviors. And there seemed no behavior more questioned, especially among those married to an addict, than that of one's spouse immediately clicking out of the computer page he or she was viewing after you had walked into the room. A behavior that happened so routinely you couldn't help but ask why, only to have your spouse say you were crazy or imagining it. But that uncomfortable feeling that washed over you every time it happened didn't feel crazy, it just felt wrong.

An addict has to convince those around him that they aren't seeing what they're seeing, aren't feeling what they're feeling, because if they begin to believe themselves more than they believe him, the lies he's invested so much in begin to fall apart and they'll learn the truth of what he has allowed himself to become. But sometimes his fear of that happening isn't so great because he knows they've got just as much invested in believing his lies as he does in telling them.

So that feeling you constantly chose to deny was telling you the truth. He was wrong. You didn't imagine it. Every time you walked in, he did click out of something he didn't want you to see. And he was right. There is something wrong with you. You will trust anyone before you will trust yourself. This is how someone gets into, and stays in, a relationship with an addict.

Most of what I'd heard about sex addiction came from sex addicts themselves, but a few times I was told what it was like to be in a relationship with one. Primarily women frequented the Codependents Anonymous (CoDA) meetings I had attended both in and outside the clinic, but I was continually surprised at the growing number of men. Rather than my initial understanding that these meetings were for anyone trying to correct unhealthy relationship patterns with others, they were really for those who wanted to establish a healthy relationship with themselves. So addicts of every kind, realizing their addictive behavior was the result of a deeper problem resulting from trauma or wrong thinking, often attended the meetings.

The CoDA meetings were much different from the AA meetings I'd attended. AA meetings always followed traditional protocol, and not once did I see a meeting or its members deviate from the scripted format.

There are the readings:
- The Preamble
- "How it works" and the Twelve Steps from *The Big Book*
- The Twelve Traditions
- The Twelve Promises

And the guidelines:
- Keep confidentiality.
- Use only "I" statements, not "you" or "we."
- Share only what has happened that day or week.
- Share on the selected topic or an experience of success, strength, or hope.
- Share for three minutes or less.
- Don't give advice or try to fix others.
- No crosstalk.

In addition to understanding that this commitment to structure was to give the addicts a place to practice something other than chaos, I'd also realized AA had had over seventy-five years to get it right. If any newcomers came in unconcerned about or uninterested in the proper procedure, the old-timers set them straight in a hurry.

Codependency and CoDA meetings were relatively new and still finding their way in the twelve-step world. And though all of the CoDA meetings I had been to were patterned after AA, the biggest difference was in how closely that pattern was followed, which was sometimes not very closely at all. Most of the deviation occurred during sharing. There usually wasn't a time limit, crosstalk was common, and the sharing could veer off into inappropriate comments about a spouse or portraying oneself as a victim. But the most interesting thing about CoDA meetings was watching a group of people, who were there specifically because their problem is fixing things and giving advice, doing everything in their power to not fix things or give advice.

At a meeting one night, mixed in with a thief, a drug addict, and the rest of us trying to make sense of our relationships was a woman so despondent over her marriage to a sex addict she could barely raise her eyes or her voice as she spoke.

The clinic was full of people who had done horrible things to themselves and others, as well as had been on the receiving end of equally damaging behavior. When the full effects of these acts became clear, some were low-spirited for a while but then fell back on the same artificial arrogance that had helped put them in this place to begin with.

Some were genuinely repentant and committed to the long process of healing—a process requiring the unwavering conviction that, no matter what someone has done or has had done to them, and no matter whether anyone else thinks otherwise, we are all worthy of change, growth, forgiveness, and a fair chance at living a happy and healthy life. But it was never easy to see and hear someone so unable to overcome her belief in her worthlessness. She said,

> Being married to a sex addict, I have no place in his heart, his mind, or his bed because he's built his life around anyone but me. Sex addicts are collectors. They store up experiences and people who can give them the high they crave. But I can't be part of the collection. I am familiar when he wants the unknown, constant when he wants change, commitment when he wants to disavow, limits when he wants indulgence, accountability when he wants an exemption, one choice when he wants it all.
>
> There are no moments, words, or places meant for just the two of us. Vacations, movies, dinners, and parties are all shared with whoever has his attention and has become the latest addition to his collection of fantasies. Anything intimate or erotic I believed he shared only with me, he has said to or done with many others. There is nothing private, nothing sacred, nothing special.
>
> I will never be enough because he spent whatever he felt for me long ago. I will always be too much because I ask for more: more communication, more time together, more emotion, more love, his touch, his kiss, his arms around me. I want to get closer. But the purpose of his life of fantasy, flirtation, and affairs is to get as far away from me and our marriage as possible.
>
> This is my life. I am here, not because of what my husband is, but because of what I am. I am someone who has believed this is what I am worth for as long as I can remember. It's not that I don't realize this life is wrong for me, wrong for anyone. It's just that I don't know any other. I don't know how to be worth more than this, because I've never been more than this to anyone, or to myself. There are times I feel what I'm sure is

an instinct to survive well up inside of me. My head and heart aren't so tired. I stand a little straighter, my legs get a little stronger, and I think I can walk away. But then I stop. I've got nowhere to go, and there's no one else I know how to be. I just don't know how.

The stories from sex addicts and the women married to them illustrated several concepts the clinic wanted us to grasp, one being that you cannot use your dysfunctional mind to get well. The choices addicts make to try to heal on their own will be inherently flawed because they are coming from a mind that is broken, angry, scared, lonely, arrogant, and insecure. The sex addict who spoke at the twelve-step meeting and his wife understood this when they chose to turn their recovery over to their support system.

There is a reason the First Step in the twelve-step program is first. Everything else in your recovery will be meaningless unless you admit you have a problem and ask for help from those who have made the journey before you. There is also a reason why the First Step is the hardest. Since addicts by definition can't be intimate, they also can't be vulnerable, and you become very vulnerable the moment you say, "Please help me."

But just admitting your powerlessness isn't enough. Without making humility an intrinsic and constant part of your life, any success you think you've had in your recovery will fall apart, which makes relapse not very far behind.

Ralph Waldo Emerson said, "No change of circumstances can repair a defect of character." A genuinely recovering addict knows you can quit drinking, using drugs, or having meaningless sex, but unless there is a true and thorough transformation of your character, you're just a dry drunk who will only replace one addiction with another. This transformational process, which substitutes the unhealthy thoughts and behaviors you've clung to for years with healthy ones, is lifelong. Addicts who don't realize this don't recover.

Addicts in genuine recovery say that it sometimes took them years to understand and apply some of what they had been exposed to during those first months of recovery. But you cannot truly recover without putting yourself in an environment that constantly promotes and reaffirms the transformation. To do this, you must first find the humility to admit to others that the place you've put yourself in isn't where you were meant to be.

It was interesting to watch the effect words like humility, vulnerability, and intimacy had on not just addicts, but on many people who swore there was nothing broken about them. Some of the strongest resistance came from men who looked at humility, vulnerability, and intimacy as a lack of power, a loss of self, a weakness rather than strength, and they convinced themselves of this with evidence from their relationships.

Because those at the love-avoidant extreme can't be intimate or vulnerable, they gravitate toward others who they think can to create balance in their lives, but not knowing balance, only excess, they choose partners at the other extreme. Men who are emotionally walled-off and unavailable form relationships with women who so completely emotionally attach that they never develop proper boundaries or the separate sense of self they need to have their own thoughts and accomplishments. So love-avoidant men use a love addict's clinging and inability to have a life outside the relationship to support their belief that intimacy equals weakness and a loss of self.

But neither completely shutting down an intimate connection nor completely attaching to one is correct. Defining intimacy with one sick mind while supporting your beliefs through the behaviors from another one equally dysfunctional will not get you one step closer to health, because what you will see as intimacy and vulnerability is neither. It is only another face of brokenness.

As I listened to those in the clinic who had lived most of their lives denying, refusing, or burying any thought of vulnerability, intimacy, or humility, I asked why, in spite of their show of invulnerability, they looked so weak and shattered. Why, if a life without intimacy was the right choice, they felt so isolated and lonely. And how, if they knew so much more than any God, loved one, or health professional, they continually made the wrong choices and ended up here.

Everything they thought would give them power, self-esteem, love, and respect had actually drained all of this from their lives. And everything they saw as a weakness was their greatest strength. I saw two sources for this upended thinking: what they thought and how they thought. The clinic's goal for every one of us was transformation, and to transform, we must redefine.

Addicts have crystal clear ideas of what is right and wrong, good and bad, true and false, acceptable and unacceptable. And what defines things like love, respect, courage, self-esteem, humility, intimacy, and power. But what they believe bears no resemblance to what is real.

Humility is the lack of false pride. False pride is believing and taking credit for something about yourself that isn't true. Far from the addict's belief that humility is a weakness, it requires that you be brave enough to admit that your idea of what defines you and your character, value, and purpose is false, and then seek what is real.

But how can you make that admission, even realize you need to, if you can't use your unhealthy mind to do it? It seems there is only one place in each of us where we find truth and pure guidance. It is from this place that the voice telling us "No" comes when we are about to do something harmful or wrong, and where we find strength, joy, and peace when doing what is right. But its name alone causes such fear in so many that we will adamantly deny or cavalierly dismiss its power and purpose, which is exactly why we had all ended up in this place to begin with. We had put all of our trust in the mind, believed it to be the source of intelligence, and faithfully followed its guidance. But through denial, justification, and arrogance you can make the mind believe anything, make it tell you what you want to hear, make any irrational thought and behavior seem completely sane, and ultimately make it ignore or overpower what is true. The mind becomes such a willing accomplice that eventually you can't tell whether you are controlling it or it is controlling you.

It was here I got my first glimpse that something I'd believed all my life might not be true. If transformation requires redefinition, then we must rethink the source of intelligence and its path. Truthful intelligence can only come from a place that can't be corrupted, a place connected to something greater, which must fulfill its purpose as the source of truth and guidance so we can fulfill ours. *Intelligence begins in the heart.* But even the clearest guidance is worthless if it isn't acted upon. *The mind transforms guidance into action.*

Master boulderer and mathematician John Gill described this process when he said that impossible-looking mathematical proofs are solved by "quantum jumps of intuition." That "quantum jump of intuition" is truthful guidance coming from the heart, and it is the mind that uses this guidance to solve the impossible-looking proof.

The true path of all intelligence, problem-solving, and conflict resolution is from the heart to the mind. But everyone in the clinic, and many others who will never find themselves in rehab, didn't just get the source and path of intelligence wrong, they omitted the heart from their lives altogether. They gave this reason, which to them sounded like truth: "My mind isn't broken. I trust it to give me truthful answers and clear guidance."

If you think your mind isn't broken, it is more broken than most. And if you think you don't need help or counseling at times, you need it most of all. We all have minds that are broken in some way and to some degree, but a healthy mind has no fear of vulnerability, truth, or the heart. It is not afraid to be guided. It is not afraid of its place or its purpose. It knows that balance, power, achievement, conflict resolution, right choices, and true love only come when both the heart and the mind work together. But when there is no heart, there can only be conflict, chaos, confusion, separation, and suffering.

The recovering sex addict's story also illustrated the clinic's teaching of redirection when he took all the time, energy, and attention he'd once put into his dysfunction and channeled it into his recovery. Minister and author Emmett Fox called redirection the Law of Substitution: replacing destructive thoughts, actions, and behaviors with what is balanced, healthy, and healing.

Buddhists say redirection happens in our "store consciousness." They believe there is a place within each of us where all our emotional, behavioral, and thought choices are stored as seeds so that, in any situation and at any moment, we have all options available to us. Our task is to nourish only those options that support our growth and healing, water only those seeds that will put down healthy roots, and leave all others dormant. It all begins with the right choice, because whatever we cultivate will escalate.

The story from the woman married to a sex addict illuminated one of the deepest problems within all addictive and dysfunctional relationships. Addicts love and trust themselves unconditionally, but not others. Enablers love and trust others unconditionally, but not themselves. Addicts believe themselves to be the highest power, what they know to be the final word. Enablers are no one and know nothing. When you don't know and don't trust yourself, you will allow others to define you and the things that are important to you. This woman, more heartbroken and lost than any I'd seen, allowed her sex-addicted husband to define who she was—her value and potential—and define love, marriage, and commitment when he was incapable of truthfully knowing any of it even for himself.

In the clinic, there was a sex addict whose definition of freedom was sex and nudity, and he called women who openly shed their inhibitions and clothing "free spirits." As I listened to him, I imagined this place he described, a place where women took off their clothes and ran around naked or had sex with him whenever he wanted; a place where he didn't have to work very hard to feed his addiction because everyone else was doing it for him; a place where the things he saw as restrictions and limitations, such as truth, honor, respect, and boundaries, didn't exist; a place where he didn't have to bother with unnecessary obstacles, like a relationship, intimacy, commitment, or love, which only got in the way of what he really wanted.

After hearing his story, I learned he'd spent nearly his whole life in this place, which he either sought out in life or created in his mind. It was hard to imagine anyone less free. He was a slave to TV shows, radio shows, movies, magazines, music, books, jokes, and stories with even the remotest sexual content or innuendo. And chained to places where if the women weren't naked or nearly so, they should be. He spent a lot of energy manipulating others into behaving or thinking like him to make what he did and thought acceptable; after all, how bad can it be if everybody's doing it?

He had made this place his home, and he was bound to the very thing he thought was freeing him, something of no substance and with no future. I said a silent prayer that one day he would find a way to be free with his clothes on.

After many stories, I could sometimes feel my clear thinking stand up to the manipulation of definitions, sense the inconsistencies when a sex addict defined love and intimacy; when a drug addict defined morals and values; when an alcoholic defined God and spirituality; and later, when athletes who used performance-enhancing drugs were allowed to define a many-year span of professional baseball as the "steroid era" because clean athletes wouldn't come out and define it for themselves. But mostly, the manipulation and distorted definitions just felt like home. I'd been accepting them my whole life. Eventually, I could bring only the most broken people into my life, trusting they could and would heal my own brokenness. I enabled those whose lives and choices were dysfunctional to think they were sound by giving them authority over my life and choices.

Figuring out *what* I found acceptable in my relationships because of my childhood was much easier than understanding *why*. I knew the discouraging comments on top of the bigger, more damaging moments were crippling. Like nearly everyone else at the clinic, I had been told clearly and often what I was—stupid and worthless—and what my life would amount to. I was sixteen and sitting on the living room sofa one afternoon, making out with my new boyfriend. We were fully clothed, our hands were nowhere inappropriate, but we were kissing like our very breath depended on it. Then my father walked in, home early from work. My boyfriend ran off. I sat perfectly still, and waited. My father thought I was too old to whip anymore, so he scarred my purpose, my potential, and my future with these words instead: "You will never be anything. And if you go anywhere, it will be on your back."

What I didn't understand was why all of this had seeped into me so deeply, reshaping me so thoroughly that I had no choice but to believe it was truly who I was. What made me different from others who could innately understand that harmful words and acts from someone else, even someone you should be able to trust, are not acceptable and not true? How did the disconnect between what my head *thought* was true and what my heart *knew* was true happen? And why would I constantly turn my heart, my beliefs, my future, my very self over to those who couldn't care less about them?

Shortly after my wedding, a New York tabloid printed on its gossip page that I was an aerobics instructor, which other media outlets have continued to report as true throughout the years. Though I would later learn the answers to my questions, at the time I didn't know who or understand why anyone would erroneously and intentionally allege this in the first place. I have never been a certified aerobics instructor. I taught aerobics for three months while in college. It was simply a summer job, much like any summer job a college student must get to pay the bills—not my profession. And I desperately needed it. I was broke, my summer tuition was due, and I got paid $8.00 for every class I taught. But when the summer ended, so did the job.

As many times and from as many different writers as this was reported, not one called to verify its accuracy. Credibility didn't seem to matter then, and since it's still being written, it doesn't seem to matter now. However, the further I got into my healing, the less it became about the journalists' inability to do their jobs properly than my inability to define myself, and what I had the right to ask of others. Could I naturally expect protection and support from a loved one in a situation like this? Or was it yet another characteristic of codependency: relying on someone to do for me something I should be doing myself? Though there was never any guarantee that anyone telling the media I wasn't an aerobics instructor would have made them want to print the truth, it wasn't just about who should tell them, but who I would say I was instead. And not having my own definition of who I was made it easy for others, some with harmful intent, to choose it for me.

When I was young, I somehow got the idea that there are those who create and those who appreciate, and I had decided I was born to appreciate the fruit of other people's talents rather than create my own, never realizing I could do both. I became the loudest cheerleader and strongest supporter of those I loved, which meant that not only did their lives, thoughts, and beliefs became mine, but also their weaknesses. If they lied, I lied to protect them. If they betrayed me, I betrayed myself by letting their idea of who I was and what I was worth become my own.

But the clinic's counselors wouldn't let this stand. Their most frequent question to me during the five weeks was who did *I* want to be and what did *I* want to do? My only answer was that I liked to write.

In grade school I would write the kinds of stories that only made sense to a kid. In middle school I'd pick a word and write as much about it as I could: its size, shape, color, sound, smell, feel, taste, what it meant to me, to you, to the world, why it was here, and what it would be like if it weren't. But any magic, comfort, or freedom that words brought me before that night of cards with my father didn't seem to do the same after. By the time I entered high school, I could easily find any way or reason to discard nearly everything but the anger.

As a teenager I wrote only when teachers required me to, but I read everything within reach of my outstretched hands. There were two books that shared a space within me, nourishing the fragile belief that maybe one day, I would write something of my own. Jack Kerouac's *On the Road* and Edith Wharton's *Ethan Frome* faithfully stood guard over that thought's faint fire, refusing to let it be extinguished.

I've been asked, "Why these two?" a few times. My answers were never about their life metaphors or deep meanings because I'm sure I missed most of that. It was simply the writing. Vastly different styles but still, I'd never known it could be like this. Words I'd known all my life were suddenly put next to others and became everything words can't describe. But honestly, just seeing the name Sal Paradise would have almost been enough.

The spark flared a bit in my twenties, when I entered college to get a communications degree with the idea of becoming a journalist. I thought if I couldn't write for myself, maybe I could write for someone else. I graduated in three years summa cum laude, was offered a job at the newspaper at which I'd interned, then said no to everything I'd worked for, every step forward I'd taken, and got married again.

There were so many times during our Group discussions when a counselor asked why, if I wanted to write, didn't I write? But after I'd heard it once too often, I said, "Why? Maybe because I'm too busy doing everything so everyone else doesn't have to. Isn't that enough?"

"I don't know. Is it enough?" he asked.

I raised my head and stared at him through fed-up eyes. "Have you looked around here lately? At the drug addicts, the sex addicts, the gamblers, the alcoholics, the depressed, and the suicidal? They are also doctors, lawyers, an architect, a professional athlete, a movie director, an author, and an entertainer. Some have money or fame, a few have both. How has it worked for them?"

He looked back with empathy. "The question is, is your life working for you? If you say it is, you can get up, walk right out that door, and no one will stop you."

But I wouldn't leave. Looking at us all it seemed one part of our lives had been working, but there was another part we simply had no idea how to embrace, and we used what we did well to keep from looking at what we were most afraid of. Someone used his money and success to get the love and respect he couldn't give. Someone used the ability to love and support others in their life's purpose to keep from finding a purpose of her own. And for the first time, I wondered what it would look like if we were curious about the things we had so far been unable to do, rather than fearful? Curious about our capabilities regarding love and our highest potential, about how far we could go if we could just let go of being so afraid of whatever we were afraid of? Because none of us could really explain what that was anymore.

While I was ready to commit to the process, I had no idea where to start. It felt like so much in my life was broken. One day, I sat out in front of the horse stables, watching someone fix a splintered fence

post, and thought of the house I had spent so many years rebuilding. I remembered that the transformation started in the only place
it could have: the foundation. And I wondered, what if I began by
redefining everything I'd learned as a child about my potential, my
purpose, and myself?

In transactional analysis psychotherapy, this is called changing
a "life script." Transactional analysis therapists believe we are born
innately healthy but develop patterns or "scripts" that match the positive or negative messages we receive from our parents or caregivers
during childhood. Based on these early influences, we unconsciously
decide to be failures or successes, dependent or confident, depressed or
happy when young, and then spend the rest of our lives making these
identities come true.

We reveal our life scripts through three observable ego forms: the
Child, the Adult, and the Parent. Only one form is active at a time, and
each is identified by different gestures, postures, mannerisms, facial
expressions, and word and sound choices.

The Child (not to be confused with "childish") is said to be the part
of us that is most likely to be free, spontaneous, creative, and joyful,
and is preserved in its entirety from childhood. When in the Child state
we sit, stand, walk, and speak as if a child. We'll say short words like
"wow," "nice," and "cool" in a high-pitched voice. The example of the
Child state Claude Steiner gives in *Scripts People Live* is of an adult
male at a sports event expressing delight or anger, or jumping for joy.
He would not only act as a young boy, but also think and feel like one.

The Adult state functions like a computer and develops gradually
from the interactions between a child and the outside world. In this
state, we take in and process information through our senses, and
make decisions and predictions completely without emotion, which
is crucial to accurately observing and judging an external situation.

The Parent is a carbon copy of behaviors from a child's parents or
caregivers absorbed whole and without modification. While in the
Parent state we will act, react, or respond to situations exactly as we
were shown by those who raised us. It holds our traditions, values, and
survival tools, and is a constant though often unreliable basis for our

decisions. Parent state behavior is learned but, most importantly, can be changed, especially through one's own healthy experiences and choices.

It seemed to me my Parent state hadn't changed much since childhood and was still running much of my life. I now understood from a deep place in my heart that my definition of "home" was so corrupted that I had almost no ability to make accurate judgments about myself, others, and life situations when I needed to most.

I was certain the world was full of those who when young had seen and heard the same things I had, and much worse, but had never claimed those childhood walls as their own. They walked out with no burden weighting their shoulders and with nothing to prove to anyone except themselves; only knowing that this place they'd been shown made them even more certain it was not where they belonged.

Sports have two ways of looking at real or perceived identities and obstacles. The "loser mentality" is where *you* make the identity or obstacle insurmountable, and losing becomes a self-actualizing, self-perpetuating inevitability. It's the team that has gotten so used to losing that everyone associated with the organization expects it to happen; the team that accepts its decades-long losing record as its identity so it no longer knows how to win, and considers it a fluke when it does; the team that won't put up much of an argument when all the other teams instantly put a mark in the schedule's "W" column before the game is even played. It's hard to leave the confines of a loser mentality when you don't believe you can.

An "underdog mentality" is where *others* see your identity or obstacle as insurmountable; where they have underestimated you and your abilities in certain circumstances and decided you are outmatched; and where you know they are wrong. It's the AFL's New York Jets victory over the NFL's Baltimore Colts in Super Bowl III. It's the USA's miracle over Russia in the 1980 Winter Olympics. It's no-shot James "Buster" Douglas beating Mike Tyson for the 1990 heavyweight championship. It's Division I-AA Appalachian State stunning Division I-A top-ranked Michigan in 2007. It's Northern Iowa taking out sure-win, top-seeded Kansas in the second round of the 2010 NCAA tournament.

I looked at those in the clinic who were twenty years younger than

I and wondered if it was too late for me to undo what had been done. Everyone else's definitions and underestimations had been mine for so long I wasn't sure I could see any other possibilities. But I no longer had a choice. I either transformed or kept on losing until there was nothing left to lose. And even when I didn't know how to do this, I had to believe the transformational process existed and was possible for me; that I could believe in it when I couldn't believe in myself.

My first attempt at transformation while in the clinic looks a lot more like arrogance than confidence to me now. I walked up to my Group counselor just before our first session and asked him to give me the books, CDs, DVDs, paperwork, homework, and handouts they'd planned to string out over the next five weeks all at once and as soon as possible. If I had to dig up my past and break up the patterns, I wanted to get in, get through it, and get out. By the time I left the clinic, I wanted to be done with all of it.

I remember my counselor trying to find the right words to tell me it doesn't work like that. Giving up on finding them, he finally just said, "Marta, it doesn't work like that."

"Like what?" I asked.

He said, "Deconstruction and reconstruction is a process. And using dynamite to try to blow it all up is no different from anyone else using a substance or behavior for the same purpose. You can't blast through, speed through, or cover up what's broken. You deconstruct and reconstruct brick by brick. We can get you started by giving you new tools and thought processes to replace the ones you used as a child that are no longer working for you, but it won't end here."

I asked him how long doing it his way would take, and when he said two years *minimum*, I thought it couldn't be true, or at least not true for me. Eventually I'd find it didn't have to be for some of the process. You can break down much of your past with some serious commitment in less than two years. But replacing the patterns is something else entirely, and putting everything you learn into practice will take the rest of your life, because you never stop learning, growing, and healing.

But I didn't know this when his response to my open-faced doubt was, "Let's just take this one day at a time."

I told him I'd give it six months.

For many, the first day in Group is the first time telling their stories, and for all of us to answer the "Why are you here?" question. But by my first day, I had already been through my husband's Family Week and Survivor's Week and had been telling my story in scared and angry bits and pieces the whole time. Perspective had helped make things a little clearer and me a little calmer, so I spoke about my life with an alcoholic father and a drug-addicted husband and said I was there to try to understand my part in all of it.

I wasn't too far into telling my story when my counselor made a derogatory remark about my husband more on top of his breath than under it, and I stopped cold. Before my previous two weeks at the clinic, I would have quickly assessed the situation as in his control and myself as powerless and allowed the comment to stand by ignoring it. But now I had been told I had boundaries, and recourse when they were breached. My concern was that his admitted negative bias against a member of my family would interfere with his ability to work with me professionally and, most of all, without judgment. And with that one comment, I felt he had lapsed in both.

Everyone in the room heard the comment, and the quiet curiosity in my story now shifted to an intense interest in what I would do next. When I knew I wouldn't ignore it, I said: "When I heard you say something negative and judgmental about my husband, what I thought about that was that your problems with my husband are going to affect our professional relationship, my ability to do my work here, and your responsibility to compassionately teach me about boundaries, rather than cross them. And I felt sad, angry, vulnerable, and betrayed."

He acknowledged my imperfect attempt at the Feedback Loop with a nod of his head but said nothing, so I went on a bit longer with my story until I gave up on it. Later that night, I wrote a letter to an administrator that relayed the incident, expressed my belief that my being a part of this counselor's Group would be uncomfortable for both of us, and asked to be moved to another. It took me three days to realize I wasn't going to get a response.

In the clinic, a word you'll hear just as often as "boundaries" is "abandonment." I didn't know whether I would get a quick or even favorable response to my letter, but I never imagined I would get none.

I had seen and would continue to watch the clinic's staff and administrators struggle with determining which of the many patient requests and complaints were legitimate and which were addiction-fueled antics, and the best way to handle them all. Sometimes they made things better. Sometimes they over- or underreacted to the point where I couldn't see much difference between their behavior and the patient's.

I went back over the letter in my mind to make sure I hadn't overreacted or insulted the counselor. Feeling confident I'd done neither, nor even asked for an apology, only to be moved, I wrote another letter to the same administrator. I decided the best way to learn about boundaries and how to appropriately handle uncomfortable relationships and situations was to put myself in the middle of them, so I asked to stay where I was. It was also ignored.

However, I did understand the reason for putting me in this Group. It was the administration's job to place patients in an environment that would provide the most benefit and the least threat. Male sex addicts were in one Group, female sex addicts in another. No men were admitted in the Group for sexually abused women.

For the most part, my Group peers and I were a wonderful fit, and I bonded so well with one that we would stay in contact for over a year after leaving the clinic. But peers came and went with regularity, which left each Group's counselor as the one constant. With my assigned counselor I quickly realized I was going to have to learn in the clinic the same way I'd had to learn my whole life—through examples of what not to do.

I believed then, as I do now, that there was one Group counselor who better fit my situation and me but, just as during my husband's Family Week, I wasn't sure what I was allowed to ask for. Alone and in the first days of my five weeks in rehab, the answer seemed to be not much that would be listened to.

However, Group was where I learned the names and faces of my patterns, defense mechanisms, and childhood survival tools. Each time I told my story in Group I went deeper, bringing up memories and emotions I had either long forgotten or buried so low I may as well have. And each time, someone heard something in my words I was not able to hear myself.

The most frequent survival tool to surface was my need for perfection in my family, my surroundings, but mostly myself. To continually put in order, straighten out, clean up, fix, adjust, repair, improve. I could take self-discipline to a punishing level. And when I allowed myself to, I could see and hear inconsistencies in people and my surroundings quicker and better than most because I had years of practice. And because it wasn't a choice.

As a child I had one goal: to make sure my father couldn't find a reason to get angry. If that meant I cleaned, washed, sat, stood, spoke the right words, or was seen and not heard, that's what I tried to do every conscious moment from my earliest memory as a four-year-old until the last time I saw him at sixteen, and was still doing unconsciously to this day. The pressure I always felt to make things right, that damaging too-high expectation of perfection, had destroyed much of my ability to be childlike and spontaneous, and I had absolutely no comprehension of anyone willingly or consciously choosing to live in chaos.

I was at Group one morning well into my stay. A peer was telling or retelling her story. Each time my eyes shifted from my peer to the counselor's socks, so did my attention. Respecting my Group and our boundaries, I kept silent as long as I could stand it. Then with the first opening I got, I asked the counselor why he was wearing two different-colored socks. It wasn't just that one was black and one was navy blue, but the pattern and even the fabric were different.

He paused for a moment. When he spoke the Group session shifted, the focus now on my father and me, and my search for perfection. Then one peer gave an example of how perfection had even invaded my time in the clinic.

Throughout our five weeks, the counselors assigned art projects to aid us in our healing. With the "trauma egg" they asked us to draw an egg shape on a large piece of paper and fill it with words and pictures of specific traumatic events in our lives, from as far back as we could remember to age seventeen.

I stood in the art room, crayon in hand, and stared at the blank paper in front of me for several minutes contemplating how I was going to draw an egg freehand that wasn't misshapen, and then began looking for an egg template.

The counselors also used letter writing as a way to get us to go even deeper, bring out unexplored feelings about specific issues, events, or people. And before that day's session was over, my Group counselor asked me to write a letter to my perfection. He gave me a few days to write the letter before he started asking for it, and continued to do so over the next couple of weeks. The more he asked, the stronger two competing and conflicting extremes rose up within me: I could be perfect, do what I was told, and write the letter, or I could prove him wrong about my perfection and refuse. I didn't write the letter. I also didn't know what I'd accomplished.

But I do know I didn't fully agree with my Group counselor's belief that the desire to make something better, to get better and be better by working toward a purer goal, was entirely unhealthy. I couldn't help feeling that my pursuit of it, however misguided, had value, even a purpose for me.

I sought the perspective of another counselor at the clinic. He was a recovering drug addict and alcoholic of many years, had been through rehab more than once, and still attended therapy and twelve-step meetings every week. It wouldn't be unreasonable for anyone to think that, with regard to recovery, if he hadn't seen it, hadn't heard it, or didn't know it, it didn't exist. But that's where we would all be wrong, where we would miss the very point of recovery and the reason why so many fail, and why he eventually succeeded.

He listened intently to what I had to say about perfection and my conflicting feelings. His hands rested in his lap, turned up and one inside the other as if he could absorb my words through the skin of his palms, and then his eyes sparked. He said,

"What if you make perfection, your childhood survival tool, work for you now rather than against you?"

Realizing it or not, with this question he connected me to the heart of any sport, whether team or individual: Never beat yourself. You can lose to a better team or athlete, but you should never lose because you turned *yourself* into your opponent by putting everything unnecessary and counterproductive between you and your goal.

I concentrated on his words. I could feel the weight of their immeasurable value. And I looked at this man. He was not perfect, but he was different from the other counselors. It was that he approached every person, every story, every question as if it were the first time, because for him, it was.

Relapsed addicts are usually those who have done a little time in rehab, read a few paragraphs in recovery books, attended a few twelve-step meetings and therapy sessions, then declared themselves all-knowledgeable, and therefore fully recovered. But the fundamentals they will always forget—and which can never be repeated enough—are that healing never stops, for any of us, whether you think you're an addict or broken or not; and healing and recovery, like all of life, are about humility. We can never, never know it all. We can only lose the joy of learning it.

"What if your journey is not a quest for perfection, but a search for a more joyful, willing, and honest way to learn?"

Far from wanting to declare himself perfect or all-knowledgeable, this counselor saw whomever and whatever was presented to him as an opportunity to learn something new. What constantly warmed me to his presence was his sense of wonder at and appreciation for each one. He never stopped learning. He never stopped growing. He never stopped loving. So he never stopped healing.

He believed the fundamental purpose of every life and every moment on this planet is to learn, and to keep learning about everything you don't know and everything you think you know. Like how to genuinely love, how to feel joy, how to rest your mind, how to be intimate, resolve a conflict, keep a vow, find your God. Even our last breath will bring us something new to learn if we are still open to it.

Perfection keeps you from learning, actually makes you believe you've nothing left to learn. You end up fighting against yourself by putting perfection between you and what you were put here to do. Attempts at perfection will always fail because the pressure and fear that undeniably come with it actually create the very thing you are trying to avoid: mistakes.

I thought of the many things we put between ourselves and self-knowledge: dysfunction, addiction, fear, low self-esteem, arrogance, hatred, ridicule, procrastination, busyness, denial, justification, and for me, perfection. We consciously create every one of them specifically to keep from learning, to keep at a distance what we don't want to know, and we don't want to know why we are so angry, lonely, and scared; why we keep getting into the same harmful relationships or can't stay in a relationship at all; and why we would rather take and do things that will kill us than admit the problem is ours, not someone else's. But not everyone sees brokenness as an opportunity. Not everyone sees refinement as noble. Not everyone wants to know the truth.

"What if you turned your desire for perfection into a passion for all that's beautiful?"

Opportunity, refinement, and truth are beautiful, and turning perfection into beauty isn't about no longer making mistakes. It's about not making the *same* mistakes over and over. The gifts of knowledge and growth and healing, especially those acquired through mistakes, are essential to our lives. Disowning them out of fear instead of joyfully, willingly, and honestly embracing them is the same as stopping your own breath.

"And what if you show others through your own life that we shouldn't fear taking a step toward a more purposeful and fulfilled life, and then taking another? Even if you only plant a seed for someone to grow in his own time, it will be enough."

Paradoxically, as clear as I was about what needed to be fixed or improved, I could also idealize those I loved to the point where I believed they needed no improvement at all. In her book *Eat, Pray, Love*, Elizabeth Gilbert described this as projecting upon our lovers and loved ones those good qualities they never actually developed in themselves.

I wouldn't fully realize I had idealized and mythologized the men in my life until years after I had left the clinic when, still in therapy, I was brought to the point where I had to recognize the pattern and completely break it if I were ever going to have a healthy relationship. And like nearly all of my childhood survival tools, this one had come from my father.

My father was tall. So tall he could reach past the bottom limb of a sky-high tree and touch the one above. His voice was deep as well water. And he was so smart he didn't have to stay in school past the ninth grade, reading about life in schoolbooks. He lived it.

In truth, he was none of this, and I knew it. But I could never allow myself to believe it. He was my father. His blood was in my body. Whatever I believed him to be, I would be too. Just like whomever I was attracted to, and who was attracted to me, would show the world what I believed I was worth. So I fell in love with the imaginable and made it my reality, and then forced upon others the possibility of being something or someone they may not have been capable of or wanted to be in the first place.

All authentic spiritual disciplines call on us to always see the goodness in everyone, regardless of the circumstance, and I try to apply this higher-consciousness approach to others. But how do you reconcile the divinity in someone with the decidedly unholy person he chooses to be at that moment? How do you recognize and encourage potential without giving credit for something not yet earned? How do you allow someone to develop integrity, morals, and values in his own time and in his own way, possibly even without you? As an enabler, I couldn't. And in Group, I had to admit it.

Group is where all patients had to openly declare their First Step of the twelve-step program: We admitted we were powerless (over our addiction or dysfunction) and that our lives had become unmanageable.

The Group counselor gave us several pages of questions and characteristics that described our particular problem. As unlikely as it may seem, it wasn't until that moment that I understood; the First Step was not just for alcoholics. All of us, including me, had to admit to being what we had become.

At one point during my stay, I was given questionnaires on several issues, such as post-traumatic stress disorder, eating disorders, and love addiction/love avoidance. The purpose was for those at the clinic to determine what I had and what I was, and then tell me. They concluded I had post-traumatic stress disorder, did not have an eating disorder, was articulate and appeared to possess above-average intelligence, was anxious due to unresolved trauma, and had self-defeating and perfectionist behaviors. For my First Step I was to admit to being codependent, rather than a love addict or love avoidant, and I felt relieved. The yes or no questions for love addiction and love avoidance filled two pages, front and back, and I had an equal number of each answer for both behaviors, so I didn't know whether I was one, both, or neither. But at this point it didn't matter what they called me, because I still didn't like being called any of it.

My Group counselor handed me the paperwork on codependency I was to read and complete for my First Step. I looked at the first line on the first page: Am I Codependent? Then at the long list of the denial, self-esteem, compliance, and control characteristics that followed—and silently answered yes to nearly every one.

It is unsettling when you see all of your damaged and unhealthy patterns and behaviors in print for the first time, line after line after line, and shattering when you realize there is a name for all of it. That this label is now who and what you are, and it usurps everything else you thought you were.

It was hard to look past this label and see the divinity in myself; there is nothing transcendent about enabling. That's the funny thing about potential; it can go either way. You can develop your highest potential or your lowest. Choose your best life or your worst. Spend your life getting closer to, even actualizing your purpose, or do everything possible to keep from getting anywhere near it.

I wanted desperately to remove that label from my life, and by now I knew there were at least three ways to do it. However, two would only buy me time until my life broke into pieces all over again. I could simply deny my dysfunctional patterns, go through the motions of completing my First Step just to appease those at the clinic but not commit to the process, then go home and live my life exactly the way I had before. I could commit to some of the process for some length of time and then quit. Or I could commit to it all, every moment of every day for the rest of my life. I knew beyond any doubt that denial was no longer an option. The Holy Hammer had struck. My Perfect Moment had arrived.

I believe there are moments when everything comes together—the right person, situation, place, and time—to create the perfect opportunity for us to change and begin living the lives we were meant to live. I've had many of these moments throughout my life: broken marriages, toxic relationships, unhealthy children, harmful friendships, overwhelming conflict and chaos. For all but one of them, I had no idea what was before me, no idea what I was being asked to do. Even if I did, I would have had no idea how to begin.

But there was that one Perfect Moment when I knew, saw, felt to the core of my heart and soul that I was being asked to change, when I knew I had been chosen. My husband, his substance abuse, and his Family Week—the right person, situation, place, and time—was my Perfect Moment.

Though everyone is chosen at some point, only a few realize it and accept. A few more realize it and refuse. But most, through denial and detachment, never see their Perfect Moments before them and live their lives unhappy, angry, scared, and lonely until their last moment on earth. However, those who are unwilling to change through knowledge and growth have all the same chances as the person who has found happiness, love, and a peaceful mind. The only difference is the openness to being chosen. But whether through denial or refusal, most do walk away. As hard as it is for those who accept, it is much harder for those who know their Perfect Moment has come, know they've been chosen, know exactly what they are and what needs to be changed, but *consciously* choose not to. Because you can walk away, say you're not ready, or say you don't want it, but you can never again say you were unaware of your Perfect Moment; never deny what your God and this universe have asked you to do; never deny that you were chosen.

By refusing knowledge, growth, healing, and change, those anxious and uncomfortable feelings, that pressure constantly building in your body, mind, and heart from trying to resist, from trying to hold back something much more powerful than you, from trying to manage everything that's overwhelming you, only gets worse.

I did not refuse my Perfect Moment, but I also knew it would be dishonest to accept it with half a heart, to only go as far as was comfortable for me and only for as long as I determined was necessary and then claim I was healed. I accepted it all, which meant I accepted pushing myself and being pushed to do things I didn't want to do, change things I didn't think I could change, and surrender to things I didn't and still don't understand; accepted the times I resisted the call to turn back around after I'd just run a mile in the wrong direction; accepted when I stopped where I stood, paralyzed with fear and anger at having to take even one more step.

But I would always turn back around, and I would always take another step, because my divinity and the purpose for my life deserved not to remain dormant and buried under everything inglorious and untrue. And because even the smallest change made the ground on which I walked bring me that much closer to home.

My confusion during my husband's Family Week about what exactly codependency was and who it applied to cleared somewhat by the time I made my First Step. But it still seemed to be so many things and apply to everyone. Or at least to those with damaged core issues, either all or in part, which still meant everyone.

I had been at the clinic a couple of weeks when I realized our Group discussions, and often those among ourselves, focused more on core issues than on our enabling and addictions. We understood that our destructive behaviors were the result, not the cause, and if we could heal the cause of our problems—the damaged core issues—our destructive behaviors would cease.

One way we tried to get closer to understanding and healing the reason for our dysfunctions was to accept one patient's suggestion of creating a new twelve-step meeting, which followed the same guidelines and traditions as the others but dealt only with core issues. There was much to understand and heal. Keeping with the twelve-step protocol of only sharing hopeful or successful experiences, we first tried to identify how we each manifested our damaged core issues, then how to rebuild them.

By now we understood that a lack of moderation leads to the extremes of controlling others or being out of control. The problem was knowing how to recalibrate after decades of being out of balance. As always, a sports analogy helped me understand the process.

In football, a quarterback finds balance when the game slows down. Within the pocket, he gets comfortable in his calm space, finds his rhythm, and moves through his "reads" or options to determine the best place to throw the ball. This is only possible when the offensive line offers him the protection he needs against the oncoming defensive threat. Without protection, he has to navigate a much wider area to avoid being sacked, has less time to find his best option, and has more of a chance of throwing an interception because the defense forced him to react to a situation he hasn't properly identified. This is exactly the kind of chaos his pursuers want to create, their only purpose being to disrupt his rhythm, flush him out of the pocket, and pressure him into making a quick decision and, hopefully, a mistake.

It works the same when you are confronted with a threat or problem—both real and imagined—in life. Just like a defensive line, destructive thoughts and behaviors agitate your mind and body, disrupt your breathing, and enlarge the present moment by including thoughts of the past and future, feelings of being overwhelmed or abandoned, beliefs in your low self-esteem and powerlessness, and everything else you imagine is real but isn't, forcing you to react too quickly and, inevitably, say or do something you will later regret.

By slowing down the situation, establishing steady and rhythmic breathing, and confining your space to this moment rather than overwhelming it with everything unnecessary and untrue from the past and future, you are able to move beyond your thoughts and into your feelings. Only in your heart will you find the truth, even if it is everything you don't want to admit to, like feeling angry, scared, abandoned, overwhelmed, threatened, lonely, or unloved. And only through your heart do you have the time to explore all of your choices before you act or speak. Making choices through your heart is not suppressing, denying, delaying, or detaching from your feelings and the situation. Rather, it is where you become further engaged and better informed through healthy core issues so you can make the right choice.

Healthy core issues are your offensive line. Your ability to stay balanced in the midst of chaos, establish appropriate boundaries, properly interpret the situation, and act out of high self-esteem and abundance rather than fear and lack will protect you as you acknowledge what you feel. If you are angry, feel anger. If you are scared, be frightened. If you are lonely, say so. Confining painful and confusing feelings to a small space makes them manageable and gives you time to determine how to use them to help rather than hurt you. Even if you choose to fight, with healthy core issues you will fight using weapons that will never cause harm to yourself or others.

By far the most important core issue is self-esteem. The health and presence of every other core issue is directly related to the health and presence of self-esteem. Without healthy self-esteem, the ability to maintain proper balance and boundaries, appropriately assert your wants and needs, and realistically assess your environment and yourself doesn't exist. But decades of misidentifying, trivializing, and underestimating self-esteem have made it as difficult to define as codependency.

One dictionary defines *self-esteem* as "a realistic respect for or favorable impression of oneself; self-respect," and *self-respect* as "proper esteem or regard for the dignity of one's character." Because the clinic used them repeatedly, two words caught my attention: "realistic" and "proper." The contradictions within and inappropriateness of our thoughts, feelings, words, and behaviors made us unable to realistically and properly assess most things, including ourselves. So my task became to learn not only what self-esteem is, but also how to strengthen it, and one of the things I did both in and outside the clinic was search for the books to help me accomplish this.

I've often heard that those who purchase self-help books usually end up with a vast personal library of books they have never read, only read once, or only read the parts that interest them or confirm what they already believe; and whatever they do read, they never actually put into practice. All the books, words, information, and guidance simply remain one more good intention and one more broken commitment to change.

Though my love of books, my appreciation of all that it takes to actually write one, and my tendency to understand most things only through the written word have resulted in a dog-eared, highlighted, read, reread, and constantly referred to collection, I fully understood that only by turning words into action would they actually change my life.

Beginning my search for a definition and answers to my self-esteem questions with Nathaniel Branden's *The Six Pillars of Self-Esteem*, I found myself drawn to one sentence: "Self-esteem, fully realized, is the experience that we are appropriate to life and to the requirements of life."

The experience that we are appropriate to life . . .

I have heard many express feelings of not belonging, of anxiety and insecurity, of awkwardness and self-consciousness, of incompetence and unworthiness, of being out of place or having no place, of feeling they should be someone or somewhere else, and that they could be living this other, better life if only *everyone else* would see how smart or creative or special they really are. These feelings came not just from those who had yet to find their life's purpose, but also from those who had but were using their gifts detrimentally to divide, control, ridicule, and create fear rather than unite, heal, encourage, and empower.

High self-esteem, meaning to have self-efficacy and self-respect, removes the obstacles to feeling appropriate to life. Self-efficacy is the confidence in yourself to take on a task and produce a desired result, whether it be learning something new, seeing something through, living authentically, facing a challenge, taking a risk, or making a change. Self-respect is the absolute belief in your own value, the conviction that you have the right to nurture and protect yourself, to treat yourself with respect and dignity and expect the same from others; have the right to make moral and ethical choices, to be trustworthy and of high character; have the right to put yourself in the best position to experience joy, fulfillment, and love.

Branden said low self-esteem "places us in an adversarial relationship to our well-being." Everything good you deserve and deserve to be, you sacrifice to feeling incompetent and unworthy. From the resulting pain, that war you are waging against everyone and everything around you is really a reflection of your war within. What you imagine as a separation from life is really the disconnected relationship you have with yourself. After all, how close do you want to get to someone you can't trust, can't respect, and who is angry, selfish, immoral, demeaning, controlling, defensive, hostile, unable to admit and correct mistakes, and unable to love—even if that person is you?

High self-esteem disarms your weapons and stops the war within. When you feel competent and worthy, you no longer need your fears, defenses, or pretenses, and no longer accept your unhealthy thoughts, feelings, and behaviors.

Branden separated self-esteem into six foundational components or "pillars": living consciously, self-acceptance, self-responsibility, self-assertiveness, living purposefully, and personal integrity.

Living Consciously
Much in the way that the health of the other four core issues—boundaries, reality, dependency, and moderation—directly relates to the health of self-esteem, I found that the strength of the other five pillars depends on how well and how consistently we practice living consciously. But I didn't need a book to define living consciously. The clinic used every opportunity to remind us that only by examining our motivation for every choice, thought, feeling, word, and act would we find the truth,

and only through the truth could we then authentically achieve self-acceptance, self-responsibility, self-assertiveness, personal integrity, and a purposeful life.

However, I did need Branden to put living consciously into perspective with this extraordinary reminder: What sets us apart from every other life form is that we have the power to choose.

> We are the one species that can formulate a vision of what values are worth pursuing—and then pursue the opposite. We can decide that a given course of action is rational, moral, and wise—and then suspend consciousness and proceed to do something else.

Only humans can choose to seek awareness and truth or actively avoid them. Only humans can choose to become enlightened or remain ignorant. And it is this first step toward building self-esteem that is the most difficult; the one of challenging our belief that we are "best served by blindness" and that only unconsciousness and detachment from the things we think, feel, do, and say will make our lives bearable. But even choosing to know the truth isn't enough. You have to choose to act on it. Because "consciousness that is not translated into appropriate action is a betrayal of consciousness; it is mind invalidating itself."

However, living consciously does not mean you exhaustively engage in mental or emotional problem-solving every waking moment; rather, you are in the mental state appropriate to what you are doing at the time. Awareness is a process of selection. There are times of activity to uncover truths and unravel problems, and times of rest and rejuvenation. There is seeking guidance verbally through communication with others, and silently through prayer. There is receiving nourishment through energetic play and exercise, and through daydreaming and meditation. And since you can neither mentally nor physically be in two places at the same time, awareness is appropriately choosing not only where to be in mind and body that will best benefit your growth and purpose, but where not to be.

Self-awareness is not self-absorption, such as in monitoring your interactions with others for approval or disapproval, or noticing their reactions to what you say, how you look, how you act, or the material things you possess. How well and how consistently you live in awareness defines your relationship with yourself. Self-esteem is an intimate experience; it is not what others think about you, but what you think about yourself. Your inability to be intimate with yourself should cause you and everyone around you to raise the question: What are you doing or thinking that is so painful or unhealthy that not only won't you let others know, you won't even admit it to yourself?

As with any effort to take your mind places it doesn't want to go, you also risk deceiving yourself into believing you are doing something you really aren't, like claiming you are still thinking through a problem or situation can give the appearance of living consciously when in fact procrastination is just another evasion tactic to avoid being authentically aware of your intentions. Branden described how avoiding consciousness is the primary motivation behind every dysfunction and addiction:

> To the addict, consciousness is the enemy. If I have reason to know that alcohol is dangerous to me and I nonetheless take a drink, I must first turn down the light of awareness. If I know that cocaine has cost me my last three jobs and I nonetheless choose to take a snort, I must first blank out my knowledge, must refuse to see what I see and know what I know. If I recognize that I am in a relationship that is destructive to my dignity, ruinous for my self-esteem, and dangerous to my physical well-being, and if I nonetheless choose to remain in it, I must first drown out the voice of reason, fog my brain, and make myself functionally stupid. Self-destruction is an act best performed in the dark.

An addict will always turn to whatever best buries his feelings of pain, low self-esteem, and powerlessness. But they will never stay buried, and in fact, will resurface with even greater intensity.

Self-Acceptance

As important as living consciously is, change and growth are impossible without self-acceptance because *we cannot change what we deny even exists.* If you are confronted with a mistake you have made, accepting that it is yours frees you to learn from it and make better choices in the future. But you cannot learn from or correct a mistake you "cannot accept having made."

Acceptance is much more than "acknowledging" or "admitting." It is a thorough and authentic examination of your thoughts, feelings, words, and behaviors to determine their source and intention. And none of this can be done quickly. You can acknowledge or admit a fact, but then move on so fast that you have really only succeeded in practicing self-deception, convinced yourself you have appropriately dealt with a problem or situation when in reality you barely touched the surface and only increased the likelihood of making the same mistake again. It is also important to know that acceptance does not mean approving, "liking, enjoying, or condoning" the unhealthy thoughts, feelings, or behaviors. Nor does it mean that accepting your dysfunctions absolves you from change or improvement.

There will always be those who are unwilling to accept what they think, what they feel, what they've done, or what they've become. Ironically, it is this "refusal to accept" that can be the beginning of transformation. If one can accept that at this very moment he *refuses to accept* his addiction or anger or pain, he will discover a profoundly important paradox: "The resistance begins to collapse." Resistance must have opposition to exist. When you fight against a block, you only add resistance and the block grows stronger. When you acknowledge the block—*I refuse to accept I am an addict, I refuse to accept I am angry, I refuse to accept I am lonely and in pain*—it begins to disintegrate.

Transformation begins by accepting where you are.

The beauty of true acceptance is that there is no rationalizing, justifying, denying, or attempting to explain, which are only obstacles to remedying unhealthy thoughts, feelings, and behaviors. You simply accept that what is true, is true. If you have done something unhealthy or immoral, you have done it. If you feel anger, pain, fear, or inappropriate lust, you feel it. If you cannot first accept that you engage in destructive thoughts and behaviors, how will you learn to think and live constructively? If you deny or disown what is, how will you be inspired to change it?

Self-Responsibility
Self-responsibility is the full understanding that you, *and only you*, are responsible for your thoughts, feelings, words, behavior, attainment of goals, and pursuit of your life's purpose. Who you want to be, what you want to think and feel, and how you want to live are entirely in your hands. If you want to be healthy, it is up to you to make healthy choices. If you want to be trusted, you must be honorable, think and do honorable things. If you want to be in a loving, intimate relationship, you must cultivate the characteristics and behaviors that can make this happen. If you want to live your life's purpose, only you can discover your place in the world. And most importantly, no one is responsible for your happiness but you.

To be "responsible for" does not mean to be blamed for, but that you are the primary generator of your wishes and desires. Nor does it mean you are the cause of everything that happens in your life. People encounter many things that occur by accident or through the fault of others. Some are within our control, others are not. But because of the connection between self-esteem and self-responsibility, if you hold yourself responsible for things beyond your control, your self-esteem suffers because your expectations cannot be met; and if you deny responsibility for what is within your control, your self-esteem deteriorates through living an unfulfilled and unaccountable life.

By taking responsibility for your own life, you recognize that others are not on this earth to meet your expectations, satisfy your needs, or fulfill your wants, desires, or wishes; likewise, you are not a means to fulfilling theirs. James Hollis, a Jungian psychologist, said that permission to live your own life is not something you ask of others, but what you seize for yourself. Too often, we surrender our personal authority to a person or group. But each of us is responsible not only for determining what is true for our own lives, but also for having the courage to live that truth.

Self-Assertiveness

Probably the most misunderstood concepts, both in and outside the clinic, are self-assertiveness and confidence. To be self-assertive means to honor your *healthy* wants and needs. It is the willingness to stand up for the character, integrity, sound morals and values, and self-respect you have cultivated in yourself over your lifetime; to live authentically, to speak and act from your innermost convictions and feelings and not out of fear or lack or low self-esteem.

Self-assertiveness is being committed to your right to exist, to knowing that your life does not belong to others, nor are you here to live up to another's expectations. Appropriate self-assertiveness is self-responsibility in action. However, to many, the thought of holding our lives in our own hands can be uncomfortable, even terrifying.

Appropriately manifested self-assertiveness stays connected to context. You can volunteer an idea; pay a compliment; offer polite silence to express non-agreement; refuse to smile at an inappropriate joke; ask for truth, openness, and reciprocity of intimacy in relationships. But to be self-assertive it is first necessary to authentically know what you think, feel, and believe through living consciously. Branden cautioned that

> self-assertiveness should not be confused with mindless rebelliousness. "Self-assertiveness" without consciousness is not self-assertiveness; it is drunk driving.

Reflexively saying *no* when *yes* would be more appropriate and beneficial is a form of destructive self-assertiveness. It occurs when the only way you feel you can assert yourself is through refusal, whether it makes sense or not, and when your power and sense of self come from your need to deny others happiness, rather than a desire to become a source of it. Using dissension to protect one's boundaries is a valuable tool, but living in a constant state of refusal and unwillingness only arrests development and stops you from growing toward a more healthy and conscious life.

Lack of self-assertiveness looks like the avoidance of healthy confrontation with someone whose morals and values differ from yours; the need to please, placate, or be someone you are not to belong or get along; and burying or ignoring your ideas, dreams, goals, wants, and needs to make someone else happy. However, self-assertiveness is not arrogance, belligerence, or aggressiveness. It does not mean enforcing your own rights while being indifferent to everyone else's. And it does not mean being superior to others or always right.

Appropriate self-assertiveness does not force someone else to be responsible for your wants and needs. If they are healthy, and not a result of codependency or enmeshment, you have the right to ask that your wants and needs be honored, but not the right to demand or expect it. What you want and need may conflict with what someone else wants and needs, and what you have the right to ask for, someone else may not have the ability to give. You have no control over what others choose to do with your self-assertiveness—only what you do with their response to it.

Adapting a theory from Sigmund Freud, Branden believed many unhealthy thoughts, feelings, and behaviors are either direct expressions of low self-esteem (feelings of worthlessness, hopelessness, or futility) or defenses against low self-esteem (grandiosity, bragging, belligerence, compulsive sexual acting out, or over-controlling behaviors). I found that nowhere was this more evident than in rehab. It seemed many of the addicts thought that if they simply talked loudly enough, or dominated, controlled, and ridiculed as many situations and people as possible, this would be enough to convince everyone of their high self-esteem and confidence. But the truth was, the loudest and most demeaning in the room were also always the weakest. Arrogance is not an example of too much self-esteem, but too little.

The position one takes during meditation is called the Seat of the Warrior. The straight back signifies a strong back, as opposed to the strong front and weak back of a coward. What dysfunction does is cover a weak back (fear and low self-esteem) with a strong front (force, arrogance, manipulation, and ridicule). Dysfunction turns people into cowards. So to keep from feeling weak, they must develop a corrupt definition of power. But force is not power, and arrogance is not confidence. They are strong fronts covering a weak back.

Greg Anthony, a former New York Knicks guard, described the difference between arrogance and confidence within a sports team: One shuts down the flow of the game by overpowering and paralyzing teammates, the other lets the game harmoniously unfold by allowing others to freely play their positions and contribute to their highest ability. But one who is arrogant is not interested in allowing others to shine, or in another point of view, or in finding a way to amicably resolve a conflict. While confidence is grace and faith in oneself and others, arrogance is belligerent and fears everyone and everything. Confidence is open and non-judgmental. Arrogance is insulated and critical. Confidence seeks harmony and balance. Arrogance is only resistance. Authentic self-assertiveness goes beyond individualism to bring the confidence and sense of purpose of one into a relationship with another or a community of many.

Living Purposefully

At some point in our lives we all ask, "What is my purpose?" It is not enough to simply exist; we want to know *why* we exist, where we belong, what we were born to contribute. In *Man's Search for Meaning*, Victor Frankl described this as the "gap between what one is and what one should become," and he believed that an "unheard cry for meaning" often results in "depression, aggression, and addiction." Branden provided the connection between existing or "what one is," and living your purpose or "what one should become," when he wrote that success "belongs to those who do."

Finding your purpose may be less about discovering *what* it is than what you *do* as you search for the answer. How many of us have said, "I have a great idea for an invention," or "I should write a book, teach, coach, paint, volunteer, go back to school, or attend church"? How many of us actually do any of it, choosing instead to wonder about our purpose rather than actually live it? You are not living your purpose if you find yourself searching for something else, thinking there must be something more, but then choose instead to remain passive and uncomfortably comfortable because you fear change or failure, or even success.

Living your purpose means you are living a life that provides an outlet for your ideas, intelligence, and creativity, that you have taken control of your right to exercise your abilities and talents. But an authentic purpose will never manifest itself in ways that escalate your weaknesses or cause harm to yourself or others, such as with pornography or drug trafficking or public ridicule and shaming, and it will not seek to create chaos or division. Authentic purpose will always unite and elevate humanity, and find ways to alleviate suffering rather than contribute to it.

Living without purpose leaves you at the mercy of chance, allowing coincidence or luck to control your existence. Your approach to life is reactive rather than proactive. The sum of your life—all your personal and professional choices—tell the rest of us what you think you are worthy and capable of, and what is possible and appropriate for you. Living purposefully means you are confident in your ability and have the discipline to turn your ideas into reality, bring your goals to fruition, and use your knowledge and services to everyone's benefit. Knowing your purpose is essential if you are to support your existence, be productive, and feel appropriate to life.

To find your purpose, you must first be aware of who you are. Living consciously, delving into your depths to discover what makes you happy and healthy, what brings you peace and a sense of place, will allow you to determine which dreams and ideas are truly worthy of pursuit. Frankl observed it is typically American that we command each other to "be happy." But happiness is not the result of some mind trick we play, or our ability to convince ourselves to feel something when we've done nothing to create or support that feeling. Authentic happiness "cannot be pursued; it must ensue." First comes the reason for your happiness—what you've thought, said, or done to cause genuine happiness—then comes happiness.

Living your purpose means living *with* purpose, and you can't do one without the other. Once you have determined a direction, if you are to succeed you need to know what you want to achieve and how you are going to achieve it. Purposeful living is not just doing your best, but requires a specific plan of action, the discipline to see it through, and a method to acquire feedback and monitor progress. "Purposes unrelated to a plan of action do not get realized. They exist only as frustrated yearnings."

Self-discipline, or the "ability to organize our behavior over time in the service of specific tasks," requires that you defer immediate gratification in pursuit of a long-range goal. If you lack self-discipline, you can never trust yourself to carry out plans to completion and achieve results. But a self-disciplined life is not without time for rest, relaxation, spontaneity, or frivolity. Regeneration is just as important to living purposefully as activity.

High achievement, money, or fame should never be used to define one's worth. Professional success can be an expression of self-esteem, but not its primary cause. You do not develop self-esteem because of your achievements or material possessions. Rather, it is the practices of integrity, fairness, and discipline that you engage in *through the process of achieving* that establish your competence, and make living your purpose possible and effective. If you are successful in your career yet irresponsible and untrustworthy in your private life, you may be able to convince yourself that money or fame or professional records and awards are all that is required to be thought to have high self-esteem and moral character. But this is only using professional achievement to excuse or avoid looking at and taking responsibility for dysfunctional personal choices. Living purposefully is not about choosing between character and accomplishment. It is about establishing both.

Branden made the observation that when most people think of living a purposeful life, they only apply it professionally, not personally, which is why more people are successful at their jobs than their marriages. They understand it takes time, energy, and focus to achieve professional success but will conversely define a successful relationship by how little effort, attention, and especially change it requires. But according to Branden, if you want something to be successful, whether personally or professionally, you must consciously establish the thought, word, and behavior choices that will make it so.

> Everyone knows it is not enough to say, "I love my work." One must show up at the office and do something. . . . In intimate relationships, however, it is easy to imagine that "love" is enough, that happiness will just come, and if it doesn't, this means we are wrong for each other. People rarely ask themselves, "If my goal is to have a successful relationship, what must I do? What actions are needed to create and sustain trust, intimacy, continuing self-disclosure, excitement, growth?"

A healthy society is the union of self-actualized people who have successfully developed both their professional and personal autonomy and the capacity for intimacy with others. The Zulu proverb *ubuntu ngumuntu ngabantu* maintains that one is "only a person through other persons," that we must extend beyond ourselves to become more of ourselves.

Personal Integrity
Having personal integrity means your words match your behavior. There is congruence between what you say your morals, standards, and convictions are and what you do. To determine the extent of your personal integrity, ask yourself: Am I honest, faithful, and trustworthy? Do I keep my promises and commitments? Do I do what I say I respect and avoid what I say is inappropriate? Do my choices remain moral during the most challenging times?

Branden believed one of the greatest self-deceptions is to tell oneself, "Only I will know." Only I will know I am a liar. Only I will know I am unfaithful. Only I will know I have no intention of keeping this promise. The implication is that only what others think of you is important. *But authentic self-esteem comes from what you think of yourself.* You may temporarily feel good after receiving a compliment or kind gesture from another, but you learn more from your own judgment of yourself than from anyone else's. Long before others know of your dishonesty, you will know. And when your behavior conflicts with your professed morals and values, your self-respect and ability to trust yourself will suffer until you are unable to trust yourself at all. Self-esteem will always become a casualty of dishonest and immoral behavior.

If you can lower your self-esteem, you also have the power to raise it. When inappropriate thoughts and behaviors damage self-esteem, "only the practice of integrity can heal it." Branden's five steps to restoring integrity are:

1. Accept and take full responsibility for what you have done, without justification, avoidance, or detachment.
2. Take compassionate but sincere steps to understand why you did what you did, without looking to excuse, rationalize, or justify your behavior.
3. If others are involved, acknowledge explicitly to them the harm you have done, the consequences and effect of your behavior on them, and convey an understanding of their feelings.
4. Take every action available to make amends for or minimize the harm you have done.
5. Firmly commit yourself to behaving differently in the future.

Having integrity does not guarantee you will always do what is right. But because it keeps you connected to your true intentions and the consequences of your thoughts, words, and actions, integrity gives you your best chance at making healthy choices. Blindness gives you no chance at all.

Without actualizing personal integrity through living consciously you run the risk of developing or absorbing irrational or inappropriate ideals and convictions, those that will do violence to your true nature and lead you toward self-destruction rather than a life of purpose and fulfillment. Instead of allowing your dysfunctions to control you, question your thoughts, feelings, words, and behaviors. Find and resolve the contradictions between what you say you believe and what you actually do. According to Branden,

> When we have unconflicted self-esteem, joy is our motor,
> not fear. It is happiness that we wish to experience, not
> suffering that we wish to avoid. Our purpose is self-expres-
> sion, not self-avoidance or self-justification. Our motive
> is not to "prove" our worth, but to live our possibilities.

Personal integrity and morals were a frequent topic in the clinic, and many of the patients used the words "values" and "morals" interchangeably. Values are the beliefs a person or social group holds in which they have a personal investment—for instance, the ideology of a particular religious or political organization. Morals are principles or convictions pertaining to right or wrong conduct, and I have seldom been in a discussion on morals when a debate on what is right and wrong, good and bad, and who decides didn't follow.

Of all the clinic's positions, the one on personal integrity resulted in my most vocal conflict. Our discussions on morality increased as patients became more forthcoming about their past inappropriate or unlawful behaviors. But it was easier to discuss morals with those who were truthful about what they had done and were making a conscious and visible effort to change than with those who continued the behavior in the clinic. Almost daily, the administration dealt with patients who went to great lengths to break rules or find ways to continue in their addictions, and it wasn't long before I saw why the clinic didn't trust us:

- Since no sugar, caffeine, or unapproved reading materials were allowed on the premises, patients had family, friends, and other enablers load up their multi-pocket cargo pants with candy, coffee packets, and tabloids and sneak them in during Family Week and holiday visits.
- The administration allowed patients to leave the clinic on Sunday mornings to attend church services. A van would drop off patients at the church of their chosen denomination. Some of the alcoholics went wherever they could drink the wine offered during the Eucharist. Others didn't go to church at all, choosing

instead to walk to the nearby convenience store to buy candy, coffee, and tabloids.

- Theft was a problem at the clinic due to at least two admitted kleptomaniacs. For some reason, the administration didn't let them room together and steal from each other, but instead split them up and placed them with others who not only had their recovery to deal with, but also had to be vigilant about protecting their property.

- An alcoholic walked off the premises undetected one night to buy a bottle of liquor. It was empty by morning.

- Two sex addicts, one of them married, were caught having sex in a bathroom.

The clinic administrators responded quickly to the instances they were told of or uncovered on their own. We knew when someone had broken a rule when it was either changed or more strictly enforced; and we knew when someone had irrevocably crossed the line when he or she was no longer there.

Generally, a counselor's response to patients' disclosures of inappropriate behavior was to remind them that everyone is moral at their core; the problem being that they have allowed their moral choices to become buried under their addictions. At some point, every addict in the clinic would be asked to repeat, "I am not my behavior." While I understood this spiritually, I struggled mightily with it everywhere else.

The first conflict I had was with the contradiction of an addict not wanting to be defined by his behavior when he did something inappropriate, immoral, or unlawful, but very much wanting to be defined by his behavior when he did something appropriate, moral, or law-abiding. However, my biggest struggle was with the clinic's belief that anyone can consider himself to have morals—even those living an immoral life. Saying someone is moral when he's done nothing moral to prove that it is true is the same as saying someone holding two sticks has fire. We all have the *potential* to be moral, to make moral choices. But being moral—like everything else—requires action, not just words. Morality is not what you think about doing or what you intend to do. It is putting your beliefs and convictions into practice. You must actually live a trustworthy and honorable life to be considered trustworthy and honorable.

I also learned that anyone could do the right thing when faced with something that poses no hardship. For instance, one addict considered himself moral because he had never killed anyone or robbed a bank. Yet, he had been unfaithful to his wife for over twenty years. Murder or money was not his problem. Sex was. The true test of his morality was not walking into a bank and choosing not to rob it, but being faced with an opportunity to cheat on his wife and choosing fidelity, even if no one would know if he chose otherwise. "Character is what you are in the dark."

What was just as interesting to me was how he justified his behavior. He said he wasn't being unfaithful to his wife, but faithful to himself by living life to the fullest because he never passed up an experience. Defining "living life to the fullest" by the number of his sexual conquests would have been less of a problem if he hadn't been married. And I couldn't help but wonder if "never passing up an experience" had ever meant also wanting to experience integrity, fidelity, intimacy, and love.

Another sex addict said he told the truth of his infidelity to his girlfriend, and that his admission had caused her so much pain that she broke down uncontrollably. He said he never again wanted to cause someone that much pain, so he would never again admit to cheating. It didn't occur to him that the way to never cause that kind of pain was not by keeping his cheating a secret, but by not cheating.

Your actions and your self-esteem are bound in a continuous loop, one feeding off the other. The level of your self-esteem affects how you act, and how you act affects your self-esteem. The depth of your self-esteem also influences your friendships, relationships, and whom you marry. We tend to feel most comfortable around those whose level of self-esteem mirrors our own. Opposites may attract in some relationship issues, but not with self-esteem, and Branden said that the most disastrous relationships are those between two people who have feelings of low self-worth.

Low self-esteem looks like irrationality, the inability to see the truth, rigidity, fear of the new and unfamiliar, inappropriate conformity or rebelliousness, denial and defensiveness, over-compliance or over-controlling behavior, and fear of or hostility toward others.

The characteristics of high self-esteem are:

Rationality: Understanding non-contradiction and relationship: "Nothing can be true and not true."

Realism: Distinguishing between real and unreal, truth and fantasy.

Intuitiveness: Being highly sensitive to and respectful of internal signals.

Creativity: Valuing, rather than discounting, the production of one's mind.

Independence: Thinking for oneself and taking responsibility for one's own existence.

Flexibility: Responding to the new and unfamiliar without clinging to the past.

Managing change: Accepting and working with change rather than fighting against it.

Admitting and correcting mistakes: Making truth more valuable than self-protective denial or defensiveness.

Benevolence and cooperation: Loving and respecting oneself, which enables one to love and respect others.

Contrary to what many believe, Branden said one cannot have too much self-esteem any more than one can be too healthy. By living your life through healthy self-esteem, you reap its reciprocal gifts. By being trustworthy, you are trusted; by being respectful, you are respected; by authentically connecting to others through love, you are loved; by making yourself responsible for your own happiness and personal fulfillment, you free others to create and be responsible for their own. But if you live contrary to a higher-consciousness life, there is no reason you should be trusted, respected, or loved, or enjoy a purposeful life, and when you don't develop these qualities on your own, you will look to others to provide them for you through lies, manipulation, and control.

I hadn't been in the clinic long before I realized there were just as many discussions about God, mostly in our twelve-step meetings and personal conversations, as there were about self-esteem. I repeatedly found a correlation between the relationships people had with themselves and others and the relationship they had with their God. Those who were angry, aggressive, defensive, and felt the most threatened lived by the "eye for an eye" stance of their vengeful God. The enablers and rescuers turned the other cheek, embracing the teaching of their God's son from the Sermon on the Mount. The most ambivalent and disconnected from life and others believed in "something" but would not give it a name or choose a specific spiritual path or teaching. The arrogant split into two groups: Those who considered themselves above rules and laws believed in God but didn't go to church, had never read the Bible, and embraced only the parts of their religion that appealed to them, disregarding anything that actually asked them to practice what they said they believed. The others didn't believe in any God at all, making themselves their own gods, the final authority, the ultimate creator.

I imagine I have been most of these at some point in my life, but in the clinic, I simply felt lost. I knew God lived and breathed, moved among the stars and planets, the earth's trees and mountains, our minds and hearts. But every physical, mental, and intuitive sense He had given me to connect to Him seemed to have completely shut down. I couldn't reach Him, and if He was trying to reach me, I didn't know how to see, hear, or feel it. I would have prayed, but I no longer knew what to say. And this separation from the one constant that connected me to myself, and me to everything else, felt like the death of my spirit, the loss of my soul.

One night, sensing the distance that surrounded me, one of my peers, a practicing Christian and Catholic, asked if she could pray with me. I wanted to correct her by saying she could pray *for* me, because I was not capable of being a participant at that time, but all I could manage was a quiet yes. I followed her to my room and was surprised when she knelt by my bed. I knelt beside her. She took my hand and started to speak as if she were in the presence of someone she felt completely comfortable with, someone she had loved and known intimately for a very long time. I don't remember her words, but seeing this connection, hearing the gentle conversation, knowing that this relationship was truly possible seemed to be enough on this night.

My peers became important to me in many ways—some as teachers, some as listeners, a few as friends. There was usually some free time after dinner and before our twelve-step meetings, and several of us would walk a few miles around the compound. I usually walked with two peers, the one who prayed for me that night, who was also an alcoholic, and another in for drug addiction, sex addiction, and alcoholism. Most of the time we sang as we walked, trying to remember the words to some of our favorite songs. I imagine we pretty well ravaged the lyrics to Pure Prairie League's "Amie" and "Space Oddity" by David Bowie, but did Lynyrd Skynyrd fairly proud on "Sweet Home Alabama." However, the highlight was always when my prayerful friend would sing church hymns in the clearest, sweetest voice of one of God's beloved. On these nights, I could almost feel God using her voice to heal my soul.

We also had some of our deepest conversations on these walks. Being in the clinic made us acutely aware that something about us—our development and our choices—was not "normal." I wouldn't realize until much later that we should have been thinking in terms of "healthy" rather than the indefinable "normal," but we all understood perfectly every time one of us asked, "If what we are and what we're doing is abnormal, then what is normal?"

In the clinic, we got our first look at "normal" through the untraumatized core issues. I went further with my study of high self-esteem. But Abraham Maslow took me far deeper by showing me what healthy, or what he called self-actualized, actually looked like through the lives of real people.

Maslow studied self-actualization, the fifth level of his Hierarchy of Needs, through a series of informal investigations beginning in 1935 that culminated in a two-year study published in 1954. His research was considered unconventional at the time; attempting to define a self-actualized person wasn't the typical subject matter for established scientific methods. However, being primarily motivated by his own curiosity, he had no intention of publishing his results until he found them so "enlightening" he believed they could be of value to others.

His subjects consisted of "personal acquaintances and friends" and "public and historical figures." Subjects had to meet both positive and negative standards. The positive criterion was evidence of self-actualization. The negative was the absence of neurosis and a psychopathic personality. Maslow found twenty-three subjects who met his criteria and separated them into the following categories:

- Seven fairly sure and two highly probable contemporaries
- Two fairly sure historical figures: Thomas Jefferson and Abraham Lincoln in his last years
- Seven highly probable public and historical figures: Albert Einstein, Eleanor Roosevelt, Jane Addams, William James, Albert Schweitzer, Aldous Huxley, and Benedict de Spinoza
- Five contemporaries who fell short but could still be used for study

A common trait in all of the subjects was that of being an adult. In fact, Maslow believed that self-actualization doesn't occur in the young because they have not yet developed their full identity, are short on life experience, and are not focused on the pursuit of wisdom. But even though he found youth to be a disqualifier, he believed the healthy young who were living a life of positive growth were on the path toward self-actualization.

Maslow found that self-actualized people possess nineteen characteristics, some of which correspond with Branden's traits of those with high self-esteem:

Perception of Reality

The self-actualized have a strong ability to determine a person's character accurately and quickly, and have an acute sense of what is false, which is especially apparent in areas such as politics, art, science, and current events. They predict future events more correctly than others by basing their perceptions on the facts available at the time rather than on prejudice, opinion, fear, optimism, or pessimism. They are interested in pure truth as it exists rather than in manipulating it to reinforce what they want to be true, such as to support a particular political or religious belief.

Acceptance

They generally accept what nature has given them and others that cannot be changed (e.g., being bald, hairy, tall, short, or old). This does not mean the self-actualized are unconditionally satisfied with their lot, or accept what can and should be changed, like laziness, arrogance, intolerance, prejudice, or rage in themselves or humanity as a whole. They lack any demonstrable amount of hypocrisy, defensiveness, artificiality, or desire to impress and are uncomfortable with these traits in others.

Spontaneity

They are not bound by conventional rules, though they don't use the unconventional for shock value. Rather it is their choices and standards that are not mainstream. A prominent distinction of self-actualized people is that they actually participate in life as it happens rather than continually prepare for it. While others look toward future outcomes and rewards, the self-actualized are involved in the process of growth as it occurs.

Problem Centering

They are more interested in problems outside themselves. Where most people are predominantly ego-centered, the self-actualized have a calling or mission that is service oriented, whether for the good of a few individuals, a nation, or all of humanity. This calling is not necessarily something they would choose to do, but rather what they must do.

Solitude
They are comfortable with being alone, even prefer it, and can do so without causing harm to themselves, unlike addicts who isolate to indulge in and protect their addictions. The self-actualized handle adversity without resorting to extreme reactions. Maslow described them as serene, able to remain above the turmoil, dignified in undignified situations, self-starters, and self-determining.

Autonomy
They are emotionally and socially independent, growth-motivated, and appreciative of what they have rather than focused on what they lack. Being self-contained, the self-actualized rely on themselves for stability and motivation. They don't allow hard times and external circumstances to cause them to lose their internal balance. While they have relationships to meet their love and belonging needs, they are not dependent upon them.

Fresh Appreciation
They have a renewing, childlike appreciation of life's simple things like sunsets, newborns, nature, animals, and beautiful music from which they derive inspiration and strength. They take little for granted, no matter how many times it is experienced. They live in fairly constant gratitude and appreciation for their blessings and good fortune. Self-actualized people lead more fulfilled lives because more things fulfill them.

Peak Experiences
They have the ability to be out of touch with time or space, to feel powerful and helpless at the same time, to be in the moment but transcend it, and to experience a loss of self and a total absorption in something else. Maslow believed that non-peaking self-actualizers are more likely to improve the world through social work and politics, whereas those who have peak experiences are inclined to write poetry and music, and delve into philosophy and religion.

Human Kinship
They relate to and have great "affection for human beings in general." The self-actualized believe humanity is one rather than many, that there is more that connects us than divides us.

Humility and Respect
They believe in unconditional equality for all and can have relationships with those of reputable character, regardless of "class, education, political belief, race, or color." The self-actualized have great humility and are "well aware of how little they know in comparison with what could be known and what is known by others."

Interpersonal Relationships
They have fewer but deeper personal relationships than most adults, are capable of great emotion and connection without ego, but are extremely selective about whom they get close to. Their relationships are usually with those who are very close to self-actualization themselves.

Ethics
They have no doubt about the difference between right and wrong. The self-actualized are strongly ethical and have definite moral standards, which is reflected in their behavior as well as their words. "They do right and do not do wrong."

Means and Ends
They can clearly distinguish between the means of getting somewhere or accomplishing something, and the result. They take as much pleasure in the process as the conclusion.

Humor
Their sense of humor is not hostile. The self-actualized don't find jokes at someone else's expense, or stereotypical or sexual humor funny. They are more likely to be self-deprecating, or laugh at humanity in general for believing it knows so much in a world of mystery. Since

they don't find funny what the average person does, they are often considered too serious.

Creativity

Every subject in Maslow's study, without exception, had a creativity of an *original* type. Maslow did not define creativity in terms of money, fame, or success. And he did not believe that genius, talent, and productivity equal health, saying many who are considered creatively brilliant—like Van Gogh, Byron, or Wagner—were not psychologically healthy.

Resistance to Enculturation

Madison Avenue has little effect on the self-actualized. They are detached from their cultural surroundings, not interested in the latest trends, have minimal or no exposure to celebrities or gossip, and have what Maslow called an "inner freedom." They are less likely to define themselves as part of a group, such as American, Caucasian, Protestant, or Republican than as part of humanity as a whole. And they are governed by the principles of their own high character rather than by what is acceptable to society; they "live by their inner laws rather than by outer pressures."

Imperfections

Self-actualized people are not gods. They have many of the same faults and bad habits as everyone else. "They can be boring, stubborn, irritating," and temperamental. Their compassion can become a fault when they get too close to dysfunctional or unhappy people. But what I believe to be the difference between the self-actualized and everyone else is that they consciously choose to identify, examine, and correct their imperfections. A self-actualized person would not ask others to accept his selfishness, arrogance, intolerance, or dishonesty because he would refuse to accept these traits in himself.

Values

A non-conflicting value system is innate in self-actualized people. Their acceptance of human nature and clear view of reality eliminate much of the struggle and uncertainty over values that non-self-actualized people may have. For most of society, "what passes for morals, ethics, and values may be simple by-products of the pervasive psychopathology of the average."

Resolution of Dichotomies

The conflicts unhealthy people experience with opposites, such as thinking and feeling, selfishness and selflessness, sex and love, rebellion and acceptance, are not present in self-actualized people. "The id, the ego, and the superego are collaborative and synergic; they do not war with each other," as is the case with those who are dysfunctional. To be selfless is acting selfishly. Love accompanies lust. Emotions are in synch with reason.

I didn't know anyone, including myself, who upon seeing this list of characteristics didn't try to apply each one to ourselves, hoping we could be considered self-actualized. But Maslow's sobering truth is that only about two percent of humanity reaches self-actualization, which is easy to believe given our billion-dollar drug, porn, diet, and tabloid industries. Maslow rejected any subjects with pathology or pathological tendencies, which led me to wonder, can such people ever become self-actualized?

I have to believe that we all can reach our highest potential if we choose to, and that authentic and lasting change is possible. It is hard to find a point to spirituality or psychology or even life otherwise. But one barrier many put between themselves and authentic self-actualization is thinking they are there when they aren't; when self-delusion and a skewed sense of reality leads them to believe they don't have to take the same long, hard road to self-actualization as the rest of us.

I was no longer surprised by the shortcuts so many took in and outside the clinic: using substances and behaviors to cover pain rather than openly facing and healing it; pretending to be everything from moral and spiritual to faithful and compassionate while doing nothing to make those more than just words; claiming to be in recovery but not doing the work required to make this true. But I will always remember one sex addict, fully aware of what he had become, of his lies and manipulation, of the pain and damage he inflicted upon himself and his family, who said, "I love my vices too much to change." Like everyone, he had a choice: self-destruction or self-actualization. And like nearly everyone—the ninety-eight percent who never fully actualize their potential and live their purpose—he chose to remain broken.

Psychologists use a test called the Minnesota Multiphasic Personality Inventory (MMPI) to determine how, and how much, one is broken. It is the most widely used mental health instrument to identify adult psychopathology, and tests the following categories: hypochondriasis, depression, hysteria, psychopathic deviate (level of conflict, struggle, anger, or respect for society's rules), masculinity/femininity, paranoia, psychasthenia (worry, anxiety, doubts, obsessiveness), schizophrenia, hypomania, and social introversion.

In the clinic, we were all required to take the MMPI, which lasted about three hours. Many of us felt some level of anxiety upon receiving our test date and time. But even more than expressions of nervousness, what I heard most often from those about to take the test was the question: Can the test be "beaten" to ensure a positive result? Over the years, I've asked several counselors, therapists, and psychiatrists whether a patient can manipulate the MMPI, and consistently got the same answer: The reason the MMPI is the most widely used test for adult psychopathology is because it is the most reliable. Hearing this from a counselor in the clinic, I decided my results were likely going to be fairly accurate no matter what I did, and that trying to skew the test in my favor would only make things worse.

During the instructions portion of the testing period, the administrator told us we would learn our results during one of our weekly psychiatrist appointments. It seems I fell through the cracks. I was never told how I tested. I hoped this meant the clinic only disclosed the test results to those who were found to be pathological in some way, and that I was, for the most part, healthy. But I would never know because I never asked. I felt I already had more than enough to handle.

While our schedules were fairly consistent, the most significant deviation came in the fourth week of each patient's five-week program. Family Week was held during the 10:00 a.m. and 2:00 p.m. blocks usually reserved for Primary Group Therapy. On rare occasions—if there were any sensitive issues involved, such as legal matters, or if the patient or any family members were public figures—the sessions would be held privately, attended only by the patient, the family members, and the counselors. But generally, a patient's Family Week was observed by the rest of his or her Group, further reinforcing the clinic's belief that everyone's process, not just one's own, is part of recovery.

I was fortunate enough to witness the Family Weeks of three of my peers, and the benefit of seeing in action much of what had been, to this point, only theory was immense: watching family members whose only way of communicating was through anger, shame, blame, and ridicule struggle to relate to each other with respect and boundaries through the Feedback Loop; watching husbands, wives, mothers, or fathers try to remain silent in the listening chair while hearing loved ones finally tell the truth about what they had become and what they had done. But as I had learned in my husband's Family Week, it is much harder to be a participant than an observer.

Only my two children chose to attend my Family Week. Walking into a rehab clinic is unnerving for even the strongest family members, but even more so for two young adults who never understood why their mother intentionally chose to check into one in the first place.

My daughter was able to settle in and even embrace much of the process. My son couldn't have been more uncomfortable. He never refused to participate, but was reticent to the point where his words and actions were at their barest minimum. The pain I felt at watching him struggle to give answers to questions he would have never asked himself was sometimes so overwhelming I wanted to jump in and rescue him, just stop the whole process and tell him I was sorry I had asked him to come at all. But I didn't. Years later, I realized the gift I'd given my son by staying still.

The clinic was never under the illusion that patients and family members would absorb, understand, and put into practice the whole of its teachings immediately after they had returned home. But it firmly believed in planting the seeds that would, at the right time and place, grow into awareness and bring healing.

A few years after I'd left the clinic, my son, home on a college break, gave a near-perfect description of what he said he now recognized to be the codependent relationship of a long-time friend and his girlfriend. I stopped everything to replay in my mind what I'd just heard. *Did he just use the word "codependent"?*

Over the years, my son had been on the listening end of his friend's complaints and confusion over an unstable relationship and had slowly begun to connect what he'd learned in the clinic to what he was seeing and hearing in real life. I don't remember what I said to him but I knew then my son was one small step closer to understanding, if not what a healthy relationship was, at least what it wasn't.

Whether viewing someone else's Family Week or participating in my own, I always came away with the same thought: If you want to know what is healthy and what is broken about you, look at your children. Whatever good I passed on to my children was never as obvious to me as seeing them repeat my destructive relationship patterns. So many of their relationship choices and behaviors mirrored mine that I decided to make my process of transformation a transparent one. I didn't try to change them, only myself, then used my life to show them the consequences of both healthy and unhealthy relationship choices. I hid nothing, neither the best nor the worst of it, and left them to make their own relationship choices and changes. I've watched them many times choose doing what feels good over what is good, but I hope that being exposed to the process years earlier than most will mean their healthy changes will be much easier and come more quickly than mine.

When my Family Week was over and my children had gone, I realized how much I wanted to go home. I was so tired. My mind could not absorb one more lesson, or even one more word. My heart still felt broken. My spirit far from healed. Maybe everything would fall into place once I left the clinic. Maybe my miracle was waiting for me at home.

I told myself that if I included my husband's Family Week I had actually already been there five weeks, so I had put in my time. I notified the administration of my decision to leave after my Family Week, then told the few peers I had grown closest to. But I could never have anticipated their reactions. One administrator whom I had developed a deep respect for called me into his office and spent the next half hour explaining the benefits of my staying for the entire program and the consequences of my leaving early. A few hours later, I was called into the office of a second administrator, who basically gave me the same lecture but just took longer to do it. After leaving her office, I was on my way to the cafeteria to have lunch when a third administrator saw me and asked me to come to his office before the end of the day. By now I knew by heart what he'd say, so I decided to spend my time packing instead.

During our peer meetings, we held graduation ceremonies for the patients who had completed their programs. The next morning, I sat at the front of the room with the rest of the graduates, partly for the closure I hoped the ceremony would bring, but mostly for the opportunity to publicly offer my appreciation and thanks to the many who had meant so much to me during my stay at the clinic. Afterwards, one of my peers gave me a gift I still have and cherish to this day.

By our second week at the clinic, we had each been asked to go the bookstore and pick out a stuffed animal that would represent our inner child for the duration of our program. Nearly everyone did so, and it wasn't unusual to see grown and grizzled men cradling their new companions in their arms or in a makeshift sling for the remainder of their stay. I never chose one. I did try once by rummaging through the assortment, squeezing, holding, and staring intently into the faces of many of the soft pets, hoping one of them would somehow reveal herself to be my inner child. None did. I couldn't help but remember being told during my Survivor's Week that I never touched the pillow on my lap that represented my inner child, and I found the thought of this self-abandonment haunting.

I had been in the clinic for two weeks when he, a born-again Christian in his early twenties with the face of an angel and a mind and body enslaved by drug and sex addiction, checked in. As he was the same age as my children, we developed an easy bond. But I imagine this was also because I am a rescuer, and this pattern wasn't anywhere close to being broken.

We talked often during our free time about family, relationships, our demons, and our Gods. And it was he who finally convinced me to attend a Narcotics Anonymous (NA) meeting at the clinic. Since I didn't have the substance or behavioral addictions covered by most twelve-step meetings, I most often chose to attend AA to try to better understand my father. However, I made a vow to myself that I would attend all of the different meetings at least once to better understand addiction in general. After a few weeks, I had been to every type of twelve-step meeting offered at the clinic except NA. I again didn't know why, but every time I tried to walk through the door to the NA meeting, I couldn't. One day I mentioned this to him, not looking for an answer, only a way to get it into the open air and off my mind, but he came up with one anyway when he reminded me I didn't have to stay. All I had to do was walk through the door, and if it felt wrong, I could turn around and walk back out. He said he'd be there if I did decide to stay, but no one and nothing was going to force me to.

"Just walk through the door," he said. "You'll know what to do next."

I did walk through the door, and I did stay. I don't remember one story anyone shared that night, but I do remember how different that meeting was from AA. Though very well attended, it was still less than half the size of the AA meeting, and it was loud and boisterous compared to AA's somber air. Most of those who attended NA were young males. AA members were predominantly older and of both sexes. While the NA meeting followed traditional twelve-step protocol, it was much looser with a steady stream of jokes and laughter. I imagined the environment of the NA meetings would change with the constant flow of new faces, so I didn't spend too much time considering the reasons for the differences. At the time, just feeling a sense of relief and accomplishment was enough.

Here he was again after graduation that morning, the boy with the angel face, calling my name, then placing something in my hands.

It was the stuffed animal he had chosen as his inner child—a Mary Meyer bulldog he had named Rocky after the movie character, and whom I often gave as the reason I had never chosen a stuffed animal for myself. I would have wanted Rocky as my inner child if I had found him first. But the more I protested that I could never accept such a gift, the more he insisted. He said Rocky had been mine all along.

Alone in my room later that night, I held Rocky in one hand, my fingers closing lightly around him. I brought my other hand up to touch his ears, his eyes, nose, and mouth, and let his soft paws tickle the palm of my hand. Slowly, I wrapped both arms around Rocky and brought him close to my heart, hoping he felt safe and loved.

After the early morning peer meeting and graduation, we were all scheduled to attend the 9:00 a.m. lecture. One of the peers I had spent those many nights singing with as we walked the compound said he wanted to talk to me, and suggested we skip the lecture and go to the cafeteria instead. Since I didn't imagine there was much the administration could do to me for my non-attendance at this point, I agreed.

We had the cafeteria to ourselves, so we sat down at the first table we came to and he wasted no time getting to his point.

"You can't leave," he said.

Reluctantly, I asked him why, thinking I was going to hear the same drawn-out reasons I had heard from the administrators earlier.

"Because you're not done."

I told him I felt done. He insisted I wasn't, that there was a reason the program was five weeks and not four, and that if I left now, I'd never know what I'd missed; maybe even something that would have made the difference when I needed it most on the outside. It might be a lecture that answered a persistent question, a clarifying statement from a counselor, a connection with a new patient, or a kind gesture from a peer who had become a friend.

His words continued to speak to me hours after I'd left him, and eventually I realized he was right. I wasn't done. During the past four weeks, I had seen many peers leave the clinic, most of them after completing their full five-week program. But three whom I had come to know well through their stories had left in the dark of the night, two a few weeks into their stay, one just a few days. We never knew when patients left before their time until the next morning when it was too late to talk them out of it, and I know I would have tried if I had gotten the chance. I would have told them they weren't done. I would have told them they might miss the piece that made all of this make sense, and maybe even a little easier. I would have told them that if they quit now, whatever enslaved them would have won again, and that at least for now, only more bondage—not freedom—lay beyond that door. All of this was just as true for me. Later that day, I made my way back to the administrators to tell them I had changed my mind. I wanted to stay.

There were a few things that made my final week different from the previous four, valuable things I would have missed if I had chosen to leave. One was attending my second graduation. I had used the first to express my thanks and appreciation, but the second I dedicated to the three peers who had left early. I told how I had nearly made the same choice, and spoke the words from the peer who made me change my mind. My hope was that if anyone present was thinking of leaving early, these words would do the same for him or her.

After graduation, the peer who sang church hymns during our walks and I announced we had a surprise for everyone and asked them all to stay a few minutes longer. We had spent the previous week going through legitimate channels trying to get a CD of a particular song to play after our graduation. We started with our Group counselor, who said no. We went to low-level administration. They said no. We went to the two highest administrators at the clinic. They both said no. The only explanation given was that the song was not on the clinic-approved music list. I thought back to our karaoke night a week earlier and wondered how Neil Diamond's "Love on the Rocks," which had been sung by a drug addict to a room full of alcoholics, had made the list but our song of determination and survival hadn't.

Not wanting to give up, we turned to illegitimate options. My peer had her daughter smuggle in a CD onto which she had tried to burn the song, but it wouldn't play. She tried it again with the same result. Finally, I went to a counselor who had helped me often throughout my stay and explained the situation. The next morning, a store-bought copy of the CD was waiting for me at the nursing station.

After the ceremony, my peer and I asked that everyone grab a chair and move it to the side of the room while we passed out pages of the song's lyrics. I pushed the play button and the room erupted with cheers at Gloria Gaynor's words:

At first I was afraid, I was petrified.
Kept thinkin' I could never live without you by my side.
But then I spent so many nights thinkin' how you did me wrong,
And I grew strong.
And I learned how to get along.

We danced with pure joy. When the song ended, the dancing continued so we played it again. The 9:00 a.m. lecture was to be held in the same room, and we barely had enough time to replace the chairs and pick up the loose papers before the counselor or guest lecturer arrived. But we managed to get everything in order on time, believing no one was the wiser.

Our 10:00 a.m. Group session primarily focused on the two of us who had graduated that morning. Our counselor asked us to discuss what we had learned during our time in the clinic, what our initial plans were once we left, and if we had any advice for the new peers who had just arrived. When it came my turn to speak, the Group counselor said he wanted to say something to me first. I didn't hear his initial words. I was looking at his eyes, which were filling with tears. I then heard him say that when he learned I was to be a part of his Group he assumed he knew me before having met me, and he believed my problems would be many. But he'd found that his premature judgments had been wrong, and that I had taught him more than he had taught me. I thanked him openly for his kind words, but thanked him silently for showing me what humility and making amends looks like.

There were good feelings all around after our Group session, until the counselor asked me and the other graduating peer to stay after for a few minutes. Once we were alone, he told us he had heard we'd played an unauthorized song during the peer meeting that morning and he wanted to know how and from whom we had gotten the CD. Neither of us spoke. He went on to tell us about the inappropriateness of our behavior, and that we had to abide by the clinic's rules even when we didn't understand or agree with them. We both apologized, but when we still wouldn't reveal the source of the contraband, he let us go.

Now looking back, even though I thought the song and my actions were harmless, I would have made a different choice. What I eventually came to understand was that while the song, the singing, and the dancing caused me no harm, I had no way of knowing whether it was the same for the rest of my peers. For all I knew, the song "I Will Survive" might have had the same effect on a peer as that on the patient who felt uncomfortable with "Dancing Queen." Today, while I would still not name the source of the CD, my apology would be much more sincere, and my appreciation and understanding of boundaries and respect for others much greater.

The clinic left one of the most important lessons and images for last. We had all heard of the Desert Walk, but none of the graduating patients would give any details to the rest of us still working our way through the program. I will not break that confidentiality here—not because of secrecy, but because of sacredness. There is something profoundly hallowed and healing about performing a closing ritual with the very people who entered the clinic at the same time, having all the same fears, as you. Here we all were five weeks later, still scared, but a little stronger and wiser because we had known each other. We had come together in the clinic out of brokenness, but bonded in the desert through hope, faith, and love.

My return flight was uneventful, but I faced a literal fork in the road when driving home. I was stopped at a red light. Left would take me to my house; right, to a road that bordered the ocean. For the past six weeks I had been in a place that controlled nearly everything but my breathing. There was so much I missed. My time in the desert had nourished me in many ways, but there were parts of me that felt parched and dry. I wanted to sing and dance to my own music, see the ocean, smell the salt air, feel the humidity soak through my skin. I wanted to go home, but I wanted to go home replenished—my mind, body, heart, and soul overflowing with the joy of possibility and second chances. The light turned green. I turned right.

I drove for several miles until I found a spot that offered some privacy. One of my favorite songs was playing, and I could feel the bass beating down to the center of my belly. I sat inside the car for a few minutes, absorbing every high and low, moving side to side until the space in which I had confined myself became too small. I rolled down all the windows, turned up the song even louder, and stepped outside, singing and dancing with the freedom and joy of a child.

In an instant I realized I was not alone.

I felt it first as a memory of a little girl with long, soft hair, curled ends bouncing to the rhythm as she danced and sang with Diana Ross without a care or self-consciousness. Then I felt her in my heart. She was my joy, my hope, my love, my freedom, my child. I stopped all sound and movement, only wanting to feel the tingling of my skin and the tears in my eyes. I had not lost my inner child after all, but I had lost sight of her. I began to tell her the only truths I knew; that I wanted more than she could ever know to keep her safe, to protect her from anyone or anything that could cause her harm, and to love her the way she deserved to be loved; and I wanted to do all of this from the deep well of abundance within, rather than from fear or that place of lack that makes so many of us believe that God will not provide us with exactly who and what we need when the time is right, that there will never be enough for us all, and that we have to use anger, lies, manipulation, and hate to divide and conquer to get our share. But also that all of this was new to me and I wasn't sure how many times it would take until I got it right. Though I could make a promise right here, right now, standing in the soft sand and salt air, before the crashing waves and my God, that I would keep trying until I did. I stood for a while longer, in the presence of this moment and this vow—then began my journey home.

Part III

The Beginning

The relapse process begins long before that first drink or pill or sexually destructive act after being sober for a time. And it can almost always be traced back to recovery's two greatest threats—busyness and complacency.

In the clinic, some patients jokingly called busyness "doism," using the now familiar "-ism" suffix to indicate addiction, and said it deserved a twelve-step program of its own. This statement may contain more truth than wit. We have built this entire world around distraction. If you don't want to think it or feel it, you don't have to. Your only task is to wade through the millions of possibilities to find the distractions that appeal to you most.

Many are obvious distractions, such as whatever it is you are engaging in to the point of addiction, which is also most likely illegal or socially unacceptable. However, today there are other distractions so socially acceptable and widespread that few see them as a problem: spending hours watching television and playing video games; obsessively checking emails, text messages, and social media; habitually reading tabloids and gossip magazines. And who could fault you for the long hours you spend at work or on family, let alone see either of these as distractions from your goal of having a healthy and balanced life? If you had just spent five weeks in a rehab clinic for substance or behavior abuse, all of those counselors and administrators whose job it was to get you well could.

Leaving the clinic for familiar surroundings was what we longed for, but the clinic counselors and administrators wanted us to step into nothing familiar. We wanted to get back to our homes, our families, our jobs. They wanted us to approach all of these necessary parts of our lives differently. No thought could be mindless. No word spoken unconsciously. No action taken without authentic awareness of what we were doing and why. Because the price was using work, or taking care of the kids, or anything else we could think of, as an excuse not to keep therapy appointments, attend twelve-step meetings, or remain a conscious and active participant in our healing. And once we became distracted, complacency wasn't far behind.

Complacency is treacherous and deceitful. It can make you think you are in recovery when you aren't anywhere near it. Complacency controls your life when you believe five weeks, five months, or even five years is enough to fully break and replace the destructive patterns you spent decades building and reinforcing; when you think you know everything—or at least enough—about recovery that continuing your transformational process simply isn't necessary; when you believe you are strong enough to have the same friends, go to the same places, do the same things you did before rehab and not relapse; and when you'd still rather avoid or distract yourself from your feelings than face them.

So within each moment a battle rages. On one side is change—a path that guarantees a better life but is so frighteningly unfamiliar it feels more threatening than comforting. On the other are the familiar distractions and complacent feelings your mind nurtures to keep change away. But so does each moment contain a choice: Use every thought, word, and act to reinforce what you had learned over the past five weeks in rehab or use them to reinforce everything that had put you there in the first place. For recovery to be authentic and enduring—it all had to change.

This idea of a process of complete change is not exclusive to recovery. Every physical, mental, and spiritual transformation requires a purification process over a long and sustained period of time to reach your goal.

To transform your body, you purify it by changing a sedentary lifestyle to one of activity, and unhealthy food and drink to proper nutrition. To transform your mind, you release yourself from the bondage of the past and future and choose freedom by living in the present moment with acceptance and without ego. And spiritually, absolutely no one goes from ignorance to enlightenment, heaven, *nirvana, samadhi, satori,* or self-actualization except through a deep and thorough awakening to the choices that lead you to your true Self within.

The first law of thermodynamics states that energy can be neither created nor destroyed; it can only change forms. While the purification process may look like elimination, ultimately it is one of exchange or redirection. You let go of something physically, mentally, or spiritually harmful to you and replace it with something beneficial, even if you replace it with nothing. You can exchange a life of materialism for a simpler, more balanced one by letting go of unnecessary possessions. You can exchange a busy, stress-filled hour for one of silence in prayer or meditation. Optimally, we should constantly be moving toward purification one small, consistent, balanced step at a time, but many of us are pointed in the opposite direction almost from birth. Not knowing there even is another path, we build up decades of wrong steps so dense it takes a catastrophic event to get our attention.

The process can begin in any one of the three domains. Some will have to conquer physical illness. Some will feel spiritually disconnected. Still others, like me, will have to break apart a belief system thought by thought. I soon realized it doesn't matter where it begins because, eventually, you will have to undergo the purification process in each one. Your individual physical, mental, and spiritual selves are connected. If you are sick in one, you are sick in all three. If you are healthy in one, it would never allow you to be anything less in the others. Your sound mind would never let you abuse your body through drugs, alcohol, smoking, overeating, or destructive sex. Your revered body, seeing itself as a beautiful gift from God given only to create love through acts of higher consciousness, would never let your mind see any part of it as ugly. And your God, who dwells in your heart, would never sit quietly by and let your mind and body do anything that would take the place of an authentic relationship with Him. He will find a way to reach you, whether through the Holy Hammer or the Perfect Moment or some other means that finally makes you realize the life you've chosen is not the life He meant you to live.

I had no idea how deeply my decision to check into the clinic would take me until many months after I'd left. But my Perfect Moment had shown me defects in my thought and behavior patterns, so that was where I began. I thought that if I could get my mind right, the rest would fall into place. My heart would heal, my body would grow strong, and I would eventually find my spiritual home.

It's hard for me to be specific about what I felt the first few days after I returned home, other than overwhelmed. I had so much information and so many new tools that I didn't know where to start. That in itself was a profound change. I had entered the clinic codependent, an enabler, and a perfectionist but didn't know it. I left the same way, though was now highly conscious of my brokenness and my understanding that it was time to heal.

In one sense, substance and behavior abusers have a clear first step in their recovery: Stay away from whatever, wherever, or whoever triggers your addiction. But a codependent's issues are tied to his or her relationships. I was married and had children and close friends, which meant I had to figure out how to pay attention to my relationships without slipping back into old habits or using them as distractions from the healing work I had ahead of me. So through one of a long line of paradoxes to come, I had to learn how to properly care for others by first learning to properly care for myself.

The clinic counselors were just as clear about what we needed to change as they were about change itself. First were the things we added to our lives to support our recovery. I was not considered appropriately discharged from the clinic until I had a lengthy interview with an aftercare coordinator and filled out a paper indicating which therapist I had chosen from the list they had given me and which twelve-step meetings I would attend. My signature at the bottom of the page was my promise that I would follow through. I kept that promise. I called a therapist and made an appointment for the following week, then found the locations of my local CoDA and Al-Anon twelve-step meetings and attended my first ones within a few days.

Next were the substitutions that initiated the purification process, what psychologists call displacement or redirecting destructive thoughts and behaviors toward a healthy outlet. This is where we took a sincere and authentic look at the people in our lives, the music and talk programs we listened to, the television we watched, and the books we read to determine whether they supported or thwarted our new lives.

I often felt that the place my purification process began was chosen for me by a higher power because I would never have consciously chosen it on my own. Like the written word, music is among the strongest influences in my life. I'm sure it was precisely for this reason that my change had to start there.

I can't tell you how it happened because, again, as throughout my life, nothing happened. No voices. No choir. No Jesus light. Just a feeling that I wanted to listen to something new. Or maybe it was something consistent—consistently loving, positive, and supportive. I had heard Switchfoot on mainstream radio and, after listening to their lyrics, realized they were a contemporary Christian rock band. I liked their music, but they were just one band. I figured the reason so few Christian bands crossed over to mainstream was because most just weren't very good. Fortunately, I was wrong.

I was soul deep into Led Zeppelin, Filter, and Bad Religion when I first came to Christian music, and I didn't see how the two worlds could coexist. I wouldn't risk stepping back into many of those old songs until years after I'd left the clinic. Maybe I could have appropriately managed my tantalizingly primal memories upon hearing "Custard Pie," but "Jurrasitol" and "A Walk" could have raised my not-so-latent anger in an instant when I hadn't even begun to learn how to use this emotion to my benefit.

However, it was voodoo that first brought me to rock music. It was the fall of 1970 and I was eleven years old. Jimi Hendrix had just died and radio stations across the country were playing his music in tribute. I can't remember whether I had heard his name before that day, but if I had heard his music it would have been impossible to forget.

Up to that point my musical taste had run to pop and bubblegum. I was sitting in the back seat of a car with a friend. Her older sister was driving. Little flinty sparks flickered in my brain with the first palm-muted sounds and wah-wah filtered notes of "Voodoo Child." Then my head exploded. Every connection I had ever made between possibility and music lay severed and dangling with each howling note that followed, only to be realigned and reconnected to that visionary's soul when he sang of his power to make a mountain crumble with his bare hands.

You could make a connection between this moment and the one that had happened with my father just a few months earlier. Or between the song's title and first two lines and what I felt about that moment with my father, and I'm sure you'd be right to. But even if everything between my father and I had never happened, Jimi Hendrix would still have found me, still have caused a shift in what I believed music looked like, and the truth. So it is about all of life for all of us. We cement ourselves in what we know to be absolutely true until something or someone comes along to show us that it's not. It's these moments, where you must choose between continued ignorance and newfound awareness, that define what we call our journey.

A few years after I'd left the clinic, I was sitting at a red light one beautiful fall afternoon, windows down, sunroof open. A truck pulled up beside me. The driver was enjoying the open air as much as I, but also the cranked-up volume of one of rock music's greatest hymns— "Stairway to Heaven." I felt myself slip into that place inside where I held for safekeeping all the memories connected to those treasured songs. But this time I went past everything I had created in this life to something that had been created for me long ago when the song reminded me that there are always two paths, and there is always another chance to choose the right one.

Suddenly, it felt like I'd always known I was on a journey where I would constantly be asked to choose between truth and illusion. Felt like I'd always known I was connected to you, him, her, them through everything and everyone. Felt like I'd always known that the second three greatest words I had learned from Led Zeppelin were only meant to be used with the first three I had learned from Buddha and Jesus Christ. And felt like I'd always known much more than I understood.

Eventually, I reconnected with many of the old songs, though not all. There were those that took on a new and beneficial purpose after I had left the clinic, and there were those that no longer had a purpose for me at all. This idea of "purpose" was most likely the reason my change in music was easier than I had imagined. Until then, I'd only seen sex addicts resisting the need to give up their "innocent" sex thrillers along with porn, or gamblers defending beyond their last breath that the lottery and bingo were games and not gambling, as examples of what the purification process looked like. But drinking muddy water from a pitcher instead of a pool isn't purification at all. When my change in music took me from deep meaning to deeper meaning, I understood its purpose. Change can leave you pruned and silent or nourished and overflowing, but it all had to bring you closer to your true nature and purest Self, not bring you new ways to remain disconnected and broken. Though many of us at the clinic thought this was too obvious to forget, it was often the last thing we remembered, and these first few steps into the world of purpose would eventually take me to one of the deepest parts of my journey.

I was interested to see how the purification process would manifest in what I read because I was already very selective. My first choice was often history, biography, or literature. Any contemporary fiction would have to capture my attention within the first ten pages to merit further time. And before entering the clinic, I wasn't very interested in what is considered "self-help," though anything I did read in this genre had a psychological and spiritual connection. I've read parts of the Qur'an, the Upanishads, the Torah and remaining books of the Old Testament; most of the New Testament and the yoga and Buddhist sutras and commentaries; several translations of the Tao Te Ching; and all of the Bhagavad Gita, which along with Psalms and Proverbs is where I first felt most at home. I had stopped reading newspapers long before I'd checked into the clinic, preferring the longer format and greater selection advantages of the Internet. And I have managed to get to this point in my life without purchasing or intentionally reading a gossip magazine or tabloid, though some of the content is so pervasive I've absorbed it simply because I'm alive. Between the celebrity magazines and tabloids, candy racks, cigarettes, and last-chance manipulation to encourage impulse buying, I've always considered the checkout aisles in grocery stores to be some of the most toxic places on the planet.

Unlike the transformation in my music, the change in what I read was subtle. At first I built upon the few books I'd been given or had purchased while at the clinic. Then someone—a friend, or his friend, or her sister, or someone I didn't know at all—would tell me about a book or author: Emmet Fox, Florence Scovel Shinn, Caroline Myss, A Course in Miracles, something from Hay House. I hadn't heard of any of them.

One day I was scrolling through the television channel guide, once again reminded that the cliché of television rarely offering anything worth watching isn't a cliché at all, when I came across a show on PBS that looked interesting. I assumed I'd tune in and tune out like I do with nearly every show that isn't on one of the two channels I most often watch, and because it was four hours long. I had come into the program somewhere in the middle but watched until the end. The next day during my therapy session, I asked my therapist if he had ever heard of someone named Wayne Dyer. He looked at me some-what surprised, then said, "Yes. Haven't you?" I admitted I hadn't. He looked at me again but in a way I didn't yet understand and said, "Marta, there's a whole other world out there waiting for you. This is just the beginning."

He was right. One book always led me to another, and to this rich, vast, fascinating, yet humbling other world inhabited by Thich Nhat Hanh, Eknath Easwaran, Shantideva, Tsong-kha-pa, Jiddu Krishna-murti, Karen Armstrong, Meister Eckhart, Georg Feuerstein, Charlotte Joko Beck, and many others I had somehow remained blinded to for most of my life. But soon it wasn't just the spiritual and psychology books I read for purification, but those about sports and business, health and aging, self-motivation and mind training, and the origins of talent and greatness. The lessons, the guidance, and the gifts of healing were being revealed to me from everywhere, in everything, and through everyone. All I had to do was be open to receiving them.

But there was one place I rarely felt enlightened, only manipulated and frustrated. I had never been attracted to reality shows, which didn't seem real at all, or sitcoms that tried to make dysfunctional families and lives funny when they aren't, or dramas that made their characters' lives ridiculously chaotic and insane so we could feel better about our own. And I had stopped watching both network and cable news channels years before because all of them—being either privately favored or openly endorsed by a particular political party or opinion media—had shed the pretense of objective reporting long ago, especially evidenced when reporters, anchors, or commentators accepted White House positions, and those who had once held political positions became affiliated with news networks.

Yet there were two channels I found myself constantly drawn to, initially for respite and entertainment, though increasingly for insight. Classic movies have to stand on the strength of the story, the characters, and the talent. There is no hiding a weakness in any of these areas behind special effects, nudity, or even color. When it's right, what you'll witness is pure, vulnerable, and raw.

I was already watching ESPN, the all-sports network, regularly before entering the clinic. It was where I went first whenever I turned on the television, and still is, but I see the competition and athletes differently now. Much like one can view the Gita's battle at Kurukshetra between the Pandavas and the Kauravas as an allegory for our internal struggle with light and dark forces, I could connect the conflict, a missed or successful assignment, or a victory or loss on the field to those occurring within me; the fear and insecurity that creates much of an athlete's off-field drama I already knew all too well. Ironically, my lowest point, just months after leaving the clinic, was also my most creative, and what appealed to me least—television—was where my creativity went first.

However, fresh out of the clinic I didn't spend much time on what lay ahead because any part of my future that included anyone other than me was not wholly in my hands. Besides, just concentrating on the one moment and one change before me took all the energy I had. I'd always understood that this journey was mine and that I'd have to do the work alone, but this didn't mean I couldn't have teachers along the way. What I had learned in my five weeks at the clinic was indispensable, but it was barely the beginning, and it was still primarily just knowledge because I had yet to put much of it into practice.

A friend once asked me, "How do you know if you need a therapist?" I said if you are asking the question, you do. Different people seek different things in a therapist. In group therapy, I've watched patients try to make a therapist become what had been missing in their lives: a nurturing parent, a loving partner, a guru with all the answers. Some came to therapy with a sincere and committed desire to grow and heal. But many considered it a place to blame or complain about someone or something, choosing to remain stuck, to keep reliving the same pain rather than make the necessary changes.

Like any sound relationship, I knew the one with my therapist had to be based on truth, mutual trust and respect, and strong ethics and boundaries. But even with all of these intact, and whether first realized by the therapist or the patient, the relationship may simply not feel right. After I decided to leave the therapist I had inherited from the clinic, it took visits to three others before I was able to make a choice, which was based not on what the new therapist was going to do for me, but what she wasn't. I didn't enter into therapy looking for someone to fill a parental or romantic void, but I was looking for answers, and I expected my therapist to provide them for me. She said no.

A good therapist, who is also usually one who has been in therapy, knows the only answers any of us really understand and incorporate into our lives are those we discover on our own. A therapist will act as a guide by asking questions, sometimes the same one many times, but we will discount or ignore any information we aren't ready to learn or accept. Preparing ourselves for some things can take months, even years. But when we are ready, the connection, that one moment of true understanding that can lead to an avalanche of insight, happens in an instant. This is when the real work begins, because the insight is only a message. Your task is to decide whether to act on it or act as if you never heard it.

Everyone knows much less than they think they do and it's therapy, or any other form of authentic self-exploration, that turns your declarative sentences into questions. "I am . . ." becomes "Who am I?" "I can't" becomes "How can I?" And all those things you are absolutely convinced are true become "Is this true?" Self-exploration and self-discovery help break the false identities you've created for yourself and others. They ask you to release the thoughts, feelings, and behaviors you took on from others that were never yours to begin with. This is where you stop blaming your parents, your spouse, your children, everything and everyone else and begin the healing process by gathering information. Because it's the questions that help transform your stagnant life of knowing it all into your true life of growth, openness, love, and, ultimately, freedom.

As important as I believed therapy was to transformation, and as eager as I was to heal, it was often difficult for me. And there weren't many times I could say it was enjoyable—only absolutely necessary. I had to keep listening to myself speak until I truly heard what I was saying; keep finding honesty in my words and feelings because only a total commitment to seeking and telling the truth would make any of this worthwhile; and keep hearing all of the questions until I was strong enough to find the answers. When I wasn't, it was sometimes because I didn't yet know how to be, sometimes because I consciously or unconsciously chose not to be. Eventually I realized that the longer I avoided the inevitable, the longer I'd be in therapy. Healing requires a lifetime commitment, not therapy.

I remember one question from a therapist—which was also the last of the three questions that changed my life—that made me angry enough to nearly walk out of my session and quit therapy altogether. She knew my reaction was important information for both of us, that there was a reason I responded with this much volatility to a simple question. But at the time, I could only wonder why she had asked it at all.

I had been out of the clinic several months and attending weekly individual therapy sessions. I don't remember what I said that prompted the question. It was most likely that this session sounded like every other session before it. But about halfway into the hour she asked, "Who are you?" I said I didn't understand the question and asked for clarification. She again responded with, "Who are you?" I gave her the answers that made the most sense to me, but to every answer she only asked another question, each one more frustrating than the last.

Who are you?
"Well, I'm a mother."

What if your children move away to build lives of their own and no longer need you or you have a falling out?
"I'm also a wife."

What if, either through his death or his choice, your husband is no longer in your life?
"I am a benefactor, too, and active in a few charities."

What if, through a bad economy or bad investments, you no longer have any money to give?
"I'd still have non-material resources. I have a degree and a résumé. And I've always wanted to write."

What if you get into an accident that leaves you unable to work or write?

Several other answers were met with the same type of question. Every time I told her who I was, or who I could be, she took it away. After a few more questions I was unnerved enough to question *her* about her motives and perceptions.

My therapist sometimes gave me homework, mostly writing assignments, after our sessions. I was certain she was going to ask me to come up with an answer she could accept by our next meeting. But she said she wasn't looking for an answer today, or even next week. In fact, I could take as much time as I wanted. I took five years.

In the meantime, therapy and twelve-step meetings remained a consistent part of my life, which I had to reconcile with actually living my life. Though both of my children were in their twenties, they were not immune to or isolated from the changes I was going through, and the instability was uncomfortable for us all. But I couldn't have stopped the forces at work in my life then even if I had wanted to, and I couldn't tell them what the future held for my marriage or my life because I honestly didn't know; I had never been here before. But I could continue to show them what the process looked like no matter how it unfolded and allow them to witness every enlightening, encouraging, painful, or fearful step if they chose to.

I told them as much as I remembered about my childhood, my parents, my relationships, and my misguided beliefs about what I thought I knew then and what I was learning now. I told them of my enabling and codependency and how it manifested in my life and theirs, and that while I couldn't keep them from making the same mistakes I did or even new ones of their own, I could give them a different perspective and other options when their time came to work through them.

Therapy and twelve-step meetings were helping me to better understand my personal life, but I still found myself searching spiritually and professionally. While an unmapped spiritual journey that allowed the sacred unknown to reveal itself to me in its own way and time intrigued and excited me, I wasn't content to let my professional life remain a mystery. There was something I was supposed to do—I just knew it. The only thing I didn't know was what it was.

I was making my way through this new world, one of lives connected through stories created out of the same need to escape fear and pain, the same desire for love and belonging, and of possible, even probable, explanations through psychology. And I wanted more. Three months after I'd left the clinic, I decided to go back to school to get my masters degree in psychology. I spent the next four weeks studying for my Graduate Record Examination (GRE), an intimidating and daunting task because of the many years that had passed since I'd graduated from college. Four months after I'd left the clinic, I took the GRE and passed with a score well above what the university I was hoping to attend required. Five months after I'd left the clinic, my husband asked me for a divorce.

Those words are as hard to hear as I'm sure they are to say. There is no easy way to thoroughly and with finality break apart a union of two lives, even one that was broken to begin with, because you can't help searching for something worth salvaging to rebuild upon—just one thing that was whole and true.

To this point, I thought my process had taken me through every level of emotional depth possible. I couldn't have been more wrong. There is a reason so many use the words of Catholic mystic St. John of the Cross—"dark night of the soul"—to describe this otherworldly place I was about to enter. There are no other words.

The darkness is not just night, but the deepest, blackest, timeless part of night. No world imagined or created by man can live or breathe here. Your soul will not allow it and tells you so. It confronts you with every illusion you convinced yourself was real, reveals the separation from your true Self that you alone created, and asks you to choose: Will you go even deeper into the dark night in search of true light, or will you stay in your world of illusion with its thin, glittering surface covering a depth of never-ending pain?

Thomas Moore, who wrote extensively on the dark night of the soul, says the dark night, no matter how turbulent and painful, can rescue us from being stuck in the small lives we've chosen, from our flawed and limited perceptions of who we are and how we are meant to live our lives.

> In the dark night something of your makeup comes to an end—your ego, your self, your creativeness, your meaning. [But] you may find in that darkness a key to your source, the larger soul that makes you who you are and holds the secrets of your existence.

This is not a darkness you can sleep through or medicate; it is not a darkness you can suppress or ignore or outwit; it is not a darkness you would ever choose until asked. But there is no other way to reach the truth of life, of love, of peace, of the reason for your being except through the dark night.

By this time I was very familiar with Elisabeth Kübler-Ross' five stages of grief: denial, anger, bargaining, depression, and acceptance. Once again, my denial took the form of sense deprivation, the numbness acting as a kind of shock absorber. As understanding slowly seeped in, I felt disoriented, as if having no ground beneath my feet. I'd soon have to take this literally as I now had to grieve not only the loss of my marriage, but also the home I had created and the life I knew, when I hadn't yet finished grieving the changes that had begun just a few months earlier.

One night the overwhelming feeling of having nowhere to go sent me to the only place that mattered—within. It began by just wanting to sit in front of the television and do nothing, but the thought of feeding my mindlessness with even more mindlessness was not enticing.

Then came a simple thought: What would television look like if I created the programming? My heart answered by desiring a place I could go to remind me of what I'd learned in the clinic, of the guidance I was getting in therapy, of the stories I was hearing in twelve-step meetings; a place that nurtured my spiritual exploration without resorting to religious exclusion or dogma; a place that believed, as I did, that each person's mind, body, and spirit are connected, and if you seek to heal one, you must do so for the others.

My heart having spoken, my mind set about the task of putting its ideas into action. Instantly I came up with a few programs I felt could help me better understand the situation I now found myself in. As I let my mind expand and refine these initial programs, more came to me—so many that after a while I didn't trust my mind alone to contain them all accurately and I began to write them down. But what started as a few descriptive words for each program soon grew to a multi-paragraph synopsis, and in some cases, a title. When I got to where I was mapping out time slots, I realized I had outgrown paper and pencil and looked for something more workable. I found nothing but a dry erase board in the kitchen that we used to leave messages for one another, which was too small to be practical.

Fueled by energy I didn't know I had, I went out and purchased the largest dry erase board I could find and began meticulously transferring onto it everything from my notepad. The more I wrote, the more programs came to mind until my thoughts were so far ahead of what I was writing I found myself constantly moving between refining what I was working on at that moment and jotting down reminders for what I'd work on later.

Hours passed and I didn't notice. I stood and wrote, I sat and wrote, I ate and wrote, stopping only when absolutely necessary and only for the briefest amount of time. I was writing when night came and still writing at sunrise. When I could go no further, I had been awake for over two days. During that time, I had come up with more than twenty of the eventual forty-two programs I would conceive for a television network I hoped someone would create someday.

But this wasn't the end. Over the next six months, rather than wane, my creative energy grew stronger and more diverse. In all, I created programming for two television networks, and had ideas for two more networks, a radio show, a global charity, and a curriculum for a private school.

The leap from creating television programming to a school curriculum wasn't very far. It was all education and information. While in the clinic, many of us had seen others several years younger than ourselves check in, and we appreciated that they had more time to acquire and practice the tools they were about to learn, and less time to cement their current destructive thought and behavior patterns. It is much easier to break down these patterns after twenty years than it is forty.

Then I wondered, why wait until the damage has already been done? What if, while we were teaching parents how to heal, we could at the same time teach their children, in depth and from their earliest years, how to establish and maintain healthy lives? What if children were taught about self-esteem, boundaries, and moderation along with reading, writing, and arithmetic? What if we showed them how to use meditation and yoga and nutrition to mitigate hyperactivity, anxiety, and attention deficits rather than medication? And what if, day after day, year after year, they were presented with better options for resolving conflict and differences of opinion than obstruction, verbal abuse, physical violence, and war?

At the time, a presidential election was just five months away, which meant we were in the heart of the civil war the candidates, their campaign managers, cable television, and opinion media wage every four years. They all spoke about loving this country, and about wanting to help make it and its people the best they can be. But no person, family, community, nation, or planet can be elevated while one half is tearing down the other half.

In our world of politics, it's the voters who get to say what is acceptable and unacceptable in everything from negative campaigning to war. So, what if we were able to raise from birth more conscious voters and more enlightened leaders? What if we were able to nurture children into healthy parents, who would have healthy children, who would then have even healthier children? And what if we started now and all across the country? What would our nation look like after just a few generations?

As I continued to build on these questions, I realized how drastically divided my life had become. Simultaneously and with absolutely no middle ground, one part of me was giving birth to an incredible amount of creativity, while another was completely deconstructing my life as I knew it. I watched as all this immense growth unfolded even as everything I'd known was dying before my eyes.

Along with my changes in music, books, and relationships, and the additions of therapy and twelve-step meetings, I began my search for a new place to live. During the summer, the university I was hoping to attend accepted my application, and it didn't take me long to find a house in the area that looked as beat up as I felt. It was about forty years old, many additions over the years had made for an awkward floor plan, and it still suffered damage from a hurricane that had passed through over twelve years earlier. It was perfect. Alone, we were broken and hurting and still carrying the weight of the past; together, maybe we could help each other heal.

Realistically, I knew the renovation could take up to two years, which meant if I purchased the house, I would still need an interim place to live. For many years I had lived in big, complicated spaces. This and the vast amount of change going on in my life had my heart asking me to do just one thing: simplify.

I was ready for simple. I was ready for small. I was ready for uncomplicated. Just prior to the divorce becoming final, I found a small apartment with Formica, linoleum, white walls, and thin carpet, and I couldn't imagine changing a thing. There was space enough for a sofa, a bed, a TV, my computer, and the clothes I needed for school. Though I left the home I had shared with my former husband with more, I gave much away. Things—no matter how beautiful or beloved—were not what I needed now.

Somewhere among changing television, radio, the education system, and my life came the day I often thought about. The divorce papers were signed. The court date for the dissolution of the marriage was the following day. It was time for me to leave. This house was no longer my home.

On that day, I stood outside and took in everything I could—every brick and blade of grass, every sound and smell, every moment and memory. I remembered how much I had learned here from all those who helped me create something beautiful out of the overflow from my heart. I remembered how much I loved here as I knelt down in the grass where Bonnie Blue's ashes lay. Inside, I walked through the house room by room. I was grateful for the soft fabrics that brushed the palm of my hand, the antiques that would now add their brief time with me to their long histories, and the beautiful paintings that never seemed to mind my staring, no matter how long or how often.

Wanting to do one last thing before leaving, I made my way down the sandy, sea grape-lined path behind the house that led to the ocean. As children, my friends and I had played a game we called Three Wishes, where we would be granted any three things we wanted, as long as it wasn't more wishes. Somewhere during my young life I had heard that three-fourths of the planet was covered with water, and I figured that if most of the world could be found under water, so could most of world's riches. I imagined not just buried treasures from sunken ships and unmined gold, diamonds, and oil, but wealth we'd not yet discovered, like cures for sick people, food that was good for you but tasted like candy, and the magic that made sad people happy again. So I would always wish for everything valuable that lay under the water that covered the earth.

I stood at the shoreline, water washing over my feet, and looked at the two gold wedding bands I had been clutching in my hand as I made my way around the house for the last time. I then drew back and threw them into the water as far and as deep as I could, where they remain today, along with the rest of my wishful thinking.

Walking back, I realized I was moments away from never seeing this house again, something I could not have imagined just a few short years ago. As sure as I was that my feet would not touch this ground again, I also knew my last thoughts about this part of my life would profoundly affect my first thoughts about everything that lay ahead.

I had built this house with love and for love, and I resolved that it would stay that way. Standing before the house for the last time, I blessed it and all who entered it, and I prayed they would feel the heart and soul that is its foundation and know love here, find joy here, be safe here.

I drove away knowing nothing about my future, though hoping I could rebuild my life as strong and as beautiful as I had built my house. But I did know that whatever lay ahead wouldn't be easy. It had been a year since I'd left the clinic and I was still trying to get comfortable with my new tools, and still trying to be grateful for all the changes in my life that had gone far beyond anything I could have imagined.

My new place and new life were indeed simple. There was nothing and no one around to complicate it. I had moved away from my grown children, my friends, my home, my identity—everything I thought made me who I was—and ended up in the complete unknown. I knew no one. I drove on streets I had never heard of. I lived within unfamiliar bare walls. And now once again a student and single, I began to look more like a past I thought I'd left behind forever than any future I had looked forward to.

I had always thought the grieving process only follows the loss of someone or something beloved. But I learned at the clinic that grief accompanies any change, no matter how big or small, welcome or unwanted, because no matter what the change, something has to die before something else can take its place. Still, it surprised me when I began to grieve the loss of the chaos and complication in my life.

My first semester of school was still several months away, so it felt to me as if my new life had not yet begun and my old life was miles behind me. I have been told more than once how fortunate I was not to have small children or need to work, which allowed me to put all of my time and energy into my healing, and it is true. But those with these compulsory responsibilities had the structure I didn't have. If you have a job, there is a specific place you have to be at a specific time. If you have small children, there is a school schedule, an afterschool schedule, dinnertime, and bedtime. All I had now was time.

But no one's time can remain empty for long. We are all compelled to fill our individual spaces—the distance between physical birth and death—with something. What that will be is always our choice, and these choices are crucial because they become the patterns, habits, and rituals that either fulfill our lives or fail them.

Thomas Moore says a healthy ritual directs its actions toward your soul. It expands imagination, emotion, and creativity. It connects you to what lies beyond the physical world. It shows you how, then constantly reminds you to live in your heart.

From spiritual and religious practices we know that rituals follow a schedule, are outside anything we consider ordinary activity, and are highly symbolic. But they need not be confined to attending a traditional house of worship, and in fact, my first rituals after the divorce were not spiritual in the classic sense. You can connect to your consciousness through nature and creativity, by maintaining physical health through proper nutrition and exercise, even by bringing order to a disorderly life through cleaning, organizing, and maintaining your appearance, home, and personal affairs. But Moore cautions that if you aren't connecting to the soul through purifying rituals, you will connect to something else through patterns and habitual behavior. And those who lose touch with their souls tend to become habitual in ways that are destructive.

> If you choose not to become involved in ritual, some form of compulsive, repeated behavior will probably enter your life anyway. Drinking, gambling, philandering, drugs— they are all full of rituals that you may feel compelled to perform, but they don't have the effect of transforming you.

Although I now had time free of distractions to develop healing rituals, it was also very, very quiet—often too quiet to think about what I wanted in my life. There were moments I would have bargained away anything to have back the chaos and complications I allowed others to bring to my life so I didn't have to. Having an answer for everyone else's confusion was the distraction I chose to keep from untangling my own and where I found purpose. While I maintained contact with my family and friends, and never doubted I was wanted, the one who really needed me now was me.

After graduating college, I moved to New York City from a much smaller, much different city in the South and faced a situation similar to the one I now found myself in. Though I was married at the time and therefore had at least one connection to the city, everything else was unfamiliar. But I fell in love with my new home at first sight and wanted to be absorbed into its energy, the flow of its people, the strength of its buildings. I could do none of this from the back seat of a cab. So I walked—everywhere—whether I had some place to go or not. Once again in an unfamiliar city, and without realizing I was establishing a ritual, I walked. I walked at the same time nearly every morning. I walked to learn street names and building locations. I walked hoping that the new sounds and smells and faces would soon feel like home.

During the day, I continued to explore and heal my life, but every night, and nearly every free moment I had, I performed another ritual. I had already been fond of books, but now I was fully enamored, reading anything and everything that sounded even remotely interesting. As my dark night progressed, I steeped myself in the works of mystics, saints, and spiritual authors, as well as the biographies and autobiographies of those such as William James, Carl Jung, and Abraham Maslow, hoping their stories and journeys would help me make sense of my own.

Far from making me feel like I was alternating between separate worlds, spirituality and psychology seemed to blend together perfectly, almost depend upon each other to provide the missing pieces. Psychology helps us find the answers to our "what" and "why" questions, but it is the spiritual, the connection to something greater, that gives us the strength to ask the questions to begin with, and lets us know we are not going into the dark night alone or unprotected.

I later discovered that not everyone agreed there needed to be or that there even was a symbiotic relationship between spirituality and psychology. Some spiritualists believe that the past, specifically what happened in your childhood, is something you simply let go of, that it is irrelevant, non-existent, or even not reality if you are truly living in the moment. Those parents whom I had seen become so outraged upon hearing that the root of many of their children's problems lay in their family of origin would readily agree. I spent a lot of time hoping this was true; that you could simply let go of the past, whatever it held, because the alternative was often too painful for anyone to willingly choose.

It took time, but eventually I got closer to what was true for me. Though for now, I would not deny or ignore my past, and would not only keep tracking my childhood memories through the core issues I'd learned at the clinic, but find other explanations for the origin and management of destructive thoughts, feelings, and behaviors.

We are anxiety management machines. Literally every choice we make is aimed at minimizing anxiety, from avoidance and attachment behaviors to addiction to psychopathology. Because everything escalates, we must take steps to understand the sources of our anxiety as early as possible, as well as learn to manage anxiety in healthy ways at its lowest levels; the more intense our anxiety, the more extreme our anxiety management systems become.

James Hollis says the feelings of "overwhelmment" and "abandonment," which exist in all of us, are what we see as the two most basic threats to our survival. To ward off these threats, we develop a "false self" or patterns of behaviors that respond automatically to control or minimize the anxiety these feelings create. The three behavioral patterns we use to manage feeling overwhelmed are avoidance, compliance, and a power complex.

There are several ways to avoid a feeling or situation we don't want to confront. We can simply forget it. We can consciously and deliberately suppress it. We can unconsciously repress it, or push it down so far we don't even know it's there. We can try to get rid of it by projecting it onto someone else—for example, a person unable or unwilling to face his own anger will accuse others of being angry. We can find something to distract us. In extreme cases, we can disassociate, or literally cause whatever is producing the anxiety to separate from the rest of our lives and operate independently, such as with a multiple or split personality disorder, schizoid personality disorder, or paranoid personality disorder, where life has become so overwhelming and invasive that one disconnects from the rest of the world.

We also use compliance, or the tendency to submit to the wishes and demands of others, to deal with feeling powerless and overwhelmed. Codependents often adopt the relinquishing of personal authority and the right to be a part of a reciprocal relationship as an anxiety management system.

Through a power complex, we try to manage our overwhelming environment by controlling it and others. We all have controlling behaviors to a degree and the power complex is active in every relationship. At its worst, it manifests as an antisocial personality disorder or as the sociopath who constantly seeks to have power over others. But power doesn't need to be destructive or dangerous. James Hollis defines it as "the exchange of energy for certain purposes" shared with "rationality and compassion." He gives education, such as learning about our individual selves, others, and the world at large, as an example of a constructive form of power.

There are also three patterns we develop to manage our feelings of abandonment: identifying with the deficit abandonment creates, narcissism, and connecting to an "other."

One can identify with the deficit or lack through self-sabotage (constantly undermining or thwarting goals and desires to confirm one's perception of being unworthy) or through overcompensation (being driven to perfection and high-achievement by an inner sense of inadequacy and low self-worth). An example of overcompensation is the "impostor syndrome" in which a successful person gets no satisfaction from his accomplishments because internally he feels like a fraud or inadequate. He keeps trying to prove his worth through achievement, which only reinforces his feelings of inadequacy.

Narcissists alleviate the anxiety and feelings of emptiness and worthlessness caused by abandonment by using others to create and prop up a positive self-image. Narcissists often have difficulty maintaining healthy reciprocal relationships as a result of being more selfish than selfless; are unable to identify with the thoughts and feelings of others; and will exploit others, sometimes their own family, for their self-aggrandizement. Hollis gives the raging little league father and overbearing stage mother as examples of narcissists placing the burden of their low self-esteem and unrealized dreams and ambitions on their children.

Feelings of abandonment and the subsequent sense of isolation can also create a desperate need to connect with an "other," whether it is drugs, alcohol, sex, work, eating, shopping, or another person. This anxiety management system can lead to addiction.

I fully understood James Hollis' assessment that the choices we make come down to relieving the pain of feeling overwhelmed or abandoned. I had seen many examples of it in many lives, including my own. In the clinic, addicts described the battle between these two extremes as "come here, go away," a constant seesaw between not wanting their addiction and not wanting to let go of it. Outside the clinic, I saw the same pattern in almost every relationship, a cycle of beckoning a loved one to come closer only to push him or her away.

I could also see how feeling overwhelmed and abandoned could distort the five core issues I had learned about in the clinic and create problems with self-esteem, boundaries, reality, dependency, and moderation. I now understood that overwhelmment and abandonment were the catalysts for destructive thoughts and behaviors, but where did these feelings come from?

Like the clinic counselors, James Hollis believes they originate in our past, and he uses Carl Jung's concept of a complex to explain the source of our patterns and dysfunctions, which resonated with me more than any other because its description so closely matched what I felt inside. A complex is an energy-charged mass of repressed and interconnected ideas, feelings, or memories, which lead to unexplained or abnormal behavior. And this combination of the unconscious forces driving our lives and our behavioral choices that follow are based in fear.

I have made many choices in my life that were more harmful than beneficial, and have reacted in ways I can't explain. It was almost as if something I didn't know, something beyond my memory was, like a knee-jerk reaction, reflexively filling in the blank spaces for me whenever something activated it. I could almost feel, somewhere deep in my core, a densely packed mass of quietly pulsating energy, alert and ready to launch its programmed response the instant it felt threatened.

When feelings of being overwhelmed or abandoned trigger a repressed or suppressed memory or thought in the complex, you react in one of three ways. The most common is repetition, meaning you obey a message you received in your past about who you are and what you deserve and allow it to control your life by repeatedly putting yourself in situations that recreate and confirm that message. Another reaction to an active complex is to overcompensate, or do the opposite, which still keeps you in bondage to the message. James Hollis gives an example I knew well: "Every time one says, 'I'm not going to be like my mother,' or 'I want to be other than my father,' one is still being defined by that 'other' in some way." Or you will treat the problem. The treatment can be therapy or some other form of deep self-exploration. But when you don't know or have the desire to discover what the problem is, the treatment is usually to self-medicate through a substance or behavior to further distance yourself from pain, rather than confront and heal it.

Though the complex consists of the repressed and often unknown elements of your life, this does not mean you aren't accountable for your thought and behavior patterns, or responsible for discovering their source. Destructive thoughts and behaviors, including depression, are how the psyche communicates to you that something repressed exists and needs to be explored. They are the physical manifestations of the unknown and denying, ignoring, suppressing, or self-medicating the physical symptoms will not get you any closer to understanding why you do what you do or think what you think, or to changing them. Carl Jung described the danger of not addressing, or intentionally keeping secret, our hidden selves:

> Everyone carries a shadow, and the less it is embodied in the individual's conscious life, the blacker and denser it is. If an inferiority is conscious, one always has a chance to correct it. Furthermore, it is constantly in contact with other interests, so that it is continually subjected to modifications. But if it is repressed and isolated from consciousness, it never gets corrected.

The concepts of overwhelmment and abandonment and the complex still intrigue me, and I have continually tried to learn by applying them to as many people and situations as I can. It is interesting to recall the many I've known, both in the clinic and in my everyday life, who had felt both overwhelmed and abandoned at the same time. Most of the stories, as well as most of the heartache, came from feeling overwhelmingly abandoned. It was more than just wanting to be loved. It was an unbearable, never-ending, bone-deep belief that not only would they never be loved, they didn't deserve to be loved; that if someone really knew them, their deepest thoughts and feelings of inadequacy, fear, confusion, anger, emptiness, and pain, no one could possibly love them. Even if they were able to fool someone into having a relationship, he or she would never stay.

I remember hearing of the longing, the profound yearning to connect with a mate in mind, body, and spirit through acceptance. A deep need to belong, to feel right for and with another, and to fit in with this time, this place, this life. The sense of isolation was at its worst when it seemed as though everyone had found this deep and meaningful connection to another and to life except them. But many felt disconnected and lonely even when surrounded by people. It always surprised me how often these stories came from those who were married and had children.

As common as feeling overwhelmed and, especially, abandoned have been in all the stories I have heard, most couldn't explain where these feelings came from. Overwhelmment and abandonment never presented themselves as what they were but rather took the form of anger or silence, sadness or distance, arrogance or acquiescence. Throughout the years of my self-exploration I have found the most basic principle of psychology to be unerringly true: "It's not about what it's about."

Before I entered the clinic, I thought the full depth of a life consisted of two layers—the situation or person one was confronted with in the present moment and the reaction that resulted—and managing those two layers was our main task. As an adult, I thought I had acquired enough information over the years through experience to do this appropriately. I knew what I liked and didn't like. The fact that I didn't know *why* I felt this way didn't seem to matter. It never occurred to me that the management methods I'd developed could be faulty because they happened automatically within split seconds, and they were based on my belief that I was a "good person." I felt that whatever intuitively happens from one who is honorable should be basically sound. Even if I had an adverse reaction I wasn't much concerned about its true origin, and seldom defined it as a feeling, such as sadness or anger, only as appropriate. This meant my two layers consisted of the situation or person I faced in the present moment and my always perfectly acceptable and understandable reaction.

The clinic took me a few layers deeper by asking me to first identify my *behaviors*, such as the words I spoke or refused to speak, my action or non-action. Then to look at the *thoughts* behind my behavior, usually that something or someone external had caused me pain. Then finally to the internal *feelings* underlying all of it. After I left the clinic, therapy took me deeper still by showing how those submerged feelings were my reactions to believing my very survival was at risk by being abandoned or overwhelmed.

Recalling my childhood, I understood how my life could become one enormous defense mechanism against feeling abandoned and overwhelmed, and that these fears were in charge of everything, made every decision about who I loved and how I lived personally, professionally, and spiritually. While I didn't remember everything, I felt I knew enough to dissipate some of the energy driving the patterns and reflexive responses of my complex. And I couldn't understand why it didn't happen. Even though I knew more about what fueled my patterns than ever before, I often found myself locked in the same thought and behavior responses whenever my complex was triggered.

It didn't take long to find where the disconnect was occurring; it was the first place I should have looked because nearly every failure to achieve a goal happens here. Though I knew a great deal about the origins of my patterns, intellectualizing my past through information alone, however abundant, would not heal me. I also had to put it into practice.

I once heard someone say he'd rather have wisdom than knowledge, believing the two exist independently of each other. But for change to occur, both knowledge (the tools and information we acquire for our healing) and wisdom (the result of putting knowledge into practice) must be present. Without applying energy to knowledge and actively incorporating it into our lives, it remains inert and of no value other than to make one a good debater. And without first acquiring the proper tools and information, activity becomes mindless and inappropriate, causing more harm than good. It is this unbroken connection between knowing and doing, consciousness and wise action that transforms a life.

I struggled as I continued to try to understand—primarily through books and therapy—how to weaken the reflexive action of my complex until my therapist said it was time to stop reading about it and start living it. This idea of living my healing rather than simply reading about it was something I understood well at that time. By then, I had been pursuing my master's degree for a year. However, I found myself wanting to write, and wanting to take what I'd learned so far into the world, more than I wanted to go to class. It wasn't long before the pages I'd written far outnumbered the classes I was attending, and I decided my master's degree would wait for me. This creative outlet, which had become such an important part of my life and healing, wouldn't.

The most important part of any sport is the fundamentals, like the proper stance, weight placement, or hip and shoulder alignment. These are the foundation upon which everything else is built, and without which your tackle, your pass, your serve, your swing, or your drive will always fail. Likewise, you cannot be a healthy, functional adult who makes conscious choices if the fundamentals you learned during childhood were born out of fear and trauma, and if this dysfunctional child within is controlling your adult life.

Trauma creates fragmented selves, each developing coping mechanisms and survival tools based on its particular dysfunction. The goal of re-parenting is to first heal the wounds, then integrate the splintered selves into one whole and healthy being.

Despite my vow to my inner child at the beach that first day out of the clinic to do my best to love and protect her, the inner child concept was extremely difficult for me to accept; even with the Survivor's Week memory of my inability to wrap my arms around the pillow representing the little four-year-old who loved snow angels and clover fields constantly reminding me of exactly where I needed to heal most.

By the time re-parenting became the main focus of my therapy, it was clear to me when I was taking conscious steps toward my healing or backsliding into past patterns. Being years into my process had made me aware of all movement, no matter the direction. So I was thoroughly unprepared when I suddenly stood still, the thought of fully connecting to the child within freezing me into a stiff resistance.

I could easily go into my past and intellectualize the trauma and the memories, but my therapist was now asking me to take all that I had learned to my deepest levels and put it to work. And I couldn't. It didn't matter that I wanted so much to transform my life, and worked harder at it than most. It didn't even matter that I knew everything I had done to this point, all my effort all these years, would eventually fall apart if I didn't go back and repair the foundation. I literally couldn't. I couldn't read any of the suggested books on inner child work. I couldn't listen to guidance on my inner child during therapy and would redirect any conversation to a different topic at the first word of it. I even quit seeing one therapist because I felt she spent too much time trying to get me to address my inner child, and I wanted to do anything else. However, I couldn't suppress my intellectual curiosity forever. When I realized what I was doing, I wanted to know not only why I was resisting re-parenting my inner child, but what re-parenting actually looked like.

One thing I knew about my childhood—it was short. Becoming an adult in mind when I was still a child in body was most likely my first survival tool. Remaining vulnerable and innocent is the worst thing a child growing up with an addicted parent can do. You have to protect yourself because no one is willing or able to do it for you. And it is often the parents themselves you need protection from. Retaining your childlike innocence, spontaneity, and simplicity in a complicated world of inconsistency and violence can be costly.

Seeing my childhood this way helped me understand why I didn't want to go back there, and why I wouldn't know how to re-parent myself even if I had wanted to. Though revisiting trauma and the intense pain that came from this was difficult, I could look at my traumatic memories as an adult, and from a distance, and tell you what happened, why it happened, and what I thought. But I was being asked to go back and relive those moments as a child, to feel vulnerable, betrayed, and without control again. I could do even this except, since I hadn't been a child for very long and didn't have a nurturing example to draw upon, I didn't know what to do once I got there. I have no greater fear in my life than going back to those moments and not being able to get out.

Eventually I found a new therapist, though continued to resist connecting to my inner child. But that didn't stop her from trying new ways and terminology, looking for the one that made the difference. She found it by replacing the term "inner child" with "re-parenting."

Parenting is something adults do, and I could relate to being an adult. I've been one nearly all my life. But as comfortable as I was with playing the part of a parent, I still had no idea what to do with the child. As always, my therapist began with a question: "What would you do for your own children?"

Most of my parenting skills came from trying to create a positive from a negative. I knew what to do by knowing what not to do. I spent time with my children, read to them, sang to them, loved them more than I thought possible, and not a day or night went by when I didn't tell them so with words, hugs, and kisses. In spite of my parenting mistakes, I learned the one thing I had done right when a counselor asked my daughter during my Family Week if I had ever made her feel unloved or abandoned. She replied, "No. She's always loved me. Always."

But even knowing this didn't help me connect to myself as a child because I had learned to give my children so much more than I would ever give myself. So I again asked what re-parenting looked like. It was when my therapist said, "It looks like re-raising her without trauma," that I recalled a man, a boy, and a story I'd had no idea what to do with at the time it was presented to me.

About eighteen months after I had left the clinic, I attended a week-long recovery maintenance program out of state. Like in the clinic, the three counselors in attendance were recovering addicts, and each one had a story. This story began with a counselor showing us a picture of himself as a small boy. He said this boy remembered all the pain that, as an adult, he used alcohol and sex to forget. But by forgetting the pain, he also forgot the little boy. He spoke of his long, often difficult journey to reconnect to this boy, his inner child, who had deserved a much better life. Eventually, he found the common ground they shared, and this one thing they both loved brought them together again.

There was something about being in a boat, just him and the water, that he'd loved from an early age. It was quiet there. It was simple there. Life made sense. As he aged, his life got busier and more complicated, but he still loved his boat and the water and went out as often as he could. Only now he was never alone. Drifting amid the silence and the calm, he would look at his inner child seated next to him and feel love, and speak to him of memory after traumatizing memory like this: "Do you remember when this happened?" describing an event that had caused the boy pain. "This is what should have happened," and he took that memory and breathed new life into it through nurturing, protection, joy, and love. "This is what you should have always had then and what I must always be mindful of giving you now."

While you can't change your past, going back as an adult and redefining what traumatic memories *should* have looked like benefits both your adult and child selves and begins integration through mutual reinforcement: A healthy adult appropriately protecting his inner child creates a healthy child who helps fulfill the adult. By recharging memories with nurturing and healing energy, you develop new adult patterns for what is acceptable and unacceptable, which then establish a new foundation upon which your child now feels safe and protected. When you no longer put yourself, and therefore your inner child, into harmful situations, your re-parented child reciprocates by providing a healthy base from which you can authentically and honorably act, think, and feel, explore and discover, and eventually release yourself from reactive bondage to trauma.

I now had a word, "re-parenting," to help me embrace the child within, and the counselor's boat visual showing me how to redefine and transform traumatic memories. What was still missing was precisely what I was to change those memories to. I could describe in ambiguous words a vague sense of what I wanted those memories to feel like—nice, calm, kind, happy. But without the proper foundation and a constant consciousness to bring about an authentic transformation through continuing health and growth, "nice" is just another word for more enabling, and "calm" just a precursor to the eventual and inevitable chaos. This was more than changing life-numbing, traumatic memories by simply exchanging them for gentle words.

This was about giving myself the correct foundational tools to live the life I was intended to live, to pursue my purpose without fear, to finally choose freedom.

If I had been at any other place in my life the moment I came across the television program that first introduced to me a blueprint for raising a healthy child, I would have passed it by so completely as to not even mentally register the name of the show, which is precisely what happened for years. Even if it had somehow entered my consciousness, I would have thought a show called *Supernanny* was a children's cartoon about a superhero endowed with the unimaginably absurd superpower of babysitting. But my life and the moment collided with my curiosity so perfectly that I could only turn on the show and watch.

I was instantly captivated, not by a method or process, but by a person named Jo Frost, and I knew beyond any doubt that she understood nurturing by having been nurtured. The depth of her ability to instill in others her unquestioned belief in their right to live their healthiest life and achieve their highest individual and family potential through appropriate expectations, discipline, rewards, consequences, challenges, laughter, spontaneity, play, warmth, and praise was not something she had learned from a book. Jo Frost had been authentically, genuinely, and fully loved. Just how well she had learned the lessons of love, and her ability to teach those lessons to others, was startling.

Duality and paradox run through all of life. Duality is the material and spiritual, the acceptable and unacceptable, what to do and what not to do; and because of paradox we can only realize something through its opposite: ultimate freedom is only attained through restraint. How well we balance the duality and accept the paradox results in how well our actions will benefit us. It is through duality and paradox that Jo Frost teaches parents how to first re-raise themselves so they can then properly raise their children.

The families who call on Jo Frost for help are in high states of distress. Through various ways, out-of-control children have brought their overwhelmed parents to the point of repeatedly giving in to violence or giving up altogether. Both result in the family ceasing to be a family at all.

Jo herself is a vivid example of the mutual reinforcement between a nurturing adult and a healthy inner child, first through her appearance, then her method. She arrives at a family's doorstep as a tightly bunned, no-nonsense English nanny, complete with proper accent and prim demeanor, to observe the family interactions. She is confident, capable, and efficient, and she becomes background, isolating herself from activity as events unfold around her. During the ensuing parents' meeting, Jo tells them what she has seen. Children without appropriate boundaries never know how far their healthy freedoms can take them. Children without appropriate expectations only grow their limitations. Children without appropriate support, praise, and love treat everyone on the outside as worthless as they feel on the inside. Children consistently surrounded by inconsistency—one parent requiring one thing while the other requires something else, or parents having one set of rules for themselves and another for the children—believe that everything, including truth, morality, responsibility, and accountability is subject to personal whim. Children without appropriate discipline not only don't learn the corrective process, they don't think anything about them needs to change, and are destined to spend their adult lives still acting as children, resisting all healthy growth and development, making only self-centered choices. Whether coming from child or parent, all of this looks like hitting, punching, cursing, yelling, spitting, shaming, belittling, dishonesty, detachment, bribery, inattention, inconsistency, enabling, and self-medicating with things such as television, sugar, drugs, alcohol, work, the computer, outside activities, and inward withdrawal.

Once the passive part of the process is completed, Jo switches from observation and isolation to active participation when presenting the various techniques she uses to break unacceptable behavior. Gone are the tightly wound bun, knee-length skirt, and lace-up shoes, replaced with long, free-flowing hair, casual pants, and bare feet. The confident, capable, and efficient adult is still very present as she shows parents how to remain calm, firm, and committed to changing their behavior so they can then change their children's. But then you see her, little Jojo Frost, sitting cross-legged on the floor and surrounded by children as she uses play to illustrate sharing, or running carefree, laughter trailing behind her, when using a team activity to demonstrate sibling support.

We are all resistant to change, preferring to remain stuck rather than face the unknown, remain limited rather than commit to a higher expectation. It is in showing us how to break through the resistance that Jo Frost is at her best.

By the time I was introduced to Jo, my resistance to re-parenting myself was at its all-time high, manifesting primarily through my inability to write. Shortly after I had left the clinic, I found myself writing often enough for me to consider it another ritual. But while writing has always come to me, it hasn't always come easily. Writing about these moments and memories has many times left me painfully aware I had no other choice but to keep searching for healthy and enduring ways to rebuild; that is, until the day I was asked to go back to the four-year-old within and sit with her cross-legged on the floor, run with her through the clover field, laugh with her, sing with her, welcome her into my arms and say, "This is what it should have looked like." On that day, I said no, and didn't write again for weeks.

It was the image of parent after parent repeatedly putting his or her errant child back onto the naughty chair or into bed to teach the consequences of inappropriate behavior that showed me what breaking through resistance looked like. For sometimes hours, a parent chased down a child trying to escape his discipline and put him back in the place where he had to reflect on his actions. The running, screaming, kicking, crying, laughing, or cursing child's frustrated and exhausted parents wanted to revert back to whatever disciplinary methods they had used before, usually physical or verbal violence, or resignation. But Jo Frost would not allow parents to relapse into their own inappropriate behavior. Discipline should be education, not punishment. Nor would she let them quit, like they always had before, when establishing appropriate behavior for both parents and children got too hard or took too long. Your job as a parent is to keep taking that child by the hand and walking him back to where he must accept his consequences for as long as it takes to prove to the child and yourself that this time is different. This time you actively confront your resistance to change.

This time you go through the pain, inch by inch and step by step, until you break free of the bondage keeping you from the life you and your family were meant to live.

For me it was not the naughty chair but my desk chair that I had to keep putting myself into, hour after hour, day after day, as I wrote my way through and eventually actively participated in my re-parenting process. There were times I sat in front of a blank page for hours, mentally forming then discarding sentences I had no confidence in, then learning to write down even those, reworking them until I had something that made sense to me. Some days I walked away having only written a few paragraphs, other days several pages. But every day, I walked away feeling the warm presence of my precious four-year-old, courageous eleven-year-old, and gifted sixteen-year-old within and said, *Well done*—those two words, and every word I'd written, slowly replacing all those spoken by others who told me I was without ability or worth or a purpose in this world.

However, there is a drawback to watching any transformation occur within one hour of television. You don't get the full picture. While *Supernanny* does give a family update at the end of the show, you don't see how the family confronts the inevitable tendency to relapse back into old behaviors, or the resurrection of resistance to the new changes that have to occur for health and growth to continue. It takes a relentless commitment to time, to energy, to education, and to an active participation that never ends to transform a life, a family, an organization, a nation, or a world. Functional lives are not born. They are built. And they are built on love.

The clinic was the first step on a road that I thought would be built solely on my personal changes, my internal healing. And it made sense that I would think this. All of the clinic's teachings, every lecture I heard, every self-help book I read was about me exploring, understanding, breaking down, building up, and healing myself. From the core issues, the concepts of overwhelmment and abandonment, the complex and its reflexive defense mechanisms, and the re-parenting of my inner child to the hundreds of stories of trauma, pain, love, and transformation through twelve-step meetings, group therapy, and everyday life—I was given tools, I was taught, and I was told how to help me know me.

But no one told me the rest of the story.

I understood my internal unrest while in the clinic, even expected it to continue once I left. What I wasn't prepared for was also feeling overwhelmed by the upheaval and anxiety of a country immersed in a presidential election and two wars. I just couldn't seem to get comfortable, not with the vitriolic presidential campaigns nor the two wars I was being asked to support. There could very well have been a presidential candidate who was a perfect match for my vote. And the two wars may just as likely have deserved my support. But I could no longer overlook my uneasiness when faced with something about the world and my country I didn't understand. And I couldn't base decisions as important as these on blind allegiance to a political label or party. So just as the clinic taught me to do with my personal life, I decided to let information and history fill in the missing pieces regarding the outside world as well.

Between my leaving the clinic and writing this sentence there have been three mid-term and two presidential elections. Each one brought the hope that I would find my place as a voter, confident in a system and in a people who really did believe in change, morals and values, conflict resolution, and the dignity of all human beings. But each one only pushed me farther away, only reinforced the status quo of division, obstruction, verbal and emotional violence, and power struggles.

The 2000 presidential election was the last time I proactively voted for a candidate rather than against another; the last time I didn't choose between the lesser of two evils; the last time I believed change, character, and politics could coexist. It was also the last time I voted.

Two factors influenced my decision to vote for George W. Bush in 2000. The first was that I was drawn, as I have been most of my life, to whatever and whoever sounded like they had found answers to my most persistent questions. And I had been trying to grasp the concepts of confidence and self-esteem since I was first told by a teacher as a grade-schooler that girls didn't have it and boys were born with it. At the time of the election, George Bush sounded like he had at least part of what constitutes personal conviction figured out. The second was that he also had the sound of spiritual conviction. Understanding a candidate's position on pressing issues was necessary, but if he or she didn't have the character, however acquired, to follow through on what was best for the country rather than a party, personal interest, or lobbyists, none of it mattered.

However, the evangelical side of George Bush's Christianity did concern me, primarily because of most evangelists' impatience with people like me. The religious environment within which I was raised taught that if you weren't Catholic, not only would you never see God or get anywhere near heaven after death, you would burn in hell. Literally smell your skin scorch and feel your organs combust over and over and over for all eternity. There was not even the slightest hope of redemption or salvation. You had missed your chance.

I spent my teenage years rebelling against the "only one way and it's our way" claim of many religions and the idea of such an unreasonable and unfeeling God. But rather than walk away from religion, I pursued every path put before me hoping to find what I was looking for, while not even close to knowing what that was. I went to a synagogue, Baptist worship services, and Pentecostal retreats; was counseled by a Mormon elder and preached to by Jehovah's Witnesses; and was given my first Bhagavad Gita by a Hare Krishna who was passing out copies in front of my high school.

I was also still reading the Bible during this time, which looking back seemed to be for two very paradoxical reasons. One, the writing, the stories, and the poetry were to me a literature of beautiful human outpouring. But I was also looking for something very non-human within those pages, something that could not be contained within or owned by one religious organization or group of people, some universal principle that welcomed everyone through any authentically practiced spiritual philosophy. And somewhere between the Old and New Testaments, my teenage years and the first years after leaving the clinic, those early spiritual seekers helped me make a glorious discovery.

The God of the Old Testament spent his time threatening and carrying out those threats on those He saw to be wicked in the hope they would change their ways. He smote and blinded them; destroyed their homes with fire; sent plagues of frogs, gnats, and locusts; diseased their livestock; covered their skin in boils; killed their firstborn male children. He threatened to destroy His beloved Israel after He caught the Israelites—whom God finally had led to freedom after 400 years of slavery—breaking His second commandment by worshipping a calf made of gold, and nearly did destroy with a flood every living creature He had made and once declared "very good." He even took away the property, children, and health of one of His most humble and righteous followers in order to silence Satan.

But then came Jesus, and everything changed. Jesus healed the sick and lame. He brought the dead to life. He remained humble even during his most triumphant moment by entering Jerusalem on the back of a common donkey rather than a thoroughbred. He calmed a turbulent sea. He forgave his executioners. And he said those who followed his example would perform even greater miracles than these.

I often thought about the people of the Old Testament. How frightening a world with no understanding of physics, astronomy, meteorology, biology, or anatomy must have been. No scientists. No doctors. No medicine. How did one make sense of this threatening and unknowable world other than to believe it was a reflection of the God who created it? That the floods, droughts, famines, and sickness were God's wrath upon an immoral and irreverent people? And if treating wayward souls with anger, vengeance, and violence to get them to change was good enough for God, it was good enough for those He created, so they learned to treat each other the same way. But over time, they learned something even more valuable: It didn't work. No one changes through anger. No one changes through vengeance. No one changes through violence. And they allowed God to come to the same conclusion and transform Himself into a loving and forgiving God through a man, a prophet, a son.

While I didn't yet see the universal spiritual principle so clearly in front of me at the time, I did understand that Christianity was built on acts of transformation and stories of redemption, and that testimony is how Christians show non-believers the power of their God and His word. So I was surprised at George W. Bush's reaction after a DUI he had received when thirty years old became public during his 2000 presidential campaign. What I thought would be a triumphant example of a young man's salvation humbly put forth for all to witness seemed shrouded in embarrassment and secrecy. But we each come to terms with our mistakes and bad choices in our own way, and I thought, maybe this was his. With the ease of an enabler with years of practice, I excused then buried the accompanying uncomfortable feeling until I could ignore it altogether.

After the election and inauguration, I settled into the political comfort zone of a voter whose chosen candidate was now in office. For nearly a year, I understood and had confidence in my choice. But then this one man and one historic moment came together to change everything.

9/11. America's Holy Hammer, George W. Bush's Perfect Moment, and the catalyst for all my political clarity and confusion to come. Along with the rest of the world too numb and bewildered to move, I watched the towers burn and crumble again and again while rescue workers and government intelligence agencies sprang into frenzied action. Later that night, President Bush told the nation, "Our way of life, our very freedom came under attack in a series of deliberate and deadly terrorist acts." Nine days later in his address to a joint session of Congress, the president gave the terrorists a name, al-Qaeda; a leader, Osama bin Laden; and a base of operations, Afghanistan. And the names and places, beliefs and behaviors that had been so unfamiliar and distant became an inescapable part of American everyday life from that moment on.

Operation Enduring Freedom, America's response to the attacks, began on October 7, 2001, with air strikes against al-Qaeda training camps and the military installations of Afghanistan's governing Taliban regime, as well as airdrops of food, medicine, and supplies to its affected citizens. It seemed a just response to a heinous and unprovoked attack on innocent Americans, and I supported the operation and its primary focus of disrupting or eliminating sources of terrorist activity. A conclusion that made sense at the time and to someone who didn't know the alternative to feeling threatened, vulnerable and, for the first time, unsafe within the boundaries of what most Americans had come to believe was hallowed ground beyond all attack or any war. But in the following months the war in Afghanistan was overshadowed by another, more familiar threat.

The contemporary and convoluted relationship between the United States and Iraq can be traced back to the Cold War (1946–1991), which was an extension of the political, military, and economic tension existing at the end of WWII between the USSR and Western powers, primarily the United States. Though allies during the world war, the two superpowers became rivals over how post-war Europe would be configured. The resulting "cold" war was fought not with direct military action, but through a mutually escalating nuclear arms buildup, a technology competition, a space explorations race, and proxy wars in countries such as Afghanistan, Korea, Vietnam, and Angola.

Not only were Iraq and the Soviet Union allies throughout much of the Cold War, but the United States was also concerned about Iraq's animosity toward Israel and its support for various Arab and Palestinian militant groups, which led to it being placed on a list of states that sponsored terrorism. But all of that was put aside when the United States chose to aid Iraq during the Iran–Iraq War (1980–1988) over oil, borders, and regional dominance. At that time, President Ronald Reagan believed Iran to be a bigger problem than Iraq and decided that the United States "could not afford to allow Iraq to lose the war to Iran," and that it would "do whatever was necessary and legal to prevent" this, which meant billions of dollars, technology, weaponry, intelligence, training, and direct involvement in warfare against Iran.

However, in 1990, Iraq invaded neighboring Kuwait. In response to the invasion and seven-month occupation that followed, U.S.-led coalition forces launched a military intervention called Desert Storm, also known as the Gulf War, but which Iraqi president Saddam Hussein declared would be the "mother of all battles." George Herbert

Walker Bush was the president who authorized U.S. military force against Iraq. He was also the father of George W. Bush, who would himself become president just ten years later.

The combined air and ground attacks resulted in a liberated Kuwait and a clear victory for the coalition forces after just one hundred hours. However, the Bush administration was criticized for allowing Saddam Hussein to remain in power rather than having the military continue on into Baghdad and overthrow his regime. In 1992, then Secretary of Defense Dick Cheney—who later became George W. Bush's vice president—justified that decision:

> I would guess if we had gone in there, I would still have forces in Baghdad today. We'd be running the country. We would not have been able to get everybody out and bring everybody home. . . . I don't think you could have done all of that without significant additional U.S. casualties. And while everybody was tremendously impressed with the low cost of the conflict, for the 146 Americans who were killed in action and for their families, it wasn't a cheap war. And the question in my mind is, how many additional American casualties is Saddam worth? And the answer is, not very damn many. So I think we got it right, both when we decided to expel him from Kuwait, but also when the president made the decision that we'd achieved our objectives and we were not going to go get bogged down in the problems of trying to take over and govern Iraq.

George W. Bush had been president for just eight months when, on September 11, 2001, four fuel-laden domestic jets were redirected by al-Qaeda terrorists and flown into both World Trade Center towers, the Pentagon, with the fourth possibly meant for the White House but which instead crashed in a Pennsylvania field. In the months that followed, while the rest of America was focused on the nation's new color-coded threat level index and military action in Afghanistan, some of the president's closest advisors were looking at Iraq.

According to notes taken by an aide in the National Military Command Center just hours after the 9/11 attacks, U.S. Secretary of Defense Donald Rumsfeld directed General Richard Myers, Chairman of the Joint Chiefs of Staff, to get "[b]est info fast. Judge whether good enough [to] hit SH [Saddam Hussein] at same time, not only UBL [Osama bin Laden]." The notes also indicated Afghanistan was never the only intended objective: "Hard to get a good case. Need to move swiftly. Near term target needs: go massive—sweep it all up. Things related and not."

During his address to the nation on October 7, 2001, the president himself stated that his intentions to combat terrorism went far beyond Afghanistan:

> Today we focus on Afghanistan, but the battle is broader. Every nation has a choice to make. In this conflict, there is no neutral ground. If any government sponsors the outlaws and killers of innocents, they have become outlaws and murderers themselves. And they will take that lonely path at their own peril.

I don't think I could have listened closely enough to that speech and come anywhere near to predicting what was to come, or to realizing that the eighteen-month circuitous route the president took through Congress and the United Nations Security Council (UNSC) would, in hindsight, seem to be more about justifying a decision to invade Iraq that he'd already made rather than determining whether war was necessary at all.

Just four months after the 9/11 attacks during his State of the Union address, the president spoke of his goal to keep countries that support terrorism from threatening America with weapons of mass destruction (WMD), and pointed to the "axis of evil"—North Korea, Iran, and Iraq—as posing a "grave and growing danger." But on October 11, 2002, the U.S. Congress singled out Iraq and authorized the use of military force against the country citing human rights violations, the harboring of terrorists, an assassination attempt on former President

George H. W. Bush, and the continued development of WMD in violation of the U.N. resolutions enacted after the Gulf War as among the reasons for a potential invasion.

Americans heard a lot about WMD in the months that followed due to the passing of UNSC Resolution 1441 which, once again, called for Iraq's immediate and complete disarmament as well as a full disclosure of all chemical and mass destruction weaponry. We also had reason to doubt President Saddam Hussein's willingness to openly and honestly comply as a result of his well-documented lack of cooperation with U.N. weapons inspectors in the years after the Gulf War, including expelling them from the country altogether in 1998. But just days after the passage of Resolution 1441, President Hussein allowed inspectors back into Iraq after a four-year absence.

However, in February 2003, both the U.S. and Great Britain continued to lay the groundwork for an invasion by presenting to the UNSC their evidence of Iraq's existing and potential WMD, as well as ties to al-Qaeda. But they had already convinced the American public. A *CBS News/New York Times* poll taken a month earlier found that eighty-five percent of Americans believed Iraq had WMD, but they differed on whether the weapons would ever be found by inspectors. What Americans weren't willing to agree to just yet was military action. In the same poll, seventy-seven percent wanted inspectors to keep looking if they hadn't discovered weapons by the imposed deadline.

But President Bush believed he'd made a compelling case and on March 17, 2003, said, "Saddam Hussein and his sons must leave Iraq within forty-eight hours. Their refusal to do so will result in military conflict, commenced at a time of our choosing." Saddam Hussein rejected exile, and President Bush chose March 20, just three days later, to begin bombing Baghdad.

It took just three weeks for Baghdad to fall to the coalition forces, and the "wrenching down" of the large iron statue of Saddam Hussein in Firdos Square still remains one of the two most dramatic and lasting images of that event for me. The second, occurring a few weeks later, was of President Bush landing on the aircraft carrier USS *Abraham Lincoln* in an S-3B Viking jet to announce the end of major combat operations in Iraq and declare, "The tyrant has fallen, and Iraq is free," with a highly visible "Mission Accomplished" sign as his backdrop.

Also during this speech, the president reconfirmed two justifications he'd given for waging war against Iraq. The first was his belief in the connection between Iraq and terrorist activity, specifically the 9/11 attacks:

> The liberation of Iraq is a crucial advance in the campaign against terror. We've removed an ally of al-Qaeda, and cut off a source of terrorist funding. . . . We have not forgotten the victims of September 11th—the last phone calls, the cold murder of children, the searches in the rubble. With those attacks, the terrorists and their supporters declared war on the United States. And war is what they got.

However, in a news conference three years into the war, which by then had become increasingly unpopular with the American public, President Bush was questioned about his decision to invade Iraq. He asked us to imagine a world with a man in power capable of making WMD, who funded suicide bombers to kill innocents, and had committed grievous acts against humanity, including his own people; a world where this man was "stirring up even more trouble in a part of the world that had so much resentment and so much hatred that people came and killed" Americans. When then asked what Iraq had to do with the 9/11 attacks, President Bush replied, "Nothing."

It was also during the "Mission Accomplished" speech that President Bush reasserted his conviction that Iraq possessed WMD:

> And this much is certain: No terrorist network will gain weapons of mass destruction from the Iraqi regime, because the regime is no more.

Actually, no terrorist network would gain WMD from the Iraqi regime, because there weren't any.

Shortly after the invasion, the Iraq Survey Group (ISG), an international team charged with the task of locating and eliminating Saddam Hussein's WMD, entered Iraq. The eventual discovery that there were no WMD in Iraq resulted in the resignation of the head of the ISG after six months and his admission before the Senate Armed Services Committee that "it turns out that we were all wrong."

While admitting his pre-war intelligence differed from the findings of the ISG, the president defended his decision to invade Iraq and reinforced the two main premises of what came to be known as the Bush Doctrine: pre-emptive action against America's potential enemies and the promotion of democracy through regime change.

It was difficult for me to accept that waging war was now considered a pre-emptive measure rather than a last resort. Pre-emptive actions are to avert or minimize catastrophes, not create them. Waging war to prevent war and killing to stop killing are not pre-emptive, they are contributive. And I later found that, long ago, others had discovered peaceful ways not only to pre-empt war, but also to heal the separation and distrust between regions and religions that fear and misunderstanding create.

However, I did understand the desire to promote democracy and freedom—though I believe that if we want others to embrace democracy, we must first show them that it works. They can see for themselves what freedom looks like in the hands of the many who are incapable of personal restraint through our multibillion-dollar porn, diet, drug, and alcohol industries. They can hear how democracy sounds through the violent, abusive, and manipulative speech over our public airways. And it seems reasonable to ask, does what we say about freedom and democracy match what we do? If this is truly what freedom and democracy look like, why would others choose the path of those who treat themselves and each other so inhumanely? Too few recognize that the freedom and democracy in our hands are gifts we should spend all of our lives earning and honoring by elevating ourselves and others to our greatest potentials, not our lowest and most destructive.

I had recently left the clinic when the world learned that Iraq had no WMD. It was also when I began to realize there was something terribly wrong with the way the president had chosen to try to liberate Iraq.

In addition to being my first year out of the clinic, 2004 was also a re-election year for George W. Bush. But unlike the previous presidential election, I was sure about nothing. Now seeing the candidates and their speeches, debates, and behaviors differently, it simply became harder for me to rationalize or even understand much of it.

Despite George Bush's optimism as he spoke onboard the aircraft carrier the previous May, the war was far from over, and Iraq was not really free. Though one tyrant had fallen, another had taken his place in the form of the Sunnis' and Shi'as' bloody conflict over his replacement—succession having also been the source of their original split in 632 AD after the death of the prophet Muhammad, when they battled over who would be the successor and how he would lead the Muslim community.

In April 2004, reports and photos of Americans looking far from benevolent themselves began to surface. Abu Ghraib prison, located about twenty miles west of Baghdad, stood vacant and looted—Saddam Hussein having granted amnesty and the release of its prisoners just prior to the Iraq invasion—when coalition forces took it over to use as a detention center. The prisoners were reportedly treated so well there that the American commanding officer said their "living conditions now are better in prison than at home. At one point, we were concerned that they wouldn't want to leave." However, the graphic videos, photos, and descriptions of emotional, psychological, and sexual humiliation, and of the torture, sodomy, rape, and murder of prisoners by American soldiers showed something much different.

Exposure of the Abu Ghraib ignominy revealed much about America, including who wanted to learn from and heal the damage through disclosure, who wanted to manipulate it for political gain, who wanted to minimize or ignore it as harmless, and who wanted to keep it hidden altogether. Over the next few years, I understood through news reports, investigations, and documents released through the Freedom of Information Act not just more about the U.S. military's and CIA's treatment of prisoners in Iraq, Afghanistan, and Guantanamo Bay, but about American soldiers themselves, their commanders, and, ultimately, their commander-in-chief.

The disclosure of the prisoner abuse and torture at Abu Ghraib coincided with the verbal brutality occurring simultaneously in the United States, to which all American citizens are exposed during every election year. This is when the negative ads and campaigning, the verbal and emotional violence, the mudslinging and dirt peddling, the finger-pointing, sarcastic quips, manipulation, half-truths, and outright lies reach their all-time high. Some voters who so personally identify with a particular candidate or party endorse, encourage, even participate in the behavior. Some who believe this was, is, and always will be the way of our political process justify then ignore it. Still others who believe casting their vote is their civic duty simply endure it. For the first time, I did not find myself in any of these groups. Because this time, as I watched the negative ads, the vitriolic debates, and the manipulative speeches at campaign stops, I could only shake my head in bewilderment and say, "*This* is how I am being asked to choose the leader of the greatest nation in the free world? And these are my choices—loud or louder, angry or angrier, manipulator or hypocrite, misleader or deceiver?"

In the past, I had always been able to overlook or underestimate any uncomfortable feelings the campaign process raised and somehow find my way to the voting booth. But something, or maybe many things, had changed, though it was still too soon for me to understand what. With Election Day just months away and America stuck in the bowels of both the presidential campaign and the ongoing revelations of U.S. treatment of its wartime prisoners and detainees, I could only sit with my vote in my hands and wonder, *What do I do now?*

Unable to defend or even comprehend any of the candidates who had the greatest chance of being elected, I decided to keep my vote and, with the help of the new tools and perspectives I had recently acquired from the clinic, spend my time observing and gathering information to better prepare myself for participation in our next presidential election.

After the initial disclosure of the prisoner abuse at Abu Ghraib, I had an increased appreciation for President Bush when he, rather than a subordinate government official, went to Arab news outlets to denounce the abuse as "abhorrent." And when the Arab-language news station al-Arabiya likened the U.S. treatment of detainees in Abu Ghraib to that under the Saddam Hussein regime when the prison was notoriously known as a place of torture, President Bush made a clear distinction between a free country and an oppressed one that both his supporters and detractors could understand, when he replied, "A dictator wouldn't be answering questions about this."

While he did not offer an apology—only the "mistakes were made" passive amends many in leadership use to put distance between themselves and everything from errors in judgment to heinous acts—he did vow that the investigations would continue, that justice would be served, and the behavior corrected. But I felt conflicted when the president described these as the "actions of a few." While the investigations would indeed continue, the Army revealed it had already spent the previous sixteen months conducting criminal investigations into the misconduct of American captors in Iraq and Afghanistan. One investigation was specifically organized to look into the Abu Ghraib torture allegations and resulted in the Taguba Report, which the president said he had no knowledge of until the media disclosed it two months after its completion.

From this report, we learned the details of the "numerous incidents of sadistic, blatant, and wanton criminal abuses" inflicted on several detainees; that the "systemic and illegal abuse of detainees was intentionally perpetrated"; and that there were videos and photographs to prove it. But the report also revealed the conditions under which the military personnel were asked to carry out their duties, among them a lack of leadership and supervision, no training in the standard operating procedures regarding detainee internment and interrogation, insufficient manpower and resources, and shared duties with Iraqi guards whose counterproductive ethics and loyalties had them providing inmates with "contraband, weapons, and information," all taking place in a facility where the rioting and escaping prisoners had significantly exceeded the maximum capacity.

None of this excuses or justifies even one second of the abuse and torture perpetrated by American soldiers on Iraqis detained at Abu Ghraib, but it does allow a deep appreciation for those precious few who, when faced with everything that comes with war and fear and being pushed to the breaking point, still did what was right: the specialist who "discovered evidence of abuse and turned it over to military law enforcement"; the lieutenant who stopped an abusive action in progress and reported the incident to the chain of command; the master-at-arms Navy dog handler who refused to participate in improper interrogations despite pressure from Military Intelligence personnel.

Ensuing investigations and news reports showed that, far from being the actions of a few rogue soldiers, the abuse was much more widespread among military personnel and the CIA and not contained within Abu Ghraib, but included prisons and American bases in Fallujah, Afghanistan, and Guantanamo Bay.

Inevitably, extremists in both politics and opinion media went to even further extremes to verbally manipulate the events at Abu Ghraib to their advantage. While one side used them to gain a political edge over their opponents currently in office, the other tried to minimize them by comparing them to "the kind of thing that you might find on any college campus." However, it was these same events that caused one Republican senator, after reviewing evidence of the abuse and torture at Abu Ghraib, to clarify: "The American public needs to understand we're talking about rape and murder here. We're not just talking about giving people a humiliating experience."

Within eighteen months of the Taguba Report's release, soldiers who had personally tortured Iraqi prisoners at Forward Operating Base (FOB) Mercury near Fallujah in Iraq gave testimony to a human rights organization about the abuse. It was their words that made it clear this was a time for neither politics nor pandering if this country were to ever take full advantage of the opportunity to learn from these events. One made possible through necessary public disclosures—from the leaked torture photos at Abu Ghraib, the document releases, and the many investigations to the few whose personal convictions caused them to come forward and take responsibility for their actions.

The 82nd Airborne soldiers of FOB Mercury were proud of the nickname The Murderous Maniacs given to them by the local Iraqis.

They called their Iraqi prisoners PUCs—persons under control—and practices such as "fucking a PUC" and "smoking a PUC" were routine.

> To "fuck a PUC" means to beat him up. We would give them blows to the head, chest, legs, and stomach, pull them down, kick dirt on them. This happened every day. To "smoke" someone is to put them in stress positions until they get muscle fatigue and pass out. That happened every day.

And the prisoners were "smoked"—which included holding five-gallon water cans in both hands with outstretched arms or doing push-ups—for up to twelve hours. The soldiers also deprived them of sleep, water, and food; put chemicals on exposed skin and in eyes; subjected them to extreme heat and cold; and broke their bones with baseball bats.

One soldier testified that he knew the behavior was "wrong," but that "this was the norm." He said, "Leadership failed to provide clear guidance so we just developed it. . . . As long as no PUCs came up dead, it happened."

It was a captain stationed at Mercury who revealed just how difficult it can be for someone to do what is right when others with higher authority would rather keep damaging information buried. The captain, a West Point graduate who served in both Afghanistan and Iraq, said he had tried to raise the matter of detainee abuse at Mercury with his superiors seventeen months earlier. His company commander told him, "Don't expect me to go to bat for you on this issue if you take this up," and, "Remember the honor of the unit is at stake." And he believed the Army investigators were more interested in discovering the identities of the soldiers who had spoken to the human rights organization than uncovering and correcting the systemic abuse of prisoners.

When the first photos of the detainee abuse at Abu Ghraib were released to the public, there were attempts to deflect attention by those who were more "outraged by the outrage" many Americans felt upon

learning of the torture than by the torture itself. One Republican senator and member of the U.S. Senate Committee on Armed Services said,

> If they're in cellblock 1A or 1B, these prisoners—they're
> murderers, they're terrorists, they're insurgents. Many
> of them probably have American blood on their hands.
> And here we're so concerned about the treatment of those
> individuals.

But according to the Taguba Report, those held at Abu Ghraib
were largely criminals who had engaged in local crime, rather than
terrorists. And one soldier from Mercury testified that about half of the
prisoners at the base in Fallujah had no part in the insurgency against
Americans. "If he's a good guy, you know, now he's a bad guy because
of the way we treated him."

While still coming to terms with the detainee abuse and torture
in Iraq, Americans also learned what had been happening behind
closed doors at the U.S. military prison at Guantanamo Bay. Government memos released in 2004 showed that FBI agents and officials
had been questioning the highly aggressive interrogation practices at
Guantanamo Bay since 2002, more than a year before the Abu Ghraib
abuse became public.

In May 2005, Amnesty International kept the focus on Guantanamo
Bay by releasing a report calling the military prison the "gulag of our
time." The White House, through its spokesperson, took exception to
comparing a U.S. military prison to the forced-labor prison camps in
the former Soviet Union, where over a million prisoners and political
dissidents died of hunger, cold, and abusive treatment, asserting:

> We hold people accountable when there's abuse. We take
> steps to prevent it from happening again. And we do so
> in a very public way for the world to see.

While all of that sounded righteous, only some of it was accurate. Not only have the doors to Guantanamo Bay been closed to the

American public, they have also been closed to most human rights organizations and the media. The first photographs at Camp X-Ray of bound and blindfolded detainees being led to interrogation in orange jumpsuits were not authorized or released by the American government or military, but were instead "courtesy of Cuban leader Fidel Castro, who allowed an American photographer unprecedented access to a sensitive border post" between Cuban territory and Guantanamo to embarrass his American enemies.

At the time of the Amnesty International report, about 540 men were being held at the Guantanamo Bay prison on suspicion of having ties to al-Qaeda or the Taliban, and the Bush administration was coming under harsh criticism worldwide for not charging the detainees with crimes or allowing them to be tried in the U.S. court system. The administration countered that, since the detainees were classified as "unlawful enemy combatants" rather than prisoners of war, they could be held indefinitely, without being charged, and outside the laws of the Geneva Convention.

Defense Secretary Rumsfeld defended the military's handling of its Guantanamo Bay detainees, but also criticized the media for putting too much focus on prisoner abuse allegations and too little on "U.S. policy guidance to treat detainees humanely." I had two concerns with his statement. First, as had become known, there was no "policy guidance," no uniform standard operating procedure regarding detainee internment and interrogation that applied to all sectors involved: the military, the FBI, and the CIA. And second, it seemed the secretary was asking the world to put more faith in the words of U.S. policy than in the actions of its citizens. But the only way to prove a policy was actually being enforced and followed was to allow full access to the prison.

For twelve years and with seventeen U.N. resolutions, the United States had repeatedly demanded that Saddam Hussein open up his country to weapons inspectors. If we were indeed proud to be an example of honorable and lawful behavior during wartime, we should have done no less at Guantanamo Bay.

As the wars raged abroad, Americans back home were continually faced with the challenge of reconciling what they saw with what they were being told. And as reports of secret CIA prisons, extraordinary rendition, "enhanced interrogation techniques," and secret Justice Department memos authorizing torture surfaced, it became easier for me to see a disconnect between what I had learned in the clinic about dysfunctional and addictive behavior and what was considered acceptable in politics and war. The foundational characteristics of truth, openness, accountability, and authenticity—where internal and external lives are synonymous and words match behavior—that the clinic believed were so essential to the health of every person, family, community, or nation didn't seem to matter to those in some of the most important decision-making positions in the world.

An American economist and political commentator wrote, "A democracy needs informed citizens if it is to thrive, or ultimately even survive." While I agree, I also know that truthful information requires two parties: one able to speak it and one willing to hear it. Though I was willing and deserved to hear the truth, it now seemed impossible to find.

While trying to understand many of the Bush administration's responses to news reports and investigations, I couldn't help but recall the often-quoted Chinese proverb: "The beginning of wisdom is to call things by their right names." During a May 2004 press briefing just after the Abu Ghraib detainee photos became public, Defense Secretary Rumsfeld parsed, "What has been charged thus far is abuse, which I believe technically is different from torture. . . . I'm not going to address the 'torture' word."

It was difficult to give Secretary Rumsfeld the same appreciation I had given to President Bush when he declared to the Arab media that, unlike a brutal dictator, he answered the tough questions. However, within a month, I became unconvinced of even the president's willingness to provide authentic answers to difficult questions when, during a post G-8 Summit press conference, he was asked three times by different reporters about a recently disclosed 2002 memo written by the Justice Department at the request of the CIA, which stated that torturing al-Qaeda terrorists in captivity abroad may be justified, and that international laws against torture "may be unconstitutional if applied to interrogations" conducted in President Bush's war on terror. And three times he avoided giving a direct answer.

When more Justice Department memos were released by the succeeding administration, we learned that, in the United States, the law and torture are open to interpretation and dependent upon circumstance and the parties involved. And the Bush administration interpreted depriving a prisoner of sleep for over a week, throwing him against a wall thirty consecutive times, forced nudity, a liquid-only diet, face and abdominal slapping used in combination with water dousing, stress positions and wall standing, and, according to one memo, "the most traumatic" interrogation technique—waterboarding—as not being torture when administered as outlined in the memos, by the CIA, to "high-value" detainees.

Much of the debate surrounding the memos focused on whether waterboarding—or "simulated drowning" by covering an inclined prisoner's breathing passages with cloth and pouring water over his face to trigger the gag reflex—was torture. President Bush said it wasn't simply because, "we do not torture." Though we do perform "enhanced interrogation techniques" and "alternative procedures" on "unlawful enemy combatants."

However, the U.S. Congress admitted to what the secretary of defense and the president would not by passing an amendment to a $440 billion military spending bill called the Detainee Treatment Act of 2005, which states, "No individual in the custody or under the physical control of the United States Government, regardless of nationality or physical location, shall be subject to cruel, inhuman, or degrading treatment or punishment." This meant no more beatings or burnings, sexual humiliation or acts, forced nudity, mock executions, hypothermia, or waterboarding now applied to everyone—except the CIA. In 2008, the president vetoed legislation that would have also prohibited the CIA from using any interrogation techniques not authorized in the Army Field Manual.

But is waterboarding torture? William Schweiker, a professor of theological ethics at the University of Chicago, listed five characteristics common to acts of torture:

1. At least two persons are involved; torture excludes self-abuse.
2. One person has physical or psychological control over another.
3. They are extreme, purposeful, and systematic rather than unintended or accidental.
4. Their purpose is to *dehumanize* an individual to obtain a result, such as a confession, information, punishment, intimidation, or a political or religious conversion.
5. They can be applied to an individual directly to achieve the above results or to a third party with information about or access to the target individual.

He also states that one must make several assumptions to justify the use of any means to achieve a goal, which in this case would be using torture to maintain the security of the United States and the safety of its citizens: that we could infallibly know someone had information that would save lives (the "ticking time bomb" argument); that torture would extract this information without distortion; that the procedure would work infallibly; and, if the information were secured truthfully and infallibly, it could be used in a timely manner.

Regardless, we would have been able to determine for ourselves whether waterboarding was torture if the CIA hadn't destroyed the interrogation videos.

But I needed to look no further than my own backyard to find the answer. I live in a state surrounded by water, and I've heard dozens of stories of near-drowning from those caught in riptides, or from others who, after falling overboard—and through either panic or intoxication—found themselves disoriented and attempted to surface from directly under the boat rather than beside it. It didn't matter how long ago the near-drowning occurred, to the person who had experienced it *only once*, the psychological trauma was still very real and very active even decades later. Imagine feeling like this for five days within one month, two sessions a day, with six simulated-drowning pours per session, each lasting up to forty seconds, which is what was sanctioned by the Justice Department under President Bush; or being subjected to eighty-three pours in one month, as was one high-value prisoner in August 2002, or 183 pours, as was another in March 2003.

Along with the disclosure of the torture methods came the information that physicians and psychologists—who are ethically and professionally bound by their oaths to heal—took part in evaluating the prisoners subjected to them. The memos stated that the ultimate goal of the interrogation techniques was to make a detainee feel that "he has no control over basic human needs."

Abraham Maslow showed us that when a human being is reduced to having to meet his most basic needs he will sacrifice everything else to achieve this, including the self-esteem gained by telling the truth—making his statements suspect—and even his personal safety. A current example of this is America's inability to secure its border shared with Mexico. Each year, thousands of immigrants risk being shot and killed by border patrol while attempting to attain in America something they can't in Mexico: a wage sufficient to meet the basic needs for themselves and their families. Those who are successful are met with hatred, ridicule, prejudice, and rejection.

It was interesting to me that anyone would think the immigrants looking for wage-paying jobs would rather subject themselves to death and cruelty than live in their homeland, surrounded by their families and countrymen. I believe our focus, as a great nation, should not be to shame them away from our country, but to help establish an environment that will allow them to stay in their own. It should be our purpose to interact with everyone, even and especially terrorists, in a way that can cause them to become more enlightened, not less than human. Because if you can understand how one is broken down, either by force or circumstance, to his most basic survival needs, you can also understand how he can be elevated to achieve his highest potential and be a healthy, functional contributor to humanity. It was the events of 9/11, our unending war on terror, and the toll our actions and reactions to all of it took on our own, both military and civilian, that eventually showed me we no longer had a choice.

However, at the time I could only wonder: if the president and his administration considered waterboarding legal and not torture, why did it take the CIA four years after the first memo was leaked to even admit they had used the technique, and the president over six years to do the same, which was eighteen months after he had left office? Waterboarding is not new. A form of it dates back to the Spanish Inquisition, and it has been used in several wars by several countries, including members of the Gestapo and the Khmer Rouge, throughout history. So the argument of needing to keep the method a secret for fear the enemy would suddenly develop training to resist its effects didn't seem to be much of one. Neither did the discovery of the Manchester Manual by British police establish that al-Qaeda members had, in fact, successfully developed advanced methods to withstand interrogation, as was suggested by the Pentagon official overseeing detainee operations.

But waterboarding was a secret the Bush administration was determined to keep, though it wouldn't be the only one. In November 2005, the *Washington Post* revealed the existence of foreign covert prisons called "black sites" where the CIA transferred high-value prisoners. This practice, known as extraordinary rendition—or "torture by proxy" by its critics—allowed the CIA to secretly abduct suspected terrorists and transport them to foreign countries where they could be held indefinitely without charge and where torture was an accepted interrogation technique. Since it is illegal for the government to detain prisoners in unknown locations within the United States, the CIA began developing a secret prison system shortly after 9/11 with eventual sites—most having been built and maintained with funds appropriated by Congress—in at least eight foreign countries. Neither the government nor the CIA would acknowledge their existence. However, the CIA did ask the Justice Department to launch an investigation to determine whether the information on the secret prison network had been illegally disclosed to the media.

During this time, I was often reminded of the clinic adage: No addict can be an addict by himself. Which means everyone who is addicted or dysfunctional, lies or denies, manipulates or keeps secrets must have help from those who allow and enable him to. In the case of torture, secret prisons, and extraordinary rendition, it was the accommodating countries that allowed the Bush administration to use them for this purpose, then refused to acknowledge it. Most notable Great Britain, which denied in 2005, 2006, and 2007 that it had been used in any U.S. rendition flights. It wasn't until 2009 that Foreign Secretary David Miliband admitted to and offered an apology for two flights that had landed in Diego Garcia, a U.K. dependent territory. It was also the CIA who carried out the rendition flights and interrogations. It was the physicians and psychologists who were party to acts of torture in direct conflict with their oaths to heal the physically and mentally wounded and do no harm. It was the military leadership who tried to minimize or cover up the abuses perpetrated by American soldiers on foreign detainees. It was the Bush administration Justice Department that attempted to find ways to legalize torture. It was the president's like-minded advisors. It was all those who were willing to keep President Bush's secrets—and the truth—from the rest of us. And it was the rest of us who believed torture and secrets were acceptable, defensible, even noble.

The reason I've heard most often for allowing presidents latitude in having secrets and withholding information from citizens is that they know more, have a broader picture of most situations than the rest of us, and therefore are in a better position to determine what is best for the country. I believe this can be true, but a president must be trustworthy to be given this benefit of the doubt. Trust is earned through trustworthy behavior; it is not bestowed simply because one becomes president. If all I had learned so far about what the Bush administration believed to be trustworthy behavior wasn't enough for me to question whether it actually could be trusted to keep secrets and withhold information for the good of the country rather than its own political interests, two other words would be: Pat Tillman.

It is no secret that power comes from information, not status, sex, or even money. Whoever has the information holds the power. One who is properly motivated can use truthful information to create understanding, unity, growth, and healing; or if not, can use misinformation, manipulated information, lack of information, even factual information to deceive, divide, and destroy. Neither can there be truth by omission. Telling the truth is more than not telling lies. It is knowing that every word, every act, every thought, and every choice made by one affects us all.

The truth that information is power is not lost on terrorists, who go to incredible depths to protect it, or on the U.S. government and military, who went just as low to acquire it. However, a great nation should be concerned not only with gathering information, but also with doing so in a way that doesn't jeopardize its citizens, and the world, for generations to come.

The foundational concept of Buddhism is cause and effect, or "this is because that is." After years of searching for the path to enlightenment, a dejected Siddhartha Gautama sat under a bodhi tree and vowed not to get up until he had found the truth. After forty-nine days, Buddha Shakyamuni arose, filled with the knowledge of the Four Noble Truths: There is the effect that is suffering; there are the causes of suffering, which are ignorance and craving; there is the effect that is the elimination of suffering; there is the cause of the elimination of suffering, which is the Noble Eightfold Path.

Equally as important to Mahayana Buddhism is the Heart Sutra of the Prajnaparamita, which contains a sentence that has been the source of much condemnation when misinterpreted, but deep joy when fully understood. "Form is emptiness, emptiness is form" is not Buddhism's description of nihilism. It does not mean nothing exists and nothing is real. Instead, it succinctly and profoundly reminds us all that nothing, not one thing, exists separately from anything else. There is no thought, no feeling, no word, no act, no physical object that contains an independent entity, nothing that would have come into being or continue to be if something else ceased to exist. *All form is empty of an inherent existence. Everything empty of inherent existence is created through the form of something else.*

There is no independent entity that is this book. It would not exist if you took away paper. Paper would not exist if you took away trees. Trees would not exist if you took away sunlight, water, or carbon dioxide.

There is no independent entity that is You. Your physical body would not exist if you took away breath or blood. Breath or blood would not exist if you took away water or carbon dioxide. And these would not exist if you took away oxygen, hydrogen, carbon, or subatomic particles.

You may identify yourself by a name, a profession, or a religious or political affiliation, but all of these are either an acceptance of or rebellion against what you learned from your caregivers, and what they learned from theirs, and so on. Not even your thoughts, feelings, or behaviors are distinctly yours but come from interactions with your environment, which is composed of other interactions that have been in motion since the beginning of time.

The Sufi mystic and poet Rumi said, "There is nothing in the universe that you are not." The components that make You are the same components that make everything and everyone else. If something affects one, it affects all. Cause and effect and the absence of an inherent existence are what connect all of us to everything and to each other, both saints and sinners. Only when you understand that compassion is not just something to talk about or only give to those you think are deserving, but something you must do always and give to everyone, will you have truly chosen peace over terror. Only when you know to the depth of your soul that you will eventually and equally share every choice you make with those you love and those you hate, with those you know intimately and those you will never know, with those here today and those many lifetimes away, will you choose love in all you think, say, and do.

In describing how far the White House would go to protect Americans, former Vice President Dick Cheney said, "We also have to work . . . the dark side." But when they chose the dark side, they chose it for all of us.

The war in Iraq was just over two years old when President Bush stated that the violence and bloodshed were horrifying and the suffering real, but it was "worth it." However, as the toll on military and civilians in Afghanistan and Iraq as well as on the home front grew more dev-astating, I knew this was something one with only a political career to lose could say.

By mid-2005, a U.S.–British non-governmental agency survey found that nearly 25,000 Iraqi civilians, police, and military recruits had been killed by U.S.-led forces, insurgents, and criminal gangs. Six years into the war, the Iraqi death toll reached over 100,000, includ-ing 66,000 civilians.

In 2006, a study contracted by the Pentagon found that the Army presence in Afghanistan and Iraq had been overextended to the breaking point, a "thin green line" ready to snap unless the combat brigades cur-rently deployed were given some relief. But some retired and active-duty soldiers found relief on their own. From 2005 to 2007, the suicide rate for eighteen- to twenty-nine-year-old veterans had increased twenty-six percent. By late 2009, the number of suicides among active-duty Army soldiers had already reached 133, which was eighteen more than the previous year. A total of 245 soldiers had committed suicide by the year's end. In June 2010, the thirty-two Army suicides within a single month were a record high. According to the Department of Veterans Affairs (VA), currently more than 6,000 veterans commit suicide each year.

For many others serving in Iraq and Afghanistan, death was not a choice. Seven years into the war in Iraq, at least 4,416 members of the U.S. military had died, and 31,770 had been wounded in hostile action. And while I was writing this, a twenty-one-year-old reservist from Williamsport, VA, became our 1,205th casualty in Afghanistan.

To some, these are just numbers. But to their loved ones, this is a child a mother had lovingly carried in her womb, a son or daugh-ter a father had patiently taught to swim, fly a kite, drive a car; the sweetheart someone had fallen in love and planned a future with; the husband or wife of someone who will never again see the face, hear the voice, or hold close the body of his or her beloved. This is the father or mother of children who are now left only with knowing their par-ent was capable of such a profound sacrifice; but during homework, heartache, weddings, graduations, holidays, birthdays, and every day when the only one who can make a difference is mom or dad, this hardly seems enough. And to the rest of us, this is the person who would have stopped to help us change a flat tire, the coach or teacher who would have changed our lives, the firefighter or doctor who would have saved our child, the scientist who would have found a cure, the man or woman who would have become a great leader by healing and uniting a nation and a world.

Among those who survived, many found they didn't have a home to return to. Between 2001 and 2004, divorces among active-duty Army officers and enlisted personnel nearly doubled, from approximately 5,600 to over 10,000. In 2006, the VA determined that about 1,500 veterans from Iraq and Afghanistan were homeless, a young and growing segment of the estimated 330,000 veterans who were homeless that year.

Homeless veterans are well known to us. The Civil War created thousands of them. Known as tramps, they wandered the country looking for jobs, often still nursing their wounds, and frequently addicted to morphine.

In the 1930s, the Bonus Army—a mass of 43,000 WWI veterans, their families, and protesters—descended on Washington demanding immediate payment of the wartime bonuses promised to them. In 1924, Congress had voted to compensate the veterans for their service in the form of certificates to be redeemed twenty years later. However, in 1932, homeless and unable to find work due to the Depression, the vets set up camp in an area of mud and swamp across from Washington, hoping to convince Congress to immediately release the badly needed financial relief. Washington's response was first to dispatch the police who, when met with resistance, shot and killed two veterans, and next to send in Army regiments commanded by Gen. Douglas MacArthur and six battle tanks commanded by Maj. George S. Patton. The cavalry charged with fixed bayonets and adamsite gas and forcibly evicted the veterans and their families from the camp, as civil service employees lined the street to watch the U.S. Army attack its own.

While all wartime veterans must deal with the physical and emotional wounds of war in some way, none have had to bear the additional burden of America's anti-war scorn like Vietnam veterans. Theirs was a homecoming of rejection and disdain, not parades, flag-waving, or yellow ribbons. They have "struggled for decades for acceptance and many are still fighting for veteran's benefits." The VA estimates that nearly half of today's homeless veterans served during the Vietnam era.

For some survivors of our most recent wars, even coming home didn't mean leaving the war behind. In 2008, a lawsuit against the VA revealed that of the 300,000 veterans of the Iraq and Afghanistan wars treated at VA hospitals, more than half had been diagnosed with a serious mental health condition. About 68,000 of those were cases of post-traumatic stress disorder (PTSD), a severe anxiety disorder that can develop after exposure to a psychologically traumatizing event—such as the threat of death, or being subjected to acts of physical, sexual, or psychological abuse—which overwhelms one's ability to cope. Family members of those who experienced the trauma can also develop PTSD.

The lawsuit was filed on behalf of veterans of both wars to dispute the VA's claim that the soldiers were not "entitled" to five years free health care after returning from combat as mandated by Congress in the Dignity for Wounded Warriors Act. The VA also asserted that medical treatment was discretionary and based on the amount of funding available in the budget. But the lawsuit described how the VA's non-action on military health care would have desperate and far-reaching consequences:

> Unless systemic and drastic measures are instituted imme-diately, the costs to these veterans, their families, and our nation will be incalculable, including broken families, a new generation of unemployed and homeless veterans, increases in drug abuse and alcoholism, and crushing burdens on the health care delivery system and other social services in our communities.

This means the decision to go to war and the consequences of war will affect you, your children, your grandchildren, and their children, regardless of whether anyone personally known to you has actively served, and possibly in ways you could not have imagined.

Commanders of the 4th Brigade Combat Team commissioned an Army study after Fort Carson soldiers committed fourteen homicides and attempted murders over a three-year period. The report found that a "toxic mix" of combat stress, drug and alcohol abuse, and mental illness had contributed to the unusual cluster of violence. But therapists and counselors found something else unusual about our returning soldiers:

> We're used to seeing people who are depressed and want to hurt themselves. We're trained to deal with that. But these soldiers were depressed and saying, "I've got this anger, I want to hurt somebody." We weren't accustomed to that.

Repressed, suppressed, or self-medicated pain or shame or guilt will remain active at an unconscious level and can be felt internally as depression, anxiety, or rage. When these feelings become too painful and overwhelming to be restrained, a person may try to get rid of them by projecting them onto something or someone outside himself. When he has transferred onto others what he does not want to own or is no longer capable of internalizing, he can now see them, rather than himself, as responsible for his pain or actions and deserving punishment. To those in Fort Carson, the punishment included the rape and murder of a nineteen-year-old girl, the gunning down of two men with an AK-47, the murder of a taxi driver, one soldier killing his infant, another killing his friend with a fire poker, and still another killing his wife and then himself.

In addition to fighting physical pain, the psychological demons created by war, and the consequences of self-medicating, veterans also found themselves waging internal battles mired in culture and confusion. Men, especially male soldiers, are not supposed to ask for help. Soldiers are the protectors, not the protected; our saviors, not the saved; the strong taking care of the weak; the brave doing what the rest of us spend our lives avoiding. And much of the pressure to just "suck it up, rub some dirt on it, and you'll be fine" comes from the military itself. A member of Iraq and Afghanistan Veterans of America testified before the House Veterans Affairs Committee that

> the heavy stigma associated with mental health care stops many service members and veterans from seeking treatment. More than half of the soldiers and Marines in Iraq who tested positive for a psychological injury reported concerns that they will be seen as weak by their fellow service members.

The words I have heard most often from those discussing or dismissing all that our soldiers face, whether in battle or at home, are "this is war," as if these three words are all I need to understand, even accept as normal that we first overwhelm our men and women soldiers with trauma and then require them to make a decision about their own life and death—whether to get help or not get help—with a mind that is broken. But even with trauma, some soldiers come to know that the life valuable enough to save is now their own, and they do seek help. Though for too many, the help they get can be as damaging as their original trauma.

Warrior Transition Units (WTU) were created to better care for soldiers with physical wounds and severe psychological trauma, and to allow the injured to recuperate and either return to duty or process out of the Army. But what some had hoped would be a healing sanctuary one soldier called "just a dark place." He said, "Being in the WTU is worse than being in Iraq."

The soldier, an Army sniper, was said to be overflowing with confidence before his tour in Iraq. After suffering two concussions from roadside bombs and watching several platoon members burn to death, he returned emotionally broken and attempted suicide with a bottle of whiskey and an overdose of painkillers. However, far from being a therapeutic way station, his transition unit prescribed a "laundry list" of medications that left him disoriented and lethargic, provided only a once-a-week counseling session with a nurse case manager, and meted out harassment or discipline when he was late to formation or broke rules. Within months of being transferred to the unit, he was "begging to get out."

Many soldiers in this transition unit believed doctors were too quick to prescribe psychotropic drugs and narcotics, which were so abundant that soldiers would "openly deal, buy, or swap" prescription medication. The result was addiction to pills or to heroin, which was also easily obtained on the barracks. "We're all on sleep meds, anxiety meds, pain meds," said one soldier from the WTU. "The heroin is all that wrapped into one."

Inevitably, a new battle arose between the overly medicated and listless soldiers who were unable to get out of bed in time to make formation or perform all-night guard duty and the non-commissioned officers who disciplined them; and between the now addicted soldiers who would do or say anything to get their drugs and the supervising officers who chose to punish rather than treat those with physical or mental health injuries. But while some soldiers felt that contempt for those who came back from the war with emotional wounds only exacerbated the problem, their leadership offered a different perspective. One sergeant from Fort Carson said he had been exposed to the same horrors of war and did not mentally fall apart.

> Stuff happened in Iraq, people died, you know, I under-stand. But then again, I lost two of my friends and I don't have a problem, you know. I mean, I'm sorry they died and all, but you've got to go on with life.

The sergeant said that some of the returning soldiers who claimed mental health problems were the same soldiers who had to be routinely disciplined for avoiding work, being late, being dirty, lying, or abusing drugs—which was substantiated by Army records—and were using PTSD to avoid punishment. He also believed studies showing that these behaviors are symptoms of an emotional disorder are still no excuse for a soldier. Another Fort Carson sergeant said there was a different reason soldiers might fake emotional problems: "They don't want to go back to Iraq and they're trying to blame all their life's problems on PTSD."

Eventually, soldiers wanted to tell their stories more than numb their minds and souls, and they felt abandoned by broken marriages and homelessness, abandoned by the military and VA administration when it came to their health and benefits, and abandoned by their own countrymen, with whom they no longer had much in common. A soldier who has personally experienced war must navigate two very different worlds: the battlefield, where he has seen the horror of death and learns what is important in life, and the home front, where the most important things to many are gossip, junk television, and mass communicating opinions or the mundane details of one's day on social media. As one retired soldier explained, someone living two different lives really has no identity, or even much of an existence at all.

> [The war in Iraq] is kind of like an invisible war. Everyone here kind of goes about their everyday life totally unaffected by what's going on over there, and you say, "You know what? I'm just going to go to the liquor store, grab a 12-pack, and go back to my room."

Soldiers described being overwhelmed by broken bodies, burned bodies, dead babies, bloodied children, pain, fear, loneliness, confusion, sadness, and guilt. And I wondered why anyone would want to return to war or how anyone could remain unaffected by it. It was then I realized that those who did not want to go back and those who were mentally broken by their war experiences were the sanest of us all.

No one should be unaffected by brutality and murder. There is a reason the psyche rebels against violence and inhumane acts. It is because they are unnatural and unholy. And absolutely every soul will rebel. Some will suppress it better or for longer than others, and it might look like isolation, lack of intimacy, lack of communication, or arrogance rather than addiction, an emotional disorder, or suicidal thoughts—at least in the beginning. But as one soldier described, eventually war breaks everyone.

> There are times when you literally will beat your chest: I am all that is man, fear the flag, we're Americans and we're going to do what we can to protect our culture and our way of life. And then there are times when you are bankrupt. You're just spiritually drained. And you realize, maybe a part of me is dying, maybe the humanity. Maybe you lose your soul in combat.

A June 2010 news story shifted my curiosity from the consequences of President Bush's choices during his eight years in office to how he made them. In a speech to the Economic Club of Grand Rapids, visibly relaxed and comfortably seated in an upholstered, high-backed chair, former President Bush admitted, "Yeah, we waterboarded Khalid Sheikh Mohammed. I'd do it again to save lives," and felt that "getting rid of Saddam Hussein was the right thing to do and the world is a better place without him."

His nonchalance over his part in the torture and death of other human beings startled me. I then realized there was one thing I never saw in him when faced with the kinds of decisions that should throw anyone's humanity and spirituality into crisis: sadness. And one word I never heard from him: forgiveness.

I am not naïve to the ways a powerful nation becomes one, so my confusion was less about the decision to wage war than it was that this man decided it. This man who loves Jesus. This man who believes Jesus saves, Jesus heals, Jesus transforms, Jesus forgives, and Jesus gives life, not destroys it.

Understanding more about how trauma shapes our choices and reflexive reactions, I wanted to know George W. Bush's story, the real story realized through years of honest and committed self-exploration and told with authenticity, not through justification and defensiveness. Because I couldn't help but wonder what had happened to him that he could be so cavalier about choosing brutality over compassion, harm over healing, death over life. More importantly, what had happened to his Christianity?

However, I did know his choices were not new, and I now wanted to explore rather than justify or ignore them. There is a saying that money doesn't change you, it only makes you more of who you already are, which works just as well for politics. Because power doesn't change you, it only makes you more of who you already are. And the wars in Iraq and Afghanistan allowed President Bush to escalate in number and consequences the kinds of choices he was already willing to make.

In the same speech where President Bush asserted that the torture at Abu Ghraib had been the actions of a few, he also said something that took me back to his years as governor of Texas.

> [The people of Iraq] must also understand that what took place in that prison does not represent the America I know. The America I know is a compassionate country that believes in freedom. *The America I know cares about every individual.*

As governor of Texas from 1994 to 2000, George W. Bush presided over 152 executions—nearly one execution every two weeks after his election—a record for the state and more than any other elected official in the recent history of the United States at the time.

The executions were controversial primarily because George W. Bush had positioned himself as a "compassionate conservative" during his 2000 presidential campaign. But the reality of a pro-life, anti-euthanasia lover of Christ who was not only governor of a death penalty state but also instrumental in the deaths of 152 people—including two in one day, one of whom was described as mentally handicapped, and a record thirty-seven inmates in one year—seemed to represent a deep disconnect between what George W. Bush said he was and what he actually did.

There were also concerns about the validity and fairness of the Texas judicial system as well as Governor Bush's review process for capital punishment cases. A thirty-three-year-old man with the communication skills of a child of seven never had his mental handicap presented to the jury or the court who condemned him to death, nor had his trial lawyer called a mental health expert to testify on his behalf. It was not until his post-conviction lawyers took over his defense that anyone learned he and his ten siblings had been "beaten regularly with whips, water hoses, extension cords, wire hangers, and fan belts." He was executed in May 1997. In 1998, two Texas defendants were executed for crimes they had committed when they were seventeen or younger. In that same year, of the seventy juveniles on death row in the United States, twenty-six were being held in Texas. And then there was the very high-profile case of Karla Faye Tucker, the first woman to be executed in Texas since the Civil War.

In June 1983, Karla Faye Tucker and her boyfriend entered the home of Jerry Lynn Dean with the intention of stealing his motorcycle to settle a grudge. Dean and a female companion had been asleep in his bedroom, and by the end of the night, both were dead. Karla Faye Tucker had hacked Dean over "twenty times with one of his own tools—a three-foot-long pickax." The woman was also struck multiple times as she begged for her life. She was found with the pickax embedded in her chest.

In April 1984, a jury found Karla Faye Tucker guilty. A few days later, the court sentenced her to death by lethal injection. In 1987, she began an appeals process that lasted over ten years, which included the U.S. Supreme Court twice refusing to hear her case. And on February 3, 1998, George W. Bush placed a checkmark next to the word "Deny" on the clemency memo submitted to him by his general counsel and signed his name, thereby giving his consent to proceed with the execution of Karla Faye Tucker. Later that same night, and just eight minutes after lethal drugs had been injected into her veins, she was pronounced dead.

As governor, George W. Bush received a clemency memo, also called an execution summary, for death row inmates, usually on the day of the execution. Each memo was about three to seven pages long and consisted of a "brief description of the crime, a paragraph or two on the defendant's personal background, and a condensed legal history." Of the 152 execution summaries George W. Bush reviewed, fifty-seven had been prepared by Alberto R. Gonzales, whom Bush later appointed as his secretary of state and to the Texas Supreme Court when governor, then as White House Counsel when president. These memos, as well as an oral briefing with Alberto Gonzales also usually taking place the day of the execution and lasting no more than thirty minutes, were the primary sources of information Governor Bush used to decide whether someone would live or die.

He used the execution summaries to satisfy three standards: whether there were "new facts or evidence of which a jury was unaware"; whether the defendant had received "a fair hearing and full access to the courts"; and whether there was any doubt about the defendant's guilt. It was in this last requirement to determine clemency that I felt the biggest conflict between the man and the Christian.

Karla Faye Tucker's 1998 execution summary was one of the few that showed any evidence of significant discussion between George W. Bush and Alberto Gonzales. It was also the only instance where Alberto Gonzales included additional documentation. Karla Faye Tucker herself eliminated any doubt regarding two of Governor Bush's criteria for deciding clemency when she admitted to her crimes and said she had been treated fairly by the courts and deserved to be punished. Yet despite what appeared to be an easy case, George W. Bush wrote in his autobiography, *A Charge to Keep*, that he anguished over his decision, had trouble sleeping the night before her execution, and that reading his statement to deny clemency was "one of the hardest things" he had ever done. Karla Faye Tucker, like George W. Bush, had become a born-again Christian.

Karla Faye Tucker's parents divorced early in her childhood, and during the proceedings she learned she had been the result of an extra-marital affair. She first smoked pot at eight years old. "By the time she was thirteen, she was shooting heroin. A year later, she dropped out of high school and followed her mother into prostitution." It was her mother who first took her to a place frequented by men to "school" her in the act of selling her body. It took the next ten years for her behavior to escalate to murder. Karla Faye Tucker was twenty-three years old on June 13, 1983. That night, her years of pain, dysfunction, and addiction collided with a weekend drug and alcohol "orgy of methadone, heroin, Dilaudid, Valium, Placidyls, Somas, Wygesics, Percodan, Mandrax, marijuana, rum, and tequila" and ended the lives of three people—the two Karla Faye Tucker murdered and, eventually, her own by both spiritual transformation and lethal injection.

Karla Faye Tucker's spiritual conversion began the only way it could—with one foot planted firmly in the only life she had ever known and the other taking a step toward not just the unknown but the inconceivable when she stole a Bible during her first days in prison, not realizing it was free. Far from being a premeditated and conspicuous gesture in an effort to save her life by claiming to have "found Jesus," this furtive first step toward redemption seemed uncertain, even an embarrassment.

Over the next fourteen years in prison, she had a virtually spotless disciplinary record and was described by prison officials as a model prisoner. And there were those both in and outside the prison who believed she had achieved not only a successful rehabilitation, but also an authentic spiritual transformation.

As her execution date approached, Karla Fay Tucker had many supporters, including the homicide detective who had originally recommended she receive the death penalty for her crimes. Pat Robertson, founder of the Christian Coalition and usually an advocate of the death penalty, said she should be spared to be able to preach God's word to other prisoners. Pope John Paul appealed for a "humanitarian gesture" on her behalf, as he had for several other U.S. death row inmates. Appeals for clemency also came in from the United Nations, the European Parliament, Italian Prime Minister Romano Prodi, the World Council of Churches, and one of George W. Bush's own daughters.

But George W. Bush repeatedly cited a Texas statute that says a governor can do nothing more than grant a one-time thirty-day reprieve to a death row inmate unless the Board of Pardons and Paroles (BPP) has recommended commuting the sentence. The governor appoints BPP members to six-year rotating terms, and by the end of his governorship, George W. Bush had appointed all eighteen members. And did, in fact, intervene with the board in the Orange Socks case, so called because these were the only items of clothing on the unidentified woman when her body was found. After Henry Lee Lucas was sentenced to death in 1984 for the murder, two successive Texas state attorneys general concluded he had been wrongly convicted since he wasn't in the state at the time. Unwilling to execute a man for a murder he didn't commit, Governor Bush got word to the BPP before it had even sent him a recommendation. In return, the BPP approved the governor's predisposition by commuting the death sentence by a 17–1 vote. George W. Bush's intervention seemed to prove his assertion that he takes each case seriously because it's a matter of life and death. But to me, it also proved that it was within his power to commute a sentence or otherwise prevent an execution, which he confirms in his autobiography: "I guess I could have tried to tell the board how to vote. The members were, after all, mostly my appointees."

However, clemency for Karla Faye Tucker was unlikely. Not only was she guilty, no one on Texas' death row had ever been pardoned based on religious conversion. Of the thirty-six pardons that have been granted to Texas death row inmates since the death penalty was reinstated in 1976, not one has been solely for humanitarian reasons.

It took me years to question why a Christian governor wouldn't have reformed, or at least challenged, these positions. And years to try to understand why those most anxious for her death were also those who most vocally claimed to love and follow the path of Jesus, among them former Texas Christian Coalition president Dick Weinhold:

> This case has two main themes. One is compassion, and one is consequences. I have a lot of compassion for Karla Faye Tucker. She seems to have strong testimony. Her salvation and conversion seem to be . . . very genuine. And her life seems to really have undergone a transformation. So I'm delighted. That is great. . . . [However],

the consequences of her crime call for her death. I don't believe the compassion side should overrule the consequences in this case.

The consequences of her crime call for her death.

By the time he was crucified, Jesus hadn't slept for nearly thirty-six hours and had walked two and a half miles from his trial before Caiaphas and the Sanhedrin to Pontius Pilate to Herod Antipas then back again to Pilate, who gave the command to have Jesus flogged in preparation for his execution.

At a wooden post, soldiers stripped Jesus naked and bound his arms high above his head leaving his body exposed from his neck to his heels. Two Roman lictors—those charged with carrying out the sentences of criminals—positioned themselves on either side of Jesus. Preparing to alternate blows, each gripped a flagrum, a wooden-handled whip consisting of nine thick leather thongs about six to seven feet long. Attached to the end of each thong were two small balls of lead, and attached to the lead balls were ragged pieces of sheep and cattle bone. The sharp bone fragments of a single thong could leave an open wound two inches long and nearly an inch deep that would require about twenty stitches to close. With the first snap of the whip, the pounding lead balls caused deep bruising as the bone fragments cut into the surface layers of flesh. With each succeeding blow, the lead balls and bone tore deeper into the open wounds, first producing oozing blood from capillaries and veins, then spurting blood from arteries as the thongs ripped into the muscles in his neck, shoulders, arms, back, buttocks, and the back of his legs, calves, and heels. The lashes continued shredding his skin until it hung in ribbons and pulverizing his flesh even though it had become an unrecognizable mass of blood and tissue. As long as it stopped short of death, it was left to the lictors to decide the number of lashes one would receive.

Soldiers then tied the crossbeam, upon which Jesus would hang, onto his shoulders forcing him to carry his own deathbed. With the over one-hundred-pound beam biting into his lacerated shoulders,

Jesus, two thieves, and the execution detail of Roman soldiers led by a centurion began the 650-yard journey to the crucifixion site called Golgotha, or Place of the Skull. Exhausted, dehydrated, in shock, suffering from blood loss, and unable to withstand the weight of the crossbeam, Jesus fell. The centurion, intent on keeping the procession moving, commanded North African Simon of Cyrene to carry the crossbeam for Jesus as he followed.

At Golgotha, the Roman soldiers stretched Jesus' arms across the crossbeam now lying on the ground, felt for the depression in the back of his hands, and drove through the blunt, square-ended iron nails. Using a tool similar to a pitchfork, the soldiers raised the crossbeam onto the upright post already in place, which bore the inscription, "Jesus, King of the Jews." Then, placing one foot over the other and pressing them into the post, a soldier pounded one final nail through both feet and deep into the wood.

Hanging by his hands, the sagging weight of Jesus' body threatened his breathing. To exhale, Jesus had to relieve the weight and create room in his lungs and diaphragm by pulling up with his spiked hands and pushing down against the nail through his feet, which also caused his flayed back to scrape against the splintered wooden post. Since one speaks when exhaling, the words Jesus spoke on the cross were brief, costly, and therefore, to many Christians, so precious not one should be taken lightly.

A common method to end a crucifixion was by crucifracture, or breaking the bones in the legs to prevent one from lifting himself up to exhale, which resulted in suffocation within minutes. Soldiers would repeatedly swing a spear like a baseball bat to break the fibulas and the large, strong shinbones. The two thieves crucified with Jesus were subjected to crucifracture, but when the Roman centurion came to Jesus, he found he was already dead. Wanting to be certain, the centurion drove his spear between Jesus' ribs and into his heart, and the wound poured out blood and water.

The Bible records the few sentences Jesus spoke before he died. The first of these he said as he looked down upon the soldiers who crucified him: "Father, forgive them for they know not what they do."

Surely the consequences of this crime, the crucifixion of an innocent man, would call for death. Yet, Jesus' last words did not reflect anger or retribution. He did not ask God to avenge his death. He did not command his mother or the disciple weeping at his feet to rise up and slay his distracted executioners, who were throwing dice for Jesus' robe just a few feet away. Not only would his executioners be allowed to live, they would be forgiven.

I don't believe the compassion side should overrule the consequences in this case.

Jesus' message as he hung on the cross was clear: *Compassion overrules everything.* In his autobiography, George W. Bush wrote, "Some advocates of life will challenge why I oppose abortion yet support the death penalty; to me, it's the difference between innocence and guilt." During Jesus' life and through his death, was there any liar, thief, torturer, persecutor, adulterer, or murderer he excluded from his mercy? No, not one. He never asked God to first determine guilt or innocence, knowing that all had caused—or eventually would cause—harm. He only asked that they be forgiven.

We all have the ability to be vengeful. However, Jesus showed us that the human need for vengeance should never overrule the spiritual act of compassion. Not only is being forgiving and compassionate what is required of Christians, it is what we are all called to be as more enlightened humans.

However, forgiveness does not mean there are no consequences. All of life is based on consequences, the rhythm of cause and effect. None of us will escape the consequences of both the good and the harm we cause, no matter how hard we try. But any consequences within our earthly power should only be those that will achieve the greatest benefit, not only for the individual, but for all of humanity.

Consequences are meant to transform a life, to bring it closer to its most loving, healing, and humble place, not contribute to more anger, vengeance, and violence. Guilt is not a disqualifier for forgiveness, redemption, and transformation but a requirement. The guiltless don't need redemption, and the pure don't need transformation. It is for all thoughts, words, and acts against humanity and God that transformation exists. But no one can transform if he or she is dead.

Karla Faye Tucker was willing to accept her consequences, even if it meant her death, but she believed that allowing her to live would serve a greater purpose.

> I see people in here in the prison where I am who are here for horrible crimes and for lesser crimes, who to this day are still acting out in violence and hurting others with no concern for another life or their own life. I can reach out to these girls and try and help them change before they walk out of this place and hurt someone else.

Karla Faye Tucker was not asking to be released from prison, but to be allowed to spend the rest of her days there telling her story; one that showed that redemption is possible and Christianity can transform even the most broken lives. This was more than telling searching souls at a church service or prayer meeting on the outside about the power of God to transform. This was a thirty-nine-year-old double murderer locked in a maximum-security prison for the rest of her life reaching out to other inmates who were on the verge of escalating their lives beyond control unless they were shown the way and a reason to have a different and more purposeful life. She could have shown them how valuable their lives were and how each of them was an important and irreplaceable part of this world. She could have caused them to feel—probably for the first time in their lives—love, understanding, and forgiveness so that they in turn could give this to others rather than the hatred, rage, and violence they'd always known. They would have listened because she had once been, in many ways, just like them—lost, alone, abused, addicted, angry, vengeful, a criminal. And in one way was still just like them—an inmate.

We will never know how many prisoners' lives she could have changed before they were set free to take the hard-earned possessions or the cherished lives of others—maybe your possessions or your loved one's life. We are only left with the question: Wasn't the transformation of even one inmate, which in turn would have meant keeping the victims of his or her future crimes safe from harm, worth saving Karla Faye Tucker's life?

In *The Alchemist*, Paulo Coelho wrote, "Anyone who interferes with the Personal Legend of another thing will never discover his own." If it is true that George W. Bush let perish one of the redeemed, someone chosen by God to heal and transform others, not only did he interfere with God's plan for Karla Faye Tucker, he is also responsible for all those inmates whose transformations never occurred because she was not alive to help them achieve it, as well as all their future victims.

One can become so focused on someone else's accountability that he forgets about his own. However, the universe will always hold accountable anyone who contributes to the dysfunction of a person, community, nation, or planet. It constantly puts us all into situations that allow us to back up what we say we are with our behavior. Those who say they are filled with compassion and forgiveness will be called upon to consistently be compassionate and forgiving. Those who talk about morals and values will be asked to prove they have them. Those who claim to have inner peace and balanced lives must demonstrate they have actually done the work to earn them. And those calling themselves Christians, Jews, Buddhists, Muslims, Hindus, Yogis, or followers of any religion or spiritual discipline must show it is true, show that their path and practice is authentic in every way, but especially when faced with the most difficult choices and circumstances.

As governor of Texas, George W. Bush was put in the position to show us all what a Christian looks like 152 times. As president, George W. Bush was again asked to choose between compassion and retribution on September 11, 2001. On that day, he could have stood before the world and, following in the footsteps of Jesus, forgiven the nineteen hijackers who intentionally murdered nearly 3,000 innocent Americans, or he could have launched a tidal wave of revenge in two countries that increased the death toll of innocent men, women, and children to horrifying numbers.

Time after time, George W. Bush was asked by his God not only to become a great leader, but to greatly contribute to the healing of a life, a nation, and a world through forgiveness and compassion. You may not have liked the choice of forgiving the nineteen hijackers, and he may not have gotten re-elected in 2004. Also, forgiveness alone wouldn't have prevented another attack or addressed a president's responsibility to protect American lives. But this was not something he was being called upon to do against his will. Forgiveness and compassion is the path George W. Bush freely chose when he declared himself a Christian. The rules of Christianity are clear. And regardless of the situation, no one gets to change them. Any attempt to do so is an admission that Christianity works in theory but not real life, which then makes the Bible nothing more than a fairy tale.

I know it is much easier to criticize a president than be one. I also know there is a lot of goodness in a man who wants to love his God so deeply. From this goodness will come the desire and ability to heal rather than destroy. From this goodness will come the deepest understanding that we all can transform lives, our nation, and this world by putting into unambiguous action our spiritual paths, and mending what we each have broken.

No one but George W. Bush knows the ways he was and will continue to be asked by his God to more authentically live the words of Jesus Christ. It may be a call to abolish capital punishment nationwide. There are only two first-world countries where the death penalty is a legal form of punishment—Japan and the United States. Which means America, in this instance, is no different from Iraq, Iran, North Korea, Afghanistan, Pakistan, Syria, Saudi Arabia, Lebanon, China, Cuba, and the Sudan. It may be prison reform. You cannot expect someone to change unless you show him, by example, what it is he should change to. And he can be shown through information and education, through his value and purpose for being, and through the lives of those inmates who have successfully found their paths to transformation. Give him a way to understand who he is and why, and the opportunity to be a relevant and contributing member of humanity while in prison, rather than someone who simply exists because his basic needs are being met. I do not presume to know the complexities of prison life. But I do know that if you can find the way to transform someone who can rape and strangle a woman to death, then tie her two young and still very much alive daughters to their beds, drench the house in gasoline, and light a match, you will also have found the way to transform all those others you think the world is better off without.

Words are only what you hope to be. Actions are what you are. But what allows one to speak so eloquently of compassion and forgiveness, yet disconnect from these sacred intentions so completely when the time comes to put them into action? While the details may differ, the answers are always the same—one being avoidance. Simply find a way to distance yourself from the consequences of and accountability for your choices. It is easy to see a criminal as nothing more than his crime when you choose not to personally visit him to put a face, a voice, a soul, the whole story to the name before putting him to death. It is easy to disconnect from your decision to execute another human being when you don't have to watch him die. It is easy to justify cruel, even fatal interrogation techniques when you don't have to conduct or witness the interrogation yourself.

In 2007, as the debate over whether waterboarding was torture or simply another interrogation technique continued—its proponents including those who had neither seen nor experienced what they endorsed—there emerged a soldier who could lay claim to it all. Malcolm W. Nance, a former Master Instructor and Chief of Training at the U.S. Navy Survival, Evasion, Resistance, and Escape School (SERE), not only personally conducted, witnessed, and supervised hundreds of waterboarding sessions, as a member of the SERE staff he was subjected to the procedure to its fullest extent.

In a piece written for smallwarsjournal.com, Malcolm Nance brought his considerable background in counterterrorism, terrorism intelligence, and terrorist tactics and procedures to the waterboarding debate. When it became public that George W. Bush had authorized waterboarding as an interrogation technique, proponents pointed out that it was the methods from our own Army and Navy SERE interrogation manuals that the CIA was using on its terror suspects. What Malcolm Nance revealed was that the manuals were designed to describe the techniques and prepare American soldiers for what could be used *on* them by despotic regimes; the techniques were not meant to be used *by* them. For Americans, training—not torture—is the only purpose for water-boarding. American leaders and soldiers are to be aware of and ready for whatever those without honor and conscience could subject them to, but Americans were never supposed to become like them.

Malcolm Nance says the interrogation techniques are not dangerous when used as a training exercise for short periods of time. However, when used on an unsuspecting prisoner, especially in combination with other methods, not only is waterboarding terrifying, it also "shocks the conscience," which our statute forbids. From his personal experience Malcolm Nance described that, because the lungs fill with water, waterboarding is not a "simulated" drowning. It is an actual drowning. How much the victim is to drown depends on how quickly the interrogator gets his desired result—meaning, acceptable answers to his questions—and the strength of the subject's resistance.

As devastating as experiencing a hostile waterboarding is, Malcolm Nance also says most couldn't withstand conducting or even viewing a high-intensity interrogation—because torture cripples the torturer as well as its witnesses.

> One has to overcome basic human decency to endure watching or causing the effects [of torture]. The brutality would force you into a personal moral dilemma between humanity and hatred. It would leave you to question the meaning of what it is to be an American.

To be considered great, a leader must always be accountable for and never shield himself from the consequences of his choices. For a president who authorizes controversial and potentially fatal interrogation techniques, this means he must not only publicly disclose it, he must also watch each interrogation session on every prisoner considered important enough in our fight against terrorism to require such treatment. For a governor of a pro-death-penalty state, this means he must witness every execution that bears his signature as it is carried out.

Because one will neither run from nor keep secret anything he truly knows to be reasonable, acceptable, moral, or honorable.

Another way to disconnect the words forgiveness and compassion from their practice is through justification. By saying, "Unfortunately, some criminals are beyond rehabilitation," George W. Bush was able to justify his part in the death of Saddam Hussein, the waterboarding of prisoners in our war on terror, and the executions of 152 Texas inmates by declaring them incapable of redemption. But if you believe that through God all things are possible, then you must believe that *anyone* can transform. And herein lies the one universal spiritual truth: Transformation is God's gift to every one of us, not just those of one religion or spiritual discipline, or those any one person deems worthy or capable. Everyone can have the scales fall from his eyes, can stand and walk, can rise from the dead. Everyone can forgive and be forgiven of even the most heinous acts. Everyone can heal. All it takes is his pure intention and just one person with authentic love and forgiveness to show the way.

The way is not retribution or execution. It is not destructive words or violent acts. It is not bombs, weapons, or war. The way is when your hands and feet are driven through with nails, your side torn open by the thrust of a spear, your head dripping with blood as thorns pierce through to the bone, your heart broken by betrayal, bigotry, hatred, abandonment, rejection, ridicule—you love and you forgive. This is what Jesus, Muhammad, Buddha, and Krishna taught. Just because we haven't yet found the way to heal the most broken among us, this doesn't mean the way doesn't exist. All we lack are those willing and courageous enough to keep looking.

Don't think I don't know how naïve and impractical this sounds. Angrily and forcefully standing up for what you believe, no matter how wayward it may be, appears principled and honorable. Standing in love and forgiveness while someone ridicules you, shames you, blames you, lies about you, steals from you, or is violent toward you, your family, your community, or your country looks weak and cowardly and stupid.

And don't think I haven't asked many times: How do you love Hitler away? How do you look in the eyes of a murderer or rapist or pedophile and not only forgive, but also love? How do you believe in non-violence without appearing tolerant of abusive, destructive, or deadly behavior? How do you defend your principles, your country, your life without becoming like those who want to destroy them? How do you stand in the presence of verbal arsonists, whose words are intentionally meant to destroy everyone and everything they are threatened by, and feel compassion? How do you reconcile protection with peace?

I believe finding the answers to these questions is the reason we are here. And to one day have more of those who live and govern by the answers than those who don't. On that day, we will have a world far different from the one we have today. On that day, we will truly be God-filled instead of godless.

At its heart, ours is a good and giving country. The wonderful things we have done to help others in times of hardship should only encourage and embolden us to look deeply and honestly into what we could have done better, or shouldn't have done at all. Greatness wants to do right and know goodness. It acknowledges and repairs what it has broken. It does not fear correction, improvement, or change. And it does not cover mistakes with myth.

The clinic had its own way of describing the law of cause and effect: Past behavior decides the present, just as the choices we make today determine the future. Meaning, the only way to understand who we are today, and how to change, is to look at what was done in the past. With individual dysfunction and healing, the historical perspective is through one's childhood. With national or global dysfunction and healing, it means going back as far as necessary until the connections and consequences lead us to understand and acknowledge our contribution to the world we have today. Just as one must want to know who he or she is in order to change and heal, we must also want to examine our actions—as a family, a community, and a nation—and the consequences of those actions on the rest of the world.

Over the years, both in and outside the clinic, I have been continually reminded of the violence we do to ourselves through dysfunctional thinking and behavior. That violence is not contained. The harm we do to ourselves, we do to everyone around us. Just how many that includes depends on how many lives we are connected to. The dysfunctional behavior of an individual will touch family, friends, and co-workers. The dysfunctional behavior of a nation will touch millions.

I wasn't out of the clinic long when I realized that three places were always in the news—Africa, Afghanistan, and Pakistan—and never for anything good. The more comfortable I became with examining my own behavior and its consequences, the more natural it felt that my healing within would lead me to examine the violent world we live in, and ask whether our nation contributed to it, either knowingly or unknowingly, and what we could have done differently to create a different result.

The extent of Africa's suffering—the Sudan, Somalia, Uganda, Ethiopia, Niger, Chad, Zimbabwe, Sierra Leone, Central African Republic, Guinea-Bissau, Union of the Comoros—overshadows its beauty and its promise. But it is the belief of one senior researcher for Human Rights Watch that "if you want peace in Africa, then you need to deal with the biggest country right at its heart," the Democratic Republic of the Congo (DRC).

The DRC is a nation of over seventy million people and has been called one of the "worst places on earth," the "worst place in the world to do business," the "rape capital of the world," and the "ultimate hellhole." And its only crime seems to be that it is rich in all the things we consider valuable.

The Congo's soil is said to contain every mineral listed on the periodic table in concentrations high enough to make a mineralogist weak in the knees. It holds the world's largest supply of high-grade copper; sixty percent of its cobalt; eighty percent of its coltan; thirty percent of its diamond reserves; millions of tons of zinc, manganese, and uranium (Congolese uranium was used in the atomic bombs dropped on Hiroshima and Nagasaki); and two major gold sources: the 711-square-mile Kilo-Moto greenstone gold belt in Oriental province, and the 130-mile Twangiza-Namoya gold belt in Kivi. According to *African Business* magazine, the total wealth of the DRC is estimated to be $24 trillion—the equivalent of the gross domestic product of Europe and the United States combined.

Take a minute and think what you would do to acquire the wealth you have always imagined. Then know that the men, women, and children of the DRC experience daily the unimaginable at the hands of those who value money over human life.

Nearly three-fourths of the DRC's economy relies on mining. However, the country neither benefits from nor has access to as much as forty percent of the revenues generated by its mineral resources. The bulk of the mining activity is located in the eastern and southeastern parts of the country—areas under the control of rebel groups who fled there after carrying out the Rwandan genocide, a mass killing of an estimated 800,000 to one million Tutsis and moderate Hutus by extremist Hutu militias in just one hundred days, and which contributed to the First Congo War from 1996 to 1997. Then, in August 1998, barely enough time for the innocent millions caught in the middle to take a breath let alone recover, the Second Congo War began.

With an estimated four million people having died from war-related causes, the five-year-long Second Congo War has the appalling distinction of being the deadliest conflict since WWII. Despite a peace agreement signed in 2003, the fighting continues in the eastern part of the country. In this region, armed rebel groups, local militia, and the Congo's own military prey upon the unprotected civilians without fear of punishment, killing—along with rampant disease and malnutrition "that wouldn't exist in peaceful times"—approximately 45,000 each month.

Continuing the fight against Rwanda's Tutsie government gives the Hutu militias the perfect means to exploit the DRC: Use the rebellion against Rwanda as a cover to plunder the Congo's natural resources and use the natural resources to finance the rebellion. But as always, it is the innocent millions who pay the highest price by suffering indiscriminate killings, mass rapes, mutilations, and forced child-soldier recruitment in the areas under control, taking the Congo's plight far beyond money or politics to one affecting its humanity.

Throughout the DRC, armed rebels and militia groups use sexual violence against women as a weapon of war in an effort to intimidate and coerce their male family members. According to a 2011 study by the *American Journal of Public Health*, more than 1,100 women and girls are raped each day in the Congo, and the sexual violence is carried out with extraordinary brutality. Rapists use objects such as gun butts, knives, and bayonets. They shoot bullets up women's vaginas. Gang rape is common and done in public for "maximum humiliation." The United Nations Population Fund has estimated that 200,000 Congolese women and girls have been victims of sexual violence since 1998. Roughly fifty percent of the rape victims do not have access to medical treatment, and less than two percent of the perpetrators are brought to court. But it isn't enough for grown men armed with weapons to terrorize women and girls. They also traumatize young boys through forced recruitment into their militias and rebel groups.

Child soldiers are well known throughout the continent. Nearly half of the world's 300,000 child soldiers are in Africa. There may be as many as 30,000 child soldiers in the Congo alone, where it is believed "armed militia groups are now targeting entire schools" for forced recruitment. An estimated thirty to forty percent are girls.

Most child soldiers are between fifteen and eighteen years old, though some are as young as seven. Those who are not fighters are used as runners, scouts, porters, sex slaves, cooks, or spies. Child soldiers are also "subjected to brutal initiation and punishment rituals" and hard labor. Many are given drugs and alcohol to break down their normal psychological barriers against committing or witnessing atrocities, such as rape and murder.

There are several reasons the practice continues. One is that children are cheap and easily manipulated; they eat little and can be molded into obedient and effective fighters. Another is that they are available; in the areas subjected to persistent conflict, there is a shortage of adult males. Also, due to the proliferation of light weaponry, young children are now able to carry and use small arms. Still another, more chilling reason is that they are expendable. But most agree that the primary reason armed rebels and militias recruit children as soldiers is "because they can."

There is not much about the Congo's current environment to feel good about. It ranks 168th out of 183 countries on the Corruption Perceptions Index, which rates the level of corruption perceived to exist among public officials and politicians. The Human Development Index—based on a country's education, income, life expectancy, and standard of living statistics—places the DRC dead last: 187th out of 187 countries. Poverty is widespread; over seventy percent are living on approximately one dollar a day. Also, the Congo has perhaps the most extensive collection of known and developing infectious diseases in the world, including plague, malaria, tuberculosis, sleeping sickness, river blindness, hookworm, and typhoid. Many in the sub-Sahara are harboring two or more parasites, which can affect cognitive functions and the ability to earn a living, even result in death.

Some say it is not the U.N. that will eventually heal the Congo, but its own future generations. It is they, through grassroots organizations, who will establish peace and prosperity in their country. But I wonder, with the many traumas the Congolese children continue to suffer—rape, murder, poverty, starvation, disease, illiteracy, forced recruitment, abandonment, shame—what will be left of those who survive? And how will they know how to heal, to lead, to change a country when all they know, all they've been shown, is anger, vengeance, and violence?

You may be asking, *What does this have to do with the United States?* Here is the answer: Throughout the Cold War, the United States delivered over $1.5 billion in weaponry to Africa, which "helped build the arsenals of eight of the nine governments directly involved" in the Congo wars. Between 1991 and 1998, U.S. training and weapons delivered to Africa totaled more than $227 million. It was also in 1998 that "Africa suffered eleven major armed conflicts, more than any other continent." And "U.S. Special Forces have trained military personnel from at least thirty-four of Africa's [fifty-four] nations, including troops fighting on *both sides*" of the Congo Wars. Rwanda was importing U.S. weapons as late as 1993, one year before the Rwandan genocide.

In 2010, hoping to contribute to its healing, the U.S. provided $306 million in aid to the DRC. The United States is also the largest donor to the U.N. peacekeeping mission in the Congo, contributing nearly one-third of its $1 billion annual budget. But more than three decades earlier, in 1976, former President Jimmy Carter pointed to a contradiction in U.S. foreign policy that still applies today and that no one, regardless of party affiliation, should take lightly: "We cannot have it both ways. We can't be both the world's leading champion of peace and the world's leading supplier of arms."

The United States has been the world's top weapons exporter for all but one year in the past twenty years. From 1986 to 1995, the U.S. delivered $42 billion in weaponry to parties at war worldwide. In 1993–1994, of the "significant ethnic and territorial conflicts," forty-five out of fifty—or *ninety percent*—"received U.S. weaponry or military technology in the period leading up to the conflict." In 2008, the Bush administration launched a surge in weapons deals due to the wars in Iraq and Afghanistan and the instability in North Korea and Iran. That year, the Department of Defense agreed to "sell or transfer more than $32 billion in weapons and other military equipment to foreign governments." It is these weapons orders, continuing several years into the future, that could be considered George W. Bush's most lasting legacy.

One frequent argument in support of aggressive arms activity is that it creates stability in unstable environments. Or as one Air Force undersecretary stated, "This is not about being gunrunners. This is about building a more secure world." But the consequences of the arms and training the United States provided much of the world during the Cold War—particularly to the Afghan rebels in the 1980s—now force us to ask: Is this true? Does the proliferation of weapons create a more stable and secure world?

Afghanistan has been in a continuous state of war for over thirty years. The Saur Revolution in 1978 brought back to power the communist Democratic Party of Afghanistan and its socialist agenda, which included state-sponsored atheism in spite of a population deeply immersed in Islam. In July of the following year, President Jimmy Carter signed the first directive to supply secret financial aid to Muslim rebels, the Mujahideen, who opposed the pro-Soviet regime in Afghanistan as well as its anti-Islamic policies. And on December 27, 1979, the Soviet Union landed 80,000 troops in Afghanistan, launching a war that lasted nine years.

President Ronald Reagan increased U.S. financial aid to the Mujahideen, whom he called "freedom fighters," and included weapons and training. Averaging $600 million in funding per year—nearly $7.5 billion total—the CIA covert program known as Operation Cyclone became one of the longest and most expensive ever authorized.

The CIA did not deal directly with the Mujahideen but instead used an intermediary, Pakistan's Inter-Services Intelligence (ISI), as a conduit for the financial aid and weaponry. Another function of the CIA–ISI alliance was to expand the jihad beyond the Afghan rebels and recruit a force of militant Islamists from around the world to fight against the Soviets. The ISI—with assistance from the CIA, the U.S. military, and Britain's MI6—trained over 100,000 Islamic militants in Pakistani bases and camps between 1986 and 1992. Among them, an estimated 35,000 militants from forty-three countries fought alongside the Afghan rebels. Though prone to factionalism and infighting, the jihadis had one thing in common at the time: They were all anti-Soviet.

If a primary goal of Operation Cyclone was to use Pakistan to unite jihadis worldwide to fight against the Soviets and promote their militant culture, the creation of new madrassahs was an essential part of it. Madrassahs were originally established as centers of learning for future Islamic scholars and clerics. But the CIA–ISI union forged during the Soviet invasion was a driving force in the escalation of madrassahs in Pakistan, which grew from 700 in 1980 to approximately 20,000 by 2000.

Public health and education were routinely a low priority for the Pakistani government and both received little funding. This put an education out of reach for most of the population, especially those living in rural areas and the poor. And if those in power cared so little for their own people, they would care even less for the millions of Afghan refugees pouring into Pakistan after the Soviet invasion forced them from their homes.

The Soviet invasion of Afghanistan created "one of the biggest humanitarian crises of modern history, with over [six] million refugees fleeing to Pakistan and Iran and another two million displaced internally." Poor, homeless, and unemployed, many Afghan refugees saw Pakistani madrassahs as the answer to a prayer. Funded by the United States and its close ally Saudi Arabia, madrassahs provided not only schooling for refugee children, but food, clothing, and lodging. They also acted as orphanages for those children who had lost parents in the Soviet–Afghan war. But since madrassahs were not subject to state supervision, each school determined for itself what it would teach—and what it would preach.

One consequence of the CIA–ISI plan to unite and train militant Islamists to fight the Soviets in Afghanistan was that a small but potent number of madrassahs in Pakistan came under the control of extremist Muslim religious and political groups, who used them to "teach a distorted view of Islam" and display a steady stream of images of Muslim repression around the world. This militarization of madrassahs had meaningful consequences for Americans. The graduating classes from hundreds of militant madrassahs eventually became effective recruiters of future terrorists. The 55th Arab Brigade, "an elite guerrilla" coalition of foreigners recruited, sponsored, and trained by Osama bin Laden's al-Qaeda, was integrated into the Taliban army from 1997 to 2001; the brigade members were products of Pakistan's madrassahs. One of the most popular and influential madrassahs, Dur-ul-Uloom Haqqania, includes among its alumni most of the Afghan Taliban leadership. Its student body, starting at age six, consists of 1,500 boarding students and 1,000 day students. Over 15,000 applicants from poor families compete for the 400 available openings each year.

In 1985, new Soviet president Mikhail Gorbachev brought domestic and foreign reforms to his country, which included the withdrawal of Soviet troops from Afghanistan. Once the Soviets removed the last of its forces in early 1989, the United States was no longer interested in

Afghanistan. It decided not to help rebuild the devastated and war-ravaged country, ensuring that the people of Afghanistan—already among the most impoverished and uneducated in the world—stayed that way.

Although Afghanistan was the recipient of humanitarian aid after Soviet withdrawal, much of it went to support the Mujahideen as they continued to battle the country's communist government. The United States greatly reduced its financial assistance to Pakistan in 1993, then stopped it altogether and imposed economic sanctions after the country began nuclear testing in 1998, even though the U.S. had helped Pakistan obtain nuclear capability.

In 1974, India carried out its first nuclear weapons test, code-named Smiling Buddha. In response, Pakistan's prime minister Zulfikar Ali Bhutto declared, "If India builds the bomb, we will eat grass and leaves for a thousand years, even go hungry, but we will get one of our own." In just a few years, events unfolded that allowed them to do just that. The Soviet Union invaded Afghanistan, and President Reagan—who frequently proclaimed his commitment to the Nuclear Non-Proliferation Treaty—ignored Pakistan's single-minded quest to acquire nuclear weapons and sold its government forty F-16 fighter jets, which were configured to drop a nuclear bomb; he ignored the millions of dollars of "restricted, high-tech materials" that had been purchased in the United States and used to assemble Pakistan's nuclear arsenal; and he ignored the two laws that cut off all economic and military aid to any non-nuclear country attempting to import nuclear materials from the United States, one of which specifically applied to Pakistan. The Pressler Amendment to the Foreign Assistance Act required President Reagan to certify every year that Pakistan did not have nuclear weapons. Without certification, Pakistan could not receive U.S. financial aid. And without giving Pakistan financial aid, President Reagan could not use the country as an intermediary to get funds, supplies, and weapons to the Mujahideen in Afghanistan in their fight against the Soviets. As Seymour Hersh described in the *New Yorker,*

> The certification process became farcical in the last
> years of the Reagan Administration, whose yearly

certification—despite explicit American intelligence about Pakistan's nuclear weapons program—was seen as little more than a payoff to the Pakistani leadership for its support in Afghanistan.

We may never know just how much U.S. money given to Pakistan during the Soviet invasion was used for its nuclear weapons program. But we do know that President George H. W. Bush was ready to sell another sixty F-16 jets to Pakistan before CIA operative Richard Barlow blew the whistle on the illegal sale in an incredible story of honor and great self-sacrifice. We do know that Pakistan sold its nuclear weapons technology to Iran, Libya, and North Korea. We do know that President George W. Bush continued to compensate Pakistan in exchange for its help in our war on terror. And we do know that the WMD were in Pakistan, not Iraq.

When the prosperity that fell to Pakistan due to the massive influx of wartime U.S. aid was squandered by widespread corruption and poor governance, education continued to be a victim of the country's subsequent economic decline, which only gave new life to the madrassahs. The removal of U.S. financial support did not end the proliferation of madrassahs in Pakistan. After nearly twenty years of funding and encouragement, the schools had perfected their role as purveyors and recruiters for their militant message.

The plight of the Congo led me to ask what becomes of children who know only violence and suffering. I found the answer in Afghanistan and Pakistan. Captain Tarlan Eyvazov, a Soviet soldier during the war in Afghanistan, unknowingly predicted the future of its refugee children— the formation of the Taliban and its relationship with al-Qaeda—when he said, "Children born in Afghanistan at the start of the war . . . have been brought up in war conditions; this is their way of life."

Poverty, illiteracy, lack of health care, and decades of violence reinforced from an early age have created what some call a "lost generation" of Afghan children. In their book *Afghanistan: Mullah, Marx, and Mujahid*, Ralph H. Magnus and Eden Naby described the consequences of this, not just for Afghanistan, but for us all:

Truly this became a generation that sacrificed itself. A world that does not help to reconstruct their country and find meaning for their loss may pay the price in warriors for hire, which disrupts not just Afghan tranquility, but stability in many corners of the world.

There is some debate as to which action by the United States most contributed to the world we have today: a war in Afghanistan against al-Qaeda and the Taliban over a decade old, a global war on terror that may never end, and nuclear weapons in one of the most unstable regions on the planet. It could have been the strategy to unite, train, and arm militant rebels from around the world. It could have been the choice of several administrations to either aid or ignore Pakistan's pursuit of nuclear weapons. Still others believe that the presence of the United States in Afghanistan before the Russian invasion was actually a premeditated attempt to draw the Soviets into a war they could neither win nor afford. This is based on an interview President Jimmy Carter's national security advisor, Zbigniew Brzezinski, gave to a French news magazine in 1998, in which he is reported to have said that the covert CIA operation was intended to lure the Soviet Union into an "Afghan trap" that would have resulted in miring them in their own Vietnam War. In denying the accuracy of the quote, Zbigniew Brzezinski said something I found even more interesting. While he agreed with President Reagan's decision to expand U.S. aid to the Mujahideen to include weapons and training because it was "important in hastening the end of the conflict" and the Cold War, he didn't believe our presence had enticed or encouraged the rebels to fight.

They would have continued fighting without our help because they were also getting a lot of money from the Persian Gulf and the Arab states, and they weren't going to quit. They didn't decide to fight because we urged them to. . . . In my view, the Afghans would have prevailed in the end anyway, because they had access to money, they had access to weapons, and they had the will to fight.

So, what if thirty years ago, as the Mujahideen fought, we had put the billions of dollars we gave them for war and weaponry—which Zbigniew Brzezinski contends they didn't need anyway—toward creating life-sustaining environments in Afghanistan and Pakistan, rather than contributing to their destruction through war, death, poverty, homelessness, and hopelessness? What if thirty years ago, our focus, our energy, and the billions of dollars we unconditionally gave to a Pakistani government desperate for money had come with a requirement: All of it must be used to transform lives and two countries into something greater through schools, universities, hospitals, homes, and a healthy infrastructure—which are true pre-emptive measures? What if thirty years ago, one full generation had been brought up in a nourishing atmosphere, had been given the freedom of choice between an existing madrassah and a different educational opportunity that would have brought into the world a new and vibrant population of Afghan and Pakistani doctors, teachers, artists, engineers, scientists, and responsible leaders who would have far outnumbered the future rebels and terrorists? What if this generation, now giving birth to the next, had vowed that education and compassion, not violence, would be their way of life? And what if, when the war had finally ended, we didn't walk away? Thirty years. One generation. Billions of dollars.

It was a mistake then for Ronald Reagan to mythologize the Mujahideen as "freedom fighters" to justify his purposes and deny their drug trafficking, repression of women, intolerance of dissenting beliefs, and tendency toward violence. And it is a mistake now to denigrate them as uncivilized, as savages, and as incapable of transformation. Because there was a time when Afghanistan's most violent and hardened people—the Pashtun ancestors of the Taliban—showed us differently by doing something the United States has never done: create a culture of non-violence.

Through the Congo and Afghanistan I learned how we have contributed to the world's violent present. But it was through a more unlikely source—the revenge-driven Pashtuns—that I found how we could have contributed greatly to its healing.

The Pashtun tribes have inhabited the inhospitable and treacherous mountain regions of current-day Afghanistan and Pakistan since at least the first millennium BC. For much of its history, the territory and its people have remained outside the control of any ruler or government. They instead used Pashtunwali, an unwritten code of ethics, to govern themselves. *Sabat* demands loyalty to one's family, friends, and fellow tribe members. *Tureh* is bravery against tyranny and the defending of one's name, property, and family—especially women—against dishonor. And then there is *badal*, the ruthless code of revenge. *Badal* obligates the Pashtun to avenge even the slightest insult. Once anything from disrespect to bloodshed occurs, only the complete annihilation of the offending party can settle the matter, and the responsibility for this is passed from father to son until it is accomplished. There is no escape from retaliation. For Pashtuns, a man who refuses to avenge an offense is not a man. To seek revenge, even if one dies as a result, is not just the honorable way, it is the only way. He must kill, even though only suffering follows. Children are left fatherless and traumatized; families distrust their neighbors; anger and violence control one half of every Pashtun life, while fear controls the other. Yet the myth of the "avenging hero" remains the primary source of Pashtun status and passion, despite it bonding them to unending tragedy and pain.

However, the British, through two Anglo-Afghan wars, provided the Pashtuns with plenty of reasons for exacting revenge. In the 1830s, Great Britain controlled India, the crown jewel and the "greatest source of wealth" in the British Empire. At the same time, Russia was making it clear it had its own interest in controlling more of Asia by conquering khanates and tribes on its southern border. Caught between these two powers and countries—India and Russia—was Afghanistan. Britain's greatest fear was that Russian expansion included India, and that Afghanistan would be the staging ground for the invasion. To prevent this, Great Britain decided to invade Afghanistan first, and in April 1839, its army marched into Kabul unchallenged.

For three decades following the end of the First Anglo-Afghan War, the Russians continued to advance toward Afghanistan, first annexing Tashkent and Samarkand, then subduing the ruler of Bukhara with a peace treaty. Not one to stand idly by as Russia inched closer to India, Britain sent frequent expeditions—called the Butcher and Bolt policy by critics—into the Pashtun's hills and shelled their fortresses, burned "their villages, and beat, flogged, and jailed" the Afghans by the thousands. During what may have passed for peaceful times, the British attempted to bribe the Pashtuns into submission. But nothing worked for very long.

In 1878, Britain formally invaded Afghanistan again. By the end of the war two years later, it had occupied much of the country and had secured a treaty that recognized Afghanistan's domestic sovereignty, but put the British in control of foreign affairs and various frontier areas, including the strategically essential Khyber Pass—the passage through the Hindu Kush mountain range considered the gateway to India. Unable to fully subjugate the Pashtun tribes, the British Empire simply used the treaty to cut their homeland into pieces.

Into this life, in 1890, was born Abdul Ghaffar Khan. He was descended from Pashtun farmers who had settled in Afghanistan's fertile Peshawar Valley, located at the east end of the Khyber Pass. His father, Behram Khan, was the chief of Utmanzai, a village about twenty miles north of Peshawar and whose tribe, the Muhammadzais (sons of Muhammad), was smaller than most but generally prosperous and peaceful. Behram Kahn himself was considered wealthy, owning all the neighboring fields stretching along the river Swat. But Behram Kahn would give to Ghaffar, his youngest son, something much more valuable than land.

In 1901, Peshawar, including Behram Khan's village, and four other districts became known as the North-West Frontier Province under the control of a British chief commissioner. The province was further dissected into three geographic groups: the Agencies in the north, the settled districts—where Ghaffar Khan resided—between the Indus River and the hills, and the free areas along the western border, where hill tribes were left to govern themselves under Pashtunwali.

One purpose for creating the North-West Frontier Province was to further insulate India from a Russian invasion. Another was to better control the unruly Afghan hill tribes by isolating them. Far from a Pashtun homeland, Ghaffar Khan grew up in this newly formed province—now a British military post and police state.

Ghaffar Khan's life was steeped in contrast. On one side he was surrounded by British conflict and occupation, foreign-imposed borders dividing his country and its people, and the Pashtuns' relentless code of revenge. On the other was his father's deep commitment to forgiveness. Behram Khan believed honor could be obtained in ways that were more enduring and more in keeping with God's will than *badal*. For any insults he may have suffered, he chose to forgive rather than seek retribution.

After finishing school, Ghaffar Khan considered his future. Descending from farmers, he chose to honor this by working in his father's rich fields along the Swat River. But he felt a restlessness when he looked at his people, at the poverty, the illiteracy, and the violence that surrounded them. He wanted to make life better for them all, but what could he, barely a man in age, do to bring about change? He thought of his time spent at a British mission school and of his headmaster, whom he admired almost as much as his own father, and then he knew. He could read and he could write. He would start a school.

Ghaffar Khan was just twenty years old in 1910 when he opened his first school in Utmanzai. The North-West Frontier Province had been in existence for nearly a decade, but so had its British laws and restrictions. The hill tribes still remained isolated from the settled districts, which meant Ghaffar Khan could not enter the tribal areas without British permission. The Frontier Crimes Regulations allowed for a man to be sent to a foreign penal colony for life without benefit of counsel or trial, and public gatherings were illegal except in mosques. There was a standing army of 10,000 soldiers that secured the province along a 200-mile perimeter, and a 6,000-man police force maintained order within.

Still, Ghaffar Khan's school was such a success that he started several more in neighboring villages and in a short time had attracted a large number of students. It was suggested that Ghaffar Khan build schools among the hill tribes, where education was needed most. Though he explained that regulations prohibited settled Pashtuns like himself from even speaking with a member of the hill tribes, he eventually agreed.

Ghaffar Kahn chose the small village of Zagai, which was remote enough to shield him from unwanted attention, and sent word to workers in the settled areas to join him. Hiding in the woods from the authorities, Ghaffar Khan waited for his help to arrive. Days passed and no one came. Looking down into the valley below he understood—while he was willing to risk capture and imprisonment to help educate his people, others were not. British tyranny and fear ruled everything and everyone.

Ghaffar Khan returned to the villages and re-opened the schools the British had closed and started new ones. In three years, he visited every one of the 500 villages in the Frontier's settled districts, determined to encourage the villagers to improve their lives. Along the way he heard about a man called Gandhi and his non-violent campaign for independence from the British that was beginning to take hold in India. Ghaffar Khan's calling took on new meaning. It was more than helping to transform and enrich the lives of his Pashtun countrymen and women. It was about freeing them—without firing a single shot.

The villagers began to understand Ghaffar Kahn and his unique mission as he made his way across the Frontier, leaving schools and a passion for a new life in his wake. It was a group of khans meeting at the mosque in Hashtnagar who honored him with the name that would define him for the rest of his life. During the meeting, Ghaffar Khan had roused the excitement of the other khans to such a high pitch that one called out, *Badshah Khan!* Soon the entire group picked up the cry, and Ghaffar Khan forever became known as Badshah Khan—the king of khans.

During WWI, the British passed emergency restrictions in India aimed at uncovering rebellious activities, even though the country was contributing greatly to Britain's war effort. Over a million Indian soldiers and laborers served during the war, and more than 43,000 died. After the war, the Rowlatt Act kept the restrictions in place, which included a curfew, a ban on public gatherings, and the detainment and arrest without warrant of any persons suspected of treasonous acts.

The continued repressive laws, as well as inflation, heavy taxation, the high number of wartime casualties, and an influenza epidemic—to which Badshah Khan lost his wife—brought the suffering and unrest in India to the breaking point. In a non-violent response to continued British repression and occupation, Gandhi called for a *hartal*, a day of fasting and prayer, which was tantamount to a nationwide strike that shut down entire cities. In the Frontier Province, thousands of Pashtuns gathered in Utmanzai to hear Badshah Khan speak. The British were listening too and declared martial law. Badshah Khan was arrested and sentenced—without a trial—to six months in prison.

In April 1919, one month after the passage of the Rowlatt Act, and in spite of Gandhi's insistence on non-violence, areas of India were deteriorating rapidly, particularly in the northwestern province of Punjab. The British responded by placing most of the province under martial law, banning any gatherings of more than four people.

The enforcement of martial law coincided with *Vaisakhi*, one of the most significant Sikh religious holidays in northern India, particularly in the Punjab. On April 13, thousands of men, women, and children gathered at Jallianwala Bagh, a garden in Amritsar, to celebrate. Later in the afternoon, a political meeting was held, of which many of those who had arrived at the garden for the holy day may have been unaware. An hour after the meeting began, Brigadier-General Reginald Dyer marched sixty-five soldiers into the garden—fifty were armed with rifles. Two armored cars with machine guns blocked the main entrance, too wide to make it through. General Dyer ordered his troops to kneel and fire into the densest part of the crowd. They continued shooting until they exhausted nearly 1,600 rounds of ammunition. An inquiry by the Indian National Congress put the number of deaths at 1,000.

After the Jallianwala Bagh massacre, the paths and lives of Gandhi and Badshah Khan converged at a historic meeting of the Indian National Congress, the largest and one of the oldest democratic political parties in the world. During the meeting, Gandhi persuaded even those who had come to oppose him of the need to fight for India's self-rule non-violently. On that night, Badshah Khan listened as the party, for the first time, resolved to openly and non-violently pursue India's full independence from Great Britain.

Although Badshah Khan felt a kinship with Gandhi and his non-violent message, politics held no attraction for him. He wanted to find a way to make life better in the province, not get caught up in the endless disagreements, stalemates, and displays of ego that largely make up a political environment. So along with his schools, Badshah Khan helped create a non-political missionary organization that supported economic, social, and educational reforms in the Frontier. When the British commissioner learned of the organization, Badshah Khan was arrested and sentenced to three years in prison with hard labor. He began his sentence with two months in solitary confinement.

During Badshah Khan's years in prison, India went through great struggles as it attempted to transition from violent rebellion to non-violent resistance. The change was neither quick nor easy. However, in 1924, Badshah Khan went home after his release from prison and found that his imprisonment had served to strengthen his movement and further encourage the Pashtuns to fight for progress and freedom non-violently. But he knew the centuries-old code of *badal* still remained his biggest obstacle. No one was more aware of the power revenge wielded over the Pashtuns, and the steep price they "were paying for their infatuation with violence." Yet Badshah Khan understood that the violence was a consequence of ignorance, superstition, and the crushing weight of tradition, not innate savagery. He only needed to show them how to redirect the extraordinary courage, honor, and determination they misused for violence toward truth and love.

Hoping to continue educating the next generations, Badshah Khan created the Pashtun Youth League, which drew its members from the graduates of his schools. One young man was present during a speech Badshah Khan gave in Utmanzai. The next morning, Badshah Khan found the young man banging on the gate of his courtyard, determined to speak what was in his heart. He said the Youth League was good for social reform, but what they needed were men willing to die for their freedom, and for each other. What they needed were soldiers.

Badshah Khan fell in love with the idea. There was no question the Pashtuns were fighters, but most fought either for the British or against each other. Instead, he envisioned something the world had never seen before—a non-violent army. The soldiers would be uniformed, disciplined, and take part in drills. There would be officers to organize and train them. And there would be a pledge to fight—not with weapons, but with their own lives.

They called themselves the Khudai Khidmatgar, Servants of God. Under the leadership of Badshah Khan, they became known as the world's first professional non-violent army. Any Pashtun was welcome. But every Pashtun who joined was required to take and abide by the army's oath. In Pashtun culture, once a promise is given it cannot be broken; even a Pashtun's enemies can rely on him to keep his word, and he will keep his word even at the risk of losing his own life.

Within just a few months, the non-violent army had 500 recruits.

In Lahore on January 26, 1930, five thousand delegates of the Indian National Congress declared all men, women, and children of India free from British rule. All they needed to do now was convince the British. It was Gandhi's job to choose when and how they would begin. And on April 6, he chose to make salt.

Not only did the British control the manufacturing and selling of salt in India, they levied a tax on each purchase, making salt a large source of revenue for Great Britain. In a tropical environment, one must replace the salt sweated out. And in India, everyone—whether rich or poor—had to use salt. Everyone was affected by the salt tax law, which to Gandhi meant everyone could be persuaded to break it.

On March 12, Gandhi left his ashram on the Sabarmati River and began his journey to the seaside village of Dandi. Seventy-eight members of his ashram accompanied him. By the time he reached Dandi twenty-four days later, the procession had become two miles long. After prayer at the Dandi seashore, Gandhi held a lump of salty mud and declared, "With this, I am shaking the foundations of the British Empire." He then boiled it in seawater, thereby not only making his own salt, but doing so without paying the British tax.

Mass civil disobedience swept through the country as millions of Indians broke British laws by making or buying illegal salt. But as the Indian non-violent movement grew, so did British determination to break it. The army and the police beat unarmed crowds with steel-tipped staffs, "raided Congress [party] offices, confiscated property, and eventually arrested every major political leader except Gandhi."

After several Khudai Khidmatgar leaders were arrested, a large crowd gathered at the Qissa Khawani Bazaar in non-violent protest. Troops arrived from the nearby army base with three armored cars, which were driven at high speed into the protestors, causing several injuries and deaths. The crowd offered to disperse after they collected the dead and wounded and if the troops left the square. In what amounted to a standoff, the British refused to withdraw, and the protestors would not leave without the dead and injured. The British made the first move by firing into the unarmed crowd. In his study of non-violent movements, Nobel Peace Prize nominee Gene Sharp described the Khudai Khidmatgar response:

> When those in front fell down wounded by the shots, those behind came forward with their breasts bared and exposed themselves to the fire, so much so that some people got as many as twenty-one bullet wounds in their bodies, and all the people stood their ground without getting into a panic. . . .
>
> The Anglo-Indian paper of Lahore, which represents the official view, itself wrote to the effect that the people came forward one after another to face the firing and when they fell wounded they were dragged back and others came forward to be shot at. This state of things continued from 11 till 5 o'clock in the evening.

Whether persuaded by Badshah Khan or British brutality and repression, the Khudai Khidmatgar non-violent army numbered nearly 100,000 at its peak. Badshah Khan spent fifteen years in British prisons, or about one day in jail for every day he was free. And he believed his only crime was that he had been born in the Frontier Province—the gateway to India.

It took seventeen more years of non-violent resistance for India to achieve independence from Great Britain—and just minutes for the country to become violent again. On August 14, 1947, at 11:57 p.m., the Governor-General declared a partitioned area of India a separate nation called Pakistan. Five minutes later, he declared India free. The result was the displacement of over twelve million people as Hindus fled their homes—in what was now Muslim-controlled Pakistan—for India, and Muslims left India for Pakistan. The transition left several hundred thousand to one million people dead as the two religious groups clashed along the way.

For almost three decades, Hindus and Muslims stood side-by-side in their non-violent fight for an independent India. They found common ground in their quest for freedom, hardly aware of their religious differences. Partition quickly reminded them. The first war between India and Pakistan began in October 1947, just two months after independence.

The Khudai Khidmatgar did not survive partition. Their decline began with a rift within the movement. Then the Pakistani government outlawed the organization until 1948. Despite being a Muslim, Badshah Khan opposed the creation of a separate Muslim state, believing the two religious groups should continue to work together in India nurturing what they had in common, rather than divide, which would only escalate their differences. However, Badshah Khan took the oath of allegiance to Pakistan during the first session of the new nation's Constituent Assembly. Still suspicious of what was considered his anti-Muslim positions, the Pakistani government placed Badshah Khan under house arrest without charge from 1948 to 1954. He was arrested again in 1956 for opposing Pakistan's merger of four provinces to create West Pakistan in order to politically dominate East Pakistan—now the nation of Bangladesh—and the government again banned the Khudai Khidmatgar. Badshah Khan was released in 1957, only to be re-arrested in 1958 until 1964. In 1973, Prime

Minister Zulfikar Ali Bhutto's government arrested him again. Badshah Khan died in Peshawar under house arrest in 1988. He was buried in Afghanistan, as he had wished. Although the Pakistani government lifted the ban against the Khudai Khidmatgar in 1972, it was too late. The non-violent movement "had been broken."

Badshah Khan was alive in 1978 when the United States chose to finance the Mujahideen rebellion in Afghanistan. Badshah Khan was alive in 1979 when the Soviet Union invaded Afghanistan and the United States spent billions of dollars providing weapons and training to the Mujahideen rebels, and gave billions more to Pakistan as payment for its role as an intermediary. Badshah Khan was alive and in Pakistan when the United States gathered militant jihadis from around the world and put them all in one place—Pakistan. The soldiers of the Khudai Khidmatgar non-violent movement disbanded after partition and had most likely scattered during the Soviet invasion, but they were alive. How different would the world be today if the West had aided Badshah Khan and the Khudai Khidmatgar in their mission to transform the Pashtuns—especially members of the hill tribes who would later come to be known as the Taliban—into a non-violent and enlightened people, rather than continually thwart him and his movement through repression, occupation, and violence? How different would the world be today if the United States had given its support and billions of dollars to the remaining members of the Khudai Khidmatgar for rebuilding and recruiting, instead of to the Mujahideen and the Pakistani government? And how different would the world be today if the United States had united the scattered Khudai Khidmatgar, not the jihadis?

Badshah Khan wrote that "all the horrors the British perpetrated on the Pashtuns had only one purpose: to provoke them to violence." The British knew only one way to fight—violently. They had neither experience with nor an understanding of non-violent resistance or non-violent responses. So if they could incite the Pashtuns to retaliate through violence, "the British would be back on familiar ground."

Americans, too, keep returning to the familiar ground of violence. In this country, we have the Department of Defense, formerly the Department of War. It employs 700,000 civilians, 1.4 million military personnel, and over a million in the National Guard and Reserve forces. And in 2011, it accounted for the largest allocation of the federal budget—$712 billion. We do not have a department dedicated to global non-violent pre-emptive measures. We do not have a department assigned to researching non-violent methods and responses. We do not have a department of anthropologists, sociologists, and psychologists to offer alternatives to any discussion of war, violence, or retribution, or to describe the future consequences of these actions for our country. We do, however, have psychologists to assess the human damage *after* our men and women soldiers return home from war with broken minds and bodies—when it's too late.

I strongly support our military. I support them having a fair chance to live their lives without unnecessary trauma. I support them having a fair chance at a loving marriage through intimacy. I support them having a fair chance to raise happy, healthy children in a family that remains intact. I support them having a fair chance to communicate their wants, needs, and vulnerabilities without fear of ridicule. I support the purpose of the military to no longer be one of killing people and breaking things, but of healing people and mending things. And I support our government no longer creating or contributing to situations that require the lives of American men and women, especially when those situations are avoidable through legitimate pre-emptive measures.

The words love and forgiveness—like intimacy and humility—are easy to dismiss. They don't appear to have substance, and they don't seem to be the instant antidotes to our pain that we demand. You can translate anger, hatred, and revenge into a physical reality and see their effects immediately. Our angry words can bring tears to another's eyes. Our hatred can draw blood. Our revenge can blow off arms and legs, burn skin, make someone deaf or blind, or simply cause him to no longer exist. But our choice, both as individuals and as a nation, is to decide how we want to get our power: through someone else's pain or through his healing and enlightenment. There has never been an instance where to put out a fire you add more fuel. There has never been an instance where to stop a boat from sinking you fill it with more water. And there will never be an instance where you stop violence by creating more violence.

If violence to deter violence worked, violent confrontation or retaliation would have ended when the first caveman threw a rock at his cave neighbor's head; but like everything else, it can only escalate.

There are those who believe that certain ends can be achieved only through violence, but we have not devoted the time, energy, or financial resources to determine whether this is true, or to determine the future consequences of returning violent acts with even more violence.

In his 1998 interview, Zbigniew Brzenzinski was asked if he had any regrets about U.S. activity in Afghanistan prior to the Soviet invasion. He had none. The interviewer continued with this question:

Q: And neither do you regret having supported Islamic fundamentalism, having given arms and advice to future terrorists?

ZB: What is most important to the history of the world? The Taliban or the collapse of the Soviet empire? Some stirred-up Muslims or the liberation of Central Europe and the end of the Cold War?

It may have been an interesting response in 1998, but it sounds far different today. The choice between ending the Cold War and losing nearly 3,000 Americans on 9/11 was not one we should have ever had to make. And it is my hope that one day we will do whatever it takes to find how we could have done one without contributing to the other. That one day, we will vow to never again sacrifice our peaceful future to the violence of the present.

In this country, any discussion of the consequences of unprovoked violence will always begin and end with 9/11. It is not possible for me to understand the pain of those personally affected by those acts of terror. I knew no one who died on that day, and I did not have to rebuild my family or my life afterwards. But it is of them I think when trying to understand what we can do differently now, so that no one else need suffer similar trauma in the future. Fortunately, there are people who have spent their lives researching proper responses to violent actions that don't escalate situations or result in equally grave future consequences. There is Kenneth Boulding's theory of transarmament; and Gene Sharp, who in 1983 founded the Albert Einstein Institution, identified 198 methods of non-violent action to counteract violence and oppression. Non-violent options deserve a voice. Our future depends on it.

We can learn many lessons from 9/11. One is that WMD are not necessary to cause large-scale death and destruction. Another is that being the world's top military superpower with the largest arsenal of the most advanced weaponry will not prevent an attack on our soil. It does, however, allow us to react to an attack quickly, extensively, and with intensity—which only creates more death and destruction.

I still believe George W. Bush was on the right path when he spoke so often of compassion, whether referring to America as a compassionate country or to himself as a compassionate conservative. Because I still believe that any response to verbal, emotional, or physical violence has to start with forgiveness.

It has been interesting to see the immediate and visceral reactions to any discussion that puts forgiveness and the 9/11 hijackers in the same sentence. Some were from Christians, who thought the idea was ridiculous, but most came from those who claim that feelings should have little or even no place in anyone's decision-making process. However, any act of revenge or violent retaliation to any degree is one hundred percent pure emotion.

I think the problem many have with applying forgiveness to violent acts is that they equate forgiveness with coddling the offender or ignoring a legitimate offense. Forgiveness does neither. There are always consequences—some the offended will be a part of, some they will not. But what forgiveness does first is defuse the emotion. Then it guides you toward determining the appropriate response to a violent act that will *de-escalate* the situation and achieve the best present and future consequences. While anger and revenge offer immediate, though temporary, relief, they are the primary obstacles to resolution and healing.

I remember a few years after I had left the clinic I became frustrated over my continued inappropriate reactions to situations that emotionally triggered me. I was still making too many missteps in response to wounds I should have healed long ago. A counselor told me that, much like someone who wants to lose weight must burn off more calories than he consumes, I needed to make more correct choices whenever I found myself in situations that were uncomfortable or painful to me than incorrect ones for my healing to continue to progress.

Right now we are weighted heavily on the side of returning violence with violence, hatred with hatred, division with more divisiveness, separation with even more isolation. But we can begin today to make more choices that shift the balance in the other direction, until those making conscious decisions to use their thoughts, words, and actions to heal greatly outnumber those who project anger, hatred, and violence. Even the smallest acts can make a difference. If someone burns the American flag, raise yours higher. If someone creates art you think is sacrilegious, create something honoring your faith, or live your life even more in keeping with the teachings of your religion. But all we are able to do through acts of revenge is stay within two steps of the violence others wish to do us. Unfortunately, those two steps will always be *behind* those who do us harm unless we acknowledge our place in the chain of cause and effect, accept responsibility for our part in the world's dysfunction, and begin to redirect our thoughts, words, and actions toward healing.

If it is true that guns don't kill people—people kill people—then it must also be true that guns don't create a secure and stable environment. People do. We can establish a different way of pre-empting and resolving conflict. We can create a peaceful world.

The world is full of opportunities for constructive change. America can show the way with a leader of extraordinary vision, courage, and a commitment to weaning us all off our dysfunctional reliance on violence and weapons.

In 2008, presidential candidate Barack Obama ran on a platform of change. However, once he became president—and despite becoming a Nobel Peace Prize recipient—the only change regarding the U.S. military and weapons manufacture and exports was an escalation of the policies already in place. The United States currently accounts for forty-three percent of the world's military spending. And though our nation is also the world's largest weapons supplier, controlling thirty percent of the market, the Obama administration has begun "modifying export control regulations" with the objective of doubling exports by 2015. In October 2010, the administration affirmed that intention by announcing its plan to sell Saudi Arabia "aircraft and other weapons" totaling $60 billion, making it the largest arms deal in U.S. history. That same year, the United States approved $200 million in military sales to Bahrain, $760,000 of which was spent on "rifles, shotguns, and assault weapons"; $91 million to the Egyptian government headed by President Hosni Mubarak just months before he was forced to resign; and $17 million to Moammar Gadhafi of Libya before he began his brutal retaliation against anti-government forces—all of which raises the possibility that American-made weapons were used against pro-democracy demonstrators during the recent protests against these Middle East governments. Also in 2010, the Department of Defense, which administers arms sales to foreign countries, "told Congress of plans to sell up to $103 billion in weapons to overseas buyers." A veteran defense consultant stated, "Obama is much more favorably disposed to arms exports than any of the previous Democratic administrations." Or as the deputy director of the Arms Control Association described it, "There's an Obama arms bazaar going on."

American-made weapons are widely coveted because they are considered to be the best in the world. However, critics contend that supplying unstable regions such as the Middle East with advanced weaponry will most likely backfire. Though the United States is said to sell arms only to its allies, past and current events have shown that simply being a U.S. ally does not guarantee that a foreign government or ruler is benevolent. Neither has any U.S. administration been willing to place how a potential importer of American weapons governs its people over how much it will pay. Since power can shift quickly in volatile countries, many U.S.-supplied arms have outlasted the governments and conflicts for which they were intended, which means yesterday's weapons are finding new uses today.

However, the consequences of our passion for arms proliferation may be as close as our own backyard. Federal agents have made almost no progress in stopping the flow of guns into Mexico. Over a two-year period, increased inspections of travelers crossing the border netted 386 guns. The problem is an estimated 2,000 guns make it into Mexico *each day.*

I understand arms proliferation is about more than attempting to create a stable and secure world through weaponry. It is about money and jobs. One hundred and three billion dollars is a lot of money, and the arms deal to Saudi Arabia alone will support approximately 75,000 jobs. But the time has come for America to define what it means to be a great country. Is it one that contributes to global death and destruction through weaponry? Is it one that contributes to generation after generation of trauma and dysfunction through violence? Or is it one that creates, transforms, and heals? Present actions determine the future. And every day brings another chance for us to choose a future that includes a healthy and peaceful world.

I wasn't surprised by President Obama's decision to continue the existing policies regarding our defense spending and weapons exports—though I had very much hoped to be. However, in early 2008, I realized no candidate had been able to show me what constructive and positive change looked like during the campaign process. I had no reason to believe it would be any different after one got elected. Instead, "change" was simply another strategy the party currently not in power used to try to oust the party that was.

The "change" strategy is not new. It has been a part of every election and the campaign of any candidate who hopes to convince voters that he or she is "different." Some will use words like hope or civility or compassion. Others will talk of a new day and a new way for our country. But in 2008, it seemed the only thing that was different was me.

Just out of the clinic in 2004, I had decided to hold on to my vote until the next presidential election when I thought I'd be better prepared to make an appropriate choice through the tools I had acquired during my time there. Four years later, I still had my tools, which had become deeply rooted through my continued commitment to my growth and healing. And I still had my vote. I now felt ready to use them.

I had been an engaged voter for several presidential and mid-term elections. I heard the strategies of the typical campaign as background noise, and would pluck out what sounded true from the din. But during the 2008 presidential election, for the first time I didn't hear what was being said—I saw it. I saw they were not strategies. They were not tactics. They were weapons. And the candidates had armed themselves with the same artillery as every candidate in every election before them. The labeling of the opposition as the party of obstruction, or of fear, or of no ideas; the claiming of one's own party as the one standing for jobs, or for freedom, or for America; the party out of power declaring their intention to "take back the country"; the party down in the polls promising to better explain their core principles; Republicans arguing over who was most conservative to attract the extreme wing of their party, while Democrats fought over who was least liberal to run away from the extreme wing of theirs; both parties vowing to go on the offensive and not let the opposing party dictate the message or frame the debate; and every candidate denouncing the mudslinging and negative campaigning, while every candidate was immersed to their mouths in it.

The eighteen-month-long presidential campaign season weighs dark and heavy on the country. The hostility between rival candidates seeps into our lives, turning family members, friends, and co-workers with opposing party loyalties into combatants. Even those who try to distance themselves from the candidates' rancor may find that difficult. In October 2008 alone, 1.41 million political ads aired on local TV and radio stations across the country, and an average of fifty-two percent of political ads for the candidates vying for the 2008 presidential nomination were negative.

Every sports fan is familiar with trash talk and its purpose, which is not about getting in someone's face. It's about getting in his head. Politicians aim their trash talk at two targets, one being their opposition. There is a curious mindset in politics; candidates do not want to compete against an able opponent or compelling ideas to show they are the most capable within a group of many worthy choices. No candidate will give respect to a good opponent and then set out to be better. No candidate will appreciate an opponent's good idea and then refine it to make it exceptional. They would rather, through negative campaigning, try to get their opponent off balance and off message by making him spend his time addressing accusations instead of discussing policy—the goal being to sabotage the opposition's chances to present a plan that might appeal to or benefit citizens and thereby secure their votes. Or they will use negative campaigning to exploit an opposing party's vulnerabilities, such as low approval ratings, intra-party divisions, or scandal. But no voter can feel good about electing a candidate to lead this country who only feels strong when his opponent is at his weakest.

The second target is the voter, whom the candidates mire deepest in the negative squalor, hoping to create enough confusion to capture his or her vote. The result is that voters never choose the greatest from among our very best, but the least flawed and corrupt from among the available evils.

It wasn't long into the 2008 campaign season before the negative ads and contentious speeches began to overwhelm me. It seemed the clinic had given me tools to better understand my life, but nothing to help me make sense of our political campaign process. But then I remembered a sentence the counselors repeated often, though I just as often found easy to forget: Every time one speaks, he tells me who *he* is. With every negative political ad and campaign speech, a candidate was not telling me about his opponent. He was not telling me what I should do or think as a voter. He was telling me about himself. From that moment, every time I heard a hostile political message, I no longer looked at the target of the hostility, but at the candidate who delivered it. Because every word told me not only how he was running his campaign and his life, but how he would run the country if elected.

In November 2007, the Dallas Cowboys defeated the New York Giants in New York. However, one taunting and two unnecessary roughness penalties against the Cowboys that came after plays had been whistled dead cost them points, and could have cost them the game. The head coach of the Cowboys responded to the unprofessional behavior by requiring his players to sign a pledge that they would avoid senseless penalties in the future. "I want their word that they're going to try to do the right thing," he said.

Throughout the presidential campaign season, I often wondered what would happen if voters required every candidate to sign a pledge against negative campaigning. My first thought was that no one would sign it, and any who did wouldn't be able to honor his or her word. In truth, either of those actions would tell me more about a candidate than any political ad or campaign speech ever could.

The debates were even more difficult for me, and I never saw one in its entirety. As the campaign season wore on, I became more frustrated over what, as a voter, I had a right to ask for from the candidates. I wanted to elect a leader for who he or she is, not who the other candidate isn't. Maybe we will never have an election free of negative campaigning, but do we have a right to one debate, just one, where presidential candidates are barred from speaking negatively about their opponents?

During debates, every candidate desires just one thing: time to speak. What if for every negative reference a candidate makes about an opponent in one designated debate, he or she is docked an amount of speaking time, and that time is then given to the opponent? Would there be so many negative references that the minutes would simply be shuffled and re-shuffled among the candidates? Or at some point would each candidate have accumulated so many penalties that none could speak? Which would mean the candidates were either speaking negatively about an opponent or not speaking at all. That, again, would tell me all I needed to know.

Maybe a debate conducted in this manner would teach the candidates the value of time, which is as precious to voters as it is to candidates. And maybe it would teach the candidates that if they don't use time productively, they will lose it.

This does not mean a candidate's character and personal life shouldn't be a part of the campaign process. They absolutely should.

If you are asking for something from me—such as my respect, my time, or my vote—you are also attempting to establish a relationship with me, and a relationship is reciprocal. I can only know how you will conduct yourself in a relationship with me if I know your relationship with yourself. You will only be as honest with me as you are with yourself; you will only be as open with me as you are with yourself; you will only hold yourself accountable for promises you made to me if you have done the same with those you made to yourself; and you will only be able to resolve conflicts with another person or party or country if you have been able to resolve the conflicts within yourself.

Rather, my concern is with *who* is pointing out the flaws in an opponent's character or the problems in his personal life. When it comes to the opposition, every candidate's motives are suspect, and none are above embellishing or fabricating information about an opponent if it will cast doubt on his integrity and weaken his position among the voters.

I believe there are better ways to address a candidate's character issues. One is through the mainstream media. Each election, the media gets closer to squandering whatever good name it has left through biased political reporting. However, it is still bound by more checks and balances through its editing and fact-checking processes than any politician. Another is through the candidate whose character is in question. Ultimately, voters should hear the full and timely truth about any mistakes or character issues from the candidates themselves. This doesn't mean through a rehearsed statement that simply minimizes the offense, but through journalists, interviewers, and debate moderators who will ask the questions a candidate didn't think to ask himself, and who will continue to seek answers until all that should be revealed has been.

However, it often seems journalists are so busy thinking about their next question that they don't listen to the answer to the one they just asked. This allows candidates to get away with answers that aren't really answers at all, and it keeps journalists from asking the proper follow-up questions that would get us all closer to what we truly need to know. What is important about the disclosure of any inappropriate behavior is not the details, *but the steps the person took to change it.* What did he do to transform himself? What does he continue to do to make sure he stays that way? It is not enough to put on display the family members who are standing by him. What does he do day by day, step by step to ensure he isn't simply surrounding himself with enablers who ignore or deny his problems rather than encourage him to address them? It is not enough to check into a rehabilitation clinic for a few weeks; change, health, and recovery require a lifetime of commitment. What does he do day by day, step by step to continue his growth and healing? It is not enough to claim a transformation through God. What does he do day by day, step by step to support and stay grounded in his religious conviction? What changes has he made and will he continue to make that will convince us he won't engage in behaviors such as ethics violations, fraud, theft, addiction, or adultery in the future? Or merely exchange one corrupt or immoral behavior for another?

Debate moderators can also ask better questions that will give voters a clearer idea of who the candidates really are. While policy questions are important, so are personal ones. During a debate in which candidates are barred from making negative references about their opponents, moderators could use that time to ask candidates to speak about themselves. What are a candidate's weaknesses and how does he use them as strengths? What are a candidate's strengths and how does he use them to benefit others? What is the best thing he has done in his life? What is the worst and what changes did he make as a result? What qualities make up a life of morality and character? Does he consider himself to have these qualities and, if so, what actions does he take on a daily basis to support them? What did conflict resolution look like in his childhood home? How does he resolve conflict as an adult? How will he use these skills to bridge the political divide in the White House and in the country if elected? What would be his alternatives to war? What one thing does he like about his opponent politically? What one thing does he like about his opponent personally? These and other questions like them would give us the answer to the most important question of all: Who are you?

A candidate's personal life will always be as important as his professional goals and accomplishments, because we cannot know how any candidate will lead the country until we know how he leads himself.

Whenever someone is involved in scandal, there is always talk about whether he has the ability to compartmentalize, or separate his personal mistakes from his professional responsibilities. This capacity to compartmentalize is often seen as a favorable trait. It isn't. While it may have the short-term effect of allowing one to distance himself from shame or accountability, the long-term consequences are always catastrophic. Compartmentalization is simply denial and justification—two dysfunctional mind games aimed at keeping reality from breaking through. And the reality is that what you are willing to do in one part of your life is what you are willing to do in every other part of your life. A person will not have one set of values for his private life and another for his career, and a candidate will not act one way during a political campaign and another after elected. If he sells himself to lobbyists or tries to minimize an opponent through obstruction and mudslinging during the campaign, he will do so when he governs. If he feels powerful as a candidate only when others are weak, he will feel this way as a husband, a father, a friend, an employer, and a president.

While the following explanation of this concept of individual connectedness by Sharon Salzberg, a Buddhist teacher and author, may seem directed toward students of Buddhism, it applies to every one of us.

> In order to live with integrity, we must stop fragmenting and compartmentalizing our lives. Telling lies at work and expecting great truths in meditation is nonsensical. Using our sexual energy in a way that harms ourselves or others, and then expecting to know transcendent love in another arena, is mindless. *Every aspect of our lives is connected to every other aspect of our lives. This truth is the basis for an awakened life.*

Determining how a candidate has authentically created a life of character through his actions also keeps him from simply staking a claim to it through his words. Exit polls from the 2004 election showed that twenty-two percent listed "moral values" as their highest determining factor when voting for a president, ranking it above the war in Iraq, terrorism, and the economy. However, when George W. Bush won the election, some translated this to mean that not only had the voters overwhelmingly concluded he was the candidate with the highest character, but also that the Republican party itself was the party of "morals and values." Character and morals do not belong to a political party. They belong to all individuals—regardless of party affiliation or religious preference—who continually and consciously practice moral behavior in their lives. Voters have a right to choose a leader based not on who a candidate or his supporters say he is, but on what he can show he has done.

Amid the hostility of the 2008 election there was, however, an encouraging moment. Presidential candidate Barack Obama had written a memoir as a young law school graduate in which he spoke of his teenage drinking and drug use, which included cocaine. Something that may have seemed like a good idea long before he ever considered running for president was now getting a lot of attention.

It was not so long ago that such candid admissions would have ended his hope for a life of public service, or at the very least opened him up to an onslaught of personal attacks from opponents. Two decades ago, a U.S. Court of Appeals judge for the District of Columbia Circuit was forced to withdraw as a nominee for the Supreme Court after it was revealed he had used marijuana as a law professor. In 1992, one presidential candidate thought his previous marijuana use was more of a liability than lying about it and claimed to have smoked the drug but not inhaled. And in 2000, another presidential candidate steadfastly deflected questions about his past by acknowledging he had been "irresponsible" but offering no details.

But Barack Obama never distanced himself from his past choices nor expressed regret for his candor, saying he would tell the same story today "even if certain passages have proven to be inconvenient politically." Neither did he minimize them as youthful mistakes. Instead, he recognized his actions and their consequences for what they were:

lessons, change, and growth. Speaking to students at a New Hampshire high school, he told them, "[I] got into drinking. I experimented with drugs. There was a whole stretch of time that I didn't really apply myself a lot. It wasn't until I got out of high school and went to college that I started realizing, 'Man, I wasted a lot of time.'"

However, to me, the reactions to Barack Obama's disclosures were even more compelling than the disclosures themselves. One 2008 presidential contender with a past of three marriages, adultery, and a connection to an indicted police commissioner defended Barack Obama, saying he respected his honesty. While two other contenders, one of whom had also married three times and admitted to adultery, made pleas to keep the candidates' private lives private. But the most interesting reaction came from a Republican candidate who said Barack Obama had made a "huge error" in revealing his past mistakes.

> It's just not a good idea for people running for President of the United States who potentially could be the role model for a lot of people to talk about their personal failings while they were kids because it opens the doorway to other kids thinking, "well I can do that too and become President of the United States." . . . It is just the wrong way for people who want to be the leader of the free world.

While I could appreciate his contention that adults should set good examples for our nation's children, I couldn't agree with how he thought we should do this. No one learns anything from an example of lying by omission except how to lie by omission. And a child who has been taught that lying is acceptable, even by well-meaning parents, will do so to everyone—including those well-meaning parents.

What this candidate saw in Barack Obama was someone who used drugs and became president. What I saw was someone who used drugs, came to know the behavior was damaging and unproductive, and changed it—and absolutely no inappropriate thoughts, feelings, or behaviors can be changed if they remain hidden. One of the most valuable gifts we can give our children is to show them how to free themselves from their mistakes and transform their lives, with the focus being not on the mistake, but on the process of correction. Giving them the mechanisms to suppress errors only teaches them shame and self-hatred, and creates a life of illusion, not truth.

Every day I see how important it is to be mindful of what we teach our children. I look around at our country's twenty-year-old young men and women, at what television shows they watch, what music they listen to, what they read, what they consider valuable, what their intimate relationships look like, how they communicate, how they spend their free time, how they treat others, and how they deal with anger, fear, failure, and mistakes. All they have been exposed to is what adults have created for them. How they live their lives is the result of what adults have shown them is acceptable. We will see how well we have done in thirty years, when we must choose our next president from among them.

While this candidate may have thought he was telling me his opinion of Barack Obama's disclosure of past drug use, what I heard was him telling me about himself. I learned that this candidate would lie by omission when it served a purpose he could justify—in this case, to protect children. Since I knew that what a person does in one he does in all, I wondered what other circumstances in his life might justify lying by omission. Would he lie to protect his reputation? Would he lie to save his marriage? Would he lie to get my vote as a candidate? Would he lie to keep his job as president? Despite my questions about the characters of all the candidates, I came away knowing at least one thing: I hope that one day, change means politicians will try as hard at telling the truth as they do at telling what they want voters to hear.

But this change, or any other that was promised during the 2008 campaign season wasn't likely. Any dysfunctional relationship, family, organization, process, or system can only attract dysfunctional people, because no healthy or highly functional person can operate within one. They simply cannot do what would be required of them to maintain it. And everything about the political behavior in this country, from campaigning to governing, is dysfunctional. There is nothing healthy, productive, or constructive about lying, secrecy, sabotage, obstruction, corruption, manipulation, verbal violence, influence peddling, or fiscal irresponsibility, which means anyone who actively seeks to be president isn't worth electing, and the only people worthy of the job don't want it.

Not even the candidates themselves believe there is anything healthy about our political system. If they don't think it is broken, why does every one of them promise to change it? Even if someone within the system made an authentic attempt at change, he would be outnumbered. Much like an addict must maintain his dysfunctional environment to support his addiction, there are too many people—from politicians and campaign managers to lobbyists and opinion media—whose careers and very sense of self depend on making sure our campaigning and governing processes stay dysfunctional. There is not now, and never has been, an incentive to unite the country. Anyone who gets his identity, his power, or his money from one political party will do or say whatever it takes to ensure the other party fails. All the political energy in this country goes to dividing, disrupting, and corrupting. It does not go to cooperation. It does not go to resolution. It does not go to change. This behavior is unstable, unsupportable, and should be unacceptable to any country that considers itself great, moral, and compassionate.

One of the most disappointing things to come out of the 2008 presidential election was the redefining of what it means to be a strong woman. At one time, it meant conducting oneself with integrity, grace, self-reliance, and individuality. However, in this election it not only meant continuing the dysfunctional behaviors previously established by others, but escalating them. Having the ability to out-bully, out-humiliate, out-manipulate, or out-trash talk any man is not strength. Neither is strength simply giving the appearance of being civil by turning the dirty work over to someone else, such as a vice-presidential nominee during a campaign or a cabinet member after the election is won. Strength is conviction without arrogance. Strength is passion without ridicule. Strength is principles without hatred. And this can only come from one who is highly conscious, courageous, and balanced.

The universe strives for balance because it is essential for survival. Whenever extremes are present, a moderator will always arise to restore equanimity. This looks like Freud's Ego acting as mediator between the self-indulgent Id and the austere Superego; the Holy Spirit bridging communication between man and God; Buddha's Middle Way showing that neither asceticism nor excess leads to liberation; and the center heart chakra building harmony between the three lower physical chakras and the three higher spiritual chakras. Stagnation and decay lie in extremes, and because anything extreme is defective, it cannot be sustained. It will, eventually, destroy itself. Movement is always in the middle, and because balance supports life, growth, and creativity, it is from here that all true power comes.

There are those who have made attempts to bring the middle way into our politics. They are called independents, moderates, or centrists; but because no functional person can survive in a dysfunctional system, they rarely last. In 1996 alone, ten senators with strong bipartisan credentials chose to retire rather than run for re-election. Not long ago, senate seats were among the most coveted in the country. But today, many believe the $174,000 salary isn't worth the gridlock and obstruction the extremists in the two major parties actively endorse, the crushing weight to conform to the dysfunctional system, or the attacks from opinion media. In 2010, we saw a similar exodus of bipartisan leaders in both the House and the Senate, as well as some new faces refusing the chance to run. One retiring congressman, who had reached the conclusion that he could get more done in the private sector, said there is "too much narrow ideology and not enough practical problem-solving. I do not love Congress."

Just after the contentious 2004 presidential election there came a plea from within Congress to conduct business with civility. Two House members—one Democrat and one Republican—created the bipartisan Congressional Civility Caucus aimed at fostering civil debate in politics. Organized bipartisanship has been attempted at least once before. A civility retreat for members of the House met in 1997. It met again in 1999 but was poorly attended, and efforts at bipartisanship ended soon afterward due to a "lack of interest." The Civility Caucus seems destined for a similar fate. After two years and a less than encouraging response by fellow House members, the Civility Caucus was renamed the Civility Task Force; however, the two founders remained its only members. In January 2011, they vowed again to establish a Civility Caucus in Congress stating that "true leaders guide with compassion and by example." As of this writing, there are still only two members.

One way political extremism tries to obstruct and diminish independent politicians and voters is by disparaging them as unprincipled. But it's not that political independents don't have convictions, passions, or principles—they just don't believe simply belonging to a political party creates them. A person with principles has a commitment to the truth wherever it is found. But when you attach to one person or one entity, you become limited by their limitations, and most people limit their principles to words, not actions. For a political independent, it will never be enough to hear about principles, no matter how loudly or arrogantly they are voiced. They must be proven through behavior.

Principled behavior does not fear close examination. Passion does not fear improvement. Conviction does not fear growth. However, political extremism fears all of this and anything else that threatens its perceived relevance and power. Extremism can never be powerful in its own right, but only through its attempts to make others weak through division, obstruction, and ridicule. While political extremists may spend all their time talking about others, what they say can only tell us who they are. The chaos they create is a reflection of the chaos in their own lives. The conflict they provoke allows them to avoid facing their own conflicts within. Escalating the dysfunction in others enables them to normalize the dysfunction in themselves. Because extremism is inherently weak, it will only attract the weak among us—those with prejudice, hatred, and anger. And we can always be controlled and manipulated through our fears.

While balance is always the answer, mythologizing the middle as quick or easy is a mistake. There is a reason extremism is more prevalent than balance: It is quick and it is easy. You simply choose a position, then proceed to point out and distance yourself from anything or anyone who acts or thinks or believes differently from you, no matter how beneficial it may be. Extremism can only survive through differences, which are easy to escalate and manipulate. However, balance must take the time to make sense of our differences, find out how they work together to everyone's greatest benefit. Most importantly, balance must constantly remind us of all we have in common, because it is on our common ground where we treat each other with love and respect, and where we encourage each other's growth, healing, and creativity. Not many are able to celebrate what we share—acknowledge that we are truly all the same, with the same fears, same hopes, same struggles— and still feel personally powerful. Most settle for false power through our differences, because it is only when one believes he is apart from others that he can also believe he is above others.

However, Republicans and Democrats have found a few areas where they agree. Unfortunately, their bipartisanship extends only to those things that are dysfunctional and detrimental to our country, such as scandal, adultery, lying, secrecy, obstruction, corruption, manipulation, verbal violence, influence peddling, and fiscal irresponsibility. Nearly every year, a politician from one party or the other resigns in disgrace, declaring he is doing so because he doesn't want his personal failings and mistakes to "get in the way of doing the people's work." Which always leads me to wonder why he didn't feel that way before he got caught doing whatever it was that caused him to resign.

The truth is, just as no addict can be an addict by himself, a politician can only do what voters allow him to do. And voters are not only enabling dysfunctional political behavior, they are engaging in it. During the 2004 election, researchers monitored the brains of Democrat and Republican voters with strong party allegiances as they were asked to evaluate negative information about several candidates. Both groups were quick to identify "inconsistency and hypocrisy—but only in candidates they opposed." When presented with negative information about their preferred candidate that could not be rationally ignored, not only did partisan voters find ways to justify it, but brain scans showed their reward centers were activated afterward. Emory University psychologist Drew Westen said, "Essentially, it appears as if partisans twirl the cognitive kaleidoscope until they get the conclusions they want, and then they get massively reinforced for it." He also observed there are parallels between a partisan voter's behavior and that of addicts, who also find ways to justify and then reward themselves for their dysfunctional actions.

However, voters have clearly stated their political concerns and expectations. According to a Pew Research Center poll, seventy-two percent of voters said there was more mudslinging in the 2004 presidential election than in previous campaigns. In 2005, a Harris poll found that seventy-nine percent favored moderate candidates. In that same poll, fifty-three percent said extreme conservatives have too much influence in the Republican party, and thirty-eight percent believed extreme liberals have too much influence in the Democratic party. In 2008, another Harris poll found that sixty percent of voters said there is too much partisanship in Washington, with more Republicans believing this than Democrats. Eighty-nine percent said it was important for the president elected in 2008 to reduce the partisanship and hostility, which was a priority for more Democrats than Republicans.

But are voters truly prepared to not just demand, but accept what they say they want? In 2008, it seemed the answer was no.

While no one can change a dysfunctional system by working within it, one can change a dysfunctional system by operating outside of it, much like we have seen with independent filmmakers and musicians. In 2006, a political organization was formed to try to do just that. Unity08 attempted not only to minimize the partisanship and mudslinging by seeking to recruit a bipartisan ticket to run in the 2008 presidential election, but also to eliminate corporate influence bought through big corporate money by relying on small donations to fund the campaign. However, Unity08 suspended operations even before the 2008 election was held.

One obstacle the organization faced was convincing candidates with viable bipartisan credentials to take part in the election. Once again, those who had already left political life declined to get back in, and those still in politics chose to retire rather than seek re-election. I imagine they realized that, while they would be running a different type of campaign, they would still have to govern within the same dysfunctional system. A bipartisan ticket may affect the mudslinging and negative campaigning during an election. If a bipartisan candidate were elected, eliminating corporate donations would mitigate corporate expectations, and creating a bipartisan cabinet would encourage all viewpoints in the executive branch. But these do not address the main problem: Congress. Members of the legislative branch are not interested in bipartisanship, but in either passing one's own partisan agenda or finding effective ways to obstruct someone else's.

The other problem was the voters themselves. Independents and moderates simply weren't joining the organization in numbers the polls say exist, which made sense to me. Political independents already endorse the bipartisan concept, which in effect means they've already signed on. What they are waiting for are credible candidates. So while political independents may give their allegiance to bipartisanship, their money will only go to candidates capable of putting it into action.

There are most certainly other reasons for voter reluctance. I have seen and been a part of a lot of change not just in my own life, but also in the lives of those I have been privileged to know who have chosen the same path, and I can say this with certainty: *All* change is difficult and terrifying. Because of this the known, even when it is uncomfortable or dysfunctional, is often chosen over what is unknown. Which means voters may choose to remain in their own cycle of familiar dysfunction rather than take a risk on something new.

About every eight years, the disillusionment with one party becomes unbearable and voters shift power to the other after falling prey to its promises of "change," as well as the four words that are the mantra of every enabler: This time is different. But a reactive backlash is not change, and it is not balance. It is simply swinging the political pendulum from one dysfunctional extreme to the other. There is no difference between two political parties that are part of the same dysfunctional system.

Any change we wish to see outside of ourselves must first start within. This means that to change our political system and attract better leaders, we must first become better voters. Do you want the truth, or do you want your party to win? Do you want an end to negative campaigning, or do you want your party to win? Do you truly want to find common ground, or do you want your party to win?

For authentic change to happen, voters must have the courage to no longer get their identities from a political party, but only from the truth. By demanding authenticity and accountability you will not betray your country or yourself, but by accepting dysfunction on any level, you betray them both. Voters must also be willing to hold themselves accountable for their part in this country's political dysfunction. Our politicians will only do what we have shown them we are willing to accept. And accepting dysfunctional behavior during a campaign, then expecting it to change after a candidate gets elected is like accepting dysfunctional behavior while dating, then expecting it to change after you are married. Justification and denial have no place in any relationship that is based on truth.

Stepping into this political dark night will most certainly be difficult and terrifying. But if we can stay committed—day by day, step by step—it will be worth every moment.

In 2008, realizing that we were no closer to authentic change long before Election Day arrived, I again made the decision not to vote. If you find yourself critical of this, you are not alone. My inner circle holds many active voters, and few were supportive of my choice to be a political abstainer. Most of them remind me quickly and often that voting is a privilege, and that it is my right as an American citizen to let my voice be heard.

Therein lies the problem. If I vote, I am saying I accept our dysfunctional political system, and I do not. I do not accept the lying. I do not accept the secrecy. I do not accept the obstruction. I do not accept the corruption. I do not accept the manipulation. I do not accept the verbal violence. I do not accept the influence peddling. And I do not accept the fiscal irresponsibility.

Some have responded to my non-acceptance by saying, "What do you expect? They are politicians." On this we agree. It is always bewildering to me whenever a politician is given a diplomatic position. Politicians by their very definition are not diplomats. They have neither experience in nor an inclination toward bridging differences or negotiating compromises. Politicians operate solely in division and obstruction, which means when you vote, you are not electing a representative or a leader; you are simply hiring a professional politician.

But it is not because I believe my vote means so little that I abstain. It is because my vote means so much. However, I am not advocating nationwide political abstinence. It is likely that non-action on Election Day is not right for anyone else. It is only that, at this time, it is right for me. The truth is, there really is no place for me or my vote in our political system; but I've been told politicians don't want my vote anyway. There are definitely much easier votes to be had. Mine will always require the conditions I have repeated so often when attempting to explain my political positions that they've been christened my Maranda Rights:

> Truth over illusion
> Action over words
> Openness over secrecy
> Accountability over denial

While these may not be my rights as granted by our Constitution, they are my hopes for the country I love.

Everything good is found through the truth. It is the heart of change, consciousness, salvation, liberation, happiness, and love. The truth makes our lives authentic. The truth makes our world compassionate. The truth makes our survival possible. But to gain the truth you must give up everything else—everything you thought you knew, but most of all, everything you think you are. You cannot find the truth through your ego. You cannot find the truth through an identity. And you cannot find the truth by believing you have already found it.

Very few people are able to consistently let go of themselves when seeking the truth. Our egos—the creation of a self through our histories, our politics, our religions, possessions, jobs, and relationships—are the strongest forces in our lives. We feel powerful through our identities. We feel important through our opinions. And the truth too often becomes a casualty if it conflicts with the need to feel powerful and important. This is what makes authentic truth-seeking so difficult and so rare;

and why, though we have an entire professional calling dedicated to discovering and telling the truth, so few succeed.

It has become commonplace to criticize the mainstream media. Some criticism is unwarranted. There are many who couldn't do their jobs if the media didn't do theirs. I couldn't have written this book, and opinion media couldn't broadcast their radio and television shows without them. Despite disparaging mainstream media for its bias, opinion media rely on its work daily to support what they already believe, or find arguments against what they don't. However, mainstream media has brought much of the criticism upon itself.

"I wonder how intelligent citizens can profess love for their country and so much hate for their fellow countrymen" are among the most appropriate words of our time. But the response requires just one: money. Politicians discovered long ago that there is no money in unifying the country. Media opinionists followed right behind when they learned there is no money in treating fellow countrymen who disagree with their views with respect. Mainstream media took note of it all and realized there is no money in the truth. But there is money—big money—in division, in verbal violence, and in bias.

In this country, those who have the toughest or most dangerous jobs are among our lowest compensated. The incomes of our police officers, firefighters, teachers, and military can in no way be defended against the multimillions paid to actors, athletes, media personalities, and reality show stars. But this is how a democracy works. Any demand will create a market, and we prefer to be well entertained rather than well educated. We would rather have what we already believe reinforced than be shown the truth.

There has always been a feeling among journalists that they are not performing a job, but answering a calling. That much I believe is true. But long ago, the call to find the truth became the call to change the world. However, journalists are not here to change the world, but to bring the world to the rest of us to change through the truth.

"A fish cannot see the water it is swimming in" explains how someone can be oblivious to something so obvious to others. And one of the most important things to happen to journalism was the public's awareness of a clear bias in the media and their demand that journalists see it too. This created an opportunity to bring the corrective process into journalism and into the public. This was the time for change. But like every entity or individual who embarks on change, the media and its viewers, readers, and listeners did not find balance. They simply swung the dysfunction to the other extreme. The answer to liberal bias is not conservative bias. The answer is the truth.

Change is a process. Our first action upon becoming aware of dysfunction will always be to take our behavior to the opposite extreme, which is equally destructive and unsustainable. However, the hope is that an entity or individual will stay connected to the corrective process and continue to bring the behavior—day by day, step by step—closer to the center, and closer to the truth. But because the public did not continue the process, the demand for the truth became the demand to have what they already believed proven right; and because the media did not continue the process, the business of finding the truth simply became a business.

Today, every American with a political bias knows where to go to get their views reinforced; former politicians, political speechwriters, campaign managers, and White House staffers know where to go to get jobs; and businessmen know where to go to make money. There is a place for all of them in network and cable news. But it is not too late for journalists to return to their purpose. They are here not to be of service to themselves by injecting their own beliefs into their work or inflating their self-image by socializing with those in power, but to be of service to the world through the truth. The ability to do this lies solely in their hands.

There are enough journalists who have become celebrities with celebrity-sized money and power to create their own news network; one run and staffed only by journalists. No businessmen, no political professionals, and no one who hasn't been educated in or bound by the highest standards, requirements, and ethics of journalism. I understand the news business is still a business, but it is a dysfunctional one, and you cannot change a dysfunctional system by operating within it. This is your moment to create a new and authentic way. This is your moment to honor your calling. You have shown us you will defer to businessmen and politicians. You have shown us you will compromise your integrity and profession through bias. It is now time to show us the truth.

In the news media, the messenger must never be greater than the message. In today's opinion media, the messenger seeks not only to be greater than the message, but above the need for responsibility and accountability. It may be true that opinion is where the passion is. Unfortunately, it is also where the prejudice, hatred, anger, dysfunction, and verbal violence are. But it doesn't have to be this way.

One's opinions and how they are expressed are a reflection of not only the number and kinds of experiences he has opened himself up to, but also how well he has translated them. Since no one is able to have every experience in his lifetime, the beauty of being exposed to the opinions of others is to reveal all that is possible. The broader one's experiences and willingness to be open to the new and unknown, the more beneficial and accessible his views are to others. The narrower one's experiences and thinking, the more rigid and inaccessible his opinions become. Because when one speaks he is telling me about himself, every time he gives an opinion, he is telling me which path he has chosen.

For an opinion to properly serve its purpose, it must be developed by one with a healthy and open mind and not just be an attempt to validate an already-held dysfunctional and inflexible belief. And you will always know that an opinion is from a healthy mind and serving its purpose if it creates, unites, resolves, and heals through understanding and compassion.

However, opinion has become less about the benefits of the statement than about the way it is expressed. And today it seems the only way an opinion can be expressed is through ridicule, anger, hatred, and divisiveness, which only makes the opinion accessible to those who live their lives the same way—through their brokenness. But whenever one gives an opinion he always has a choice. He can communicate a position or disagreement with dignity, with the goal of accomplishing what is good for all, or through verbal violence that can only provide a dysfunctional sense of relevance and importance for one.

Throughout my life, there have been those who tried to convince me to include hockey among the sports I enjoy. While I'm certain there is a legitimate sport in there somewhere, I have never been able to find it with so much malicious and intentional violence blocking my way. So it is with opinion media. There are many valid points being made every day in opinion media that are obscured by verbal violence, and that remain inaccessible to everyone except the opinionist's like-minded core believers. But as politicians have shown us, there is big money and power in appealing to a base of people who only want their opinions validated—not expanded or changed—and who will remain loyal regardless of which political party is in office.

With opinion, it is easy for one to confuse his prejudices with his principles, and another way to determine whether an opinion has been formed through a healthy or a dysfunctional mind is by observing how much time he devotes to pointing out the weaknesses, hypocrisy, and failures of others, and how much he devotes to exploring and disclosing his own. In today's opinion media, "just saying what everyone else is thinking" or "just telling the truth" is always relayed through ridicule or anger and only applies to one's adversaries. Opinionists never seem to "just tell the truth" about themselves. So what if for every book sentence or broadcast minute spent criticizing perceived enemies through verbal violence, media opinionists had to apply the same amount of time and level of scrutiny to themselves and those things they favor? Would they be able to tell us whether they have ever had their minds changed through ridicule? Would they be able to tell us how hatred and anger ever resolved a conflict? Or would they find a more sophisticated, educated, and beneficial way to express opinion? And if our country's opinion media finds it is too much to ask that opinionists deeply and authentically examine the way they have chosen to assert their views over the years, maybe it is simply time to ask ourselves, how is our country better for it?

You can often tell those who have not only gone through their personal dark nights, but stayed there until they found answers to questions they never knew to ask, unearthed feelings they never knew existed, and discovered truths they never thought possible. There is a richness about them when they come through the other side, a depth to their souls, a mindfulness to their words and behaviors. There is also the realization that we too often mainstream and make acceptable those things we once considered extreme. Today this means we accept that our country best expresses itself through verbal violence. However, this changes when we no longer focus on what one is saying about the subject of his derision, but on what he is saying about himself; when verbal attacks are no longer valued over accuracy and accountability; when having influence is no longer determined by how much the other side hates you; when being relevant is no longer accomplished by minimizing everyone else; when cleverness is no longer defined by sarcastic quips or the ability to disparage those who disagree; when blaming self-created enemies can no longer be used to avoid taking responsibility for one's own words and actions; and when it is no longer acceptable to hate, manipulate, degrade, and divide and call it patriotism, party loyalty, Christianity, spirituality, recovery, growth, or health.

You can have principles without hostility. You can have pride without ridicule. You can make a point without being polarizing. But how can you love your country while expressing so much hatred for your fellow countrymen? The truth is, you can't.

If applying all I had learned since my time in the clinic to the media and our political system was often dark and difficult, my spiritual exploration was a joy, which was completely unexpected. For most of my life, so much about God and religion and spirituality seemed complicated and enigmatic. So I was surprised when the deeper my curiosity and questions took me, the simpler and clearer God became.

Christianity is my spiritual foundation. Though my childhood religious examples were inconsistent and incongruent, the heart of

Christianity made sense to me. Because of my history of sexual abuse, I would never again feel safe in the Catholic Church. However, I was comfortable gathering with like-minded souls and felt nourished by religious and spiritual rituals—the hymns, the prayers, the sermons, and the Scripture. All I had to do after I'd left the clinic was find a church and a congregation that felt comfortable with me: those who would accept my spiritual curiosity just as I accepted their spiritual certainty; allow me to take the Bible seriously just as I allowed them to take it literally; and let me use them to grow my soul just as I let them use me to grow their wealth.

After a few years, my search became less about the place I was supposed to find than the people I was supposed to meet along the way. It was in churches where I came across some of the rare few who not only lived their religious conviction as if it were an honor, but lived it joyfully. To them, making spiritual choices was not a hardship. They didn't complain about or struggle with or feel conflicted over doing what is spiritually right. They simply did it. And they rarely used words like morals or values, leaving them for those who were spiritually contradictory, those who had to use the words in their speech because they didn't live them through their behavior. But there was something else they showed me, something I would have to go back 2,500 years to understand.

However, even as my spiritual journey was bringing more authenticity into my life than I had ever known before, it was also helping me better understand how we took everything glorious about God and religion and spirituality and broke it.

There are two ways to legitimize dysfunction. One is to legalize it; the other is to spiritualize it. Anyone can find justifications for hatred, revenge, bigotry, murder, adultery, and sex addiction in the texts and practices of every religion and spiritual discipline. You only need to manipulate and interpret them to fit your chosen dysfunction, or join with others who have done this for you. And most will choose to seek out or create environments that support their dysfunction rather than strengthen their divinity.

Looking closely at or questioning another's spiritual life and choices is an extremely sensitive undertaking, especially when it is more important to look closely at and question one's own. I try to be mindful of this and keep my focus on my own spiritual weaknesses and strengths rather than someone else's, except when I am being asked for something, such as when George W. Bush asked for my vote. However, my attempts to reconcile the president's Christian beliefs with his political behavior were rarely tolerated by his fellow Christians. It was their view that asking a human being to act like a divine one was asking too much; that no person can ever live up to the life of Jesus Christ. We can only spend our lives trying.

I understand this. And I respect anyone's right to believe that Jesus was a God who became man, and far exceeds anything any one of us could ever imagine or emulate. But it also feels like a way to justify not even trying, a way to avoid having to consistently apply one's spiritual beliefs to his or her behavior, especially when faced with the most difficult people and circumstances. Christians are not expected to perform divine miracles. You don't need to walk on water, feed the multitudes with a handful of food, or raise the dead. The human miracles of forgiveness, mindfulness, tolerance, and compassion will always be enough. But while believing in these sacred intentions is important, they will never work in your life, or in the world, unless you live them.

Just as when I was younger, after I left the clinic my spiritual curiosity led me to other disciplines. The Hindu scripture, the Bhagavad Gita, once again became a source of inspiration; I began to practice yoga; and Buddhism brought a clarity and deep sense of awe to my spiritual life I had only hoped one day to find. But I have never called or considered myself a Christian, a Hindu, a Yogini, or a Buddhist. To me, claiming these identities means one has achieved actually living his or her life more in keeping with one's religion or spirituality than not, and I am a poor practitioner of all my spiritual beliefs.

Ironically, it is the addicts I have known who showed me what authentically turning a life over to a higher power looks like. That God is not a person or an idea or a belief, but an act.

All addicts deeply immerse their behaviors in whatever god they are convinced will ease their pain, never leave them, always love them. And I saw how powerful total acceptance of any chosen way of life can be. Whether it is a spiritual healing God or a material destructive one, you will become what you choose.

Everyone has a god—even those who say they don't—and sometimes more than one. You always hope the higher power you choose most often is one that causes you to live your life closer to your divinity: forgive someone who hurt you, say a kind word to someone who insulted you, love someone whom you didn't think deserved your love. But many choose gods that can only put everything unholy between themselves and a more enlightened life. And while most use only words to honor their spiritual God, you will always know your true higher power through your actions.

Your god is anything you believe you can't live without, what causes you anxiety at the thought of it being taken away, and what you devote most of your time, energy, or money supporting and protecting. Your god is what you sacrifice everything to: your family, your health, your morality, your freedom, your life. And your god is the god of one—you. Its only job is easing your pain, finding you love, getting you what you want, and taking away what you don't, and it makes every dysfunctional and self-centered dream, goal, demand, or desire a reality. It can be alcohol, drugs, or sex; money, your career, or your public image; your relationships or your possessions; your desire for power, relevance, or acceptance. It can be your need to be right, your need to be in control, your need to be validated and appreciated, or your demand to be seen and heard. But at its core, your god is your disappointment in the life you have—you should be happier, wealthier, more attractive, more desired, shine bigger, better, brighter; your god is your fear that you will not be or get everything you think you deserve.

Your God is none of this.

One day I came across a friend who was with someone I had never met. After a brief catching up, she asked me if I was still going to the Dharma center about an hour away from my home. Her friend looked bewildered for a moment and said, "How can you be a Buddhist? Your God isn't a living God."

It seemed to me such a curious thing to say. I don't remember what I said in response, but I remember what I thought. *I have the same God you do. Even if I believe in a different God, I have the same God you do. Even if I didn't believe in God at all, I'd still have the same God you do.*

Cause and effect is the one constant. You can have faith that dysfunctional choices will create only dysfunctional consequences, and healthy choices will create only healthy consequences. Mercy is that this is always true. However, being human poses two problems for us. One is that we think our dysfunctional choices are healthy; the other is that everything and everyone is connected through continuous interaction. You simply cannot always know, or even be capable of understanding, the impact what has happened at another time or place will have on your life. But every act of love, healing, and truth will create loving, healing, and truthful consequences. They may not happen when or how you think they are supposed to, but they will happen when and how they should.

The principles of cause and effect apply to every one of us all the time. Dishonesty, theft, abuse, adultery, addiction, murder—no matter what you've done or how much suffering your past dysfunctional choices have brought to yourself and the world, each moment brings another chance to make a healthy choice that creates a healthy consequence. While you must always be responsible for your past mistakes, cause and effect allow you to come just as you are right now and make the choices that will let you become who you were always meant to be.

God is all of those loving, healing, and truthful choices that create loving, healing, and truthful consequences. And whatever religion or spiritual path that consistently causes you to make authentic spiritual choices is the right one for you. It may be Scripture, the Eucharist, and Jesus on the cross; the Talmud, the Noble Eightfold Path, or the Yamas and Niyamas; the Bhagavad Gita, Lam Rim, or the Tao Te Ching; the Qur'an, *amal, yakeen,* and *muhabat*; sutras, yantras, mantras, or meditation; rosaries, malas, candles, or incense. But you will always know that your path is authentic—and being practiced authentically—if it contributes to the growth, unity, healing, and liberation of not just yourself, but the world. An authentic spiritual path practiced authentically will never contribute to dysfunction.

Love is the highest act that creates the highest consequence, and God is love. There was never a time when that concept was advanced that I didn't hear someone question, "But what about me? Am I supposed to quietly accept everything everyone does? Am I supposed to act happy when I'm not? How is being kind when I'm angry, or loving to someone I don't even like being true to my feelings?" And there was never a time when it didn't sound as if the questions were coming from those who wanted to be true to their dysfunctions, not their feelings.

It is not healthy for you to give yourself everything you want, any more than it is healthy to give others everything they want. Sometimes love sounds like yes. Sometimes love sounds like no. Sometimes love looks like doing for others. Sometimes love looks like allowing others to do for themselves. Sometimes love is accepting help. Sometimes love is helping yourself. But you must have a healthy mind to know the difference between dysfunction and love, because a healthy mind will demand that you determine your true intention for every choice. Knowing your true intention requires only one question: Are your choices about healing yourself and others, or about protecting your dysfunctions, like low self-esteem, enabling, and addiction?

Having a healthy mind doesn't mean you never get angry, or never feel disrespected, unappreciated, or misunderstood. But some who have reached a high level of health and mindfulness say that those times are few because they no longer give control of who they are and how they feel to others. There isn't the grasping and forcing and demanding that others fill the needs you should be filling yourself. Your value comes from a healthy and honorable you, not a dysfunctional something or someone else. You assert yourself appropriately rather than angrily and aggressively. And healthy boundaries allow you to determine what is your concern and what is not, where you belong and where you don't.

Everyone seeks happiness, and your happiness is true if your intention to heal yourself and others is true. Any choice you make with a dysfunctional ulterior motive can never bring happiness. But the truth is, as long as you inhabit both a body and a soul, you will struggle with making spiritual choices in a physical world, with finding balance between what your mind says you want and what your God says you already have. However, peace comes when you realize that the exact same circumstances will create the exact same consequences a million out of a million times. And if you change just one thing—an angry word into a kind one, a vengeful act into a loving one—you change everything.

Most religions and spiritual disciplines give us four principles that, when practiced authentically, will ease our suffering: no expectations, non-attachment, surrender, and non-judgment. And there is no doubt that craving, whether it is for a particular outcome, identity, person, thing, or circumstance, causes pain. However, rather than the acceptance of these four principles, the most compelling part of my spiritual journey was my resistance to the total elimination of their opposites. I had been steeping in psychology for too long not to wonder how much of my resistance came from genuinely exploring my spirituality and how much came from protecting my dysfunctions.

The concept of "interbeing"—that all phenomena are connected through a chain of cause and effect that has no beginning or end—most clearly shows the need for eliminating expectations; you can never acquire all the information you need to fully understand how continuous dependent events, often years ago and miles away, will affect the consequence of any choice made here and now. This is important to remember every time you place your expectations on another person or circumstance. If you are like most people, what you authentically know about yourself is next to nothing. What you authentically know about others is truly nothing. You know what they show you, and what you have judged to be true about what you have been shown, but because most operate out of their dysfunctions, neither is likely to be the truth. And if you have had no inclination to devote the time and effort to what *can* be known through self-exploration to better understand who you are, you will do even less to understand anyone else.

Yet, despite our dysfunctions and lack of truthful information, we place great expectations on other people and circumstances. We do or say something and expect love, respect, understanding, appreciation, happiness, or wealth from people and situations that we not only don't authentically know or understand, but have absolutely no control over. When our expectations are not met, which is the only possible outcome, we suffer.

You only have control over you. You truly know this if you no longer concentrate on what you expect from anyone or anything else as a result of your actions, but only on your actions, ensuring that each one comes from the highest and healthiest intentions. But for most, it has never been enough to live consciously and compassionately because that is who we are. Instead, we ultimately use our words and actions to get something in return.

In his thought-provoking book *The Prodigal God*, Timothy Keller uses the Parable of the Prodigal Son to illustrate how our lives are driven by our expectations of not only other people and circumstances, but God Himself. Most often the focus of this parable is on the wayward young son who finds his literal and spiritual way home. However, Timothy Keller believes that to end the parable there is to end it too soon, because as the story states, "There was a man who had *two* sons."

Although the youngest son had abandoned his family and squandered his inheritance, his father welcomed him home and prepared a great feast in his honor. The elder son, who had all the while remained loyal and obedient to his father, was furious at the warm reception and refused to attend the celebration. To his father's pleas to reconsider, the elder son replied,

> All these years I've been slaving for you and never disobeyed your orders. Yet, you never gave me even a young goat so I could celebrate with my friends. But when this son of yours who has squandered your property with prostitutes comes home, you kill the fattened calf for him!

The parable shows that, while the elder brother's choices were moral, his intentions behind those choices were not. He didn't remain at home to tend his father's fields and care for his livestock out of love. He expected something in return: an outward demonstration of his father's appreciation.

We all become Elder Brothers when we put God in our debt or attempt to control Him by making spiritual choices in order to get something from Him in return, or in effect tell God, "I did this for you, now you must do this for me." However, living according to your morals, your principles, or your spiritual path should not be a part of some bargain you've made with God. Doing what is loving, healing, and truthful with the expectation of waking up one morning to have all of our hopes and desires fulfilled is something we should have outgrown long ago. God is not Santa Claus.

You do not act to receive. You act to be.

You do not act God-like in return for answered prayers. You act God-like to be more like God, to be a mirror of His compassion and forgiveness. You do not say and do loving things for others in return for their devotion and appreciation. You are loving simply to be loving. You are kind to be kind. You are honest, faithful, supportive, and hardworking because this is who you are and will continue to be regardless of whether you get everything in return or nothing at all.

By now it was clear to me that a healthy life meant one could not depend upon another person or thing for his happiness or sense of self. However, non-attachment doesn't mean we should never have people or things in our lives. It is the "exaggerated seeking and clinging" that creates suffering. Most of our mental and physical energy is obsessively devoted to the object we desire. If we don't have it, we will either do anything to get it or endlessly mourn its absence. If we have it, we live in constant fear of losing it.

Expectations play a large part in attachment. What we cling to is less about having possessions, relationships, and identities than about what we expect them to provide for us. And we expect all that we acquire to make us feel loved, appreciated, or important. It is this dysfunctional perception that is at the root of all attachment. "Whether it is an object or a person, we give it meanings and values that do not exist."

Non-attachment is not detachment. Detachment is a dysfunctional defense mechanism and pain management system that results in mental, emotional, or physical isolation. However, detachment doesn't just block pain from one's life, it blocks the flow of all energy, and eliminates any chance of healthy interaction with the people and circumstances that are essential to heal dysfunction. Rather, non-attachment is an act of compassion and healing. There is no conscious manipulation of choices and consequences out of fear. When we relinquish control and release our grasp, energy flows, allowing our lives to grow, change, and heal through all that comes and goes.

Many say it is this very relinquishing of control—or the surrendering of our expectations and attachments to something greater than ourselves—that is the heart of any authentically practiced religion or spiritual discipline and the foundation of every healthy life. Unfortunately, it is also the most difficult spiritual principle to practice.

In the physical world, our expectations and attachments have substance. We can explain, describe, point to, even hold in our hands what we want or who we think we are. Such substance and certainty are comforting. However, spiritual authenticity requires that we surrender all we know or think we know, everything we want or think we deserve to something we've never seen and can't definitively explain. It asks us to willingly give up the known for the unknown, leave the comfort of substance and certainty and enter a world of Mystery. For most, this exchange is hardly enticing.

Like everything spiritual, it is much easier to talk about or give the appearance of surrender than authentically live it. And there is likely no other saying used more often to give the appearance of surrender than "it is what it is." Many times the message behind these words is, "Since whatever harm I have caused cannot be changed, I am going to accept it and forget it, and this is what the rest of you should do too." However, acceptance is not an opportunity to be dismissive. It does not mean you escape responsibility for your actions. And it is not a justification for future inaction, or a way to disregard the lesson that must be learned. "It is what it is" does not provide you with a convenient ending, but a necessary beginning. Because it is meant to help you heal and grow by asking the question: While you cannot change the past, how will you change your future?

Many don't surrender until they are forced to, until they have exhausted every justification or attempt to control. However, surrender isn't a last resort. It isn't failure. It isn't submission, giving in, or giving up. Surrender is a way of life.

About 2,500 years ago a spiritual philosophy emerged based on a collection of verses called the *Tao Te Ching*. The Chinese word *tao* can mean way, path, or road, as well as knowledge. Taoism was founded on the principle of a harmonious relationship between all that exists, or "when the walker and road become one." Most of our time and energy is spent in struggle, in forcing our will upon our surroundings in total opposition to all that is natural and true. Taoism teaches there is a rhythm to the universe that, when surrendered to, brings us in harmony with existence. Musicians hear rhythm in their environment. Writers hear rhythm in their words. But those whose lives flow with the universe *feel* its rhythm in their bodies and souls. Their actions are fluid, simple, but most of all, effortless. Taoists call this *wu wie*—action without action.

Whether in churches, the spiritual community, or everyday life, you know when you come across the rare few whose lives are in step with the universe. They are not those who suppress their anxiety or talk about never feeling stress to give the appearance of a calm life. They are not those who tell others to relax or lighten up. They accept your struggles just as they accept their own, not with a sigh of resignation, but with the ease of surrender. They have made their peace with Mystery and live to honor it through their humility, because with each step they are joyfully aware that "the road is wiser than the one who walks its path."

There is likely no other principle more discussed in the spiritual community than non-judgment. I have always found it interesting that most only mention the need to practice non-judgment upon hearing a negative comment about someone or something, but never a positive one. However, non-judgment means to have no judgment at all, whether positive or negative, because its goal is to free us from the painful cycle of attaching to things we desire and avoiding things we don't. But eliminating all judgment never seemed particularly healthy, or even possible, to me. It was Buddhism that got me closer to understanding why.

I was at a spiritually themed lecture one evening when someone made a comment someone else considered negative.

"We should only observe, not pass judgment," he said, and the inevitable discussion on non-judgment followed.

I listened as the many good reasons for practicing non-judgment were offered by several of those present, but something about the conversation troubled me.

"Weren't you judging when you said the person who made the comment should observe and not judge?" I asked.

"No," he replied. "I made an observation."

I asked again, "But isn't deciding that you made an observation rather than a judgment making a judgment?"

It seemed to me it takes judgment to conclude that someone has judged. And calling one's own behavior an observation or discerning or a choice rather than a judgment also requires that a judgment be made to determine the most appropriate label. When you choose one thing, you must reject something else. And determining that observation is good and judgment is bad sounded like judgment to me.

Literally every moment of our lives contains judgment. We accept what we judge to be favorable to us and reject what we don't. The shirt you're wearing, the car you drive, the spouse you married, the career you have, the pet you choose, the food you buy, whether to walk, sit, stand, sleep, eat, watch, listen, or speak all require you to make a judgment that, if you are like most, is more often made through dysfunction than not. Buddhism taught me that our goal should not be to eliminate judgment, but to judge properly.

As with everything in life, whether your judgment is appropriate or not depends on your motivation. Do you use judgment as a weapon, as a means to raise your self-esteem by degrading or ridiculing others? Or do you judge to determine which choices contribute to balance, love, growth, truth, and the healing of yourself and others? Through the Noble Eightfold Path—right view, right intention, right speech, right action, right livelihood, right effort, right mindfulness, and right concentration—Buddhism showed me the way to a healthy life through healthy judgment. It also showed me that, while judgment is necessary, having an opinion about everything and everyone is not.

When I saw the necessity for judgment as well as non-judgment, I also realized there is a time for commitment and a time for surrender; a time for healthy attachment to the things that support love, healing, and truth and a time to be free of attachments that can only bring suffering; a time for balanced expectations and a time for no expectations at all. Everything has a purpose. Often it is to show us what is possible through its opposite: you understand love when you've seen hatred, kindness when you've seen anger, life when you've seen death. There is even an appropriate place for the one thing many in the spiritual community believe should be completely eliminated: the ego.

I had been out of the clinic a few years when a book by an author known primarily to the spiritual community had captured the interest of a much wider audience. I had read his first book while in the clinic, and though he disagreed that understanding and dismantling one's dysfunctional past was essential to having a healthy life, I thought his book incredibly insightful and was happy to see his next one get worldwide attention. I bought and read the second book and was grateful to be reintroduced to some of the concepts I had found so enlightening in his first, among them how much suffering we bring upon ourselves and the world when we identify with our egos. As I held the book in my hands I noticed a few things. One was that his name on the front cover was twice as big as the book title. Another was that the back of the book featured a good-sized photograph and a short biography labeling him a spiritual author and teacher. Such labels and identifications are ego in its purest sense. In this case, the ego was used to bring others closer to an awakened life. Everything in the physical world—ego, identity, labels, form—has a place, which is to always serve a spiritual purpose: one of love, healing, and truth. It is when we choose not to use something, including ourselves, for its true purpose that suffering occurs. This journey is not about finding your happiness. It is about finding your meaning, and using all of the gifts in the physical world to live it for a spiritual purpose.

Meditation is a foundational component of many Eastern religions and spiritual philosophies, and my initial exposure to the practice, through Buddhism and yoga, astonished me. For decades, I'd simply had no idea my mind was nowhere close to functioning as it should.

While some use it as yet another way to numb or distance themselves from their lives, meditation is not a lack of awareness or unconsciousness. It is a hyper-consciousness that will bring you closer to understanding not only yourself, but all existence.

Though meditation can take many forms, there are basically two types: insight (vipashyana) and concentration (shamatha). Insight meditation uses self-observation and introspection as a means of transformation. When meditating, the mind and body can become overrun with thoughts, feelings, and sensations. Through insight meditation, one neither attaches to nor avoids the sensory activity, but rather simply observes all that occurs in the mind and body. The image I have heard used most often to describe the process likens the meditator to a river and the sensory activity to the debris flowing through it. With the arising and passing of thoughts, feelings, and sensations, the meditator sees the ultimate impermanence of all things and the senselessness of attachment and avoidance.

Concentration meditation is where one focuses on a single object or thought to achieve one-pointedness, and it can be anything from a mantra to a candle flame to the virtue of loving-kindness to consciousness itself. My first experience with meditation was to concentrate on my breath. I only had to focus on breathing in and breathing out, ten breaths at a time, for fifteen minutes. If a thought, feeling, or sensation arose in my mind or body at any time during the course of ten breaths, I had to start over. It took me nearly six months to make it to ten without my mind or body demanding attention.

Today, while I am much stronger in my meditation practice, there are still times when I simply cannot quiet my mind. I was at a group meditation session one morning and asked the facilitator, whose meditation practice spanned twenty years, how many minutes out of his daily sitting was he where he wanted to be. He said there are times—after work, the kids, bills to pay, and chores to do—when just making it to his cushion at the end of the night was the strongest part of his practice. He explained that it is this "coming back" that defines any process. It is coming back to your cushion to meditate when you would rather sit on the sofa and watch television. It is coming back to breath number one after a thought or feeling, once again, interrupted you before you had reached breath number ten. It is coming back to being an observer after you attached too long to a thought or feeling you should have let pass by. And it is coming back to your commitment to living an honorable, compassionate, and forgiving life after you reacted to something or someone in a dishonorable, angry, or vengeful way. Every errant step gives us another chance to come back to love, healing, and truth.

Ironically, the concept of "coming back" is essential to enlightenment. Most imagine enlightenment to be the ultimate goal. One that, once achieved, transforms a human being into a perfected one free of all anger, fear, pain, ego, judgment, and difficulties, who lives his life in complete surrender, and radiates pure love and truth. And who would ever want to leave any of this? However, in his book *After the Ecstasy, the Laundry*, Jack Kornfield explains, "There is no such thing as enlightened retirement."

> Enlightenment does exist. It is possible to awaken. Unbounded freedom and joy, oneness with the Divine, awakening into a state of timeless grace—these experiences are more common than you know, and not far away. There is one further truth, however: They don't last. Our realizations and awakenings show us the reality of the world, and they bring transformation, but they pass. . . . We all know that after the honeymoon comes the marriage, after the

election comes the hard task of governance. In spiritual
life it is the same: After the ecstasy comes the laundry.

However, Jack Kornfield isn't saying that since enlightenment can't
be continually sustained in the physical world we should settle for the
mundane. He is asking the question that is at the very heart of our
existence: "Is there a wisdom [that] includes both the ecstasy and the
laundry?"

Currently and throughout history, there are countless examples of
individuals and institutions that claim to have achieved everything from
unimpeachable integrity to a godliness untouched by worldly dysfunction, while their actions show this to be untrue. The result has been and
continues to be some of the most destructive people and communities
among us. This happens because the rest of us so desperately want to
believe the myths those we identify with cover themselves in that we
deny the obvious: No individual or institution is without dysfunction.
Not one. Individual and institutional health is not defined by the lack
of dysfunction, but by how well and how quickly the dysfunction is
addressed and remedied when it is revealed, and by how well and how
quickly the rest of us admit to and heal our need to protect our own
dysfunctions by enabling the dysfunctions of others.

With awareness comes the realization that there are times of deep
compassion, great wisdom, boundless joy, and ultimate freedom that
coexist with times of fear, pain, struggle, and brokenness. By refusing
to acknowledge and address the shadow that accompanies life, we
never receive the gift it yearns to give us. The physical world, with all
its pain and problems, is not here to thwart our enlightenment, but to
strengthen it. With every *satori*, or enlightenment experience, we come
back and hone what we've learned against the challenges in our lives
and in this world; we come back to show others what love, healing,
and truth look like in a world of anger, pain, and dysfunction. Or in
the words of Suzuki Roshi, "There are no enlightened people, there is
only enlightened activity."

Yet enlightenment through resisting, denying, or ignoring the
lessons of the world rather than embracing them continues to be a

preoccupation of many, often in conflict with some of spirituality's core principles. An authentic spiritual life is not possible without humility. Which means you would rarely, if ever, know who has achieved *satori*, so deep would be his commitment to this virtue. But there are those who regularly describe what they have determined to be an enlightened experience, or express their desire to generate one. There is a sense of using this experience not to strengthen their humility, but to escalate their need to feel special, chosen, or more connected to God than others. Not only does this eliminate humility as one of the benefits of the experience, but it also undermines the very purpose of enlightenment: to become one with the Divine and all that exists, not separate, different from, or better than. There are also times when it is difficult to see a difference between the way a seeker uses enlightenment and an addict uses alcohol, drugs, or sex. Both want an escape from the life they have created, rather than a doorway to their truth and healing.

However, the biggest conflict is that in desiring an enlightenment one has yet to attain, one has to deny the present moment just as it exists. The concept of "being in the moment" is the bedrock of spiritual practice. It is in the moment where we become one with the Divine and all of existence, and it is only in the moment that enlightenment can occur.

I once heard being in the moment described through an exercise for practicing non-judgment. The idea was to go somewhere densely populated, such as an airport or park, and just observe those near or passing by without judging, labeling, or forming an opinion; or, while on a walk, simply become aware of your environment: the blooms of the flowers, the expanse of the sky, the feel of the day. Some who performed the exercise described being able to successfully observe others without judgment, or appreciate their present environment without their mind wandering into the past or future. This sounded to me like a valuable first step, but still a distance away from actually being in the moment. If you are aware of how well you are practicing non-judgment or appreciating your surroundings, two things are occurring. First, you may not be judging others, but you are judging yourself to determine how well you are performing your task, and maybe even congratulating yourself on your high level of awareness. Second, you are still operating in a duality—the experience and the observer—that cannot exist when in the moment. When you are in the moment there is no self-consciousness, no separation between you and the experience. You are the experience. You would not be able to describe how well you practiced non-judgment or appreciated the day, because you wouldn't have observed the others or your environment, you would have become them.

Duality was the easiest thing about Christianity for me to let go of. Christians more often create God in their own image, rather than allow God to make them in His. And their God is somewhere "out there" or "on high," separate from humanity. The idea of a distant benevolent presence constantly watching over you, unconditionally loving you, answering your prayers is comforting—until things go horribly wrong. The Bible and Christian songs are full of pain over feeling abandoned or rejected by God in one's darkest hour or time of greatest need. But when your God lies within your own body and soul, when you make choices that honor and strengthen the divinity within, rather than expect an outside presence to rescue you or do your bidding, you hold the greatest power on earth: the power to manifest God, to bring Him into the world through every loving, healing, and truthful thought, word, and act.

Life is about integration: speech and behavior, inner and outer lives, the individual and the community, the material and the spiritual, but above all, your God and you.

It would be difficult to have any relationship with Buddhism and not hear of the plight of Tibet. For 700 years, Buddhism has been essential to the lives of Tibetans, who take its teachings—among them *ahimsa*, or non-violence—not as beliefs or ideas, but as solemn vows that must be diligently practiced. With Christianity, I look for how well and how effectively its foundational teachings of forgiveness and compassion can be applied by its followers in times of greatest provocation and suffering. I can do the same with Buddhism as China, day by day, gets closer to eliminating an entire culture and people. I had hoped that after 700 years of faithful Dharma practice, Tibetans would no longer exist because they had been released from *samsara*, the cycle of birth and death. Instead, they are being violently obliterated. We still mourn civilizations lost centuries ago, yet watch passively as one is disappearing before our eyes. Maybe the loss of Tibet is meant to teach us more about ourselves than about the effectiveness of Buddhism and non-violence in the face of brutality. Maybe only when we are faced with what remains after it no longer exists will we see the true value of Tibet. Or maybe we can awaken for just a moment and see it now.

My years since leaving the clinic have been spent relearning the world I live in, and God, politics, war, honor, authenticity, love, what is valuable and acceptable, and what is not all look different to me now. But by far relationships, of every kind, have been the most difficult to see clearly. And the truth is, there is still much I don't understand.

The counselors recommended that all single patients, and those who soon would be, not enter into any intimate relationships for a year after leaving the clinic. I waited two. The profound changes in my life required so much of my time, energy, and attention there was little left over for establishing a healthy, intimate relationship. Eventually I realized not even two years was long enough.

I wasn't pursuing a relationship, but after those first two years out of the clinic I felt ready if it should happen. And just like that, I found myself in two brief relationships. One felt like every relationship I have ever known. The other felt closer to nothing like I have ever known. I thought it interesting that I was uncomfortable in both. It was a magazine interview with a professional golfer discussing his swing change that showed me why. He explained that when he first began making changes, everything new felt unnatural and uncomfortable, and he kept finding his way back to his old swing. After time and practice, he came to an even more uncomfortable middle ground, where neither his old nor his new swing felt right. Eventually, through even more hard work, his old swing was no longer where he wanted to be and his new swing felt like home. And I realized that, even two years after leaving the clinic, I was still in the murky middle where neither a dysfunctional relationship nor a potentially healthy one felt comfortable.

I spent the next several years observing those in committed relationships. Some people I knew well. Others were simply the result of being in the same place at the same time. I know now that authentically healthy and loving relationships—where two people truly want to be where they are and with whom they are committed—are rare. Mostly, people in relationships are in a constant state of annoyance, inconvenienced by those they claim to love. Spouses and children are regularly treated as nuisances to be tolerated, dealt with, or ignored. Dishonor, disrespect, personal insults, power struggles, and sabotage, whether passive or aggressive, are rampant. And the way people in relationships speak to each other, if they speak at all, is enough to break your heart as well as your belief that authentic love is possible. Even when spoken, those extraordinary three words between lovers are often reduced to just words—without feeling, thought, or meaning, and without the actions that would make "I love you" true.

A healthy relationship is not about finding a partner you believe is unbroken. No such person exists. It is about finding one who has committed to continual self-exploration, the truthful disclosure of what has been found, and transformation. But from the beginning, we consciously choose to mythologize our lovers and relationships rather than look at them honestly, afraid of what we may see, and even more afraid of, once again, finding ourselves alone. So we imagine relationships that more resemble a holiday form letter that only admits to marriages, births, graduations, awards, and exotic vacations but never divorces, arrests, school suspensions, infidelity, or stays in rehab.

However filled with passion and possibility, we actually enter into relationships through our dysfunctions. It is at that moment when we must choose between two paths: we can either make each other sicker or help each other heal. Soul mates are not found. They are created. And it is healing along with your beloved that creates a soul union.

In a healthy relationship, when we commit it is to the mutual process of self-discovery, truthful disclosure, and transformation, not to another person. But the chance is far greater that you'll find someone who will insist that you "take me as I am," rather than "take me as I am right now." And the more committed we are to our dysfunctions, the more popular the concept of unconditional love has become. It is always much easier to find someone to agree to love us unconditionally than it is for us to authentically transform our dysfunctions. Over and over, I have seen the highest spiritual act of unconditional love used not to heal, but to protect what is broken.

More often than not, when one speaks of unconditional love it has nothing to do with how he feels about you, but how he wants you to feel about him and the dysfunctions he has no desire to heal. However, unconditional love does not mean unconditional acceptance. While you can feel compassion for one's trauma and pain, you cannot accept dysfunctional ways of suppressing or managing them. If you do, you are not loving unconditionally. You are enabling.

Unconditional love also includes unconditionally loving oneself. It means I will no longer consciously expose myself to or remain in the presence of dysfunctional speech and behavior, but I will love you. And it means continuing to love myself, as I no longer accept my own dysfunction.

Love is unconditional, but a relationship is reciprocal. There are too many who claim to be in relationships they are refusing to participate in. And there are too few who truly know how to make love outside of the bedroom, who understand that passion and physical attraction cannot survive without the mental and emotional connection created through mutual self-discovery and growth.

Today, my respect for intimate relationships is greater than ever before. I have seen the complexity, but also the joy of them. I do not know what lies ahead for me, but I will continue to let others teach me all that is true and beautiful about intimacy and relationships. And, for the first time, I will wait.

I have met many who have committed to transforming their lives. Some are addicts. Some are enablers. Some are those who have simply awakened to the knowledge that who they are is not who they are meant to be. But whether their transformations began in a place of worship, a rehab clinic, a therapist's office, or elsewhere, most spoke of having to find the strength and courage to make a painful choice if they were to not only get healthy, but stay that way.

Our dysfunctions cause us to try to resolve conflict or trauma by repeatedly recreating it in our lives. The process of recovery and healing breaks this destructive pattern, and includes removing oneself from a dysfunctional environment to discover and experience what is healthy. But what if this environment is one's own family?

Many families are dysfunctional systems. Often, only one family member chooses to break the patterns passed on to him or her during childhood. The rest remain trapped in a cycle of pain and dysfunction, usually for the rest of their lives. The hope is that the one who is healing will be strong enough to operate outside the dysfunctional system and preserve family relationships. But most only get sucked back into what is guaranteed to trigger the very things one is trying to heal. Ultimately, the transformation of the entire family is ideal. But the truth is, it is just as painful for many parents and siblings to admit to contributing to another family member's dysfunction as it is to admit to their own. They hear the lessons of healing not as essential information, but as blame. So to avoid accountability, they choose their dysfunction over transformation, their pain over their child, brother, or sister. Too often, this means the one committed to healing must choose between recovery and family.

Many times I have seen grown men and women weep uncontrollably over losing their families twice: once through dysfunction or addiction, and again through healing. And the thought of one day hearing of their estranged mother or father's passing drops them to their knees. How do they mourn? How do they honor someone in death they couldn't be in the same room with when alive?

Since leaving the clinic, I have struggled with mending and managing family relationships. The most difficult by far have been with my children. When choosing to give my children a much different life than my own, I simply raised them through the other extreme, which created just as much dysfunction. Enabling is doing something for someone they should be doing for themselves; loving someone more than they love themselves. It took me most of my children's lives to figure that out. But I recommit every day to my growth and healing so my children can live the lives they were meant to, and because the alternative is no longer an option.

When you refuse to recognize and heal your own dysfunction, you destroy any chance of your children living healthy lives, because all that you have protected and preserved *will* be passed on to them. If they are lucky, they will spend all of their lives trying to undo the damage you have done. If they aren't, they will spend all of their lives living out the dysfunctions and addictions they've inherited—broken, shamed, scared, angry, and alone. And all of this will be passed on to their children, your grandchildren, and every generation thereafter until someone rises up and says, "This stops here."

The process of loving and forgiving my father began when I understood that everything he passed on to me had been passed on to him. It isn't often likely one is born with the capacity to sexually abuse children. He is taught. I spent many nights asking my father, *Who hurt you?* But the question would forever remain unanswered. My father had committed suicide years before.

For most of my life, I was angry with my father for shattering my innocence and my childhood. After the clinic, when I realized transformation was possible, I was angry because he either couldn't or wouldn't heal himself, and because I had paid too high a price for him loving his dysfunctions more than he loved me. However, I knew my anger was not only slowing my healing, but causing me even further harm, and I had to find a way through it.

If healing a dysfunctional relationship with one still living is difficult, it is even more so with one who isn't. I began the only way I knew how: I wrote to him. For years I told my father everything I had always wanted to say, but was too young or scared to. There were times I couldn't stop crying long enough to finish what I needed him to hear. And times when what I had written and remembered made me so physically ill I had to burn up or tear up the words until they no longer existed. But one night, I wanted to show him not what my childhood looked like, but my life as an adult. I told him out loud how much he still controlled my choices, my relationships, and my life, whether I wanted him to or not, and despite his death.

All of my life you have abused and abandoned me. And now when I want you to leave, you refuse. I want to heal, and I want to live my life, not yours. So I am begging you, please, let me go.

I did not hear, but instead, felt these words:

I am part of your healing, and I will not leave you.

Today, my father does for me in death what he was not able to do while alive. Whenever I get too tired or frustrated with all that it takes to heal, he shows me the consequences of quitting; he bares his pain and brokenness so that I may know what love and honor and truth look like; and he leads me away from accepting his life as my own and toward something far greater than I ever imagined. Through this, he loves me.

Epilogue

A few years after leaving the clinic, I came across a friend of a friend of someone from my life long ago. As we spoke, she said she had expected me to be someone other than who she found me to be, then repeated what others had used to define my life. As she reconnected me to a place and a people from a life long past, I replied, "I appreciate them all." She said she didn't understand how I could appreciate unkind words or acts from another. I explained I had been blessed by those—all of them great teachers—who saw only faults and failures, and blessed to have lived in environments lacking in love, truth, and humility, because every unkind or dishonest word or act led me to continually seek, and often find, my true Self within. And led me to the homes, the arms, the open hearts of those who showed me what an awakened mind, an honest life, an authentic relationship, and true love look like. For this, I can only be grateful.

As I walked away, I became aware of a deep joy in my heart and of the words a man had spoken to me many years before, but which I didn't understand until that moment. It was after my former husband had asked me for a divorce. I was still sitting in the same place I had lowered myself into after hearing those words the day before, when my therapist walked in. He sat across from me, took both of my hands in his, and began to speak. He was asking questions, this I knew. But I could only ask a question of my own: "What am I to do?"

He replied, "Anything you want."

When it was clear I didn't understand, he squeezed my hands tighter as if he could press into me all the joy and excitement and anticipation he was feeling, and said, "Marta, don't you realize? You are free. You are finally free."

I remember thinking the only thing I was capable of thinking at the time: *But I don't want to be free.* But on this day, I stopped and listened more closely to the question that had been echoing in my heart for so many years now. *Who are you?* And then I knew.

I am free.

Free to learn.

Free to grow.

Free to heal.

Free to forgive.

Free to laugh and dance and sing with the joy of a child.

Free to love with intimacy, integrity, and vulnerability to the core of my soul and only give myself to one who can do the same.

Free to no longer be reckless with my heart, my mind, my body, my soul, my life.

Free to find loving ways to resolve a conflict.

Free to know that emptiness does not mean empty.

Free to know my God is within.

Free to hear anger and hatred and ridicule from another and feel only compassion for the pain they carry inside.

Free to know that a life without authentic humility is a weak one.

Free to know that confidence looks nothing like arrogance.

Free to look at one who has done something unimaginable against the laws of man and nature, through loving eyes and a merciful heart.

Free to know one cannot solve a problem with the same broken mind that created it.

Free to know that every dysfunctional choice works—until it doesn't.

Free to embrace everything that is valuable to me, even when it looks like nothing anyone else would choose, even when it isn't a thing at all.

Free to be unafraid of the life I was always meant to live.

Free to be the person my words say I am.

Free to stop shackling myself to pain and anger, to thoughts and behaviors, to judgments and identities that were never mine to begin with.

Free to know I was never in bondage at all.

The journey is not becoming free. It is realizing I always was.

I am, and forever will be, free.

And so are you.

tayatha om gate gate paragate parasamgate bodhi svaha

Acknowledgments

The content of one's life is a product of all who have been a part of it. Because I am conscious of just how true this is for me . . .

To those who walked away, thank you for the lessons you left behind. To those who stayed, thank you for the love and blessings you bring to me each day, and for knowing I could never have done this without you.

Jutta, thank you for holding on when I was letting go, for never giving up when I wanted to quit, for knowing when to speak and when to stay silent, and for understanding that sometimes I needed to walk away so I could come back. Thank you for your kindness, wisdom, and unconditional support and belief in me during those times I couldn't give these to myself. And thank you for constantly saying to me those most beautiful words: I am here. For all of this and so much more that may be left unspoken or unwritten, but always felt in my heart—I am forever grateful.

To Charles Googe, my attorney and second-favorite quarterback, I would not have found my way through the publishing world and all of my missteps if it weren't for your exceptional and always compassionate guidance. And a special thank you to Michael Bogner, Caroline Barnard, Angela Abbott, Linda Laager, Arlene Prunkl, Fiona Raven, and David Coldiron. I couldn't have asked for a better offensive line.

Nancy, without your ability to navigate the world of permissions and licensing agreements, this book would still be unpublished. Thank you hardly seems enough.

To my editors Dania, Irene, Judith, Lynne, and especially Paula, thank you for carrying out the most difficult task of all with such grace. Professionally analyzing someone's creativity while balancing that critique with a respect for both the work and the person is something only a rare few in the publishing industry have the ability to do. Making a difficult job even harder, not only did you have to repeatedly read an over 500-page manuscript, you also had to try to convince me to make changes. Many of your suggestions made this a much better, stronger book. But I am most grateful to you for accepting with understanding and compassion those times when I chose to remain with what I had written, even if it only made sense to me.

My boundless gratitude to H.H. the 14th Dalai Lama of Tibet and Healing the Divide. I have had many moments during the past several years that have impacted my healing and consciousness. But to be taught the Dharma by His Holiness for a precious twelve hours in New York City has been one of the most lasting and profound. Those days spent hearing the teachings of a spiritual discipline that is essential not only to my life but to the world, in a city that I love, shared with cherished family and friends were as close to miraculous as I've ever known. So much so that I didn't want to leave, believing the feeling would end when I returned home. It didn't. The awareness, love, strength, and newfound sense of direction I gained during that time have remained with me to this day. And my deepest gratitude to Amanda and her son, Nicholas, for allowing me to experience all of this from the sixth row.

To my peers and counselors at the clinic, the effect you have had on my life, whether through showing me what to do or what not to do, is without measure. And so is my appreciation.

Sam, Rick, and Mary Kate, the real freedom was on the inside. I hope you found your way back.

Steve, you saw it in me first. Thank you for saying the three words that helped me see it too.

To Barry, Ralph, and Sandra, thank you for helping me build more than a house.

Cameille and Susan, you didn't have to care so deeply about me or my book, but I am so grateful you did. Both are better because of you.

To my dear friends and compassionate teachers, without whom this book would be far different, thank you for your love, kindness, and support, particularly Beata, Bette, Bonnie, Dana and Tom, Janine and Kerry, Jenn, JoAnn and Jim, Laura and Tom, Lynda and Dave, Mark, Michael, Nancy, and as always, William.

To Jeremy and Sarah, you truly kept me honest and made me live my words, not just say them. I know the new path shown to us those many years ago has not been easy and didn't often make sense. But I promise you, this is what love looks like.

To Bunnie, you are the reason this stops here.

And to my Bonnie Blue, not a day goes by . . .

~ Bonnie Blue ~

Notes

Front Matter

vii   *If nothing has changed*: Hollis, James. *Through the Dark Wood: Finding Meaning in the Second Half of Life*. Sounds True Audio Learning Course, 2009, disc 3.

vii   *Never think you've got it*: Simms, Phil. 2009 AFC Championship, *NFL on CBS* broadcast, January 24, 2010.

vii   *As I turn to you and I say*: Starsailor. "Good Souls." *Love Is Here*. EMI Records Ltd., 2002.

vii   *The moment you see*: Mallika Sutta. Samyutta Nikaya, Chapter 3, Sutta 8, cited in Hanh, Thich Nhat. *Teachings on Love*. Berkeley, CA: Parallax Press, 2007, p. 22.

ix   *It's a long, hard road*: Sexton, Charlie. "Everyone Will Crawl." *Under the Wishing Tree*. MCA, 1995.

3   *love and fear cannot breathe the same*: Inspired by Caroline Myss.

Part I
The End

8   *newly adopted Title IX*: Title IX was the 1972 landmark legislation that banned sex discrimination in schools in both athletics and academics, and required that women students be afforded the same opportunities and financial support as men. While athletic equality garnered much of the initial attention—and controversy—the

amendment was responsible for some significant academic advancement for women, including:

- Women received thirty-eight percent of medical degrees in 1994, compared with nine percent in 1972.
- Women received forty-three percent of law degrees in 1994, compared with seven percent in 1972.
- Women received forty-four percent of doctoral degrees in 1994, compared with twenty-five percent in 1977.

(See "About Title IX." http://bailiwick.lib.uiowa.edu/ge/aboutRE.html; United States Department of Labor. Office of the Assistant Secretary for Administration and Management. "Title IX, Education Amendments of 1972." http://www.dol.gov/oasam/regs/statutes/titleix.htm.)

11   *My father simply drank*: While there were stretches where my father didn't appear to drink, he was never sober. He always manifested the behaviors and attitudes of an addict, whether or not he was drinking or engaging in his other addictions.

13   *Steve Howe was a hard-throwing . . . in his blood*: "Steve Howe (baseball)." Wikipedia.org. http://en.wikipedia.org/wiki/Steve_Howe_(baseball) (accessed January 4, 2012); "Cocaine, Fame Led to Tragedy of Steve Howe." Associated Press, October 12, 1985. http://articles.latimes.com/1985-10-12/sports/sp-14579_1_cocaine-dependence (accessed January 4, 2012); "Steve Howe." BaseballLibrary.com: The Home of Baseball History. http://www.baseballlibrary.com/ballplayers/player.php?name=Steve_Howe_1958 (accessed September 29, 2011); "Steve Howe." Historic Baseball: Bringing Baseball to Center Field. http://www.historicbaseball.com/players/h/howe_steve.html (accessed September 29, 2011); "Steve Howe Statistics and History." Baseball-Reference.com. http://www.baseballreference.com/players/h/howest01.shtml (accessed January 4, 2012); "Autopsy: Howe Had Meth in System at Time of Crash." Associated Press (Riverside, CA), June 28, 2006. http://sports.espn.go.com/mlb/news/story?id=2503090 (accessed September 29, 2011).

13   *Fifty-seven minutes . . . was legitimate*: Kreidler, Mark. "The Record Doesn't Matter, the Legitimacy Does." ESPN, January 7, 2002. http://espn.go.com/columns/kreidler/1307290.html (accessed September 29, 2011); New York Giants 2001 Schedule. National Football League. http://www.nfl.com/teams/newyork%20giants/schedule?team=NYG&season=2001&seasonType=REG (accessed January 4, 2012); Freeman, Mike. "On Pro Football; Cheap Sack Will Cost Favre and Strahan." *New York Times*, January 7, 2002. http://www.nytimes.com/2002/01/07/sports/on-pro-football-cheap-sack-will-cost-favre-and-strahan.html (accessed January 4, 2012).

13 *negatively alter the destiny of another person*: Minnesota Vikings defensive end Jared Allen had 22 sacks during the 2011 regular season, just a half sack shy of Michael Strahan's 2001 single-season record of 22.5. (See Sessler, Marc. "Vikes' Allen on Missed Sack Record: 'I just kind of ran out of time.'" NFL.com, January 3, 2012. http://www.nfl.com/news/story/09000d5d825af748/article/vikes-allen-on-missed-sack-record-i-just-kind-of-ran-out-of-time [accessed March 13, 2012].)

14 *"I'm angry that what I've done"*: "Clemens Vehemently Denies Steroid Use." *60 Minutes*, January 6, 2008. http://www.cbsnews.com/2100-18560_162-3671585.html (accessed October 1, 2011); "Roger Clemens Statistics and History." Baseball-Reference.com. http://www.baseball-reference.com/players/c/clemero02.shtml (accessed January 4, 2012). Roger Clemens was charged with two counts of perjury, three counts of making false statements, and one count of obstructing Congress after testifying at a hearing in February 2008 that he had never used performance-enhancing drugs. He was acquitted of all charges on June 18, 2012. (See White, Joseph. "Baseball's Roger Clemens Acquitted of All Charges." Associated Press [Washington], June 18, 2012. http://www.boston.com/sports/other_sports/articles/2012/06/18/roger_clemens_acquitted_on_all_charges/ [accessed June 19, 2012].)

19 *On the floor, propped up*: The Meadows Family Week Workbook. "Overview of Developmental Immaturity Issues," p. 12. Copyright © Pia Mellody. (Originally published in *Facing Codependence: What It Is, Where It Comes From, How It Sabotages Our Lives* by Pia Mellody, with Andrea Wells Miller and J. Keith Miller. New York: HarperCollins, 2003, p. 118.)

25 *"other-esteem"*: Mellody, Pia, with Andrea Wells Miller and J. Keith Miller. *Facing Codependence: What It Is, Where It Comes From, How It Sabotages Our Lives*. New York: HarperCollins, 2003, p. 9. (Originally published in 1989.)

28 *was spent on the Dance*: The Meadows Family Week Workbook. "Addictive Cycles in Unhealthy Addicted Relationships," p. 44. Developed by Pia Mellody; Loose page from the author's personal library: "The Dance of the Love Addict & the Love Avoidant." Copyright © Pia Mellody, 2003.

28 *making it impossible for him*: While I use a male pronoun for the Avoidance Addict and a female pronoun for the Love Addict, neither is gender specific.

32 *three parts to the Feedback Loop*: The Meadows Family Week Workbook. "Feedback Loop," p. 24. Copyright © Pia Mellody.

A fourth part can be what one would like to have happen in the future: What I would like/prefer is . . .

33 *addict's mind and pain cycle*: The Meadows Family Week Workbook. "Pain Cycle," p. 36. Diagram adapted by Clint Withrow from Johnson, Vernon E. *I'll Quit Tomorrow: A Practical Guide to Alcoholism Treatment*. New York: HarperCollins, 1980, Revised.

50 *standing too close . . . breaking commitments*: The Meadows Patient Handbook. "Boundary Violations," p. 15; Loose pages from author's personal library: "External Physical Boundary Violations," "External Sexual Boundary Violations," p. 3; "Internal Boundary Violations," p. 5.

Part II
The Clinic

67 *Group in-box*: Much like I have capitalized Survivors Week and Feedback Loop, I capitalize Group to differentiate the therapeutic process and environment ("Primary Group Therapy") from the general use of the word ("the group sang a song").

72 *Jack Kerouac called it blue air*: Kerouac, Jack. *On the Road*. New York: Viking Compass, 1959; New York: Penguin Books, 1976, p. 96. Citation refers to the Penguin edition.

87 *Much like Larry Darrell*: Maugham, W. Somerset. *The Razor's Edge*. New York: Doubleday, Doran and Co., 1944; New York: First Vintage International, 2003, p. 284. Citation refers to the First Vintage International edition.

92 *"I will take the ring"*: Lord of the Rings: Fellowship of the Ring. New Line Film Productions, Inc. (New Line Cinema), 2001. Based on Tolkien, J.R.R. *The Fellowship of the Ring*. New York: Houghton Mifflin Company, 1994, p. 271. (Originally published London: George Allen & Unwin, Ltd., 1954.)

96 *view the behavior as thrilling . . . courage, and optimism*: "Newcomers." Sex and Love Addicts Anonymous. http://slaadfw.org/newcomers/terminology.html (accessed October 3, 2011).

111 *"sex is not the search"*: Bell, Rob. *Sex God: Exploring the Endless Connections Between Sexuality and Spirituality*. Grand Rapids, MI: Zondervan, 2007, p. 123.

113 *Many have been raised*: "What Causes Sexual Addiction?" Psych central.com. http://psychcentral.com/lib/2006/what-causes-sexual-addiction/ (accessed October 3, 2011).

114 *"the feeling of being a man"*: Bell. *Sex God*, p. 126.

115 *if we don't model healthy choices*: Inspired by Rick Levine and Jeff Jawer. http://www.tarot.com.

115 *National statistics indicate . . . "kids even know about this?"*: "Sex Offenders Getting Younger, More Violent." Associated Press (Stockton, CA), June 9, 2007. http://www.msnbc.msn.com/id/19143411/ns/us_news-crime_and_courts/t/sex-offenders-getting-younger-more-violent/ (accessed January 10, 2012).

117 *Hierarchy of Needs*: Maslow's Hierarchy of Needs—Motivation Theory. http://www.abraham-maslow.com/m_motivation/Hierarchy_of_Needs.asp (accessed March 8, 2012). Abraham Maslow later added a sixth level to the Hierarchy of Needs called self-transcendence. At the fifth level of self-actualization, an individual seeks to actualize his own potential, which can still be viewed, in some measure, to be self-aggrandizing or contributing to personal gain. At the sixth level of self-transcendence, being of service to others is one's primary motivation and will always supersede service to benefit oneself. (See Koltko-Rivera, Mark E. "Rediscovering the Later Version of Maslow's Hierarchy of Needs: Self-Transcendence and Opportunities for Theory, Research, and Unification." New York University and Professional Services Group, Inc., p. 306. *Review of General Psychology*, 2006, Vol. 10, No. 4, pp. 302–317. Copyright 2006 by the American Psychological Association, 1089-2680/06, DOI: 10.1037/1089-2680.10.4.302. http://docbk.com/a/download/rediscovering-the-later-version-of-maslow-shierarchyof-needs-self.pdf [accessed January 10, 2012].)

119 *"what a man can be"*: Maslow, Abraham H. "A Theory of Human Motivation" (1943). http://psychclassics.yorku.ca/Maslow/motivation.htm (accessed January 10, 2012). (Originally published in *Psychological Review*, 50, pp. 370–396.)

135 *"No change of circumstances"*: Emerson, Ralph W. "Character." *Essays: Second Series*. New York: Houghton, Mifflin Company, 1844; Charleston, SC: Nabu Press, 2010. p. 83. Citation refers to the Nabu Press edition.

137 *whether you are controlling it*: Tolle, Eckhart. *The Power of Now: A Guide to Spiritual Enlightenment*. Vancouver, Canada: Namaste Publishing, 2004, p. 16. (Originally published in 1997.)

138 *impossible-looking mathematical proofs*: Krakauer, Jon. *Eiger Dreams: Ventures Among Men and Mountains*. New York: Lyons & Buford, 1990; New York: Anchor Books, 1990, p. 16. Citation refers to the Anchor Books edition.

138 *"quantum jumps of intuition"*: Ibid.

138 *Law of Substitution*: Fox, Emmet. *Around the Year with Emmet*

Fox. New York: HarperCollins, 1992, p. 23. (Originally published in 1958.)

144   *Transactional analysis therapists . . . come true*: Steiner, Claude M. *Scripts People Live: Transactional Analysis of Life Scripts*. New York: Grove Press, 1974, back cover.

144   *the Child, the Adult, and the Parent*: Ibid., pp. 27–30.

152   *Perfection keeps you from learning*: Perfectionists can be identified by their over-controlling behaviors, which act as defenses against the vulnerability, fear, and chaos they feel within. They seek to control not only their environment and others, but also the image they project because they get their identity from being thought of as rarely making mistakes, of having a perfect life; or as being the one with all the answers, the ultimate problem-solver. Ironically, controlling and perfectionist behaviors are an indication of the very things perfectionists are trying so hard to hide: vulnerability, fear, and internal chaos. However, they will rebel at being labeled as controlling or a perfectionist, or considered dysfunctional in any way, never realizing that the need to control and the need to be perfect—as well as thinking that one is without dysfunction— is dysfunctional. There is a place for healthy self-assertiveness, but it requires one who lives his or her life in balance and with openness, one who acknowledges vulnerability and is eager to learn and grow, to know what it looks like.

153   *projecting upon our lovers*: Gilbert, Elizabeth. *Eat, Pray, Love: One Woman's Search for Everything across Italy, India, and Indonesia*. New York: Penguin Group, 2006, p. 65.

157   *Within the pocket*: A spiritualist would use the image of one standing within the motionless hub of a wheel as the rest spins around him.

158   *"a realistic respect"*: Dictionary.com, s.v. "self-esteem." http://dictionary.reference.com/browse/self+esteem (accessed January 12, 2012).

158   *"proper esteem or regard"*: Dictionary.com, s.v. "self-respect." http://dictionary.reference.com/browse/self+respect?s=t. (accessed January 12, 2012).

159   *"Self-esteem, fully realized"*: Branden, Nathaniel. *The Six Pillars of Self-Esteem*. New York: Bantam Books, 1995, p. 4. (Originally published in 1994.)

159   *High self-esteem, meaning*: Ibid., p. 26.

160   *produce a desired result*: Ibid., p. 33.

160   *absolute belief in your own value*: Ibid., p, 26.

160 *"places us in an adversarial"*: Ibid., p. 17.

161 *"We are the one species"*: Ibid., p. 31.

161 *"best served by blindness"*: Ibid., p. 50.

161 *"consciousness that is not translated"*: Ibid., p. 69.

161 *exhaustively engage in*: Ibid., p. 70.

161 *Awareness is a process of selection*: Ibid.

162 *give the appearance of living consciously*: Ibid., p. 69.

162 *"To the addict, consciousness is the enemy"*: Ibid., p. 81.

162 *resurface with even greater intensity*: Ibid.

163 *we cannot change what we deny*: Ibid., pp. 93, 96.

163 *"cannot accept having made"*: Ibid., p. 93.

163 *Acceptance is much more*: Ibid., p. 92.

163 *You can acknowledge*: Ibid., pp. 92, 93.

163 *increased the likelihood*: Ibid., p. 93.

163 *"liking, enjoying, or condoning"*: Ibid.

163 *absolves you from change or improvement*: Ibid., pp. 100, 101.

163 *"The resistance begins to collapse"*: Ibid., p. 99, 100.

163 *there is no rationalizing, justifying*: Ibid., p. 92.

164 *If you cannot first accept*: Ibid., p. 101.

164 *you, and only you, are responsible*: Ibid., pp. 105, 106.

164 *To be "responsible for"*: Ibid., p. 106.

164 *you are the cause . . . unaccountable life*: Ibid., p. 109.

164 *permission to live your own life*: Hollis. *Through the Dark Wood*, disc 1.

165 *To be self-assertive means*: Branden. *The Six Pillars of Self-Esteem*, p. 118.

165 *Self-assertiveness is being committed . . . even terrifying*: Ibid., p. 120.

165 *Appropriately manifested self-assertiveness*: Ibid., p. 119.

165 *"self-assertiveness should not be confused"*: Ibid., p. 120.

165 *Reflexively saying no*: Ibid.

166 *Lack of self-assertiveness . . . to everyone else's*: Ibid., p. 118.

166 *it does not mean being superior*: Ibid., p. 37.

166 *Adapting a theory from Sigmund Freud*: Ibid., p. xiv.

166   *Arrogance is not an example*: Ibid., p. 19.

167   *the difference between arrogance and confidence*: Greg Anthony played in the NBA from 1991 to 2002. After his retirement, he became an analyst for ESPN on programs that included *NBA Shootaround* and *NBA Fastbreak*. I believe his discussion on the difference between arrogance and confidence originated from one of these two programs, however, the video is unavailable for confirmation.

167   *"gap between what one is"*: Frankl, Victor E. *Man's Search for Meaning*. Boston, MA: Beacon Press, 2006, p. 105. (Originally published in German under the title *Ein Psycholog erlebt das Konzentrationslager* in 1946.)

167   *"unheard cry for meaning"*: Pattakos, Alex. *Prisoners of Our Thoughts: Viktor Frankl's Principles for Discovering Meaning in Life and Work*. San Francisco, CA: Berrett-Koehler Publishers, 2008, p. 71.

167   *"depression, aggression, and addiction"*: Ibid.

167   *"belongs to those who do"*: Branden. *The Six Pillars of Self-Esteem*, p. 134.

168   *living a life that provides an outlet*: Ibid., p. 130.

168   *leaves you at the mercy of chance*: Ibid.

168   *The sum of your life*: Ibid.

168   *command each other to "be happy"*: Frankl. *Man's Search for Meaning*, p. 138.

168   *happiness "cannot be pursued"*: Ibid.

169   *need to know what you want*: Branden. *The Six Pillars of Self-Esteem*, p. 133.

169   *requires a specific plan of action*: Ibid.

169   *"Purposes unrelated to a plan"*: Ibid., p. 132.

169   *"ability to organize our behavior"*: Ibid.

169   *a self-disciplined life is not without*: Ibid., p. 133.

169   *it is the practices of integrity*: Ibid., pp. 131, 136.

169   *more people are successful at their jobs*: Ibid., p. 132.

170   *"Everyone knows it is not enough"*: Ibid.

170   *A healthy society is the union*: Ibid., p.123.

170   *"only a person through other persons"*: Pattakos, Alex. *Prisoners of Our Thoughts*, p. 150.

170   *congruence between what you say*: Branden. *The Six Pillars of Self-Esteem*, p. 143.

170   *Am I honest, faithful, and trustworthy*": Ibid., p. 144.

170   *"Only I will know*": Ibid., pp. 145, 146.

171   *Long before others know*: Ibid., p. 146.

171   *when your behavior conflicts*: Ibid., p. 143.

171   *always become a casualty*: Ibid., p. 146.

171   *"only the practice of integrity*": Ibid., p. 144.

171   *five steps to restoring integrity*: Ibid., pp. 148, 149.

171   *Having integrity does not guarantee*: Ibid., p. 144.

171   *absorbing irrational or inappropriate ideals*: Ibid., p. 149.

172   *"When we have unconflicted self-esteem*": Ibid., pp. 20, 21.

172   *Personal integrity and morals*: Lawrence Kohlberg, a psychologist who extensively researched moral development, believed that at the highest stage of moral development people act from "their own internalized standards of right or wrong," not from fear, or what is socially acceptable or lawful. This requires that they not only hold themselves to a higher standard, but must also possess a highly developed conscience, which allows them to determine and then put into practice what they consciously know to be moral. (*"their own internalized standards*": Dacey, John S. and John F. Travers. *Human Development: Across the Lifespan*, 6th ed. New York: McGraw-Hill, 2006, p. 257.)

174   *"Character is what you are in the dark*": Moody, Dwight L. Quotationsbook.com. http://quotationsbook.com/quote/6021/ (accessed January 16, 2012).

174   *bound in a continuous loop*: Branden. *The Six Pillars of Self-Esteem*, p. 4.

174   *We tend to feel most comfortable*: Ibid., p. 6.

174   *the most disastrous relationships*: Ibid., p. 7.

175   *Low self-esteem looks like*: Ibid., pp. 5, 6.

175   *The characteristics of high self-esteem*: Ibid., pp. 45–48.

175   *"Nothing can be true and not true*": Ibid., p. 45.

175   *cannot have too much self-esteem*: Ibid., p. 19.

177   *Pure Prairie League's "Amie*": The title of this song has also been written as "Aimee."

178   *Maslow studied self-actualization*: Maslow, Abraham H. *Motivation*

and Personality. Boston, MA: Addison-Wesley Educational Publishers, 1970, pp. 125, 126. (Originally published in 1954.)

178   *"personal acquaintances . . . historical figures"*: Ibid., p. 126.

178   *Maslow found twenty-three subjects*: Ibid., pp. 127–128.

178   *self-actualization doesn't occur in the young*: Ibid., p. xxvi.

178   *possess nineteen characteristics*: Ibid., pp. 128–149.

181   *"affection for human beings in general"*: Ibid., p. 138.

181   *"class, education, political belief"*: Ibid., p. 139.

181   *"well aware of how little they know"*: Ibid.

181   *"They do right"*: Ibid., p. 141.

182   *many who are considered creatively brilliant*: Maslow, Abraham H. *Toward a Psychology of Being.* New York: John Wiley & Sons, 1999, p. 151. (Originally published in 1968.)

182   *"inner freedom"*: Maslow. *Motivation and Personality*, p. 121.

182   *"live by their inner laws"*: Ibid.

182   *"They can be boring"*: Ibid., p. 146.

183   *"what passes for morals"*: Ibid., p. 147.

183   *"The id, the ego, and the superego"*: Ibid., p. 149.

191   *At first I was afraid*: Gaynor, Gloria. "I Will Survive." *Love Tracks.* Polydor, 1978.

Part III
The Beginning

201   *displacement or redirecting*: A person can also displace a thought or behavior with one equally or more destructive.

202   *first two lines and what I felt*: I initially had hoped to include the first two lines of "Voodoo Child (Slight Return)" in the book, however, Experience Hendrix, LLC refused my request for permission to reprint. The company's board objected to the subject matter of the book, stating that it "does not license music or any other rights for projects that contain the following: Alcohol/Drug Use, Excessive Violence, Sexual Content, Vulgar/Abusive Language." But I encourage you to read for yourself the first two lines of "Voodoo Child (Slight Return)," not only to place this part of the book in a more accurate context, but also because they are among the most powerful and poetic lyric lines written. But don't stop with the lyrics; listen to the song. And when you find you still need more, listen to the cover by Stevie Ray Vaughan.

210   *stuck in the small lives*: Moore, Thomas. *Dark Nights of the Soul: A Guide to Finding Your Way Through Life's Ordeals.* New York: Gotham Books, 2005, p. 13. (Originally published in 2004.)

210   *"In the dark night"*: Ibid., p. 5.

210   *not a darkness you would ever choose*: Ibid., p. xv.

211   *five stages of grief*: Kübler-Ross, Elisabeth. *On Death and Dying: What the Dying Have to Teach Doctors, Nurses, Clergy, and Their Own Families.* New York: Scribner, 2003, pp. 51–146. (Originally published in 1969.)

216   *healthy ritual directs its actions*: Moore. *Dark Nights of the Soul*, p. 45.

216   *rituals follow a schedule*: Ibid., 46.

216   *connect to your consciousness through nature*: Ibid., 45.

217   *those who lose touch with their souls*: Ibid.

217   *"If you choose not to become"*: Ibid.

219   *"overwhelmment" and "abandonment"*: Hollis. *Through the Dark Wood*, disc 1.

219   *"false self"*: Ibid.

219   *three behavioral patterns we use to manage*: Ibid.

219   *There are several ways*: Ibid.

219   *We also use compliance*: Ibid.

219   *Through a power complex*: Ibid.

219   *"the exchange of energy"*: Ibid.

220   *There are also three patterns*: Ibid.

220   *One can identify with the deficit*: Ibid.

220   *Narcissists alleviate the anxiety*: Ibid.

220   *need to connect with an "other"*: Ibid.

221   *originate in our past*: Ibid.

221   *A complex is an energy-charged mass*: Dictionary.com, s.v. "complex." http://dictionary.reference.com/browse/complex (accessed January 19, 2012).

221   *react in one of three ways*: Hollis. *Through the Dark Wood*, disc 1.

221   *The most common is repetition*: Ibid.

221   *overcompensate*: Ibid.

221   *"Every time one says"*: Ibid.

221   *treat the problem*: Ibid.

222   *how the psyche communicates*: Ibid.

222   *"Everyone carries a shadow"*: Jung, C. G. *Psychology and Religion: West and East.* 2nd ed. New Jersey: Princeton University Press, 1989, p. 76, paragraph 131. (Originally published as The Terry Lectures. New Haven, CT: Yale University Press, 1937; London: Oxford University Press, 1938.)

223   *"It's not about what it's about"*: Hollis. *Through the Dark Wood,* disc 1.

236   *"Our way of life"*: Bush, George W. Address to the Nation, September 11, 2001. http://www.presidency.ucsb.edu/ws/index. php?pid=58057 (accessed January 19, 2012).

236   *gave the terrorists a name*: Bush, George W. Address to Joint Session of Congress, September 20, 2001. http://edition.cnn.com/2001/ US/09/20/gen.bush.transcript/ (accessed January 19, 2012).

236   *Operation Enduring Freedom*: Bush, George W. Address to the Nation, October 7, 2001. http://www.press.uchicago.edu/Misc/ Chicago/481921texts.html (accessed January 19, 2012).

237   *The contemporary and convoluted relationship*: "Cold War." Wikipedia.org. http://en.wikipedia.org/wiki/Cold_war (accessed January 19, 2012).

237   *list of states that sponsored terrorism*: In 1979, the U.S. State Department created a list of countries that sponsored terrorism. Iraq, Libya, South Yemen, and Syria were the inaugural members. Iraq was removed from the list in 1982 during the Iran-Iraq war, then put back on in 1990 after Saddam Hussein invaded Kuwait. It was removed from the list again in 2003 after an interim government replaced the Hussein regime. (See Beehner, Lionel. "What Good is a Terrorism List?" *Los Angeles Times*, October 20, 2008. http://articles.latimes.com/2008/oct/20/opinion/oe-beehner20 [accessed January 21, 2012]; Miles, Donna. "U.S. Removes Iraq from List of State Sponsors of Terrorism." American Forces Press Service, October 22, 2004. http://www.defense.gov/news/news article.aspx?id=25006 [accessed January 21, 2012].)

237   *"could not afford to allow"*: Declaration of Howard Teicher. U.S. District Court, Southern District of Florida, January 31, 1995. http://www.webcitation.org/5flvP0UgC (accessed January 21, 2012).

237   *"do whatever was necessary and legal"*: Ibid.

237   *billions of dollars, technology*: Ibid.

238   *"I would guess if we had gone"*: Cheney, Dick. Discovery Institute Speech in Seattle, August 1992. http://www.democraticunder

ground.com/discuss/duboard.php?az=view_all&address=103x76369 (accessed January 21, 2012).

239 *"[b]est info fast"*: Notes from Department of Defense staffer Stephen Cambone in September 11, 2001 meeting with Defense Secretary Donald Rumsfeld. Petitioned by Thad Anderson under the Freedom of Information Act. http://blog.outragedmoderates. org/2006/02/dod-staffers-notes-from-911-obtained.html (accessed January 21, 2012).

239 *"Today we focus on Afghanistan"*: Bush. Address to the Nation, October 7, 2001.

239 *"axis of evil"*: Bush, George W. State of the Union Address, January 29, 2002. http://www.washingtonpost.com/wp-srv/onpolitics/transcripts/sou012902.htm (accessed January 21, 2012).

239 *"grave and growing danger"*: Ibid.

239 *authorized the use of military force*: Bush, George W. "Joint Resolution to Authorize the Use of United States Armed Forces Against Iraq." White House Archives, October 2, 2002. http://georgewbush-whitehouse.archives.gov/news/releases/2002/10/20021002-2.html (accessed January 21, 2012); Mitchell, Alison and Carl Hulse. "Threats and Responses: The Vote; Congress Authorizes Bush to Use Force Against Iraq, Creating a Broad Mandate." *New York Times*, October 11, 2002. http://www.nytimes.com/2002/10/11/us/threats-responses-vote-congress-authorizes-bush-use-force-against-iraq-creating.html?pagewanted=all&src=pm (accessed January 21, 2012).

240 *UNSC Resolution 1441 . . . four-year absence*: "Iraq Disarmament Timeline 1990–2003." Wikipedia.org. http://en.wikipedia.org/wiki/Iraq_disarmament_timeline_1990–2003#1998 (accessed January 21, 2012); "Chronology: The Evolution of the Bush Doctrine—The War Behind Closed Doors." *Frontline*. PBS. http://www.pbs.org/wgbh/pages/frontline/shows/iraq/etc/cron.html (accessed March 9, 2012).

240 *both the U.S. and Great Britain*: While "Great Britain" is more commonly used in America (and used in this book for consistency and familiarity purposes), the correct identification in this instance would be the United Kingdom. Great Britain is a geographical entity and only one part of the political entity known as the "United Kingdom of Great Britain and Northern Ireland."

240 *A CBS News/New York Times poll*: Cosgrove-Mather, Bootie. "Poll: Talk First, Fight Later." *CBS News/New York Times*, conducted January 19–22, 2003. http://www.cbsnews.com/2100-500160_162-537739.html (accessed January 21, 2012).

240   *"Saddam Hussein and his sons"*: Bush, George W. Address to the
       Nation, "Iraq: Denial and Deception," March 17, 2003. http://
       georgewbush-whitehouse.archives.gov/news/releases/2003/03/
       print/20030317-7.html (accessed January 21, 2012).

240   *President Bush chose March 20*: "U.S. Launches Cruise Missiles
       at Saddam." CNN World, March 20, 2003. http://articles.cnn.
       com/2003-03-19/world/sprj.irq.main_1_coalition-forces-coalition-
       attack-military-action?_s=PM:WORLD. (accessed January 21,
       2012). Thursday, March 20, 2003, refers to Arabia Standard
       Time (AST), which would have been Wednesday, March 19, 2003
       Eastern Standard Time (EST).

240   *"wrenching down"*: Antonowicz, Anton. "Toppling Saddam's
       Statue is the Final Triumph for These Oppressed People." *The
       Mirror*, April 10, 2003. http://www.thefreelibrary.com/GUL+W
       AR+2%3A+ANTON+ANTONOWICZ+WAT%20CHES+THE
       +FALL+OF+BAGHDAD%3A+Toxppling-a099844046 (accessed
       January 21, 2012).

241   *"the tyrant has fallen"*: Bush, George W. "President Bush
       Announces Major Combat Operations in Iraq Have Ended."
       Address to the Nation, May 1, 2003, from the USS *Abraham
       Lincoln*. http://georgewbush-whitehouse.archives.gov/news/
       releases/2003/05/20030501-15.html (accessed January 22, 2012).

241   *"The liberation of Iraq is a crucial advance"*: Ibid.

241   *"stirring up even more trouble"*: Bush, George W. News confer-
       ence, August 21, 2006. http://www.washingtonpost.com/wp-dyn/
       content/article/2006/08/21/AR2006082100469.html (accessed
       January 22, 2012).

241   *"Nothing"*: Ibid. Supporters of President Bush protested when
       journalists and bloggers ended his response with the word, "Noth-
       ing." In fact, he did go on to explain, "Nobody has ever suggested
       in this administration that Saddam Hussein ordered the attack."
       However, not ending his quote with "Nothing" would require one
       to do something far worse—enable the president to manipulate
       words and their meanings to avoid accountability.
          While he did not specifically use the words, "Saddam Hussein
       ordered the 9/11 attacks," he did more than suggest it by stating
       there was proof of a deep Iraq/al-Qaeda connection, and that he
       believed in the very real, if not imminent, possibility of an Iraqi-
       sponsored mass chemical or biological attack in his State of the
       Union address on January 28, 2003:

          Evidence from intelligence sources, secret communications,
          and statements by people now in custody reveal that Saddam
          Hussein aids and protects terrorists, including members of

al-Qaeda. Secretly, and without fingerprints, he could provide one of his hidden weapons to terrorists, or help them
develop their own. Before September the 11th, many in the
world believed that Saddam Hussein could be contained.
But chemical agents, lethal viruses, and shadowy terrorist
networks are not easily contained. Imagine those nineteen
hijackers with other weapons and other plans, this time
armed by Saddam Hussein. It would take one vial, one
canister, one crate slipped into this country to bring a day
of horror like none we have ever known.

(See http://georgewbush-whitehouse.archives.gov/news/releases/
2003/01/20030128-19.html. [accessed January 22, 2012].)

241   *"And this much is certain"*: Bush. "President Bush Announces
        Major Combat Operations in Iraq Have Ended." Address to the
        Nation, May 1, 2003.

242   *"it turns out that we were all wrong"*: Kay, David. Senate Armed
        Services testimony, January 28, 2004. http://www.cnn.com/2004/
        US/01/28/kay.transcript/ (accessed January 22, 2012).

242   *what freedom looks like in the hands of the many who are inca-
        pable of personal restraint*: Early morning on December 1, 2012,
        Jovan Belcher, a linebacker for the Kansas City Chiefs, shot and
        killed his girlfriend in front of his mother, and in the vicinity of
        the couple's three-month-old daughter. He then drove to the team's
        practice facility and fatally shot himself in the parking lot in front
        of his general manager and coach. The tragedy of a murder-suicide
        involving two people barely in their 20s, and an infant who not only
        will never know her mother or father but also will have to learn
        to live with the circumstances of their deaths is more than enough
        to cause us all to pause and reflect on the depth and authenticity
        of our own relationships. Or as Kansas City Chiefs quarterback
        Brady Quinn observed:

> When you ask someone how they are doing, do you really
> mean it? When you answer someone back how you are
> doing, are you really telling the truth? We live in a society
> of social networks, with Twitter pages and Facebook, and
> that's fine, but we have contact with our work associates,
> our family, our friends, and it seems like half the time we
> are more preoccupied with our phone and other things going
> on instead of the actual relationships that we have right in
> front of us.

However, it was Bob Costas, a sports broadcaster for NBC,
who turned our reflection into conversation and, some say, controversy. Because this event involved an NFL player and happened
the day before most NFL games are played, the sports media were

obligated to address it. On his broadcast the following evening, Bob Costas spoke about the "unfathomable events," but also about the need for gun control. Some thought this was the appropriate person and place to interject politics amid tragedy; some did not.

While I believe there is a proper time and place for a journalist to express an opinion—during his personal time as a guest on a television or radio talk show, but not when performing his professional duties as a journalist—this did not dampen my appreciation for the discussion that followed Bob Costas' comments. Any discussion of freedom and limits is always interesting to me because of my conflict between my belief in personal freedom and my understanding that the Second Amendment, or any constitutionally afforded right, is only as good as the people it empowers.

Without the Second Amendment, we are North Korea, Cuba, and Iran. With it, we are only as free as the least healthy among us—those who take our freedoms to destructive extremes—allow us to be. The debate should not be about whether our freedom should be limited or absolute, but how we achieve the health, as individuals and a nation, essential to accepting the responsibilities and restraints that must accompany freedom in order for it to be effective. (See Murphy, Kevin. "Anguished Kansas City Chiefs Snap Losing Streak." Reuters [Kansas City, MO], December 2, 2012. http://www.reuters.com/article/2012/12/02/us-nfl-chiefs-shooting-idUS BRE8B00aa20121202 [accessed December 3, 2012]; Boren, Cindy. "Brady Quinn on Jovan Belcher Tragedy: An Eloquent Moment for Chiefs QB." *The Washington Post*, December 3, 2012. http://www.washingtonpost.com/blogs/early-lead/wp/2012/12/03/brady-quinn-on-jovan-belcher-tragedy-an-eloquent-moment-for-chiefs-qb/ [accessed December 3, 2012]; Bauder, David. "Costas Gun Control Commentary Gets Notice." Associated Press [New York], December 3, 2012. http://tv.yahoo.com/news/costas-gun-control-commentary-gets-notice-212041088--spt.html [accessed December 3, 2012].)

242   *why would others choose the path*: Inspired by Rutherfurd, Edward. *New York: The Novel*. New York: Ballantine Books, 2010, p. 290.

243   *"living conditions now are better"*: Hersh, Seymour M. "Torture at Abu Ghraib." *The New Yorker*, May 10, 2004 (citing the St. Petersburg *Times* interview of Brig. Gen. Janis Karpinski, December 2003). http://www.newyorker.com/archive/2004/05/10/040510fa_fact (accessed January 22, 2012).

244   *"abhorrent"*: Bush, George W. Arab news outlet conference, May 5, 2004. http://news.bbc.co.uk/2/hi/americas/3685669.stm (accessed March 9, 2012). Al-Hurra is funded by and based in the United States. The al-Arabiya satellite channel is owned by Saudi Arabia and based in Dubai Media City, United Arab Emirates.

245 *"A dictator wouldn't"*: Ibid.

245 *did not offer an apology*: Ibid.

245 *"actions of a few"*: "Bush Discusses Prisoner Abuse with Arab Media." Fox News/Associated Press, May 6, 2004. http://www. foxnews.com/story/0,2933,119033,00.html (accessed January 22, 2012).

245 *misconduct of American captors*: Jehl, Douglas and Eric Schmitt. "The Struggle for Iraq: Investigations; Army Discloses Criminal Inquiry on Prison Abuse." *New York Times*, May 5, 2004. http://www.nytimes.com/2004/05/05/world/struggle-for-iraq-investigations-army-discloses-criminal-inquiry-prison-abuse. html?pagewanted=all&src=pm (accessed January 22, 2012).

245 *no knowledge of*: "Bush Discusses Prisoner Abuse with Arab Media."

245 *"numerous incidents of sadistic"*: The Taguba Report on Treatment of Abu Ghraib Prisoners in Iraq. "Article 15-6 Investigation of the 800th Military Police Brigade," Findings of Fact, Section 5. Released May 2004. http://news.findlaw.com/hdocs/docs/iraq/tagubarpt.html#ThR1.19(accessed January 22, 2012).

245 *"systemic and illegal abuse"*: Ibid.

245 *lack of leadership*: Ibid., Sections 8, 23, 34b, e, f, g, h. Other Findings/Observations, Section 2.

245 *"contraband, weapons, and information"*: Ibid., Section 29.

246 *"discovered evidence of abuse"*: Ibid., Other Findings/Observations, Section 4a, b, c.

246 *"kind of thing that you might find"*: North, Oliver. *Hannity & Colmes*. Fox News Channel. May 11, 2004. http://mediamatters. org/research/2004/05/12/oliver-north-iraqi-prisoner-abuse-the-kind-of-t/131135 (accessed January 22, 2012).

246 *"The American public needs to understand"*: Sen. Lindsey Graham, R-S.C., to reporters in May 2004, cited in "Rumsfeld: Worst Still to Come." CBSNews/Associated Press, May 2004. http://www. cbsnews.com/2100-500257_162-616338.html (accessed January 22, 2012).

246 *The Murderous Maniacs*: Human Rights Watch Report. "Leadership Failure: Firsthand Accounts of Torture of Iraqi Detainees by the U.S. Army's 82nd Airborne Division," September 23, 2005. http:// www.hrw.org/reports/2005/09/22/leadership-failure (accessed January 23, 2012).

247 *"fucking a PUC" and "smoking a PUC"*: Ibid.

247   *"To 'fuck a PUC' means to beat him"*: Ibid.

247   *the prisoners were "smoked" . . . with baseball bats*: Ibid.

247   *"wrong"*: Ibid.

247   *"this was the norm"*: Ibid.

247   *"Leadership failed to provide"*: Ibid.

247   *tried to raise the matter of detainee abuse*: Ibid.

247   *"Don't expect me to go to bat for you"*: Ibid.

247   *"Remember the honor of the unit is at stake"*: Ibid.

247   *more interested in discovering the identities*: Schmitt, Eric. "Officer Criticizes Detainee Abuse Inquiry." *New York Times*, September 28, 2005. http://www.nytimes.com/2005/09/28/international/middleeast/28abuse.html?_r=1 (accessed January 23, 2012).

247   *"outraged by the outrage"*: "GOP Senator Labels Abused Prisoners 'Terrorists.'" CNN Politics, May 12, 2004. http://articles.cnn.com/2004-05-11/politics/inhofe.abuse_1_naked-prisoners-iraqi-prisoners-james-inhofe?_s=PM:ALLPOLITICS (accessed January 23, 2012).

248   *"If they're in cell block 1A or 1B"*: Ibid.

248   *criminals who had engaged in local crime*: The Taguba Report on Treatment of Abu Ghraib Prisoners in Iraq, IO Comments on MG Miller's Assessment, Section 1.

248   *"If he's a good guy"*: Human Rights Watch Report.

248   *"gulag of our time"*: Dodds, Paisley. "Amnesty Takes Aim at 'Gulag' in Guantanamo." Associated Press (London), May 25, 2005.

248   *"We hold people accountable"*: Ibid.

249   *closed to most human rights organizations*: Ibid.

249   *"courtesy of Cuban leader Fidel Castro"*: Coughlin, Con. "Trapped in a Legal No-Man's Land." *The Telegraph*, February 17, 2006. http://www.telegraph.co.uk/news/worldnews/northamerica/usa/1510758/Trapped-in-a-legal-no-mans-land.html (accessed January 23, 2012).

249   *held indefinitely, without being charged*: During the first four years after the 9/11 attacks, the United States detained or questioned and released approximately 83,000 foreigners in the war on terror. (See Shrader, Katherine. "U.S. Has Detained 83,000 in War on Terror." Associated Press [Washington], November 16, 2005.)

249   *"U.S. policy guidance"*: Burns, Robert. "Rumsfeld Defends Treatment of Prisoners." Associated Press (Washington), June 1, 2005.

249   *seventeen U.N. resolutions*: "Iraq Disarmament Timeline 1990–2003." Wikipedia.org.

250   *"A democracy needs informed citizens"*: Sowell, Thomas. "Is U.S.
      Now on Slippery Slope to Tyranny?" Investors.com, June 21, 2010.
      http://news.investors.com/article/537967/201006211813/is-us-
      now-on-slippery-slope-to-tyranny-.htm?p=full (accessed January
      23, 2012).

250   *"What has been charged thus far is abuse"*: Rumsfeld, Don-
      ald. Defense Department Operational Update Briefing,
      May 4, 2004. http://www.defense.gov/transcripts/transcript.
      aspx?transcriptid=2973 (accessed January 23, 2012).

250   *post G-8 Summit press conference*: Bush, George W. Post G-8
      Summit News Conference, June 10, 2004. http://www.washington
      post.com/wp-dyn/articles/A32143-2004Jun10.html (accessed Janu-
      ary 23, 2012). The following are the three questions and answers
      between George W. Bush and reporters during the post G-8 Summit
      press conference, regarding the 2002 Justice Department memo
      on torture:

      QUESTION 1: Mr. President, the Justice Department issued
      an advisory opinion last year declaring that, as commander-in-
      chief, you have the authority to order any kind of interrogation
      techniques that are necessary to pursue the war on terror. Were
      you aware of this advisory opinion? Do you agree with it? And
      did you issue any such authorization at any time?
      PRESIDENT BUSH: The authorization I issued was that any-
      thing we did would conform to U.S. law and would be consistent
      with international treaty obligations. That's the message I gave
      our people.
      FOLLOW-UP QUESTION: Have you seen the memos?
      PRESIDENT BUSH: I can't remember if I've seen the memo
      or not, but I gave those instructions.

      QUESTION 2: Returning to the question of torture, if you
      knew a person was in U.S. custody and had specific information
      about an imminent terrorist attack that could kill hundreds or
      even thousands of Americans, would you authorize the use of
      any means necessary to get that information and to save those
      lives?
      PRESIDENT BUSH: What I've authorized is that we stay
      within U.S. law.

      QUESTION 3: Mr. President, I wanted to return to the question
      of torture. What we've learned from these memos this week is
      that the Department of Justice lawyers and the Pentagon law-
      yers have essentially worked out a way that U.S. officials can
      torture detainees without running afoul of the law. So when
      you say that you want the U.S. to adhere to international and
      U.S. laws, that's not very comforting. This is a moral question:
      Is torture ever justified?

PRESIDENT BUSH: Look, I'm going to say it one more time. Maybe I can be more clear. The instructions went out to our people to adhere to the law. That ought to comfort you. We're a nation of law. We adhere to laws. We have laws on the books. You might look at these laws and that might provide comfort for you. And those were the instructions from me to the government.

251   *"may be unconstitutional if applied to interrogations"*: Bybee, Jay S. "Memorandum for Alberto R. Gonzales, Counsel to the President," August 1, 2002, pp. 2, 46. http://news.findlaw.com/wp/docs/doj/bybee80102mem.pdf (accessed January 23, 2012).

251   *depriving a prisoner of sleep*: Bradbury, Steven G. "Memorandum for John A. Rizzo, Senior Deputy General Counsel, Central Intelligence Agency," May 10, 2005, no. 0000012, pp. 51, 54, 57, and May 10, 2005, no. 0000013, p. 10. http://documents.nytimes.com/justice-department-memos-on-interrogation-techniques (accessed January 23, 2012).

251   *"the most traumatic" interrogation technique*: Bradbury. "Memorandum for John A. Rizzo," May 10, 2005, no. 0000013, p. 43. The Bush administration admitted to waterboarding only three senior al-Qaeda suspects at black sites in Thailand and Poland. However, in June 2012, Human Rights Watch said it found evidence of a wider use of waterboarding by the CIA. A 154-page report featured interviews with fourteen Libyan dissidents who had set up training camps in Afghanistan, where al-Qaeda is also based. However, these camps were not aligned with Osama bin Laden. They were created with the intention of overthrowing Libyan dictator Moammar Gadhafi. The report details the close cooperation between Washington and the Gadhafi regime where opponents of Gadhafi were handed over with only "thin diplomatic assurances" that they would be treated properly. According to a counterterrorism adviser at Human Rights Watch, "Not only did the U.S. deliver [to Gadhafi] his enemies on a silver platter, but it seems the CIA tortured many of them first." The detainees described systematic abuses while being held in U.S. detention centers in Afghanistan—some for as long as two years—or as the target of U.S.-led interrogations in Pakistan, Morocco, Thailand, and the Sudan before being transported to Libya. The spokesperson for the CIA said the Justice Department had decided against prosecution after it "exhaustively reviewed the treatment of more than 100 detainees in the post-9/11 period—including allegations involving unauthorized interrogation techniques." Ironically, in 2011, the United States helped the Gadhafi opposition overthrow the dictator. Several of the fourteen former detainees now hold positions in

the new Libyan government. (See El Deeb, Sarah. "Human Rights Watch: Evidence of Wider U.S. Waterboarding Use." Associated Press [Cairo], September 6, 2012. http://www.usatoday.com/news/world/story/2012-09-06/waterboarding-cia-human-rights-watch/57626318/1?csp=34news [accessed September 6, 2012].)

251 *"high value" detainees*: Ibid., p. 6.

251 *"we do not torture"*: Bush, George W. Latin America press conference, November 7, 2005. http://www.usatoday.com/news/washington/2005-11-07-bush-terror-suspects_x.htm# (accessed January 23, 2012).

251 *"No individual in the custody"*: Detainee Treatment Act of 2005. 109th Congress Report, House of Representatives. http://www.pegc.us/detainee_act_2005.html (accessed January 23, 2012).

251 *the president vetoed legislation*: Eggen, Dan. "Bush Announces Veto of Waterboarding Ban." *The Washington Post*, March 8, 2008. http://www.washingtonpost.com/wp-dyn/content/article/2008/03/08/AR2008030800304.html (accessed January 23, 2012).

252 *five characteristics common to acts of torture*: Schweiker, William. *Torture and Religious Practice*. "Torture: Its Meaning and History." *Dialog*, 2008, 47, pp. 208–216. DOI: 10.1111/j.1540-6385.2008.00395. http://onlinelibrary.wiley.com/doi/10.1111/j.1540-6385.2008.00395.x/full (accessed January 23, 2012).

252 *dehumanize*: Emphasis added.

252 *must make several assumptions*: Schweiker. *Torture and Religious Practice*. "What Justifies Torture?"

252 *CIA hadn't destroyed*: "CIA Destroyed Interrogation Tapes." BBC News, December 7, 2007. http://news.bbc.co.uk/2/hi/americas/7132000.stm (accessed January 23, 2012).

252 *five days within one month*: Bradbury. "Memorandum for John A. Rizzo," May 10, 2005, no. 0000013, p. 44.

253 *eighty-three pours in one month*: Bradbury, Steven G. "Memorandum for John A. Rizzo, Senior Deputy General Counsel, Central Intelligence Agency," May 30, 2005, no. 0000011, p. 37. http://documents.nytimes.com/justice-department-memos-on-interrogation-techniques (accessed January 23, 2012).

253 *physicians and psychologists*: Bradbury. "Memorandum for John A. Rizzo," May 10, 2005, no. 0000013, p. 16.

253 *"he has no control"*: Bradbury. "Memorandum for John A. Rizzo," May 10, 2005, no. 0000012, p. 54.

253 *a wage sufficient to meet the basic needs*: There are those who attempt to cross the border to engage in already high-risk activities,

such as drug smuggling. We can either continue to forcefully prevent them from entering this country or not give them a reason to come here in the first place. Smugglers of illegal drugs will not go where there is no market for what they are selling, and the best way to clean our borders of this contingent is to clean our own lives and our own country of illegal drug dependency.

254   *take the CIA four years*: "CIA Admits Waterboarding Inmates." BBC News, February 5, 2008. http://news.bbc.co.uk/2/hi/americas/7229169.stm (accessed January 24, 2012).

254   *and the president over six years*: Roelofs, Ted. "'I'd Do It Again' Former President Bush Tells Grand Rapids Crowd About Waterboarding Terrorists." *The Grand Rapids Press*, June, 2, 2010. http://www.mlive.com/news/grand-rapids/index.ssf/2010/06/id_do_it_again_former_presiden.html (accessed January 28, 2012).

254   *Waterboarding is not new*: "Waterboarding." Wikipedia.org. http://en.wikipedia.org/wiki/Waterboarding (accessed January 24, 2012).

254   *Manchester Manual*: "NewsHour with Jim Lehrer, The Detainees." *Newshour*, PBS, February 13, 2004. http://www.pbs.org/newshour/bb/terrorism/jan-june04/detainees_2-13.html (accessed January 24, 2012). According to Pentagon official Paul Butler:

> There's a document called the Manchester Manual that was picked up in a search in Manchester and has surfaced in Afghanistan and elsewhere. It's the al-Qaeda manual, basically. There is a very lengthy chapter on counter-interrogation techniques. These are sophisticated terrorists who know how to avoid interrogation.

> The key components in the "Interrogation and Investigation" chapter of the al-Qaeda "Manchester Manual" entitled *Declaration of Jihad Against the Country's Tyrants*—which seemed to resemble basic avoidance advice rather than any advanced resistance training—include the following:

> • Patience, steadfastness, and silence about any information whatsoever. That is very difficult except for those who take refuge in Allah.
> • Executing the security plan that was agreed upon prior to execution of the operation and not deviating from it.
> • The worst case—Allah forbid—is when the brother breaks down totally and tells all he knows, which is due to a poor choice in the brother. Thus, it is important to test individuals prior to such work in order to ensure their steadfastness and minimize the likelihood of their breaking down. Testing may be done by accusing him of being an enemy agent and lying about the reported information.

(See "Terrorism 101: A How-To Guide." TheSmokingGun.com. http://www.thesmokinggun.com/file/seventeenth-lesson?page=8 [accessed January 24, 2012].)

254 *"black sites" . . . illegally disclosed*: Priest, Dana. "CIA Hold Terror Suspects in Secret Prisons." *The Washington Post*, November 2, 2005. http://www.washingtonpost.com/wp-dyn/content/ article/2005/11/01/AR2005110101644.html (accessed January 24, 2012). Barack Obama shut down the CIA's secret prison system and banned torture and extraordinary rendition one year after being elected president. (See Goldenberg, Suzanne and Ewen MacAskill. "Obama Shuts Network of CIA 'Ghost Prisons.'" *The Guardian*, January 22, 2009. http://www.guardian.co.uk/ world/2009/jan/23/obama-rendition-torture [accessed March 13, 2012].)

255 *Most notable Great Britain*: "UK Apology Over Rendition Flights." BBC News, February 21, 2008. http://news.bbc.co.uk/2/hi/uk_ news/politics/7256587.stm (accessed June 11, 2010).

257 *"There is nothing in the universe that you are not"*: Rumi (Jalal al-Din Rumi, Maulana). *Rumi: Thief of Sleep*. Prescott, AZ: Hohm Press, 2000, p. 94. Translation of Divan-i Shams-i Tabrizi by Shahram Shiva. (The quatrains in this book were originally published in *Rending the Veil: Literal and Poetic Translations of Rumi*, by Shahram Shiva. Prescott, AZ: Hohm Press, 1995.)

257 *"We also have to work . . . the dark side"*: Cheney, Dick. *Meet the Press with Tim Russert*. NBC, Camp David, Maryland, September 16, 2001. http://georgewbush-whitehouse.archives.gov/vicepresi dent/news-speeches/speeches/vp20010916.html (accessed January 24, 2012).

257 *"worth it"*: Loven, Jennifer. "Bush: Bloodshed in Iraq is 'Worth It.'" Associated Press (Fort Bragg, NC), June 28, 2005.

258 *non-governmental agency survey*: "Iraq War Takes Heavy Toll on Civilians—Survey." Reuters (Baghdad), July 19, 2005.

258 *death toll reached over 100,000*: Wikileaks document release, October 22, 2010. (See also "66,000 Iraqi Civilians Killed by U.S. Army–Wikileaks." http://hubpages.com/forum/topic/57438 [accessed January 25, 2012].)

258 *"thin green line"*: Burns, Robert. "Study: Army Stretched to Breaking Point." Associated Press (Washington), January 24, 2006. http://usatoday30.usatoday.com/news/washington/2006-01-24- army-study_x.htm# (accessed January 25, 2012).

258 *suicide rate for eighteen- to twenty-nine-year-old veterans*: Hefling, Kimberly. "Increase in Suicide Rate of Veterans Noted." Associated Press (Washington), January 11, 2010. http://www.armytimes.

com/news/2010/01/ap_vet_suicide_011110/ (accessed January 25, 2012).

258   *suicides among active-duty Army soldiers*: Capaccio, Anthony. "Suicides in U.S. Army are on Track to Reach New High." Bloomberg, November 13, 2009. http://www.bloomberg.com/apps/new s?pid=newsarchive&sid=aquBCzT7ZMLs (accessed January 25, 2012). Through June 3, 2012, the suicide rate among U.S. active-duty troops surged to an average of nearly one a day. The 154 suicides in the first 155 days of the year were fifty percent more than the number of U.S. soldiers killed in action in Afghanistan during the same period. After over ten years of war, two things remain true regarding soldier suicides: The military is still struggling to understand the source of suicidal behavior and the proper responses to it, and too many soldiers still believe that asking for help would be viewed as a sign of weakness. In a statement written in his January 2012 blog, Maj. Gen. Dana Pittard became an example of the first and the reason for the second:

> I have now come to the conclusion that suicide is an absolutely selfish act. . . . I am personally fed up with soldiers who are choosing to take their own lives so that others can clean up their mess. Be an adult, act like an adult, and deal with your real-life problems like the rest of us.

(See Burns, Robert. "AP Impact: Suicides are Surging Among U.S. Troops." Associated Press [Washington], June 8, 2012. http://news.yahoo.com/ap-impact-suicides-surging-among-us-troops-204148055.html. [accessed January 25, 2012].)

258   *245 soldiers had committed suicide*: Official Homepage of the United States Army. "Family Life Chaplain Promotes Suicide Prevention Month." Fort Knox, KY, September 14, 2010. http://www.army.mil/article/45171/Family_Life_Chaplain_Promotes_Suicide_Prevention_Month/ (accessed January 25, 2012).

258   *thirty-two Army suicides within a single month*: Zoroya, Gregg. "Army Reports Record Number of Suicides for June." *USA Today*, July 15, 2010. http://www.usatoday.com/news/military/2010-07-15-army-suicides_N.htm (accessed January 25, 2012).

258   *6,000 veterans commit suicide each year*: Miles, Donna. "VA Strives to Prevent Veteran Suicides." American Forces Press Service (Washington), April 23, 2010. http://www.defense.gov/news/newsarticle.aspx?id=58879 (accessed January 25, 2012).

258   *4,416 members of the U.S. military*: Anderson, Rick. "Facing Our Losses—Iraq 2010." *Seattle Weekly*, March 17, 2010. http://www.seattleweekly.com/2010-03-17/news/facing-our-losses-iraq-2010/ (accessed January 25, 2012); "Casualties of War: The Human

Toll of the Conflict in Iraq." Associated Press. http://hosted. ap.org/specials/interactives/_international/iraq_withdrawal/index. html?SITE=AP (accessed January 25, 2012).

258   *31,770 had been wounded in hostile action*: "Casualties: Afghanistan/Iraq, 2010." http://www.cnn.com/SPECIALS/war.casualties/ index.html (accessed January 25, 2012).

258   *twenty-one-year-old reservist*: "American Casualties in Iraq, Afghanistan, and Beyond." *USA Today*. http://www.usatoday.com/ news/world/casualties.htm#afghan (accessed January 25, 2012).

259   *divorces among active-duty Army officers*: Crary, David. "Iraq War Takes Toll on Army Marriages." Associated Press (New York), June 29, 2005.

259   *1,500 veterans from Iraq and Afghanistan*: McClam, Erin. "Why Does Johnny Come Marching Homeless?" Associated Press (Leeds, MA), January 19, 2008.

259   *Known as tramps*: Ibid.

259   *In the 1930s, the Bonus Army*: Ibid.

259   *Congress had voted to compensate . . . attack its own*: "Bonus Army." Wikipedia.org. http://en.wikipedia.org/wiki/Bonus_army (accessed January 26, 2012).

260   *"struggled for decades for acceptance"*: Bender, Bryan. "New Veterans Fear Repeat of Vietnam." *The Boston Globe*, May 30, 2006. http://www.boston.com/news/nation/washington/articles/ 2006/05/30/new_veterans_fear_repeat_of_vietnam/?page=1 (accessed January 26, 2012).

260   *nearly half of today's homeless veterans*: National Coalition for Homeless Veterans. "Background & Statistics." http://nchv.org/ index.php/news/media/background_and_statistics/ (accessed January 25, 2012).

260   *300,000 veterans of the Iraq and Afghanistan wars*: Leopold, Jason. "VA Official: More Than 60,000 Iraq, Afghanistan Vets Diagnosed with PTSD." Column, March 8, 2008. http://www. scoop.co.nz/stories/HL0803/S00119.htm (accessed January 25, 2012).

260   *not "entitled" to five years*: Ibid.

260   *"Unless systemic and drastic measures"*: Ibid. This prediction has come true with alarming accuracy. America's veterans of the Iraq and Afghanistan wars are on their way to becoming "the most medically and mentally troubled generation of former troops the nation has ever seen." A staggering forty-five percent of the 1.6 million veterans from our two latest wars have filed for disability

benefits, or more than double the estimate of twenty-one percent for claims filed after the Gulf War in the early 1990s. And new veterans are reporting an average of eight to nine, some as high as eleven to fourteen, ailments per soldier. Women are filing in greater numbers than in previous wars, and include among their disabilities PTSD due to military sexual trauma. Of those who have sought VA care and compensation:

- More than 400,000 have been treated for a mental health problem.
- Thousands are disfigured; as many as 200 need face transplants; and one-quarter of the battlefield injuries include wounds to the face or jaw.
- More than 1,600 have lost a limb; many others have lost fingers or toes.
- At least 156 are blind; thousands of others are visually impaired.
- More than 177,000 have hearing loss, and more than 350,000 report tinnitus—noise or ringing in the ears.

American taxpayers are only just beginning to feel the wartime financial trauma. Caring for veterans typically rises over decades and peaks at around thirty to forty years after a disability claim. A Harvard economist estimates the health care and disability costs of the Iraq and Afghanistan wars at *$600 billion* to *$900 billion*. This means Americans paid an estimated *$4 trillion* to physically and mentally break our fellow countrymen and women by sending them to war, and must now pay hundreds of billions more to try to put them back together again. (*"most medically and mentally"*: Marchione, Marilynn. "AP Impact: Almost Half of New Vets Seek Disability." Associated Press, May 22, 2012. http://news.yahoo.com/ap-impact-almost-half-vets-seek-disability-160656481.html [accessed May 22, 2012]; *$4 trillion*: Eisenhower Study Group; Brown University's Watson Institute for International Studies. "The Costs of War Project," June 2011. http://costsofwar.org [accessed May 22, 2012].)

261　*4th Brigade Combat Team commissioned*: Roeder, Tom. "Fort Carson Report: Combat Stress Contributed to Soldiers' Crimes Back Home." *The Gazette*, July 15, 2009. http://www.gazette.com/news/soldiers-58520-report-army.html (accessed January 26, 2012).

261　*"toxic mix"*: Ibid.

261　*combat stress, drug and alcohol abuse*: U.S. Army Center for Health Promotion and Preventive Medicine. "Epidemiologic Consultation No. 14-hk-ob1u-09: Investigation of Homicides at Fort Carson, Colorado, November 2008–May 2009." Released July 2009. http://www3.gazette.com/documents/epiconreport.pdf (accessed January 26, 2012).

261   *"We're used to seeing people"*: "Soldiers in Colorado Tell of Iraq Horrors." Associated Press (Colorado Springs, CO), July 26, 2009.

261   *projecting them onto something*: Tipping, Colin C. *Radical Forgiveness: Making Room for the Miracle.* 2nd ed. Marietta, GA: Global 13 Publications, Inc., 2002, p. 89.

261   *rape and murder of a nineteen-year-old girl*: Roeder. "Fort Carson Report."

261   *"suck it up"*: Hall, Kristin M. "Fort Campbell Tries to Stop Soldier Suicides." Associated Press (Fort Campbell, KY), April 25, 2010. http://www.armytimes.com/news/2010/04/ap_army_campbell_suicides_042510/ (accessed January 26, 2012).

262   *"the heavy stigma associated"*: Goodwin, Liz. "Army Suicides Hit Record Number in June." Yahoo! News, July 16, 2010. http://news.yahoo.com/blogs/upshot/army-suicides-hit-record-number-june-153452765.html (accessed January 26, 2012).

262   *Warrior Transition Units (WTU) were created*: Dao, James and Dan Frosch. "Feeling Warehoused in Army Trauma Care Units." *New York Times*, April 24, 2010. http://www.nytimes.com/2010/04/25/health/25warrior.html?pagewanted=all (accessed January 26, 2012).

262   *"just a dark place"*: Ibid.

262   *"Being in the WTU"*: Ibid.

262   *an Army sniper, was said to be overflowing*: Ibid.

262   *"laundry list"*: Ibid.

263   *"begging to get out"*: Ibid.

263   *"openly deal, buy, or swap"*: Ibid.

263   *"We're all on sleep meds"*: Ibid.

263   *overly medicated and listless soldiers*: Ibid.

263   *"Stuff happened in Iraq"*: Zwerdling, Daniel. "Soldiers Face Obstacles to Mental Health Services." National Public Radio, December 4, 2006. http://www.npr.org/templates/story/story.php?storyId=6575431 (accessed January 26, 2012).

264   *"They don't want to go back to Iraq"*: Ibid.

264   *"[The war in Iraq] is kind of like"*: Buzzell, Spc. Colby (U.S. Army Retd). "Inside the Iraq War." National Geographic Channel. (Originally aired December 13, 2009.)

265   *"There are times when you literally"*: Ibid., Bellavia, SSG David (U.S. Army Retd).

265   *"Yeah, we waterboarded Khalid Sheikh Mohammed"*: Roelofs. "I'd Do It Again."

265   *"getting rid of Saddam Hussein"*: Ibid.

266   *"[The people of Iraq] must also understand"*: Bush, George W. Interview with al-Hurra, May 5, 2004. http://www.pbs.org/news hour/bb/white_house/jan-june04/bush-alhurra_5-5.html (accessed January 28, 2012). Emphasis added.

266   *nearly one execution every two weeks*: Hitchens, Christopher. "Gov. Death." Salon.com, August 7, 1999. http://www.salon. com/1999/08/07/death_2/ (accessed January 28, 2012).

266   *a record for the state*: Berlow, Alan. "The Texas Clemency Memos." *The Atlantic Monthly,* July/August, 2003. http://www.theatlantic. com/magazine/print/2003/07/the-texas-clemency-memos/2755/ (accessed January 28, 2012). Texas Gov. Rick Perry currently holds the record for the most executions in modern history with 234. Texas is "responsible for a third of the executions in the country and has carried out two and a half times as many death sentences as the next leading state." (See Barnes, Robert. "Rick Perry Holds the Record on Executions." *The Washington Post*, August, 23, 2011. http://www.washingtonpost.com/politics/rick-perry-holds-the-record-on-executions/2011/08/17/gIQ [accessed January 28, 2012]; *"responsible for a third"*: Dieter, Richard C. "The Future of the Death Penalty in the U.S.: A Texas-Sized Crisis." Death Penalty Information Center, May 1994. http://deathpenaltyinfo. org/node/682 [accessed January 28, 2012].)

266   *including two in one day*: Graczyk, Michael. "Two Killers Executed in Texas." Associated Press (Huntsville, TX), August 9, 2000. http://ccadp.org/TX2X.htm (accessed January 28, 2012).

266   *record thirty-seven inmates in one year*: Verhovek, Sam Howe. "As Woman's Execution Nears, Texas Squirms." *New York Times,* January 1, 1998. http://www.nytimes.com/1998/01/01/us/as-woman-s-execution-nears-texas-squirms.html?pagewanted=all&src=pm (accessed January 28, 2012).

267   *communication skills of a child of seven*: Prejean, Sister Helen. "Death in Texas." *The New York Review of Books*, January 13, 2005. http://www.nybooks.com/articles/archives/2005/jan/13/ death-in-texas/?pagination=false (accessed January 28, 2012).

267   *post-conviction lawyers*: Ibid.

267   *"beaten regularly with whips, water hoses"*: Ibid. (See also Berlow. "The Texas Clemency Memos.")

267   *committed when they were seventeen*: Coordinating Council on Juvenile Justice and Delinquency Prevention. "Background Information, March 1999." http://www.juvenilecouncil.gov/summary/ juveniles.html (accessed January 28, 2012).

267   *seventy juveniles on death row*: Hitchens. "Gov. Death."

267   *Karla Faye Tucker and her boyfriend*: Clark County Prosecutor. Karla Fay Tucker #437, Summary/Fact Sheet on Karla Faye Tucker. http://www.clarkprosecutor.org/html/death/US/tucker437.htm (accessed January 28, 2012).

267   *"twenty times with one of his own tools"*: Walt, Kathy. "Tucker Dies After Apologizing; Despite Legal Blitz, Woman Executed for Pickax Slayings." *Houston Chronicle*, February 3, 1998. http://www.clarkprosecutor.org/html/death/US/tucker437.htm (accessed January 28, 2012).

267   *embedded in her chest*: Clark County Prosecutor. Karla Fay Tucker #437, Summary.

267   *a jury found Karla Faye Tucker guilty*: Clark County Prosecutor. Karla Fay Tucker #437, Procedural History. http://www.clark prosecutor.org/html/death/US/tucker437.htm (accessed January 28, 2012).

267   *eight minutes after lethal drugs*: Walt. "Tucker Dies After Apologizing."

268   *"brief description of the crime"*: Berlow. "The Texas Clemency Memos."

268   *fifty-seven had been prepared by Alberto R. Gonzales*: Ibid.

268   *lasting no more than thirty minutes*: Ibid.

268   *"new facts or evidence"*: Bush, George W. *A Charge to Keep*. New York: HarperCollins, 1999, p. 148. (Hardcover edition published in 1999 by William Morrow and Company, Inc.)

268   *"a fair hearing and full access"*: Ibid., p. 162.

268   *whether there was any doubt*: Ibid., p. 141.

268   *evidence of significant discussion . . . additional documentation*: Berlow. "The Texas Clemency Memos."

268   *"one of the hardest things"*: Bush. *A Charge to Keep*, pp. 153–154.

268   *first smoked pot . . . "into prostitution"*: Prejean. "Death in Texas."

268   *"school" her in the act*: Tucker, Karla Faye. Letter to Gov. George W. Bush, January 20, 1998. http://www.clarkprosecutor.org/html/death/US/tucker437.htm (accessed January 29, 2012).

269   *"orgy of methadone"*: Walt, Kathy. "Execution May Haunt Texas; Tucker Case Likely to Bring Unprecedented Scrutiny." *Houston Chronicle*, December 14, 1997. http://www.clarkprosecutor.org/html/death/US/tucker437.htm (accessed January 29, 2012).

269   *stole a Bible during her first days in prison*: Tucker, Karla Faye.

"Karla Faye Tucker: Live from Death Row." *CNN Larry King Live*, January 14, 1998. http://www.cnn.com/SPECIALS/1998/tucker. execution/transcripts/trans.1.14.html (accessed January 29, 2012).

269 *a model prisoner*: Zorn, Eric. "Death Row Beauty Shows Execution is Always Unfair." *Chicago Tribune*, January 22, 1998. http:// articles.chicagotribune.com/1998-01-22/news/9801220166_1_ texas-inmate-karla-faye-tucker-execution (accessed January 29, 2012).

269 *Pat Robertson . . . to other prisoners*: Leung, Rebecca. "Texas Executes Tucker." ABC News, February 3, 1998. http://www. clarkprosecutor.org/html/death/US/tucker437.htm (accessed January 29, 2012).

269 *"humanitarian gesture"*: Ibid.

269 *one of George W. Bush's own daughters*: Bush. *A Charge to Keep*, p. 147.

269 *a governor can do nothing . . . eighteen members*: Berlow. "The Texas Clemency Memos."

270 *Orange Socks case . . . 17-1 vote*: Ibid.

270 *"I guess I could have tried"*: Bush. *A Charge to Keep*, p. 151.

270 *no one on Texas' death row . . . humanitarian reasons*: Court TV Online. "Texas v. Karla Faye Tucker Background Report: A Question of Mercy." http://www.clarkprosecutor.org/html/death/ US/tucker437.htm (accessed January 30, 2012).

270 *"This case has two main themes"*: Walt. "Execution May Haunt Texas."

271 *Jesus hadn't slept for nearly thirty-six hours*: Maxwell, Dr. Keith. "The Cruxification." Speech presented in Asheville, NC. http:// www.thylacineslair.com/Reflections/Cruxification.htm (accessed January 30, 2012).

271 *nine thick leather thongs*: Ibid.

271 *open wound two inches long*: Ibid. Dr. Maxwell believes the cold night air kept Jesus from bleeding to death.

271 *the pounding lead balls . . . lashes one would receive*: Davis, Dr. C. Truman. "A Physician Analyzes the Crucifixion." http:// www.thecross-photo.com/Dr_C._Truman_Davis_Analyzes_the_ Crucifixion.htm (accessed January 30, 2012).

271 *over one-hundred-pound beam*: Maxwell. "The Cruxification."

272 *650-yard journey*: Davis. "A Physician Analyzes the Crucifixion." Today, the crucifixion path in the Old City of Jerusalem is called the Via Dolorosa, the Way of Suffering.

272 *felt for the depression in the back of his hands*: There is some dispute as to the nail location. Dr. Davis believes it was in the wrist. Frederick T. Zugibe, MD, PhD, conducted research that concluded it was in the upper part of the palm. (See Zugibe, Frederick T. "Pierre Barbet Revisited." http://www.crucifixion-shroud.com/Barbet.htm [accessed May 1, 2012].)

272 *tool similar to a pitchfork*: Maxwell. "The Cruxification."

272 *To exhale, Jesus . . . taken lightly*: Ibid.

272 *end a crucifixion . . . strong shinbones*: Ibid.

273 *"Some advocates of life"*: Bush. *A Charge to Keep*, p. 147.

274 *"I see people in here in the prison"*: Tucker. Letter to Gov. George W. Bush.

275 *"Anyone who interferes with the Personal Legend"*: Coelho, Paulo. *The Alchemist*. New York: HarperCollins, 1993, p. 138. (Originally published in Portuguese under the title *O Alquimista* by Editora Rocco Ltd. in 1998.)

275 *what a Christian looks like 152 times*: Or 153 times if the "Orange Socks" case defendant, who was exonerated, is included.

277 *someone who can rape and strangle a woman to death*: On July 23, 2007, two men broke into a Connecticut home as a doctor, his wife, and their two daughters slept. Dr. William Petit was first hit with a baseball bat, then tied to a pole in the basement, where he heard the two men beat, rape, and strangle his wife to death, and molest one of his young daughters before setting the house on fire. Dr. Petit was the only survivor. (See Wikipedia.org. "Cheshire, Connecticut, Home Invasion Murders" http://en.wikipedia.org/wiki/Cheshire,_Connecticut,_home_invasion_murders [accessed March 30, 2012].)

277 *personally conducted, witnessed*: Nance, Malcolm. "Waterboarding is Torture . . . Period." *Small Wars Journal* Blog Post, October 31, 2007. http://smallwarsjournal.com/blog/waterboarding-is-torture-period-links-updated-9 (accessed January 30, 2012).

277 *background in counterterrorism*: Ibid.

277 *Army and Navy SERE interrogation manuals*: Bybee. "Memorandum for Alberto R. Gonzales," p. 17.

277 *manuals were designed to describe*: Nance. "Waterboarding is Torture . . . Period."

278 *"shocks the conscience"*: Bradbury. "Memorandum for John A. Rizzo," May 30, 2005, no. 0000011, p. 2.

278 *not a "simulated" drowning*: Nance. "Waterboarding is Torture . . . Period."

278   *torture cripples the torturer as well*: Keller, Loretta. Opinion. *San Gabriel Valley Tribune*, November 16, 2007.

278   *"One has to overcome basic human decency"*: Nance. "Waterboarding is Torture . . . Period."

278   *question the meaning of what it is to be an American*: Personal experience also caused another soldier to struggle with humanity and hatred, and bridge the distance between his words and the consequences of his actions during the Iraq War. After a bloody, three-week battle in Fallujah, the Marines pulled out at the end of April 2004 and handed over power to an Iraqi interim government, acting only in a subordinate role to the Iraqis when fighting insurgents in the area. However, in the following months, Fallujah once again became an insurgent stronghold. And in November 2004, Operation Phantom Fury landed 8,000 U.S. ground troops in the city. But rather than sparking intense fighting, the soldiers found the city eerily quiet. The insurgents had taken cover in homes and buildings, forcing soldiers to conduct enemy searches house to house, room by room.

In one house, a soldier spotted a wounded insurgent and shot as he ran after him. The soldier chased the insurgent into a room where he then, face to face, plunged a knife deep into his chest.

> He just got weaker and weaker. [He] ran his hand through my hair, and slowly brought his hand down on my cheek. It was probably the worst moment of my life at that moment. He wasn't an animal anymore. He wasn't a bad guy anymore. He wasn't an insurgent. He was a person fighting for his life. And I was taking it.

(See "Inside the Iraq War." National Geographic Channel. [Originally aired December 13, 2009]; *"He just got weaker"*: Ibid. Bellavia, SSG David [U.S. Army Retd].)

279   *"Unfortunately, some criminals"*: Bush, George W. "Issues 2000," December 31, 1998. http://www.issues2000.org/celeb/More_George_W__Bush_Crime.htm (accessed January 30, 2012). (Original source unavailable: http://www.governor.state.tx.us/divisions/faq_index.html.)

281   *"if you want peace in Africa"*: Robinson, Simon. "The Deadliest War in the World." *Time Magazine*, May 28, 2006. http://www.time.com/time/magazine/article/0,9171,1198921,00.html (accessed February 2, 2012).

281   *"worst places on earth"*: Robinson. "The Deadliest War in the World."

281   *"worst place in the world to do business"*: Behar, Richard. "Mineral Wealth of the Congo." FastCompany.com, June 1, 2008. http://

www.fastcompany.com/849680/mineral-wealth-congo (accessed February 2, 2012).

281 *"rape capital of the world"*: Kristof, Nickolas D. "Death by Gadget." *New York Times*, June 26, 2010. http://www.nytimes.com/2010/06/27/opinion/27kristof.html (accessed February 2, 2012).

281 *"ultimate hellhole"*: Robinson. "The Deadliest War in the World."

281 *make a mineralogist weak in the knees*: "Diamond Heist." *The Washington Post*, November 28, 2001. http://www.washington post.com/wp-adv/specialsales/spotlight/congo/diamond.html (accessed February 2, 2012).

281 *largest supply of high-grade copper . . . Nagasaki*: Montague, Dena and Frida Berrigan. "The Business of War in the Democratic Republic of Congo." *Dollars and Sense Magazine*, July/August 2001. http://www.thirdworldtraveler.com/Africa/Business_War_Congo.html (accessed February 2, 2012).

281 *thirty percent of its diamond reserves*: Winter, Joseph. "DR Congo Poll Crucial for Africa." BBC News, November 16, 2006. http://news.bbc.co.uk/2/hi/africa/5209428.stm (accessed March 10, 2012).

281 *two major gold sources*: Trans Continent Exploration & Mining Company. "DRC Gold Overview." http://www.tcemco.com/drc_gold.html (accessed February 2, 2012).

281 *711-square-mile Kilo-Moto greenstone gold belt*: "Kilo-Moto." Wikipedia.org. http://en.wikipedia.org/wiki/Kilo-Moto (accessed March 10, 2010).

281 *130-mile Twangiza-Namoya gold belt*: IDE-JETRO. "Banro Corporation Company Profile and History." http://www.ide.go.jp/English/Data/Africa_file/Company/drc01.html (accessed February 2, 2012).

281 *estimated to be $24 trillion*: Warah, Rasna. "Blood Mobile Phones Fan DRC's Murderous Conflict." *Daily Nation*, March 15, 2009. http://www.nation.co.ke/oped/Opinion/-/440808/546106/-/444qqy/-/index.html (accessed February 2, 2012).

282 *nor has access to as much as forty percent*: "Diamond Heist."

282 *estimated four million people having died*: Robinson. "The Deadliest War in the World."

282 *armed rebel groups*: Bavier, Joe. "Congo War-Driven Crisis Kills 45,000 a Month: Study." Reuters (Kinshasa), January 22, 2008. http://www.reuters.com/article/2008/01/22/us-congo-democratic-death-idUSL2280201220080122 (accessed February 2, 2012).

282   *"that wouldn't exist in peaceful times"*: Robinson. "The Deadliest
       War in the World."

282   *45,000 each month*: Bavier. "Congo War-Driven Crisis Kills 45,000
       a Month: Study."

282   *indiscriminate killings, mass rapes*: U.S. Department of State.
       "Background Note: Democratic Republic of the Congo." Bureau
       of African Affairs, September 30, 2011. http://www.state.gov/r/
       pa/ei/bgn/2823.htm (accessed February 3, 2012).

283   *more than 1,100 women and girls*: "More Than 1,100 Rapes
       Daily in DR Congo: Study." Agence-France Press (Washington),
       May 10, 2011. http://www.google.com/hostednews/afp/article/
       ALeqM5iqLkVw-clmTOBS7eUTh33eI8EJog?docId=CNG.19d25
       18f55df02422e69e294f3d17a1d.51 (accessed February 3, 2012).

283   *gun butts, knives, and bayonets*: Faul, Michelle. "Congo Women
       Fight Back, Speak Out About Rape." Associated Press (Doshu,
       Congo), March 16, 2009. http://www.msnbc.msn.com/id/29719277/
       ns/world_news-africa/t/congo-women-fight-backspeak-out-about-
       rape/#.UCHYKkZvYbR (accessed February 3, 2012).

283   *"maximum humiliation"*: McCrummen, Stephanie. "Prevalence
       of Rape in E. Congo Described as Worst in World." *The Wash-
       ington Post*, September 9, 2007. http://www.washingtonpost.com/
       wp-dyn/content/article/2007/09/08/AR2007090801194_pf.html
       (accessed March 10, 2012).

283   *fifty percent of the rape victims*: U.S. Department of State. "Back-
       ground Note: Democratic Republic of the Congo."

283   *half of the world's 300,000 child soldiers*: "Too Small to be Fight-
       ing in Anyone's War." United Nations Office for the Coordina-
       tion of Humanitarian Affairs/Integrated Regional Information
       Networks. Special Report: Child Soldiers, December 12, 2003.
       http://www.irinnews.org/pdf/in-depth/Child-Soldiers-IRIN-In-
       Depth.pdf (accessed March 10, 2012); Shah, Anup. "Children,
       Conflicts, and the Military." *Global Issues*, September 27, 2003.
       http://www.globalissues.org/print/article/82 (accessed March 10,
       2012).

283   *30,000 child soldiers in the Congo*: Bell, Martin. "Martin Bell
       Reports on Children Caught in War." UNICEF Child Alert: Demo-
       cratic Republic of Congo, July 2006. http://www.unicef.org/child
       alert/drc/childsoldiers.php (accessed February 3, 2012).

283   *"armed militia groups are now targeting"*: Greste, Peter. "Congo-
       lese Children Forced to Fight." BBC News (Goma), November 12,
       2008. http://news.bbc.co.uk/2/hi/africa/7724088.stm (accessed
       February 3, 2012).

283 *thirty to forty percent are girls*: Bell. "Martin Bell Reports on Children Caught in War."

283 *runners, scouts, porters*: "Too Small to be Fighting in Anyone's War."

283 *"subjected to brutal initiation and punishment"*: Ibid.

283 *There are several reasons the practice continues*: Ibid.

283 *"because they can"*: Ibid.

284 *Corruption Perceptions Index*: Transparency International. "Corruption Perceptions Index 2011." http://cpi.transparency.org/cpi2011/results/#CountryResults (accessed February 5, 2012).

284 *The Human Development Index*: United Nations Development Program. "2011 Human Development Report." http://hdrstats.undp.org/en/countries/profiles/COD.html (accessed February 5, 2012); United Nations Development Program. "2011 Human Development Index Covers Record 187 Countries and Territories, Puts Norway at Top, DR Congo Last." Copenhagen, November 2, 2011. http://www.tr.undp.org/content/turkey/en/home/presscenter/pressreleases/2011/11/02/2011-human-development-index-covers-record-187-countries-and-territories/ (accessed February 5, 2012).

284 *over seventy percent are living on*: Central Intelligence Agency. "The World Fact Book." Democratic Republic of the Congo. https://www.cia.gov/library/publications/the-world-factbook/geos/cg.html (accessed February 5, 2012).

284 *Congo has perhaps the most extensive*: Behar. "Mineral Wealth of the Congo."

284 *Many in the sub-Sahara are harboring*: Ibid.

284 *its own future generations*: Montague and Berrigan. "The Business of War in the Democratic Republic of Congo."

284 *delivered over $1.5 billion*: Hartung, William D. and Bridget Moix. "Report: U.S. Arms to Africa and the Congo War—World Policy Institute." Arms Trade Resource Center, January 2000. http://www.worldpolicy.org/projects/arms/reports/congo.htm (accessed February 5, 2012).

284 *"helped build the arsenals"*: Ibid.

284 *"Africa suffered eleven major armed conflicts"*: Ibid.

284 *"U.S. Special Forces have trained military personnel"*: Ibid. Emphasis added.

284 *provided $306 million in aid*: U.S. Department of State. "Background Note: Democratic Republic of the Congo."

285   *"We cannot have it both ways"*: Committee on Administration, U.S.
       House of Representatives, The Presidential Campaign, 1976, Part I:
       Jimmy Carter. Washington, DC: U.S. Government Printing Office,
       1978, pp. 266–275, cited in Hartung, William D. "Report: The
       Role of U.S. Arms Transfers in Human Rights Violations—World
       Policy Institute." Arms Trade Resource Center. Testimony before
       the Subcommittee on International Operations and Human Rights,
       House International Relations Committee, March 7, 2001. http://
       www.worldpolicy.org/projects/arms/reports/testimony030701.htm
       (accessed February 5, 2012).

285   *world's top weapons exporter*: Stockholm International Peace
       Research Institute. http://www.sipri.org (accessed February 5,
       2012).

285   *delivered $42 billion in weaponry*: Hartung. "Report: The Role
       of U.S. Arms Transfers in Human Rights Violations."

285   *"significant ethnic and territorial conflicts"*: Ibid.

285   *ninety percent—"received U.S. weaponry"*: Ibid. Emphasis added.

285   *"sell or transfer more than $32 billion in weapons"*: Lipton, Eric.
       "With White House Push, U.S. Arms Sales Jump." *New York
       Times*, September 14, 2008. http://www.nytimes.com/2008/09/14/
       washington/14arms.html?_r=1 (accessed February 5, 2012).

285   *most lasting legacy*: Ibid.

285   *"This is not about being gunrunners"*: Ibid.

285   *Afghanistan has been in a continuous state of war*: "War in
       Afghanistan (1978–Present)." Wikipedia.org. http://en.wikipedia.
       org/wiki/War_in_Afghanistan_(1978–present) (accessed May
       15, 2012); "Soviet War in Afghanistan." Wikipedia.org. http://
       en.wikipedia.org/wiki/Soviet_war_in_Afghanistan (accessed May
       15, 2012).

286   *Averaging $600 million*: "Operation Cyclone." Wikipedia.org.
       http://en.wikipedia.org/wiki/Operation_Cyclone (accessed May
       15, 2012).

286   *Another function of the CIA–ISI alliance*: Pilger, John. "What
       Good Friends Left Behind." *The Guardian*, September 19, 2003.
       http://www.guardian.co.uk/world/2003/sep/20/afghanistan.week
       end7 (accessed March 10, 2012).

286   *an estimated 35,000 militants from forty-three countries*:
       Rashid, Ahmed. "How a Holy War Against the Soviets Turned
       on U.S." *The Pittsburgh Post-Gazette*, September 23, 2001.
       http://s3.amazonaws.com/911timeline/2001/pittsburghpost
       gazette092301.html (accessed February 6, 2012).

286   *Madrassahs were originally established as centers*: Singer, Peter
        W. "Pakistan's Madrassahs: Ensuring a System of Education Not
        Jihad." The Brookings Institution, November 1, 2001. http://www.
        brookings.edu/research/papers/2001/11/pakistan-singer (accessed
        March 10, 2012).

286   *which grew from 700 in 1980*: Javed, Kazy. "Scary Scenario." *The
        News on Sunday*, February, 23, 2003, cited in Ali Riaz. "Global
        Jihad, Sectarianism and the Madrassahs in Pakistan." Institute
        of Defense and Strategic Studies, Singapore, August 2005. http://
        www.rsis.edu.sg/publications/WorkingPapers/WP85.pdf (accessed
        March 10, 2012).

286   *Public health and education were routinely*: Riaz. "Global Jihad,
        Sectarianism and the Madrassahs in Pakistan."

287   *"one of the biggest humanitarian crises"*: Bhutta, Zulfiqar Ahmed.
        "Children of War: The Real Casualties of the Afghan Conflict."
        British Medical Journal, February 9, 2002. http://www.ncbi.nlm.
        nih.gov/pmc/articles/PMC1122273/ (accessed March 10, 2012).
        (See also Miller, Laura C. and Masouma Timouri, Jelleke Wijnker,
        and Jane G. Schaller. *Archives of Pediatric & Adolescent Medicine*,
        July 1994, 148(7): 704–708.)

287   *Funded by the United States and its close ally*: Riaz. "Global Jihad,
        Sectarianism and the Madrassahs in Pakistan."

287   *acted as orphanages . . . would preach*: Singer. "Pakistan's Madras-
        sahs: Ensuring a System of Education Not Jihad."

287   *"teach a distorted view of Islam"*: Ibid.

287   *steady stream of images*: Bhutta. "Children of War: The Real
        Casualties of the Afghan Conflict."

287   *"an elite guerrilla"*: "55th Arab Brigade." Wikipedia.org. http://
        en.wikipedia.org/wiki/55th_Arab_Brigade (accessed March 11,
        2012).

287   *trained by Osama bin Laden's al-Qaeda*: Osama bin Laden's pres-
        ence in Afghanistan originated during the Soviet invasion at the
        request of the CIA, who invited him there to "inspire the Mujahi-
        deen." (See Jay, Paul. "The Afghan War and the 'Grand Chessboard'
        Pt. 2." The Real News Network, January 15, 2010. http://the
        realnews.com/t2/component/content/index.php?option=com_
        content&task=view&id=31&Itemid=74&jumival=4716 [accessed
        April 11, 2011].)

287   *integrated into the Taliban army*: Gunaratna, Rohan. *Inside Al
        Qaeda: Global Network of Terror*. New York: Columbia University
        Press, 2002, p. 58.

287 *brigade members were products of Pakistan's madrassahs*: Singer. "Pakistan's Madrassahs: Ensuring a System of Education Not Jihad."

287 *Dur-ul-Uloom Haqqania . . . available openings each year*: Ibid.

288 *much of it went to support the Mujahideen*: Bhutta. "Children of War: The Real Casualties of the Afghan Conflict."

288 *The United States greatly reduced*: Ibid.

288 *sold its government forty F-16 fighter jets*: Levy, Adrian and Cathy Scott-Clark. "The Man Who Knew Too Much." *The Guardian*, October 12, 2007. http://www.guardian.co.uk/world/2007/oct/13/usa.pakistan (accessed May 5, 2011).

288 *"restricted, high-tech materials"*: Hersh, Seymour M. "On the Nuclear Edge." *The New Yorker*, March 29, 1993. http://www.newyorker.com/archive/1993/03/29/1993_03_29_056_TNY_CARDS_000363214 (accessed May 5, 2011).

288 *"The certification process became farcical"*: Ibid.

289 *sell another sixty F-16 jets to Pakistan*: "The Spider's Stratagem." *The Economist*, January 3, 2008. http://www.economist.com/node/10424283 (accessed May 5, 2011).

289 *Pakistan sold its nuclear weapons technology*: Ibid.

289 *squandered by widespread corruption*: Bhutta. "Children of War: The Real Casualties of the Afghan Conflict."

289 *The removal of U.S. financial support*: Riaz. "Global Jihad, Sectarianism and the Madrassahs in Pakistan."

289 *"Children born in Afghanistan at the start"*: "Soviet War in Afghanistan." Wikipedia.org.

290 *"Truly this became a generation"*: Magnus, Ralph H. and Eden Naby. *Afghanistan: Mullah, Marx, and Mujahid*. Boulder, CO: Westview Press, 2002, p. 157.

290 *"Afghan trap"*: Le Nouvel Observateur. "The CIA's Intervention in Afghanistan." Interview with Zbigniew Brzezinski, National Security Advisor to President Jimmy Carter. Paris, January 15–21, 1998. http://www.globalresearch.ca/articles/BRZ110A.html (accessed April 11, 2011).

290 *"important in hastening the end"*: Jay, Paul. "The Afghan War and the 'Grand Chessboard' Pt. 2." The Real News Network, January 15, 2010. http://therealnews.com/t2/component/content/index.php?option=com_content&task=view&id=31&Itemid=74&jumival=4716 (accessed April 11, 2011).

290 *"They would have continued fighting"*: Ibid.

291   *deny their drug trafficking*: Gibbs, David N. "Afghanistan: The Soviet Invasion in Retrospect." Review Essay, University of Arizona. *International Politics 37*, pp. 233–246, June 2000. http:// dgibbs.faculty.arizona.edu/sites/dgibbs.faculty.arizona.edu/files/ afghan-ip.pdf (accessed March 10, 2012).

292   *first millennium BC*: Sabahuddin, Abdul. *History of Afghanistan*. Global Vision Publishing, 2008, p. 15. http://books.google.com/ books?id=XfDYtxfOvTYC&lpg=PP1&pg=PA15#v=onepage& q&f=false, cited in "Pashtun People." Wikipedia.org. http:// en.wikipedia.org/wiki/Pashtun_people (accessed March 12, 2012).

292   *Pashtunwali, an unwritten code*: "Pashtunwali." Wikipedia.org. http://en.wikipedia.org/wiki/Pushtunwali (accessed March 12, 2012).

292   *even though only suffering follows*: Easwaran, Eknath. *Nonviolent Soldier of Islam: Badshah Khan, a Man to Match His Mountains*. 2nd ed. Tomales, CA: Nilgiri Press, 2002, p. 95. (Originally published in 1984.)

292   *"avenging hero"*: Ibid.

292   *"greatest source of wealth"*: Ibid., p. 18.

292   *through two Anglo-Afghan wars*: "The Battle of Kabul and the Retreat to Gandamak." http://www.britishbattles.com/first-afghan-war/kabul-gandamak.htm (accessed April 17, 2011); Nell, Grant Sebastian. "The Retreat from Kabul: A Bloodbath of the First Anglo-Afghan War," June 24, 2009. http://suite101.com/article/ the-retreat-from-kabul-a127375 (accessed April 17, 2011); "The Great Game." Wikipedia.org. http://en.wikipedia.org/wiki/The_ Great_Game (accessed April 15, 2011); "First Anglo-Afghan War." Wikipedia.org. http://en.wikipedia.org/wiki/First_Anglo-Afghan_ War (accessed April 17, 2011); McNamara, Robert. "Britain's Disastrous Retreat from Kabul: In 1842 Afghanistan Massacre Only One British Soldier Survived." http://history1800s.about. com/od/colonialwars/a/kabul1842.htm (accessed April 17, 2011); Szczepanski, Kallie. "What Was the Great Game?" http://asian history.about.com/od/glossaryfj/g/What-Was-The-Great-Game. htm (accessed March 12, 2012).

293   *Butcher and Bolt*: Yapp, Malcolm E. "North-West Frontier." *The Oxford Companion to Military History*. http://www.answers.com/ topic/north-west-frontier-1 (accessed April 27, 2011).

293   *burned "their villages"*: Easwaran. *Nonviolent Soldier of Islam*, p. 18.

293   *Into this life, in 1890*: Khan, Badshah. *My Life and Struggle: Autobiography of Badshah Khan*. Daily Afghanistan Times (Publisher), 2008, p. 1. (Originally published by Hind Pocket Books, 1969.)

293   *Pashtun farmers who had settled*: Easwaran. *Nonviolent Soldier of Islam*, p. 29.

293   *(sons of Muhammad)*: Ibid., p. 40.

293   *considered wealthy, owning all*: Ibid., p. 29.

293   *North-West Frontier Province*: "North-West Frontier Province (1901-1955)." Wikipedia.org. http://en.wikipedia.org/wiki/North-West_Frontier_Province_(1901–1955) (accessed April 27, 2011).

293   *The province was further dissected*: Easwaran. *Nonviolent Soldier of Islam*, p. 29.

294   *military post and police state*: Ibid., p. 66.

294   *Behram Khan believed honor*: Ibid., p. 41.

294   *he chose to forgive*: Khan. *My Life and Struggle*, p. 1.

294   *whom he admired almost as much*: Easwaran. *Nonviolent Soldier of Islam*, p. 57.

294   *He could read and he could write*: Ibid., p. 64.

294   *standing army of 10,000*: Ibid., p. 65.

295   *regulations prohibited settled Pashtuns*: Ibid.

295   *small village of Zagai . . . no one came*: Ibid., p. 70.

295   *In three years, he visited*: Ibid., p. 79.

295   *at the mosque in Hashtnagar . . . the king of khans*: Ibid., p. 79.

295   *Over a million Indian soldiers*: "Jallianwala Bagh Massacre." Wikipedia.org. http://en.wikipedia.org/wiki/Jallianwala_Bagh_massacre (accessed March 12, 2012).

295   *Rowlatt Act kept the restrictions*: "Rowlatt Act." Wikipedia.org. http://en.wikipedia.org/wiki/Rowlatt_act (accessed March 12, 2012).

296   *The British were listening . . . six months in prison*: Easwaran. *Nonviolent Soldier of Islam*, p. 81.

296   *The enforcement of martial law . . . deaths at 1,000*: "Jallianwala Bagh Massacre." Wikipedia.org.

297   *two months in solitary*: Easwaran. *Nonviolent Soldier of Islam*, p. 87.

297   *"were paying for their infatuation"*: Ibid., p. 95.

297   *a consequence of ignorance*: Ibid., p. 101.

297   *banging on the gate . . . needed were soldiers*: Ibid., p. 110.

298   *Khudai Khidmatgar . . . losing his own life*: Ibid., pp. 111, 112.

298   *500 recruits*: Ibid., p. 112.

298   *In Lahore, on January 26, 1930*: "Purna Swaraj." Wikipedia.org. http://en.wikipedia.org/wiki/Purna_Swaraj (March 12, 2011); Easwaran. *Nonviolent Soldier of Islam*, p. 117.

298   *"With this, I am shaking the foundations"*: "Salt Satyagraha." Wikipedia.org. http://en.wikipedia.org/wiki/Salt_Satyagraha (accessed March 12, 2012).

299   *"raided Congress [party] offices"*: Easwaran. *Nonviolent Soldier of Islam*, p. 120.

299   *The crowd offered to disperse*: Ibid., p. 122.

299   *"When those in front fell down wounded"*: Ibid., p. 123.

299   *non-violent army numbered nearly 100,000*: "Khudai Khidmatgar." Wikipedia.org. http://en.wikipedia.org/wiki/Khudai_Khid matgar (accessed March 12, 2012).

299   *Khan spent fifteen years in British prisons*: Easwaran. *Nonviolent Soldier of Islam*, p. 20.

300   *his only crime*: Khan, Badshah. Speech to the Indian Christian Association. Bombay, India, October 27, 1934, cited in Easwaran. *Nonviolent Soldier of Islam*, p. 147.

300   *August 14, 1947 . . . one million people dead*: "Indian Independence Movement." Wikipedia.org. http://en.wikipedia.org/wiki/Indian_independence_movement#The_non-cooperation_move ments (accessed March 12, 2012); "Partition of India." Wikipedia.org. http://en.wikipedia.org/wiki/Partition_of_india (accessed March 12, 2012).

300   *The first war between India and Pakistan*: "India-Pakistan: Troubled Relations; The 1947–48 War." BBC News. http://news.bbc.co.uk/hi/english/static/in_depth/south_asia/2002/india_pakistan/timeline/1947_48.stm (accessed March 12, 2012).

300   *placed Badshah Khan under house arrest . . . as he had wished*: "Khan Abdul Ghaffar Khan." Wikipedia.org. http://en.wikipedia.org/wiki/Badshah_Khan#cite_notePakistan:_The_Frontier_Gandhi-20 (accessed March 12, 2012).

301   *"had been broken"*: "Khudai Khidmatgar." Wikipedia.org.

301   *"All the horrors the British perpetrated"*: Easwaran. *Nonviolent Soldier of Islam*, p. 125. The direct quote came from Eknath Easwaran's book. Badshah Kahn wrote in his autobiography: "This was the reason for the innumerable cruelties they inflicted on us in 1932. All the arrests, imprisonments and other disgraceful acts of the British had only one object: to provoke the Pathans to be violent." (See Khan. *My Life and Struggle*, p. 135.)

301   *"the British would be back on familiar ground"*: Ibid.

301 *employs 700,000 civilians*: "About the Department of Defense (DOD)." http://www.defense.gov/about/ (accessed March 12, 2012).

302 *$712 billion*: Harrison, Todd. "Analysis of the FY 2011 Defense Budget." Center for Strategic and Budgetary Assessments, June 29, 2010. http://www.csbaonline.org/publications/2010/06/fy-2011-defense-budget-analysis/ (accessed March 13 2012).

303 *can be achieved only through violence*: Mattaini, Mark A. and Kristen Atkinson. "Constructive Noncooperation: Living in Truth." *Peace and Conflict Studies*, Spring 2011, 18.1, p. 7. http://shss.nova.edu/pcs/journalsPDF/pcs_spring_2011.pdf (accessed March 10, 2012).

303 *"And neither do you regret"*: Le Nouvel Observateur. "The CIA's Intervention in Afghanistan."

304 *theory of transarmament*: Transarmament is the exchange of one means of defense for another, especially from a military-based defense (conventional and nuclear military power) to a civilian-based defense (psychological, economic, social, and political resistance and counter-attack). (See Sharp, Gene. "National Security through Civilian-Based Defense." Omaha, Nebraska: Association for Transarmament Studies, 1985 (Originally published in 1970). Albert Einstein Institution: Advancing Freedom through Nonviolent Action. http://www.aeinstein.org/wp-content/uploads/2013/09/NationalSecurityThroughCivilian-BasedDefense-English.pdf [accessed March 10, 2012.]; "Transarmament." Wikipedia.org. http://en.wikipedia.org/wiki/Transarmament [accessed March 10, 2012]; "Civilian-based Defense." Wikipedia.org. http://en.wikipedia.org/wiki/Civilian-based_defense [accessed March 10, 2012].)

304 *identified 198 methods of non-violent action*: Mattaini and Atkinson. "Constructive Noncooperation: Living in Truth," 18.1, p. 7.

305 *currently accounts for forty-three percent*: "Recent Trends in Military Expenditure." Stockholm International Peace Research Institute. http://www.sipri.org/research/armaments/milex/result output/trends (accessed March 12, 2012).

306 *world's largest weapons supplier*: "India World's Largest Arms Importer According to New SIPRI Data on International Arms Transfers." Stockholm International Peace Research Institute, March 14, 2011. http://www.sipri.org/media/pressreleases/2011/armstransfers (accessed March 13, 2012). In March 2011, the Stockholm International Peace Research Institute reported that India—the founding country of *ahimsa* (non-violence), Hinduism, Buddhism, and Yoga—was the world's largest weapons importer from 2006 to 2010.

306   *"modifying export control regulations"*: Bridgeman, Maggie. "Obama Seeks to Expand Arms Exports by Trimming Approval Process." McClatchy Newspapers, July 29, 2010. http://www. mcclatchydc.com/2010/07/29/98337/obama-seeks-to-expand-arms-exports.html (accessed March 13, 2012).

306   *"aircraft and other weapons"*: Black, Ian. "Barack Obama to Authorize Record $60bn Saudi Arms Sale." *The Guardian*, September 13, 2010. http://www.guardian.co.uk/world/2010/sep/13/us-saudi-arabia-arms-deal (accessed March 17, 2012).

306   *$200 million in military sales to Bahrain*: Braun, Stephen. "U.S. Defense Sales to Bahrain Rose Before Crackdown." Associated Press (Washington), June 11, 2011. http://www.usatoday.com/news/topstories/2011-06-11-3391123216_x.htm (accessed March 13, 2012).

306   *"rifles, shotguns, and assault weapons"*: Ibid.

306   *$91 million to the Egyptian government*: Ibid.

306   *$17 million to Moammar Gadhafi*: Ibid.

306   *"told Congress of plans"*: Kimes, Mina. "America's Hottest Export: Weapons." *CNN Money*, February 24, 2011. http://money.cnn.com/2011/02/10/news/international/america_exports_weapons_full.fortune/index.htm (accessed March 13, 2012).

306   *"Obama is much more favorably disposed"*: Ibid.

306   *"There's an Obama arms bazaar going on"*: Ibid. America's gun industry also thrived during President Obama's first term in office. An analysis by the Associated Press found that major gun company stock prices rose, the number of federally licensed retail gun dealers increased for the first time in nearly 20 years, the National Rifle Association was "bursting with cash," and manufacturers couldn't "make enough guns fast enough." According to one gun industry analyst, "The driver is President Obama. He's the best thing that ever happened to the firearm industry."

While fear of stricter gun laws may have caused an initial spike in sales just after the 2008 presidential election, the industry continued to do well when it became clear President Obama did not consider gun control a priority. Under President Obama, Washington showed little interest in passing stricter gun laws, and the president made no promises for new gun control legislation during his campaign for a second term.

When not yet through President Obama's first term, the government had already carried out as many background checks for prospective buyers as it did in six years of George W. Bush's presidency. In the first three and a half years of the Bush administration, the FBI conducted about 28 million background checks compared to more than 50 million during the same period under

President Obama. The gun industry uses background checks as an indicator of consumer demand.

However, December 14, 2012, brought change, at least in the short term. On this morning, a lone gunman entered an elementary school in Newtown, Conn., armed with a large quantity of ammunition and three semi-automatic firearms: a .223-caliber Bushmaster military-style assault rifle, a 10mm Glock handgun, and a 9mm Sig Sauer handgun. Within minutes, he had murdered twenty children, all between the ages of six and seven, and six adults before fatally shooting himself when state and local police arrived at the scene. The result was that the stock prices of some of the country's largest gun makers fell, one sporting-goods chain temporarily stopped its sale of military-style firearms, and Cerberus Capital Management, a New York-based investment firm, announced it would sell the ironically named Freedom Group, Inc., the largest gun maker in the country and manufacturer of the Bushmaster semi-automatic rifle.

The questions remain, however, whether these changes were the result of conscience or of fear that the attack would soon bring stricter gun laws, how long the changes will last, and if more are coming. But as we monitor the future decisions of our investors, CEOs, and lawmakers, we must also consider, if we are only as free as the least healthy among us allow us to be, are the freedoms that we cling to so tightly only an illusion? Just how free can we be shackled to guns and violence? (See Sullivan, Eileen and Jack Gillum. "Gun Industry Thrives During Obama's Term in Office." Associated Press [Washington], October 19, 2012. http://news.yahoo.com/gun-industry-thrives-during-obamas-term-office-073353804--election.html [accessed November 1, 2012]; Kleinfield, N.R. "Gunman Took Big Supply of Ammunition to School After Killing Mother at Home." *New York Times*, December 16, 2012. http://www.nytimes.com/2012/12/17/nyregion/sandy-hook-school-shooting-in-newtown.html [accessed December 20, 2012]; "Sandy Hook Elementary School Shooting." Wikipedia.org. http://en.wikipedia.org/wiki/Sandy_Hook_shooting [accessed December 30, 2012]; Freed, Joshua. "Investors Turn Against Gun Makers After Massacre." Associated Press [Minneapolis, MN], December 18, 2012. http://news.yahoo.com/investors-turn-against-gun-makers-massacre-231352965--finance.html;_ylt=AwrBTzahaCxTdE0AbdJXNyoA;_ylu=X3oDMTEzdTE3cnU0BHNlYwNzcgRwb3MDMDQRjb2xvA2JmMQR2dGlkA1ZJUDQwMl8x [accessed December 20, 2012]; Banerjee, Devin, and David Carey and Cristina Alesci. "Cerberus to Sell Gunmaker Freedom After School Massacre." Bloomberg, December 18, 2012. http://www.bloomberg.com/news/2012-12-18/cerberus-outlay-reviewed-by-pension-after-school-massacre.html [accessed December 20, 2012].)

306   *considered to be the best*: Ibid.

306   *many U.S.-supplied arms have outlasted*: Hartung, William D. and Bridget Moix. "Report: U.S. Arms to Africa and the Congo War—World Policy Institute."

306   *yesterday's weapons are finding new uses*: Ibid.

307   *netted 386 guns . . . into Mexico each day*: Weissert, Will. "AP Enterprise: U.S. Push Not Halting Guns to Mexico." Associated Press (Brownsville, TX), March 5, 2011.

307   *support approximately 75,000 jobs*: Black. "Barack Obama to Authorize Record $60bn Saudi Arms Sale."

307   *a future that includes a healthy and peaceful world*: I understand there is incongruity between my desire for a "healthy and peaceful world" and my attraction to one of the most violent sports in our country: professional football. And I have struggled with this greatly over the past few years. When Chicago Bears safety Dave Duerson, in an incredible act of selflessness, shot himself in the chest and left instructions for his brain to be used to research the effects of brain trauma suffered by professional football players, I began to question in earnest how I could reconcile my desire for a peaceful world and my passion for football. I still don't have an answer. But I do know that, for me, football is not and has never been about the hard hits. I don't remember any of them. But I do remember New England Patriots tight end Benjamin Watson running diagonally across an entire field to tackle Denver Broncos cornerback Champ Bailey, who had just intercepted a Tom Brady pass, at the two-yard line and cause a fumble. I do remember Buffalo Bills wide receiver Don Beebe chasing down hot-dogging Dallas Cowboys defensive tackle Leon Lett, knocking the ball out of his hands, and preventing a Dallas touchdown during Super Bowl XXVII. I do remember New Orleans Saints head coach Sean Payton calling for an onside kick to start the second half of Super Bowl XLIV (my worst memory). And I do remember New England Patriots head coach Bill Belichick going for it on fourth-and-two in a regular season game against the Indianapolis Colts in 2009 (my favorite memory). Unlike some fans, media members, and even players, I welcome the changes that will make professional football safer for those who play it. These changes will do nothing to lessen my enjoyment of the sport. I will take strategy, clutch plays, and big plays over big hits any day.

308   *1.41 million political ads aired*: "In the Busiest Month for TV Political Ads, Cleveland Rocks." Nielsenwire, November 5, 2010. http://blog.nielsen.com/nielsenwire/politics/in-the-busiest-month for-political-tv-ads-cleveland-rocks/ (accessed February 9, 2012).

308   *average of fifty-two percent of political ads*: "A Report on the 2008 Presidential Nomination Ads: Ads More Negative than Previous

Years." The Brookings Institution, July 2, 2008. http://www. brookings.edu/research/papers/2008/07/0630-campaignads-west (accessed June 18, 2011).

308 *getting in someone's face . . . in his head*: Burwell, Bryan. *The Fab Five.* ESPN Films, director Jason Hehir. (Originally aired March 13, 2011.)

310 *"I want their word"*: "No-Penalty Pledge Signed by Cowboys After Some Miscues." Associated Press (Irving, TX), November 15, 2007.

313 *While the following explanation*: "Understanding 'Emotional Compartmentalization' and How It Can Affect Our Lives and the Lives of Those You Love." http://www.sixwise.com/news letters/06/11/29/understanding-emotional-compartmentalization-andhow-it-can-affect-our-lives-and-the-lives-of-thos.htm (accessed February 9, 2012).

313 *"In order to live with integrity"*: Salzberg, Sharon. *Lovingkindness: The Revolutionary Art of Happiness.* Boston, MA: Shambhala Publications, Inc., 1995, p. 34. Emphasis added.

314 *twenty-two percent listed "moral values"*: Langer, Gary. "A Question of Values." *New York Times*, November 6, 2004. http://www. nytimes.com/2004/11/06/opinion/06langer.html?_r=1 (accessed March 10, 2012).

314 *forced to withdraw . . . offering no details*: Romano, Lois. "Effect of Obama's Candor Remains to be Seen." *The Washington Post*, January 3, 2007. http://www.washingtonpost.com/wp-dyn/content/article/2007/01/02/AR2007010201359.html (accessed March 10, 2012).

314 *"even if certain passages"*: Ibid.

315 *"[I] got into drinking"*: Elliot, Philip. "Obama Says He Drank, Tried Drugs as Teen." Associated Press (Manchester, NH), November 20, 2007.

315 *defended Barack Obama*: Oinounou, Mosheh. "Rudy Defends Obama's Discussion of Previous Drug Use." Foxnews.com, November 20, 2007.

315 *made pleas to keep the candidates'*: "Gingrich: 2008 Race Should Avoid Private Lives of Candidates." Associated Press (Nashville, TN), 2007.

315 *"huge error"*: Oinounou. "Rudy Defends Obama's Discussion of Previous Drug Use."

315 *"It's just not a good idea"*: Ibid.

318 *ten senators with strong bipartisan credentials*: Kellman, Laurie and Henry C. Jackson, with Liz Sidoti. "Bayh the Latest Exit as Moderates Leave Congress." Associated Press (Washington),

February 17, 2010. In 2012, another wave of moderate senators chose not to seek re-election, including Ben Nelson, Joe Lieberman, Kent Conrad, Kay Bailey Hutchison, and Olympia Snowe. In a *Washington Post* op-ed, Olympia Snowe cited the lack of bipartisanship as the reason for her retirement, stating, "Congress is becoming more like a parliamentary system—where everyone simply votes with their party and those in charge employ every possible tactic to block the other side." And some believe moderate politicians are feeling the pressure to conform to party ideology not only from within Congress, but also from partisan voters. According to the *National Journal*, this demand from dysfunctional politicians and voters that our leaders adhere to political extremism or risk losing their jobs has resulted in the highest level of congressional polarization ever recorded. The question now is, what does everyone else do about it? There has never been an easy answer to extremism and dysfunction, but there do seem to be at least two options: overpower the extremists—not by employing their raucous and corrosive tactics, but through overwhelming numbers—or let extremists destroy themselves and each other, which they inevitably and eventually will. But in choosing the latter, independent politicians and voters must also ask, what will be left of our country after they have gone? (See Snowe, Olympia J. "Why I'm Leaving the Senate." *The Washington Post*, March 1, 2012. http://www.washingtonpost.com/opinions/olympia-snowewhy-im-leaving-the-senate/2012/03/01/gIQApGYZlR_story.html [accessed June 12, 2012]; Brownstein, Ronald. "Pulling Apart." *National Journal*, February 24, 2011. [Updated February 27, 2011]. http://www.nationaljournal.com/magazine/congress-hitsnew-peak-in-polarization-20110224 [accessed June 12, 2012].)

318   *"too much narrow ideology"*: Ibid.

318   *bipartisan Congressional Civility Caucus*: Israel, Steve and Timothy V. Johnson. "Plea from Within Congress: Let's Be Civil for a Change." USA Today, January 9, 2005.

318   *"lack of interest"*: Ibid.

319   *remained its only members*: Hearn, Josephine. "Civility Caucus? No Way!" Politico.com, June 6, 2007. http://www.politico.com/news/stories/0607/4373.html (accessed June 12, 2011).

319   *"true leaders guide with compassion"*: Capito, Shelley Moore and Emanuel Cleaver II. "Politico: Rebuilding the Civility Caucus." Capito.house.gov, February 17, 2011. http://capito.house.gov/op-eds/politico-rebuilding-the-civility-caucus/ (accessed June 12, 2011).

320   *"inconsistency and hypocrisy"*: Vedantam, Shankar. "Study Ties Political Leanings to Hidden Biases." *The Washington Post*, January 30, 2006. http://www.washingtonpost.com/wp-dyn/content/

article/2006/01/29/AR2006012900642.html (accessed March 11, 2012).

320 *"Essentially, it appears as if partisans"*: LiveScience Staff. "Democrats and Republicans Both Adept at Ignoring Facts, Study Finds." LiveScience.com, January 24, 2006. http://www.livescience. com/576-democrats-republicans-adept-ignoring-facts-study-finds. html (accessed March 11, 2012).

321 *voters said there was more mudslinging*: "Voters Liked Campaign 2004, But Too Much 'Mud-Slinging.'" The Pew Research Center, Released November 11, 2004. http://www.people-press. org/2004/11/11/voters-liked-campaign-2004-but-too-much-mud slinging (accessed November 30, 2009).

321 *favored moderate candidates*: "Partisanship is Not What Most of the American Public Desires." The Harris Poll® #43, May 19, 2005. (Original source unavailable: http://www.harrisinteractive. com/harris_poll/index.asp?PID=572.)

321 *too much partisanship*: "Partisanship and Hostility Cast a Shadow Over U.S. and Canadian Capitals." The Harris Poll® #72, July 10, 2008. http://www.harrisinteractive.com/vault/Harris-Interactive-Poll-Research-The-Printer-Friendly-Format-2008-07.pdf (accessed November 30, 2009).

321 *Unity08 attempted not only to minimize*: Haussamen, Heath. "Can Unity '08 Succeed?" NewWest.net, December 6, 2007. http://www.newwest.net/main/print/18664/ (accessed March 11, 2012).

321 *Unity08 suspended operations*: "Group Suspends Ballot Access Project for Bipartisan Ticket." Newsday.com, January 10, 2008, cited in Wikipedia.org, "Unity08". http://en.wikipedia.org/wiki/ Unity (accessed March 11, 2012).

325 *"I wonder how intelligent citizens"*: Peterson, Dale. "Common Ground." Opinion. *The Union*, November 14, 2004. http://www. theunion.com/article/20041115/OPINION/111150085&parent profile=search (accessed January 26, 2012).

327 *One's opinions and how they are expressed*: We are in the midst of what feels like an opinion avalanche. Social networking and instantly communicating thoughts and opinions in 140 characters or less may have been a good idea in theory, but it takes a healthy and functional world to make them meaningful in real life. And, for the most part, what is currently being communicated through social media is neither healthy nor functional. Just because everyone has or is entitled to an opinion, this doesn't mean everyone is entitled to have his or her opinions respected or acknowledged. Most of those mass communicating opinions today disqualify themselves, through

their anger and ridicule, within their first few words. But the good news is that social media has shown us, on a scale so large that it can't be disputed, that most opinion is simply the projection of pain—or the throwing onto others the anger, hatred, and low self-esteem one feels within that has become too unbearable to contain. And that these opinions tell us more about those giving them than anyone or anything they have chosen to talk about. It is now up to us to decide if we want to learn the lesson that is being presented to us: Offering or accepting destructive and dysfunctional opinions can only create a world that is destructive and dysfunctional.

To determine which opinions consistently deserve our time and attention, we must first learn whether the one offering the opinion has done the work, both personally and professionally, to have his or her positions valued. This means the rest of us have to do our work, that of questioning the motivations and learning the stories behind those giving the opinions, rather than just accepting one because it matches our own or because it allows us to feel better about ourselves through the ridicule and dysfunction of others. While disparaging those who disparage makes us no different from the offender, we should also avoid giving too much credit to those who haven't earned it.

328   *Opinionists never seem to "just tell the truth" about themselves*: It is the media's responsibility to ask celebrity tell-all book authors and those who make their livings destructively criticizing and ridiculing perceived opponents if they have looked as closely at their own lives, and publicly revealed what they have discovered, as they have at the person they have written or talked about. However, the problems with this are one, the media rarely, if ever, pursues this line of questioning even though it has ample opportunity since authors of celebrity tell-alls must use the media to sell their books, and two, opinionists rarely put themselves in a position to be questioned.

330   *take the Bible seriously*: Inspired by Borg, Marcus J. *Reading the Bible Again For the First Time: Taking the Bible Seriously But Not Literally.* New York: HarperCollins, 2001.

335   *"interbeing"*: http://www.orderofinterbeing.org/ (accessed January 26, 2012).

336   *Parable of the Prodigal Son*: Keller, Timothy J. *The Prodigal God: Recovering the Heart of the Christian Faith.* New York: Penguin Group, 2008, pp. 3, 6.

336   *"There was a man who had two sons"*: The Bible, New International Version. Luke 15:11. Emphasis added.

336   *"All these years"*: Ibid., Luke 15:29, 30.

337   *You do not act to receive*: Expectation is big business. There are
       books, movies, lectures, seminars, even cruises devoted to help-
       ing you manifest love, wealth, happiness or whatever your heart
       desires. The law of attraction asserts that "like attracts like,"
       meaning if you give love, you will get love; if you are charitable
       with your money, you will receive wealth; if you project happi-
       ness into the world, the world will provide you with happiness
       in return. It is hard to dispute that what you think and how you
       live your life create your reality. However, the very premise of
       the law of attraction—the expectation of getting in return what
       you give—contains the seed for its failure. The universe rewards
       those with authentic thoughts and actions; those who give love and
       wealth, and bring happiness to others simply because they want
       to make the world a better place, not because they are going to
       get something in return. Relying on the law of attraction means
       you are only trying another method—under the guise of spiri-
       tuality—to manipulate the universe into giving you something
       you are not prepared to receive. And you are not prepared to
       receive, or even recognize authentic love if you don't know how
       to love authentically—without expectation or ulterior motive.
       The universe cannot be manipulated, and the universe will not
       be tested. But it will teach you, as many times and through as
       many ways as you require, not only how to heal so you can give
       love, wealth, and happiness without expectation, but also how
       to recognize the love, wealth, and happiness you already have.

337   *in return for answered prayers*: Prayer is often another form of
       spiritual expectation. However, your God and the universe already
       know what you need. It is through your prayers that they want
       you to know it too. *Your prayers are not when you speak to God,
       but when God speaks to you.* Though it is expectation—wanting
       what you ask for to be magically bestowed upon you by a higher
       power—that renders your prayers nothing more than words. When
       you ask for love, He is telling you to do the work to understand what
       authentic love is, then discover why you don't think you already
       have or even deserve it. When you ask for happiness or patience
       or wealth or success, He wants you to do the work to get them, to
       learn what you need to learn, and seek the help of those who can
       teach you—especially about all that is truly valuable in life.
            Awareness is being in a state of authentic prayer. And as long
       as you remain unaware of the true purpose of prayer, you will ask
       but never hear.

337   *"exaggerated seeking and clinging"*: "The Misunderstandings
       Around Non-Attachment: Detachment and Aversion." Urbanmonk.
       net. http://www.urbanmonk.net/783/non-attachment-detachment
       aversion/ (accessed January 26, 2012).

337 *If we don't have it*: Ibid.

337 *What we cling to is less about having*: Sunada. "Love, Sex, and Non-Attachment." Wildmind.org Blog Post, January 22, 2009. http://www.wildmind.org/blogs/on-practice/love-sex-and-nonattachment (accessed January 26, 2012).

337 *"Whether it is an object or a person"*: "The Misunderstandings Around Non-Attachment: Detachment and Aversion."

339 *"when the walker and road"*: Ka Gold Jewelry. *Ring of Tao Product Description*. http://www.ka-gold-jewelry.com/p-products/ring-of-tao-silver.php (accessed January 26, 2012).

339 *"The road is wiser"*: Ibid.

342 *Though meditation can take many forms*: In addition to traditional types of meditation, which usually require silence and stillness, there are also active meditations (sometimes called chaotic methods) that include jumping, kicking, whirling, flailing, dancing, humming, laughing, shouting, screaming, or speaking in gibberish. Proponents of active meditation believe that, because we have evolved into increasingly stressed and suppressed beings, traditional meditation methods are no longer appropriate; that the ancient meditation practices of Patanjali and Buddha should adapt to modern man, rather than modern man try to adopt ancient meditation methods that have become outdated and ineffective.

　　While traditional meditation methods are most beneficial to me, I have used active meditation. However, what I have found interesting is that, when endorsing active meditation, proponents feel they must denigrate traditional methods. But the truth is, there is value and a place for both. On August 8, 2009, Rod Woodson, a defensive player in the NFL, was inducted into the Pro Football Hall of Fame. During his speech, he spoke of growing up as a biracial child, and of constantly being asked to choose between being black or white. He then said something I remember every time someone wants me to make a choice that isn't truthful, healing, or even necessary: "We don't have to choose."

342 *basically two types*: Along with outer object (concentration) and inner object (insight) meditations, Buddhists have as their ultimate goal a third form of meditation, no object.

343 *"There is no such thing"*: Kornfield, Jack. *After the Ecstasy, the Laundry: How the Heart Grows Wise on the Spiritual Path*. New York: Bantam Books, 2001, p. xiii.

343 *"Enlightenment does exist"*: Ibid.

344 *"Is there a wisdom [that] includes both"*: Ibid., p. xxi.

344 *claim to have achieved . . . among us*: Ibid., p. xx.

344   *protect our own dysfunctions by enabling the dysfunctions of*
       others: One of the most heartbreaking examples of this is the
       conviction of a former Penn State assistant football coach on 45
       counts of child sexual abuse; he was accused of molesting 10 boys
       over 15 years. Through an independent investigation and during
       his trial, evidence and testimony showed that many people over
       many years enabled and protected the coach: a district attorney
       who declined to charge the coach over a 1998 molestation allega-
       tion even though the investigating detective believed they had a
       solid case; a janitor in 2000, and a coaching assistant in 2001,
       who say they saw the coach engaged in sex acts with boys in the
       campus showers, yet failed to stop the abuse or immediately notify
       the authorities; school district officials who refused to believe the
       abuse claims of one of the victims; the coach's wife who, as one
       accuser testified, was in the house when he was being molested
       by the coach in a basement bedroom; and top university officials
       and the head football coach who knew of the sexual abuse, but
       are believed to have been part of a multi-year cover-up to protect
       their own and the university's reputations.

       The questions about the events at Penn State are limitless. But
       there are some that must be asked out loud and as many times as
       it takes to find the answers.

       How do you teach someone—even one capable of doing the
       unthinkable—to have a conscience? By having a conscience yourself.
       No addict or liar or murderer or pedophile can be any of these by
       himself. *The depth of the addiction or dysfunction always equals*
       the depth of the enabling.

       How far would you go to protect your reputation, your identity,
       or your brand? We are all Penn State to some degree, and we all
       need to determine which parts of our lives we are willing to justify,
       deny, ignore, or mythologize to protect. It might be a relationship,
       your career, or your religion, but there always exists something that
       we have the potential to love more than awareness and the truth.
       The root of this always lies in thinking of ourselves and others as
       objects or things, rather than human beings. You are not a brand.
       You are not your career. You are not your relationship. You are a
       heart and a soul. And your awakening depends on spending more
       time developing yourself as a heart and soul than anything else.

       How do we begin to heal the trauma and remedy the dysfunction
       associated with Penn State? First, we must understand that child
       sexual abuse is a violent crime, which not only goes against our
       laws, but against our humanity. Two ways we can begin to heal,
       as well as reduce the chances of this happening in the future, are
       through openness and education. Secrecy festers all wounds, and all
       offenders of every kind need the silence of their enablers and their

victims to carry out and continue their offenses. They will threaten and manipulate, or use labels such as snitch or narc to bully their victims and enablers into secrecy, thereby keeping everyone connected to their offenses as broken as they are. Speaking out in the midst of great shame takes great courage. But silence only increases shame and prevents healing. You must speak out to anyone and everyone who will listen, until you find one who understands.

Education about sexual predators must be thorough and begin at an early age so children can feel empowered and supported. But we each must also embrace self-education and exploration to discover our own dysfunctions and divinity. Because the more aware we are about our own lives, the less willing we will be to create or contribute to an environment of trauma and brokenness.

The sacrifice of the Penn State victims has been great: lost innocence, violated bodies, shattered spirits, broken hearts. We must learn the lessons of this tragedy, or their sacrifice will have been for nothing. (See Rubinkam, Michael. "Testimony at Sandusky Trial Shows Missed Chances." Associated Press, June 16, 2012. http://news.yahoo.com/testimony-sandusky-trial-shows-missed-chances-175240741--spt.html [accessed September 1, 2012].)

344   *times of deep compassion*: Kornfield. *After the Ecstasy, the Laundry*, p. xix.

344   *"There are no enlightened people"*: Ibid., pp. xx, xxi.

355   *one cannot solve a problem*: Einstein, Albert. "We can't solve problems by using the same kind of thinking we used when we created them." http://rescomp.stanford.edu/~cheshire/EinsteinQuotes.html (accessed January 26, 2012).